W9-CKR-702

Gift
of
the
Class
of
1992

Portraits of Pioneers
in Psychology

Portraits of Pioneers
in Psychology

Edited by

Gregory A. Kimble
Duke University

Michael Wertheimer
University of Colorado

Charlotte White
Boyden-White Vision Laboratory

 AMERICAN PSYCHOLOGICAL ASSOCIATION
Washington, DC
1991

 LAWRENCE ERLBAUM ASSOCIATES, PUBLISHERS
1991   Hillsdale, New Jersey   Hove and London

American Psychological Association
1200 Seventeenth Street, NW
Washington, DC 20036

Lawrence Erlbaum Associates, Inc., Publishers
365 Broadway
Hillsdale, New Jersey 07642

Cover and production by: Christopher Pecci

Library of Congress Cataloging-in-Publication Data

Portraits of pioneers in psychology / edited by Gregory A. Kimble,
 Michael Wertheimer, Charlotte White.
      p.   cm.
   "Sponsored by the Division of General Psychology, American
 Psychological Association."
   Includes bibliographical references and index.
   ISBN 0-8058-0620-2. – ISBN 0-8058-1136-2 (pbk.)
   1. Psychologists – Biography. 2. Psychology – History. I. Kimble,
 Gregory A. II. Wertheimer, Michael. III. White, Charlotte.
 IV. American Psychological Association. Division of General
 Psychology.
 BF109.A1P67 1991
 150'.92'2 – dc20
 [B]   91-7226
                                                                  CIP

Printed in the United States of America
10 9 8 7 6 5 4 3 2

In memory of Robert L. Thorndike

Contents

Preface   ix

Portraits of the Authors and Editors   xiii

1   A Trans-Time Visit with Francis Galton
G.E. McClearn   1

2   William James: Spoiled Child of American Psychology
Barbara Ross   13

3   The Spirit of Ivan Petrovich Pavlov
Gregory A. Kimble   27

4   Freud: 3 Contributions
Ernst G. Beier   43

5   From "Paired Associates" to a Psychology of Self:
The Intellectual Odyssey of Mary Whiton Calkins
Laurel Furumoto   57

6   The Intrepid Joseph Jastrow
Arthur L. Blumenthal   75

7   E. B. Titchener on Scientific Psychology and Technology
Rand B. Evans   89

8 Continuity for Women: Ethel Puffer's Struggle
Elizabeth Scarborough   105

**9 Harvey Carr and Chicago Functionalism:
A Simulated Interview**
Ernest R. Hilgard   121

**10 Edward L. Thorndike: A Professional and
Personal Appreciation**
Robert L. Thorndike   139

11 C. G. Jung: The Man and His Work, Then and Now
Irving E. Alexander   153

12 Perspectives on John B. Watson
Charles L. Brewer   171

**13 Max Wertheimer: Modern Cognitive Psychology
and the Gestalt Problem**
Michael Wertheimer   189

**14 Psychology from the Standpoint of a Mechanist:
An Appreciation of Clark L. Hull**
Gregory A. Kimble   209

**15 Edward Chace Tolman: A Life of Scientific and
Social Purpose**
Henry Gleitman   227

**16 Leta Stetter Hollingworth: "Literature of Opinion" and the
Study of Individual Differences**
Stephanie A. Shields   243

17 Natural Wholes: Wolfgang Köhler and Gestalt Theory
Robert Sherrill, Jr.   257

**18 General Anthroponomy and Its Systematic Problems:
A Tribute to Walter S. Hunter**
Charles N. Cofer   275

**19 Systems as Reconceptualizations: The Work of
Edna Heidbreder**
Mary Henle   293

20 Integrations of Lashley
Darryl Bruce   **307**

21 Harry Stack Sullivan: The Clinician and the Man
Kenneth L. Chatelaine   **325**

22 Robert Choate Tryon: Pioneer in Differential Psychology
Kurt Schlesinger   **343**

Index   **357**

Preface

This book presents biographical portraits of 22 of psychology's pioneers, portraits of them as men and women as well as scientists. All of these portraits, many of them offered by a descendant, colleague, or student of the pioneer, are informal. Most of them are lighthearted, even humorous, in their approach. A few are intimate and personal. Several authors impersonate their pioneers and present the stories of their lives and work in the pioneer's own words. Thus Galton, Pavlov, Freud, Wertheimer, Köhler, Hull, Tryon, and Hollingworth "return" to describe their contributions and occasionally to comment on psychology today. One portrait takes the form of an imagined interview with Harvey Carr. Others are what might be called "appreciations" of the pioneer. Typically the authors view the scientific achievements of the pioneers in the context of their times. Collectively they describe psychology's search for direction and significance in the dawning of a new discipline.

The authors of this book are recognized authorities in psychology, often in the same field as their pioneers. At least eight of them discovered their pioneers when they were graduate students and went on to study them over a period of many years. Many of the authors' own careers were influenced by their pioneers in ways that are described either in their chapters or in the Portraits of the Authors and Editors part of this volume.

All but 1 of the 22 pioneers were born in the 19th century. In this volume, they appear in order of their dates of birth. The oldest, Francis Galton, was born in 1822; the youngest Robert Tryon, in 1901. By coincidence, both of these scientists studied behavioral genetics, a topic of substantial current interest. All these pioneers were important in the early history of topics of contemporary concern: Pavlov, Thorndike, Calkins, Watson, Hull, Tolman, Hunter, Lashley, and Tryon (conditioning and learning); Freud, Jung, and Sullivan (personality and psychotherapy); Galton, Puffer, James, Jastrow, and Watson (media psychology); Jastrow and Hull (hypnosis); Hollingworth, Thorndike, and Pavlov (individual differences); James, Calkins, Thorndike, Wertheimer, Tolman, Köhler, Hunter, and Heidbreder (cognitive psychology); Calkins, Puffer, and Hollingworth (women's studies); the list could go on.

Many of our pioneers were among the founders of the traditional "schools" of psychology. These include Titchener (Structuralism); Freud and Jung (Psychoanalysis); Watson, Lashley, Hunter, Tolman, and Hull (Behaviorism); Carr, James, Thorndike, and Hull (Functionalism), and Wertheimer and Köhler (Gestalt theory). As the appearance of several names in more than one category reveals, many of these pioneers made contributions in several areas. For that reason, the book contains surprises.

The history of *Portraits of Pioneers in Psychology* goes back to the mid-1970s, when William Wilsoncroft, Patricia Keith-Spiegel, and Norma Weckler conceived the ideas of presenting the giants in the history of psychology by impersonation, and recruited a series of such presentations for conventions of the Western Psychological Association. At about the same time, Michael Wertheimer developed a similar series for conventions of the Rocky Mountain Psychological Association. Then, in 1983, Elizabeth Scarborough used a similar format for a set of invited addresses that were delivered at the convention of the American Psychological Association (APA) and sponsored by Division 1 (General Psychology) of APA. Since then the series has continued, most often under the joint sponsorship of Division 1 and Division 26 (History of Psychology).

These invited addresses have been enormously popular, often playing to standing-room-only audiences; their popularity led to many requests that they be published. This book is a response to those requests. In 1989, the Executive Committee of Division 1 of APA charged the three editors of this volume with the responsibility of producing the requested publication, timed to be available in 1992, when APA would celebrate its centennial year.

The chapters in this volume are revisions of the talks described above. That fact accounts for certain features of the book. The pioneers included are those introduced in these addresses, rather than those who might have been selected to implement some special theme. The styles and organizations of the chapters vary, because they are those that the individual authors found comfortable when they delivered their ad-dresses. In the case of those that originally were impersonations, the language is the one that the pioneer would have spoken half a century or more earlier.

This book was compiled for the purpose of making these informal talks available to graduate and undergraduate students and to scholars in the history of psychology. The final product will serve that purpose very well. Individual chapters provide a glimpse into the lives of the particular pioneers. Selected groups of chapters will yield rich material related to specific schools, topics, and perspectives in psychology. The index was prepared to facilitate such uses. The entries are cross-referenced so that the reader can locate discussions that reveal the interactions among our pioneers as well as their sometimes opposite positions on topics.

Many people helped to make this book come into existence. We want to acknowledge the contributions of Division 1 of APA, for providing financial backing for the project; Judith Amsel of Lawrence Erlbaum Associates, who gave sound editorial advice; Genevieve Offner, who took scripts from audiotapes, from manuscripts, and from disks that our computers could not read and put them into a form that we could use; John Popplestone, who provided the majority of the photographs; Carroll White, for a heroic amount of background research on some of the pioneers; and D. Bret King, who helped with the final proofreading and with construct of index.

Gregory A. Kimble
Michael Wertheimer
Charlotte White

Portraits of the
Authors and Editors[1]

Irving Alexander, who wrote the chapter on C.G. Jung, has had a continuing interest in the relationship between the life and work of prominent personality theorists. A native New Yorker, he was an undergraduate at the University of Alabama and did his graduate work at Princeton University, where he continued as a member of that faculty for 9 years after his doctorate. A sabbatical leave at the Jung Institute in Zurich heralded a change in intellectual interest, from the problems of auditory theory to those of personality theory and eventually psychobiographical inquiry. Following 4 years at the National Institute of Mental Health as a training grant administrator, Alexander accepted his primary academic appointment at Duke University, where he is currently professor of psychology. In the past, he has served as director of the Clinical Psychology Training Program and as chair of the Duke psychology department. He has held visiting professorships at Harvard University, the Hebrew University of Jerusalem, the University of Tel-Aviv, and Princeton University. Alexander's major publications include his books, *The Experience of Introversion* and *Personality: Method and Content in Personality Assessment and Psychobiology,* as well as two monographs on cross-cultural influences on the development of affective–social responses in children.

Ernst Beier, author of "Freud: 3 Contributions," was born in Germany

---

[1]These "portraits" are based on biographical statements submitted by the authors. The editors revised them where necessary to produce greater uniformity and to allow the occasional mentions of the importance of the authors' contributions to psychology.

and came to the United States in 1939. After graduating from Amherst College, he had a brief career as a chemist. In 1943, Beier joined the U.S. Army, went overseas, and was captured by the Germans. During his captivity he re-evaluated his goals and decided that, after the war, he would seek training in psychology. He received this training at Teachers College, Columbia University, obtaining a PhD in clinical psychology. Following his degree, Beier taught at Syracuse University for 5 years. Then he went to the University of Utah, where he established the Clinical Psychology Training Program. Beier joined APA in 1949. He has served on the Council of Representatives and chaired several major boards and committees. He has been president of Division 29 (Psychotherapy) and received the Distinguished Psychologist Award from that division. He has also been president of the Utah and the Rocky Mountain Psychological Associations. Beier's qualifications to write on Freud are impressive. He began reading Freud at an early age, saw an analyst as a teen-ager, and helped get funding for the Freud Museum in London. He says that Freud's influence on his life has been second to none. Beier is the author of *The Silent Language of Psychotherapy* and *People Reading*. Presently he is Professor Emeritus at Utah.

Arthur L. Blumenthal, who wrote "The Intrepid Joseph Jastrow," has long been interested in reevaluating the history of psychology. Born in Wyoming, he grew up and was educated in several western states, receiving his doctoral degree from the University of Washington. Blumenthal carried out postdoctoral studies at Harvard and at MIT, specializing in psycholinguistics. In that context he did important research on the history of psycholinguistics, which culminated in a book *Language and Psychology: Historical Aspects of Psycholinguistics*. That book was followed by a historically oriented text on cognitive psychology, *The Process of Cognition*, which shows the relevance of late-19th-century experimental studies to contemporary cognitive psychology. Most of Blumenthal's more recent historical research has focused on Wilhelm Wundt, whom he has struggled to rescue from the distortions and mistranslations that have left Wundt's "voluntaristic" psychology either unknown or confused with Titchener's "structuralist" school. Recently, the University of Wisconsin commissioned Blumenthal to recover the forgotten history of the subject for his chapter in this volume, Joseph Jastrow, who founded at Wisconsin in 1888 America's oldest continuously operating laboratory of experimental psychology. Blumenthal has taught at Harvard and the University of Massachusetts at Boston. He is now on the faculty of Sarah Lawrence College. He is a fellow of the American Psychological Association and the American Psychological Society.

Charles Brewer, author of the chapter on Watson, is professor of psychology at Furman University, Watson's alma mater. Born in Pine Bluff, Arkansas, Brewer received his education largely in that state: BA from Hendrix College, MA and PhD in experimental psychology from the University of Arkansas. His postdoctoral work was at Harvard and the University of Michigan. Brewer taught at the College of Wooster (Ohio) and Elmira College (New York) before joining the faculty at Furman (Greenville, South Carolina) in 1967. He has made important contributions to psychology as editor of the journal *Teaching of Psychology* and as coeditor of the *Handbook for Teaching Introductory Psychology* and the *Handbook for Teaching Statistics and Research Methods*. He received the first annual Meritorious Teaching Award at Furman in 1969 and the American Psychological Foundation's Distinguished Teaching in Psychology Award in 1989. Former president of the Council of Undergraduate Psychology Departments, he has also chaired the American Psychological Association's Committee on Undergraduate Education and has been president of the Association's Division 2 (Teaching of Psychology). Brewer's empirical research is in the areas of human learning and memory. A recognized authority on J. B. Watson, Brewer's sources of information included Watson's family. His chapter also contains a set of reflections by Watson's son, Jim.

Darryl Bruce, who wrote "Integrations of Lashley," was born in Dryden, Ontario, Canada. He received his bachelor's degree from McGill University and his MS and PhD from Pennyslvania State University. Bruce brings to this volume years of research into Lashley's life and work, research that grew from his scholarly interests in the areas of animal behavior, cognition, memory (both as studied in the laboratory and as it functions in the real world) and in the history of psychology. Before coming to Saint Mary's University in Halifax, Nova Scotia, Canada as chair of the Department of Psychology, Bruce's primary academic appointments were at Florida State University and Mount Allison University, Sackville, New Brunswick, Canada. He has also been a visiting professor at several universities in the United States, Canada, and England. Bruce has served on the Board of Consulting Editors for the *Journal of Experimental Psychology: General* and was a guest editor with R. H. Logie on a special issue of *Applied Cognitive Psychology*, devoted to applied cognitive psychology in the 1990s.

Kenneth L. Chatelaine, author of the chapter on Harry Stack Sullivan, was born and raised in Minneapolis. He received his BA at Saint Paul College, an MLA from Johns Hopkins University, and a PhD from the University of Maryland. He also received postdoctoral training at the Washington School of Psychiatry, founded by Sullivan. Chatelaine's program of research on Sullivan's life and work began in graduate school and culminated in a doctoral dissertation on the origins of

Sullivan's ideas. Over the years he has continued to contribute information and insight into certain phases of Sullivan's life as well as into Sullivan's thinking about human development, anxiety, and the process of mental illness. Chatelaine is the author of two books on Sullivan's interpersonal theory of psychiatry: *Harry Stack Sullivan, The Formative Years*, and *Good Me, Bad Me, Not Me*. As a faculty member of the Washington School of Psychiatry, he served on the school's Sullivan Committee, which is charged with re-editing the complete works of Sullivan. In addition to his work on Sullivan, Chatelaine's further interests and research have been in human development and in mental health. He is currently professor of psychology at Anne Arundel Community College.

Charles Cofer, who contributed the chapter on Walter S. Hunter, was one of Hunter's doctoral students. He was born in Missouri and received his doctorate from Brown in 1940. Cofer has taught at several universities, including the University of Houston, the University of Maryland, and Pennsylvania State University, where he was chair of the psychology department. Following retirement, he has had affiliations with the University of North Carolina and currently with the University of New Mexico. Cofer's research has included work on problem solving, verbal learning, memory, and motivation. He has been president of the Maryland and District of Columbia Psychological Associations and of the Eastern Psychological Association. He has served as chairman of the section on psychology of the American Association for the Advancement of Science and president of the Division of Experimental Psychology of the American Psychological Association. He has edited two volumes on verbal learning and verbal behavior. One of Cofer's major publications, *Motivation: Theory and Research*, was coauthored with Mortimer J. Appley. Cofer is currently working on biological rhythms, topic of a seminar and an anticipated book.

Rand Evans, author of the chapter on Titchener, was born in Baytown, Texas, and received his BA, MA, and PhD from the University of Texas. His doctoral work was with Karl M. Dallenbach, one of E. B. Titchener's "lieutenants." Working with Dallenbach kindled Evans' interest in the history of psychology and introduced him to Titchener's ideas. While he was trained in sensory psychology and psychophysics, most of Evans' publications have been in the history of psychology. His research has centered on early American philosophical psychology, the beginnings of experimental psychology, the development of experimental instrumentation, and particularly on the structural psychology of E. B. Titchener. His book-length biography of Titchener is currently in press. Evans has held positions at Wright State University, University of

New Hampshire, Texas A&M University, and the University of Baltimore. Currently he is chair of the department of psychology at East Carolina University (Greenville, North Carolina). Evans is a fellow of Division 26 (History of Psychology) of the American Psychological Association, past executive officer of the Cheiron Society, and a fellow of the American Psychological Society.

Laurel Furumoto, author of the chapter on Mary Calkins, has been interested in this pioneer since her days as a graduate student. After receiving a PhD from Harvard, Furumoto accepted a position at Wellesley College, where Calkins founded the psychology laboratory. Wellesley has been Furumoto's major academic appointment since the 1960s. She is now professor of psychology there. Furumoto was born and grew up in the Midwest. Her BA and MA were from the University of Illinois and Ohio State University. At Harvard, her doctoral dissertation was on experimental extinction in pigeons; her subsequent teaching and research interests have been in the history of psychology, women's studies, and experimental psychology. Over the years, Furumoto has done extensive research on Calkins's personal life, psychology, and philosophy and has generated many publications on women in psychology and their critical contributions to cognitive, comparative, and experimental psychology. With Elizabeth Scarborough, Furumoto has published the book *Untold Lives: The First Generation of American Women in Psychology.* At Wellesley, Furumoto has chaired the department of psychology. She is a fellow of the American Psychological Association and has served the association as chair of the Committee on Academic Freedom and Conditions of Employment, as a representative from Division 26 (History of Psychology) on the Council of Representatives and as a member of the Task Force on Centennial Celebrations.

Henry Gleitman, who wrote the chapter on Edward C. Tolman, was himself a student of Tolman. Gleitman was born in Germany and came to the United States when he was 14, receiving most of his education in the United States. His BS is from the City College of New York and his PhD from the University of California. Gleitman's early research was on animal learning, a field in which Tolman was a major pioneer; his later work has been in human cognition, language, and general psychology. His major academic appointments have been at Swarthmore College and the University of Pennsylvania, where he served as chair of the psychology department, and now is a professor. Gleitman is a recent president of the American Psychological Association's Division 1 (General Psychology) and is a past president of Division 10 (Psychology and the Arts). He has been the recipient of several teaching awards at the University of Pennsylvania and received the American Psychological

Foundation Award for Distinguished Teaching in Psychology in 1982. He is also the author of one of the most widely used textbooks in introductory psychology, *Psychology*.

Mary Henle, author of the chapter on Edna Heidbreder, was born in Cleveland. Her BA and MA were from Smith College and her PhD from Bryn Mawr College. She was attracted early to the work of Edna Heidbreder and to systematic psychology. Heidbreder's approach to analysis of the ideas of psychology has been essential to her own research, which has been in the tradition of Gestalt psychology. Throughout her formative years in psychology, Henle was strongly influenced by continuing interactions with the leaders of Gestalt psychology. Her initial contact with this tradition was provided by Kurt Koffka at Smith. At Bryn Mawr, she worked with Harry Helson and Donald MacKinnon. Her doctoral dissertation drew on both the Gestalt and the Lewinian traditions. She worked with Wolfgang Köhler during a postdoctoral appointment at Swarthmore College. One of Henle's major academic positions was at the New School for Social Research, whose psychology department was founded by Max Wertheimer. Henle's empirical work has been in the areas of perception, motivation, and thinking. Her honors have included two Guggenheim Fellowships, a research fellowship at Harvard, appointment as a visiting professor at Cornell, and an LHD awarded by the New School for Social Research. She has served APA as president of Division 24 (Theoretical and Philosophical Psychology) and Division 26 (History of Psychology) and on the APA Membership Committee. She has been president and a member of the board of directors of the Eastern Psychological Association.

Ernest R. Hilgard, who wrote the chapter on Harvey Carr, was born and raised in Illinois. His BS and PhD were from the University of Illinois and Yale. During his many years on the faculties at Yale and Stanford, Hilgard has made major contributions to scholarship in several areas, including learning and motivation, hypnosis and the control of pain, and the history of psychology, in which his major publication is a recent book, *Psychology in America: A Historical Survey*. Hilgard's earlier books testify to his influential role in that history: *Conditioning and Learning*, with D. G. Marquis; *Theories of Learning*, later editions with G. H. Bower; *Introduction to Psychology; Hypnosis in the Relief of Pain*, with J. R. Hilgard; and *Divided Consciousness: Multiple Controls in Human Thought and Action*. Hilgard's honors include election to the National Academy of Sciences, the National Academy of Education, the American Academy of Arts and Sciences, and the American Philosophical Society. He has received Gold Medals from the American Psychological Foundation and the International Society of Hypnosis. He served as president of both the APA and the ISH. The scope of Hilgard's services to the world community reflects the breadth and practical spirit he found in functionalism: U.S. Education Mission to Japan; National Advisory Mental Health Council, NIMH; consultant on education to James B. Conant, and to the Hebrew University in Jerusalem.

Gregory A. Kimble, editor and author of the chapters on Pavlov and Hull, was born in Mason City, Iowa. He grew up in Minnesota and attended the public schools there. His BA, MA, and PhD were from Carleton College, Northwestern University, and the University of Iowa. Kimble's doctoral research was on conditioning, a field in which Hull was the most important theorist at the time and Pavlov the leading figure in its history. Following receipt of the degree, Kimble continued to do research and publish on conditioning. In addition to reports on empirical research, he has two books in the field: *Hilgard and Marquis' Conditioning and Learning* and *Foundations of Conditioning and Learning.* Kimble joined APA in 1945 and has played many roles in the Association. He was the last editor of *Journal of Experimental Psychology: General.* He has been a member of the Council of Representatives several times and was on the board of directors from 1980 to 1983. Kimble has been president of Division 1 (General Psychology) and Division 3 (Experimental Psychology). His major academic appointments have been at Brown University, Yale University, University of Colorado, and Duke University. He served as director of undergraduate studies and director of graduate studies at Duke and as department chair at Duke and Colorado. Currently, he is Professor Emeritus of Psychology at Duke.

Gerald E. McClearn, author of the chapter on Francis Galton, was born in Sandy Lake, Pennsylvania. He first encountered the career of Francis Galton in Edwin G. Boring's *History of Experimental Psychology,* in an undergraduate course at Allegheny College, where he received a BS degree in 1951. During his years as a psychology major, McClearn developed an intense interest in heredity. This interest continued through graduate school at the University of Wisconsin, where he received a PhD in psychology with a minor in genetics in 1954. McClearn maintained his interest in behavioral genetics through academic appointments at Yale University, Allegheny College, University of California, University of Colorado, and Pennyslvania State University. At Colorado, McClearn established the Institute for Behavioral Genetics, and at Penn State he established the Center for Developmental and Health Genetics. One of McClearn's important publications is the book, *Behavioral Genetics: A Primer,* coauthored with his Colorado colleagues, John DeFries and Robert Plomin, the latter now at Penn State. A past president of the Behavior Genetics Association and recipient of the Dobzhansky Memorial Award for Eminent Research in

Behavior Genetics, McClearn is currently Evan Pugh Professor of Health and Human Development and head of the program in biobehavioral health at Penn State. His early interest in Galton was sharpened by a postdoctoral semester at the Galton Laboratory, University College, London, where memorabilia of the "Victorian genius" abound.

Barbara Ross, who contributed the chapter on William James, was born near Boston and has spent most of her life in New England. She attended St. Anselm's College and the Manchester Institute of Art, and received her BA in psychology and art from the University of New Hampshire, where she was a Ford scholar. She completed a MA in experimental psychology and a PhD in history and theory in psychology at the same university. Her mentor was Robert I. Watson, Sr. Ross, has been president of the New England Psychological Association, and of Division 1 (General Psychology) and Division 26 (History of Psychology) of the APA. Since 1974 she has served as editor of the *Journal of the History of the Behavioral Sciences,* and is on the editorial boards of *Storia e critica della Psicologia, Revista de Historia de la Psicologia,* and the *Psychohistory Review.* Ross is a recognized authority on 19th-century psychology in general and William James in particular. She is currently on the faculty of the psychology department of the University of Massachusetts, Harbor campus.

Elizabeth Scarborough, author of the chapter on Ethel Puffer, was born in northern Louisiana and left there to attend Hardin-Simmons University, where she received her BA. Subsequently, she studied at the Carver School of Missions and Social Work and at Teachers College, Columbia University, before earning MA and PhD degrees at the University of New Hampshire in experimental psychology and the history of psychology, respectively. She shares with Ethel Puffer the experience of struggling to coordinate academic and professional activities with the demands of homemaking and childbearing. Scarborough held brief appointments at several institutions prior to her appointment in the department of psychology at State University of New York College at Fredonia in 1977. At Fredonia she has served as department chair and as assistant to the college president. Her professional contributions include service to Cheiron, the International Society for the History of the Behavioral and Social Sciences (as executive officer), and to the APA through membership on the Education and Training Board, the Committee on Continuing Education, and the Committee on Undergraduate Education. She is a fellow of Division 26 (History of Psychology) and Division 35 (Psychology of Women) and a recent president of Division 26. Coauthor with Laurel Furumoto of *Untold Lives: The First Generation of American Women Psychologists,* she has published most frequently on women in the history of psychology.

Kurt Schlesinger, author of the chapter on Robert Choate Tryon, was born in Graz, Austria. After spending the war years in China and subsequently emigrating to Argentina, he came to the United States in 1954. His BA and MA are from San Francisco State University. He received his PhD from the University of California. Schlesinger's doctoral dissertation was on the genetics and biochemistry of alcohol consumption. Following receipt of the degree, Schlesinger went to the University of North Carolina. In 1966, he moved to the University of Colorado, where he has been since. He has served both as director of undergraduate studies and director of graduate studies in the psychology department at that university. Schlesinger's major research has focused on the genetic and biochemical mechanisms that mediate behavior. He has studied alcohol preference, susceptibility to sound-induced convulsions, brain mechanisms involved in neural plasticity, and the effects of a variety of pharmacological agents that affect learning and memory in experimental animals. In addition to articles reporting on empirical research findings, he has been a coauthor of several textbooks on introductory and biological psychology. One of his major publications is the two-volume work, *Topics in the History of Psychology,* coedited with G. A. Kimble.

Robert Sherrill, Jr., author of the chapter on Wolfgang Köhler, was born in Washington, DC, and raised in rural Ohio. He received a bachelor's degree from Trinity College in Connecticut in 1969, and a doctorate from the Union Institute in Cincinnati in 1974. Sherrill's interest in Gestalt theory began in his freshman psychology course, when he was struck by the concept that the whole is different from the sum of its parts. In his subsequent study of Gestalt theory, he was impressed by the researchers' cultural depth and their attempts to relate experimental psychology to other fields of study. In his first year of graduate school, he stumbled upon *Gestalt Therapy* by Perls, Hefferline, and Goodman. Eventually, he wrote his doctoral dissertation on the relationship of Gestalt theory and Gestalt psychotherapy. He later trained under the eminent Gestalt therapist James Simkin. Sherrill has been a practicing clinical psychologist in Farmington, New Mexico, since 1977. He has a specialty interest in clinical neuropsychology, and has published research on neuropsychological assessment. His clinical work is a continuation of his interest in relating meaningful psychological phenomena such as memory or problem solving to underlying brain processes, which began with his readings in Gestalt theory.

Stephanie A. Shields, author of the chapter on Leta Stetter Hollingworth, is professor of psychology at the University of California, Davis. Shields first encountered Hollingworth's name and work while a first-year graduate student at Pennsylvania State University, where she obtained her MS in 1973 and PhD in 1978. In the course of writing a term paper on psychology of women, she discovered Hollingworth's early articles and was impressed by the power of her description of the essential problem that women face in modern culture: how to make an intellectual and social contribution through work and, at the same time, fulfill one's capacity to nurture. Her interest in Hollingworth led Shields to write an account of Hollingworth's contributions to the psychology of women, which was published in 1975. Shields' chapter in this volume grew out of her contribution to a lecture series organized by Elizabeth Scarborough for the 1983 convention of the American Psychological Association to celebrate the 50th anniversary of Edna Heidbreder's *Seven Psychologies*. Shields' research is primarily concerned with the relationship between emotion as a quality of consciousness and emotion as a cultural construct, and she continues to publish on 19th-century scientific studies of gender.

The late **Robert L. Thorndike,** who wrote the chapter about his father, Edward L. Thorndike, was born and grew up in Montrose, New York. He received his BA and PhD from Wesleyan University and Columbia University. After 2 years on the faculty at George Washington University, Thorndike spent the balance of his academic career at Teachers College, Columbia University, following in his father's footsteps. Robert Thorndike and his father each spent 41 years at Columbia before their retirements. Thorndike's special interest in ability testing led to the creation of the Lorge-Thorndike Intelligence Tests (later known as the Cognitive Ability Tests) that are still in use. During World War II, he spent 4 years in the Army Aviation Psychology Program, an experience that led to his books, *Personnel Selection* and *10,000 Careers*. More books followed: *Concepts of Over and Under Achievement* and *Applied Psychometrics,* and the second edition of *Educational Measurement.* Thorndike was president of the Psychometric Society and the American Educational Research Association, and served on the APA board of directors. He was also director of the Psychological Corporation and of the American Institute for Research. Shortly before the present book went to press, news came of Robert Thorndike's death in Lacey, Washington. As part of a response to a request for biographical information for this section of the book, he had written, "I have been honored by awards from Columbia University, the Educational Testing Service, and the Division of Educational Psychology of APA. It has been a good life—better than I have deserved."

Michael Wertheimer, editor and author of the chapter on Max Wertheimer, is one of Wertheimer's sons. Born in Germany, he came to the United States with his family in 1933, and obtained his education in the United States. His bachelor's degree was from Swarthmore College, his master's from Johns Hopkins University, and his doctorate in experimental psychology from Harvard. Wertheimer taught at Wesleyan University for 3 years before moving to the University of Colorado in 1955, where he has been since. After early publications in experimental psychology, psycholinguistics, and social psychology, his major work has been in general psychology, theoretical and philosophical psychology, and the history of psychology. His books include texts for introductory psychology as well as *A Brief History of Psychology*. A former president of the Rocky Mountain Psychological Association, he has also been president of various divisions of the American Psychological Association: Divisions 1 (General Psychology), 2 (Teaching of Psychology), 24 (Theoretical and Philosophical Psychology), and 26 (History of Psychology). He also served many terms on the Council of Representatives and has chaired various APA boards and committees. Wertheimer received the 1983 American Psychological Foundation Distinguished Teaching in Psychology Award and the 1990 American Psychological Association Award for Distinguished Career Contributions to Education and Training, and was national president of Psi Chi, the national honor society in psychology, in 1990–91.

Charlotte White, an editor of the present book, was born and grew up in San Diego. Before entering the field of psychology, she was a graduate student in oriental history at Columbia University and art history at the Institute of Art History, New York University. White received an MA in child development at Mills College, Oakland, California, and a PhD in developmental psychology at Denver University. She held positions at Johns Hopkins University, University of California, Los Angeles, and California State University, Hayward, before returning to San Diego. Currently, she is associated with the University of California, San Diego, but her major work is with the Boyden-White Vision Laboratory in San Diego. Here, with Douglas G. Boyden and Carroll T. White, she is working on basic and applied problems in the area of visual electrophysiology.

Chapter 1

A Trans-Time Visit with Francis Galton

as recorded by
G. E. McClearn

I recall how intrigued I was when H.G. Wells's *The Time Machine* first was published. My first thought was that a man of science could have no greater boon than to be transported into the future and see to what advanced state his infant inquiries had developed. I am sure that you can imagine my astonishment when it happened—and I was plucked out of my present into this time, my future—by means of the marvelous time device of Dr. Kimble, Dr. Wertheimer, and Dr. White. The fare that I have been charged for this temporal journey is to tell you of my reactions.

This travel into the future is not an unmixed blessing. It satisfies the curiosity, but offers a near overwhelming frustration, as well. It is rather humiliating, for example, to discover that undergraduates of my future, your present, know more about so many things than did the most advanced scholars of my time. It disappoints me to learn that notions I fancied to be splendid and germinal have faded into obscure footnotes of scientific history. Worst of all, with the hindsight available from this future perspective, one sees how close one was at times to critical new insights—how very, very close—and yet failed to take the crucial steps.

However, let me say that to see these *savant* undergraduates assures that the scientific enterprise *is* cumulative and to learn that some of one's contributions *were* useful and are remembered, is very gratifying indeed.

I'm told that it is 1992, and that your nation is just 16 years past

---

*Photograph of Francis Galton courtesy of the Archives of the History of Psychology, Akron, Ohio

its bicentennial. In that context it might be appropriate to note that I had a grandfather, Erasmus Darwin, whose reputation was sufficient that he was invited to become court physician to King George III. Abhorring London city life, he declined. I wonder, if he had been able to minister successfully to the King's psychic ills, and if that monarch had therefore developed a somewhat more conciliatory attitude concerning taxation and representation, whether the whole unpleasantness of the Revolution might possibly have been avoided.

PERSONAL HISTORY

Perhaps a brief autobiographical statement will be an appropriate way to illustrate my life and times of science. My father, Samuel, was a successful banker, and was himself the son of a manufacturer. My mother, Violetta, was the eldest daughter of Erasmus Darwin. Their marriage resulted in nine children, of whom seven lived beyond infancy. I was the last born, in 1822 (and I note with some consternation the recent work on birth order), and being the baby of the family, I was very pampered by older sisters as well as by mother. It is not irrelevant, I believe, to note that my father was an amateur scientist, and from my very early years, I can remember various types of optical apparatus — microscopes, telescopes, and so on — about his study. Father published little, but I might note with some filial pride that some of his observations on colour vision anticipated the trichromatic theory later advanced by Young.

Education

My early education was of the classical sort — with much Latin, much Greek, much grammar and no mathematics, nor science worthy of note. My education was not, I later concluded, of very much value for a scientific career. When I was 16, I entered medical studies at Birmingham General Hospital. An empirical predilection revealed itself during my study of pharmaceuticals in a determination to administer them all to myself. I began alphabetically, but my enthusiasm for the experiment was dampened when I tried Croton oil, which is, as I discovered, a most remarkably effective purgative and emetic! I did not venture onward to the Ds! My training continued at Kings College, London, where I was particularly interested in anatomy and chemistry. Mathematics also appealed greatly to my mind, and I took time out for a degree in mathematics at Cambridge. At about this time, I may note, I had many lively and engaging conversations with my cousin, Charles

Darwin, who had just published the *Journal of the Voyage of the Beagle*. Perhaps more than I realized, my cousin's voyage contributed to my own wanderlust, which I was ultimately to satisfy quite thoroughly.

Freedom to Explore

My medical studies were interrupted by the death of my father. Upon coming into my inheritance I entered what I like to regard as a fallow period. Superficially, it was a leisurely and (I now quote myself) "very idle life, but it was not really so. I read a good deal all the time, and digested what I read by much thinking about it. It has always been my unwholesome way of work to brood much at irregular times." I traveled widely in Syria and Egypt, and resolved upon a geographical expedition to Africa. This expedition in 1850-1852 provided some exciting encounters with lions and episodes of tribal warfare, but it provided also many opportunities for geographical observation. My report to the Royal Geographical Society was well received, and I acquired some small reputation amongst English men of scientific affairs.

My time was well filled with various projects. Inspired by paternal example (and, as I believe, inheriting his proclivity) I undertook several inventions. I had already done some small things with respect to locks, and a rotary steam engine; I now turned my attention to the invention and development of a printing telegraph, underwater spectacles to be used by divers, hyperscopes (I believe you would call them periscopes) for seeing over women's bonnets at lectures and other uses.

I also became interested in meteorology and had the honour to originate weather maps. I was also able to discover the direction of flow around high and low pressure areas—a routine feature now on TV weather news.

A Turning Point

In 1859 there occurred an event that shaped my thoughts and channeled my energies for the rest of my life: the publication of my cousin Darwin's book, *On The Origin of Species*. I can illustrate the importance of this work by an excerpt from a letter that I wrote to Charles:

> [I] always think of you in the same way as converts from barbarism think of the teacher who first relieved them from the intolerable burden of their superstition. I used to be wretched under the weight of the old-fashioned arguments from design; of which I felt though I was unable to prove to myself, the worthlessness. Consequently, the appearance of your *Origin of*

Species formed a real crisis in my life; your book drove away the constraint of my old superstition as if it had been a nightmare and was the first to give me freedom of thought. (Pearson, 1924, Vol. 1, Plate II)

HEREDITARY GENIUS

From my first reading of this monumental book, my interest never wavered from what might best be described as the natural history of human faculty. In 1865, I made my first venture into this field by writing two articles, jointly entitled "Hereditary Talent and Character," which were published in *Macmillan's Magazine*. Four years later, a greatly expanded discussion was published with the title *Hereditary Genius: An Inquiry into its Laws and Consequences*.

The general argument presented in this work was that amongst the relatives of persons endowed with high mental ability are to be found a greater number of other extremely able individuals than would be expected by chance; furthermore, the closer the family relationship, the higher the incidence of such superior individuals. Applying Quetelet's "law of deviation from an average," which at the time was a fairly recent development, but which is familiar to all of you as the normal curve, I distinguished 14 levels of human ability, ranging from idiocy through mediocrity to genius.

No satisfactory way of quantifying natural ability was then available, so I had to rely upon reputation as an index. By reputation, I did not mean notoriety from a single act, nor mere social or official position, but "the reputation of a leader of opinion, of an originator, of a man to whom the world deliberately acknowledges itself largely indebted." The designation "eminent" I applied to those individuals who comprised the upper 250 millionths of the population (i.e., one in 4,000 persons would attain such a rank), and it was with such men that the discussion was concerned. Indeed, the majority of individuals presented in evidence were, in my estimation, the cream of this elite group, and were termed "illustrious." These were men whose talents ranked them one in a million.

By reading biographies, published accounts, and by direct inquiry, when possible and convenient, I evaluated the accomplishments of eminent judges, statesmen, peers, military commanders, literary men, scientists, poets, musicians, painters, Protestant religious leaders and Cambridge scholars, and their relatives. As a matter of fact, I also examined oarsmen and wrestlers of note in order to extend the range of inquiry from brain to brawn. In all, I found nearly 1,000 eminent men in the 300 families examined. With the overall incidence of eminence only

1 in 4,000, this result clearly illustrated the tendency for eminence to be a family trait; but more of this later.

This application of the normal curve gave me much satisfaction, showing, as it seemed to me to do, that psychical (you would say psychological) properties are susceptible to assessment and measurement just as are physical ones such as height or weight, and that they are also subject to the laws of inheritance.

STUDY OF ASSOCIATION

In an attempt to study the functioning of the mind in a more detailed way, I began investigations of my own processes of associating ideas. In my first such effort, I made an attempt to examine all of the associations that came to mind in a walk along Pall Mall. I was at once impressed that (again quoting myself)

> [t]he brain was vastly more active than I had previously believed it to be, and I was perfectly amazed at the unexpected width of the field of its everyday operations. After an interval of some days, during which I kept my mind from dwelling on my first experiences, in order that it might retain as much freshness as possible for a second experiment, I repeated the walk, and was struck just as much as before by the variety of ideas that presented themselves, and the number of events to which they referred, about which I had never consciously occupied myself of late years. But my admiration at the activity of the mind was seriously diminished by another observation which I then made, namely that there had been a very great deal of repetition of thought. The actors in my mental stage were indeed very numerous, but by no means so numerous as I had imagined. They now seemed to be something like the actors in theaters where large processions are represented, who march off one side of the stage, and, going round by the back, come on again at the other. I accordingly cast about for means of laying hold of these fleeting thoughts, and submitting them to statistical analysis, to find out more about their tendency to repetition and other matters.

I approached this problem by choosing 100 words, all beginning with the letter A, exposing them to view for 4 seconds, and recording all ideas that came to mind. My principal object was to show that a large class of mental phenomena, that have hitherto been too vague to lay hold of, admit of being caught by the firm grip of genuine statistical inquiry. Several salient points emerged from my analysis.

First, the average rate of production of association was about 50 per minute, which struck me as being a surprisingly slow rate.

Second, there were many repetitions of association upon repeated exposure. As I had concluded from my Pall Mall walk, the mind "is apparently always engaged in mumbling over its old stores and if any one of these is wholly neglected for a while, it is apt to be forgotten, perhaps irrecoverably."

Third, upon inspection, it appeared that most of the associations derived from early rather than recent experiences.

> In 1879, I reported these results in the journal *Brain* and concluded: Perhaps the strongest impression left by these experiments regards the multifariousness of the work done by the mind in a state of half-consciousness, and the valid reason they afford for believing in the existence of still deeper strata of mental operations, sunk wholly below the level of consciousness, which may account for such mental phenomena as cannot otherwise be explained.

Now, it is known that Sigmund Freud was a reader of this journal, and I may perhaps be excused the speculation that my observation may have contributed in some modest way to the theorizing that he accomplished with respect to unconscious mental processes.

IMAGERY AND INDIVIDUAL DIFFERENCES

Many of my scientific colleagues were perplexed by that part of my results which pertained to associations that were visual images, having apparently no experience with any such subjective phenomenon themselves. In order to explore the difference amongst people in imaging ability or proclivity implied by these comments, I devised a questionnaire that inquired concerning the respondent's ability to recollect the breakfast table that morning, and about the definition, clarity and brightness of the image, about the presence or absence of colour, and so forth.

A detailed account of the conclusions would be out of place at this time; I was principally impressed by the wide array of individual differences, ranging from those who reported no imagery whatsoever to those who claimed to see in imagery as much detail as if seeing the reality.

MEASUREMENT OF TALENT

In spite of my being engrossed in the development of these various approaches to a meaningful analysis of human faculty, I remained concerned about the element of subjectivity, and desired psychical measures as objective and rigorous as those that could be used in physics or chemistry or geology.

I did some small work on the ability to repeat numbers serially presented, comparing normal persons to idiots. I understand that Binet included a variant of this procedure called "digit span" in his later test, which had some considerable success and which has had some very successful descendants.

Being of mechanical inclination, I turned my attention to the design of instruments that might give reliable results with respect to what I then called keenness of sight, colour-sense, judgement of eye, hearing, highest audible note, breathing power, strength of pull and squeeze, and swiftness of blow.

A major problem arose in the gathering of information utilizing these instruments. Reputation I could assess from reading of documents; association I could investigate essentially by consulting myself (introspection), and imagery could be examined from questionnaires despatched by mail, and attended to at leisure by the respondent.

However, these new instruments required administration. A rather different order of logistical demands was made by this type of investigation, and you should remember that all expenses were borne by myself. I was, of course, quite comfortably established, but there were limits!

The solution to the problem was to set up a booth at the International Health Exhibition in 1884. A plentiful supply of potential subjects was assured by the great popularity of this Exhibition. More than 9,000 persons were attracted by the opportunity to be measured by my devices. Given your current frenetic system of grant seeking, you may be envious to learn that they each paid threepence for the privilege of being so measured.

STATISTICS

As will have become apparent, my career was dominated by consuming interest in applying mathematical and statistical manipulations to the measurement and analysis of data on human faculty. Now with the results from my Anthropometric Laboratory available, I possessed the necessary body of data, and I was able to indulge myself freely. I had already puzzled long over a phenomenon that appeared in my researches on heredity (about which more later). Inheritance seemed to involve partial determination, not the simple linear causality of simple physical systems. In the latter case, statements could be made that A *causes* B. In the former, A might influence B, but there are other factors at work, as well. How was one to characterize this partial causality?

The notion of *reversion* presented itself, referring to the observation that offspring of extreme parents were less extreme than their parents. I later changed the name to regression, which is, I have been told, a familiar term to you all. I take some pride in showing you now the first regression line, which I drew to illustrate the relationship of size of seed of parent and offspring pea plants.

The idea of correlation came a bit later; I understand that your symbol for correlation is still the *r* from my early work on reversion. The whole modern edifice that you have available of multivariate statistics, with multiple regressions, cluster analyses, numerical taxonomy, latent variable analysis and the like, delights and amazes me. It is here that I feel the jolt of time displacement most. What might we of my generation not have been able to do with these new techniques of studying corelationships? Nevertheless, I take pride and consolation from having pointed the way.

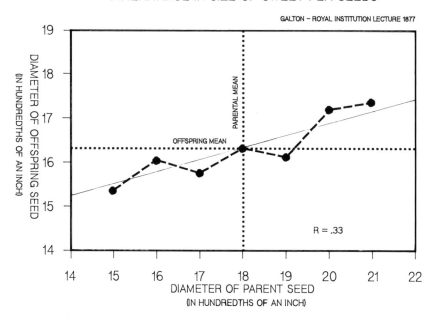

FIG. 1.1. *The first regression line.* The diameters of the seeds of offspring (vertical axis) increase with increase in the diameter of the parent seeds. Note, however, that the offspring of the largest parent seeds (21 inches) are smaller (only about 17.5 inches on the average). This illustrates the phenomenon of *regression to the mean*, one of my discoveries (from Galton's Royal Institution Lecture, 1877).

HEREDITY IN THE LABORATORY

My interest was not just in assessing human faculty, but also in studying its descent and inheritance. I did some research with rabbits in collaboration with Charles Darwin. We disagreed on the interpretation of the results, which seemed to me to call into question Charles's theory of pargenesis. I observed:

> From the well-known circumstance that an individual may transmit to his descendants ancestral qualities which he does not himself possess, we are assured that they could not have been altogether destroyed in him, but must have maintained their existence in a latent form. Therefore each individual may properly be conceived as consisting of two parts, one of which is latent and only known to us by its effects on his posterity, while the other is patent, and constitutes the person manifest to our senses.

Read today, one can see here the ideas of genetic dominance, and of the distinction between genotype and phenotype, which Mendel had seen so clearly in 1865. But my views were slightly tangential and just a bit out of focus, whereas his were direct and crisp. It is really remarkable how these views could have been so close, yet, when Mendel's laws were rediscovered in 1900, I had proceeded so far down another exploratory track that I missed the profound Mendelian discovery.

NATURE AND/OR NURTURE

It was natural enough, I imagine, that my two main interests—behavior and heredity—should have been fused. It is gratifying, indeed, to note that the test of time seems to have supported my basic premise that heredity influences behavior, as witness the now well-established field of behavioral genetics. But this field has also shown that my early conception was exceedingly simplistic. Although I then realized that both heredity and environment were involved in shaping characteristics, my regard for the influence of heredity was, I dare say, overdrawn. Even more important, I failed to understand the intricate coactivity of heredity and environment, which makes particularly clear the limitations of an either-or view of heredity and environment. (In this connection, allow me to apologize for introducing the phrase, "nature vs. nurture." It seemed at the time to capture so well, and in such easily remembered alliterative form, the essence of the inquiries into the natural history of human faculty. I can now see that the dichotomous nature of the phrase has constituted a handicap to conceptual advancement; the "nature *or* nurture" perspective clearly continues in some quarters in spite of ample demonstration that the appropriate formulation would be "nature *and* nurture.")

How I wish I could have known of this coaction of heredity and environment, and other now-commonplace conceptions that would have been revelations to me in my time: heterozygote advantage, balanced polymorphisms, Hardy-Weinberg equilibria, the conservative nature of the gene pool, and, most incredible, knowledge of the actual structure and functioning of the hereditary material! If this knowledge would have illuminated my basic science efforts, how much more might it have informed my labours in a domain that I regarded to be the obvious and urgent application of knowledge of the inheritance of human attributes to societal problems: a domain I named "Eugenics."

I defined Eugenics as the science that deals with all influences that improve the inborn qualities of a species, *and* with those influences that develop them to the utmost advantage. With this wording, I clearly included both genetic and environmental factors. I believe that I credited environment too little, however, and many of the most ardent enthusiasts in the Eugenics cause evidently lost sight of environment entirely. Furthermore, my aim was focused on the encouragement of increased reproduction of the finest of our population—positive eugenics; with the assurance of a privileged citizen of Victorian England, I was confident of my ability to identify the attributes that were good and bad, and it seemed logically compelling that it would be advantageous to our species if the "best" individuals reproduced differentially more than the "worst" individuals.

Your modern advances in genetics and in psychology make it clear that this view was not just hopelessly simplistic, both with respect to what is a "good" characteristic and also to the efficacy of reproductive differential to bring about rapid "improvement," but also dangerous. Whereas I had seen Eugenics as a force for good, it seems now to have been a prototypical case of unintended consequences of the premature, enthusiastic application of inadequate knowledge to an enormously complex situation. The notions of Eugenics, intended to uplift humankind, played a role in the unimaginable evil of genocide during World War II. With the enormously enhanced capabilities of genetic engineering now at your disposal or nearly at hand, the power to do genetic good and genetic ill is greatly enhanced. The experience with the earlier Eugenics should warn you that the application of this new power must be exercised with the greatest caution.

CONCLUSION

What message do I wish to leave behind (or ahead) with you? Simply recall that these researches of mine and those of my colleagues, which must now appear to be dry and dusty and to have been naïvely conceived and shoddily executed, had for us the immediacy and excitement that your research today has for you. We were the cutting edge then as you are now. It seems probable that a century hence, the papers you are now writing and reading will also have a musty aura to those who represent that year's cutting edge. I do not mean to suggest that you should be disheartened by this; on the contrary, you should be uplifted because we who are participants in the scientific enterprise are contributing to a *truly cumulative* effort. If I did not appear archaic to you, and if you do not to your intellectual descendants and heirs, then we shall have failed. But realization of this state of affairs may add a dash of humility to our eagerness and confidence, and sensitize us, not to what we know, but to what we don't yet know.

REFERENCES

Forrest, D. W. (1974). *Francis Galton: The life and work of a Victorian genius*. New York: Taplinger.

Pearson, K. (1924). *The life, letters and labours of Francis Galton*. London: Cambridge, University Press.

Chapter 2

William James: Spoiled Child of American Psychology

Barbara Ross

About a year and a half before his death, William James was referred to by Lightner Witmer (1909) as

> [a] philosopher-psychologist, temperamentally interested in mysticism, professionally engaged in philosophy and temporarily assuming the role of a psychologist . . . the spoiled child of American psychology, exempt from all serious criticism and the beau ideal of a large and cultured circle . . . [who] since the publication of his *Principles of Psychology*, has apparently relaxed the intellectual tradition which every man should exert over his desires.

Although James never was held completely blameless by his contemporaries, he *was* in a sense "spoiled" by them. Despite his repeated criticism of most of the experimental work being done in the German and American laboratories during the early decades of classical psychology, his colleagues granted him the highest professional honors throughout his career. He was elected president of the American Psychological Association in 1895, president of the American Philosophical Association in 1906, and received an LLD from Harvard in 1903.

EARLY YEARS

As a child, James was also spoiled in the more usual sense of that word, growing up in a well-to-do family, the eldest of five children. William

---

*Photograph of William James courtesy of the Archives of the History of Psychology, Akron, Ohio

and his younger brother, Henry, who became a major novelist, were born just 15 months apart and remained close throughout their eventful lives. They enjoyed the advantages provided by the affluence of their father, Henry James, Senior.

Henry James, Senior grew up in a large household in Albany, New York, the son of William James, our subject's grandfather and namesake. This earlier William James was an Irish immigrant who, by the early 19th century, was the wealthiest man in the state of New York, except for John Jacob Astor. Henry Senior described his mother as democratic and sympathetic, and his father as a stern man who saw to it that his children conformed to Presbyterian orthodoxy, with its emphasis on piety and frugality. Henry Senior rejected his father's religion shortly after entering Union College. He ran away to Boston and managed on his own for a few months. Then he reconciled his differences with his father, returned to Union College, and completed his degree in 1830. Two years later his father died, leaving his children enough money so that none had to earn a living (Allen, 1967).

Although Henry Senior rejected his father's Calvinist leanings, he did not abandon religion altogether. At about age 20, he was introduced to the writings of a "primitive Christian mystic," and came to believe that a person's individual salvation depends on the salvation of society. He spent his adult years writing books that were mostly on the insubstantiality of conventional morality and institutionalized religion. It mattered little that few copies of these books were ever sold.

Henry Senior's first two sons, William and Henry Junior, were born in New York City in 1842 and 1843. Later on they had two younger brothers and a sister. Possibly because of his rejection of his father's values, Henry Senior created a family situation that was spiritually and socially democratic. He provided a permissive and loving environment for his five children, and indulged them "with a sublime confidence that their characters were indestructible" (Barzun, 1983).

The Jameses were a family of travelers. They crossed the Atlantic many times. The first trip was when William and Henry were less than 2 years old. The James children did not go to regular schools, but attended private schools for varying lengths of time wherever their restless father settled: New York City, Albany, Newport, London, Geneva, Paris, and several cities in Germany.

With the exception of William's stable mother, the entire family was hypochondriacal at one time or another during their lives. When William was 2, his father suffered an unexplainable, mystical, catastrophic experience, which was unsuccessfully treated by prominent physicians and would upset the James household for almost 2 years. Finally, the reading of a Swedish mystic, Emanuel Swedenborg, provided the cure and a basis for Henry Senior's spiritual writings for the remainder of his life. Emotionally precocious, William was probably aware of his father's difficulties. At the age of 20, William also went through a traumatic time, even considering suicide. After studying anxiety himself years later, he concluded that his father's neurotic condition had resulted from suppressed childhood feelings of guilt for rebelling against his own father and his father's god.

As a young boy, William experimented with chemicals, and collected small marine animals. His father foresaw a scientific career for him. Possibly because of the vagaries of his unstructured liberal education and his general restlessness, however, William had a difficult time settling down. His first brief encounter was with art. Despite his disappointment that William had not chosen science, Henry Senior allowed William to study painting under the Newport artist, John La Farge, during 1860 and 1861. William's interest did not last.

ADULTHOOD AND THE SEARCH FOR IDENTITY

At the outbreak of the Civil War in 1861, William and Henry were about 20 years old, the right age to enlist, but neither was inclined to do so. Henry had a back ailment, and William had nervous problems. Throughout his adult life William would have recurring bouts of illness that today would probably be considered psychosomatic. Henry Senior had no difficulty allowing his two younger sons to enlist, but, because he believed that William and Henry Junior had intellectual leanings, he encouraged them to stay out of the war.

In the fall of 1861, posssibly because he felt he should be doing something constructive—and to his father's delight—William enrolled in the Lawrence Scientific School at Harvard. There he studied chemistry under Charles W. Eliot, a Cambridge neighbor of the James family who, as it turned out, proved to be a much better administrator and organizer than scientist. Eliot was later president of Harvard College and would play a significant role in William's career.

During his second year at Lawrence Scientific School, William's pains and undefinable nervousness led him to withdraw for 8 months or so to rest. When he returned to Lawrence, he shifted from chemistry to comparative anatomy, but his goals were still unsettled. After his usual painful ruminations about his place in the world, he decided to try medicine and enrolled in Harvard Medical School in 1864. Predictably, however, James's attention was soon diverted to a forthcoming expedition to Brazil to be led by the famous Harvard professor of zoology and geology, Louis Agassiz. James went along. Now 23, he hoped the trip would provide an opportunity to learn about himself and to settle on his goals in life—but it did not. Although he enjoyed parts of the expedition, he returned home physically and mentally exhausted and convinced "that each man's constitution limits him to a certain amount of emotion and action" (Allen, 1967).

DEALING WITH AMBIGUITY

James held a brief internship at Massachusetts General Hospital in the summer of 1866. Returning to his medical studies, he was beginning to believe that he actually had entered the field of medicine in order to be a physiologist. And, once again, in the spring of 1867, he interrupted his medical studies for a considerable length of time.

As it turned out, the spring of 1867 was the beginning of several years of mental and physical suffering for James. During this period, he experienced bouts of serious depression but his pliant nature allowed him to maintain basic sanity. At one point, his frequent backaches led him to Germany, purportedly for baths to relieve his pain, but he also had another reason for going. His medical studies had exposed him to German experimental physiology, which he found intriguing; he decided to see what was happening in German laboratories, and at the same time, to perfect his German.

After he arrived in Europe, James postponed the baths for a few months and enjoyed the art galleries and the theater. His correspondence during this time reveals periods of fluctuation between reinvigoration, during which he read French novels and some philosophy, and periods of poor health, marked by brooding melancholy, feelings of purposelessness and vocational doubts. In psychological terms, one might suspect that James's basic conflict was between the uncompromising spiritualism of his father and his recognition that scientific determinism as taught at the Lawrence Scientific School could be justified, at least in some cases.

James saw the universe as unfinished and in a constant state of change, providing serious challenges to the interpretation of human experience. The deterministic view made it difficult to find meaning in life; the idealists held values on such an abstract level that they were out of touch with the reality of the contemporary world. Although James found value in the deterministic view, he could not accept a determinism that gave no satisfactory explanation of evil. If evil cannot be overcome, even in part, then to believe that utter pessimism is the only escape was cynicism. If God created evil only to banish it, the human will is fiction, and life is nothing but boredom (Allen, 1967). James needed a compromise, and his later writings indicate that he had finally found one. In these writings he offered a pragmatic philosophy that he hoped would bring the conflicting views together (James, 1907a, 1907b).

In the meantime, James was groping for something personal to believe in so that he could pull himself out of his mental depression. He found a partial solution in the writing of the French philosopher, Renouvier, whom he later labeled a "nondeterminist empiricist." Renouvier's definition of free will, "the sustaining of a thought *Because I Choose To*—when I might have other thoughts," provided a handle for James. His first act of free will was to believe in free will. Later on, describing James's compromise, A. J. Ayer (1968) wrote that James "sought the advantage of being tough-minded with regard to any questions of natural fact and tender-minded with respect to morals and theology."

A PLACE IN THE WORLD

The months in Europe during 1867–1868 did not cure James's back pains nor his concerns about his future, but he did profit enormously from his extensive reading in literature and philosophy. Also, as he was gradually gaining his health in Berlin, James heard lectures on physiology by Emil Du Bois-Reymond and began to entertain ideas of approaching psychology from the perspective of physiology. The first step toward that goal was gaining a degree in medicine.

When James returned to Cambridge and thought of his forthcoming medical examination, his depression returned. In spite of all his worries, James rose to the occasion. He prepared carefully, passed the examination, and finally received the MD degree in 1869.

After receiving his medical degree, James did little of significance for several years. He spent his time reading and resting, still depressed about his lack of direction. He had decided that the physical demands of doing the rounds and laboratory research that a medical career required were more than his health could handle. More important, he found medicine lacking in intellectual challenge. Still without definite goals in life, he attended occasional lectures at Harvard. His father supported his traveling and leisure, expecting William to settle down in time.

It was at this point that James's former teacher and neighbor, Charles Eliot, helped to pull James out of his doldrums with an offer of the opportunity to teach half of a 1-year course in comparative anatomy and physiology at Harvard in 1872. Now 30 years old, William had never held a job and was still living as a spoiled child in the protected environment of the family home. He saw the offer as a godsend and, believing that it would help dispel his "philosophical hypochondria," he accepted the position.

Finally relieved of any guilt that he might have felt because of his dependency and lack of direction, William was a great success in the classroom. Having been included in intellectual discussions from an early age in his liberal household, James was at ease with students and they with him. His varied background and his attempts to relate class material to life situations were appealing to students. The breadth of his experiences and reading, his ability to communicate, and his engaging style added to his popularity. It appears that, since his reading of Renouvier in 1870, James endorsed a practical approach to learning and to life in general. Although he had been hired to teach physiology, he approached the subject broadly enough to incorporate many of his own ideas and students reacted positively. After this initial success, James was offered the whole course for the following year. Although his experience in the classroom provided self-confidence and his depression lifted, James felt that he needed another year in Europe before settling down. After that year, he was employed by Harvard for the rest of his life.

Many of the students in James's classes were to become famous. The fact that George Santayana, Gertrude Stein, and G. Stanley Hall were included in this group is well known. In addition, there were Morton Prince and Boris Sidis, both of whom made significant contributions to psychiatric and psychoanalytic thinking in America. James Jackson Putnam, a close friend of James, became an important figure in the psychoanalytic movement and might not have taken up psychoanalysis without James's influence.

James's contact with Morton Prince was a decisive factor in the latter's professional development. As had James, Prince accepted the approaches of Janet and Charcot to neurology and therapeutics and became internationally known through his writings. He championed "scientific psychopathology," founded the *Journal of Abnormal Psychology* and served as its editor for many years.

About a decade ago, David Shakow (1978) revealed that, through John Dewey, James had entered his life and had become his permanent hero. Shakow took historians to task for their "limited view" of the factors they saw as playing major roles in the development of psychoanalytic thought. He wrote:

> Such insensitivity is reflected in unmindfulness of the inferences that flow from two fundamental Jamesian principles. One is what Thorndike called James's most significant discovery in psychology: the existence of "fringes" of mental states. The other is James's emphasis on the concept,

not unrelated to the first, of "habit": the minor repetitive experiences in
our environments and in our actions . . . [that] play momentous roles in
the establishment of attitudes, receptivities [and] responses.

James shared his knowledge and his philosophies, not only with
students and professional associates, but as he became established, with
teachers, the public, and intellectuals in general (James, 1899). There
were few subjects that he did not address. He examined social and
political issues in articles on patriotism, war, lynching, the ascetic,
genius, and the hidden energies of men. James's son, Harry, described
him as "not disposed to underestimate the fighting instinct," which
James saw as a highly irritable force underlying the society of all
dominant races. He advocated international courts, reduction of arma-
ments, and other "measures that might present appeals to the war-
raging passion." James suggested that the fighting instinct should be
diverted into constructive channels, and attacked those who were
attempting to establish a social psychology based upon the supposed
hedonistic nature of man. For James, human nature was grounded in
the potential creativity of individuals, best realized in interaction with
the social order. James's concept of the social self was used in later
developments in psychological and sociological theory as a basis for
analyses of individual and group action.

IMPACT OF EUROPEAN THOUGHT

An avid reader in several languages, James was for his generation the
chief vehicle for bringing to America foreign ideas in psychology,
medicine, and neurology—particularly the work being done in France.
He reviewed Liébeault's work as early as 1868 (James, 1868). French
neurology and psychiatry were appealing to James because they were
closer to the old metaphysical conceptions than German experimental-
ism. He approved of the French attention to higher psychic functions
and the emotional and practical needs of people. French psychiatry was
particularly successful in the neurological field and in the interpretation
of organic psychoses. The clinicians were seeking underlying causes of
disease. By observing temporal changes, studying case histories, and
performing autopsies, clinicians were beginning to establish well-
defined disease entities, determined partly by their symptomatology
and partly by their underlying anatomical lesions.

Advances in the diagnosis of functional disorders also impressed
James, particularly the work of Janet and Binet on hysteria and multiple
personality. He found their work to be full of "acute psychology that

every psychologist should attend to." He predicted that the work would provoke controversy and stimulate professional interest (James, 1894a).

James's acquaintance with European psychology and psychiatry led him to promote the study of many topics that were unpopular in scientific psychology, such as hypnosis, multiple personality, hallucinations, psychical research, hysteria, the abnormal, and the studies being done in the pathology of mind in general. His promotion of such studies over the years laid much of the groundwork that compelled psychologists to pay attention to the research into dynamic processes and psychoanalytic thought (Ross, 1978).

James's account in the first volume of the *Psychological Review* of Breuer's and Freud's initial paper (James, 1894b) was the first published reference to Freud's work in America. The article claimed that hysteria is caused by a "psychic shock," reminiscences of which fall into the subliminal consciousness. If left there, they act as "thorns in the spirit," in James's words. The cure is to draw them out in hypnotism, let them produce all their emotional effects, however violent, and work themselves off. James saw nothing original here because, in England many years before, Myers had "stated that hysteria is a disease of the hypnotic stratum" and Janet's earlier work in France was simply corroborated by Freud and Breuer. At the time of Freud's visit to Clark University in 1909, when most American psychologists and psychiatrists were resistant to psychoanalytic interpretations, James wrote to Flournoy, a Geneva psychologist, that he hoped that "Freud and his pupils will push their ideas to their utmost limits. . . . They can't fail to throw light on human nature" (Le Clair, 1966).

THE AMERICAN MENTAL HEALTH SCENE

James was sensitive not only to the problematic situation of psychology during his lifetime, but also to the problems of society. In 19th-century America, materialism, giant corporations, speed, noise and status uncertainty led to nervous exhaustion, neurasthenia, or what James called "Americanitis." According to James, this new disease of the nervous system occurred because human beings, replaced by machines, feared failure and the loss of jobs, and hence experienced what we now call stress.

The traditional medical profession was doing little to solve these problems in living. There was little emphasis on therapy for the mentally ill, and not much hope for cure. The limited reforms in mental hospitals in the 1880s and 1890s did not derive from a concern for patients' welfare, but from an attempt on the part of psychiatry to achieve professional status by emphasizing physical disorders in order to gain the approval of the medical profession. Psychiatrists wanted to move psychiatry out of the institutions and into community-based programs or private practice. In his 1873 review of Isaac Ray's *Contributions to Mental Pathology*, James criticized Ray and other psychiatrists for too much focus on administration and too little concern for making new discoveries that might advance treatment.

James also made practical efforts to correct the situation. He was a charter member of the National Committee for Mental Hygiene, also known as the Beers Society, and helped its launching with a $1,000 loan. The purpose of this organization was to serve as a mediator among hospital officials, patients, and the public conscience.

James held a lifelong interest in all types of value theory, especially religion. He did not focus on the specific dogmas of particular religions, but on the personal belief of the individual believer. He saw "mindcure" or "mental healing" as an alternative to the religion of chronic anxiety that marked the earlier part of the 19th century in the evangelical circles in England and America. Religion in America was in a crisis stage during James's time. Darwin and the age of natural science made traditional beliefs in God untenable. Thomas Huxley and Herbert Spencer extended the scope of Darwin's thought so as to supplant religion altogether. Mental healing offered an optimistic scheme of life and worked for many.

Gaining momentum in America were various groups of the mental-healing and mind-cure psychotherapists, such as Christian Scientists. James firmly believed that America's greatness was due to such qualities as vigor, energy, and enthusiasm, and that a psychology of suggestion would spur on the population in the direction of success. Mind cure was designed to instill suggestions from the Scriptures in accordance with the principle that a temporary dissociation of the personality allows ready acceptance of faith-laden ideas by the subconscious. James stressed the universality of the subconscious self, which he called a "well-accredited psychological entity." He saw the mind-cure movement as practical and productive, and related these methods to the English work on subliminal consciousness and the French work on the unconscious.

From James's point of view, the great value of the mind-cure approach was that it unlocked copious human energies. James reminded readers that in physics, the conception of energy is perfectly defined and is correlated with the conception of work. Mental and moral work, however, "although we cannot live without talking about them . . . are terms as yet hardly analyzed." Unfortunately for James, the qualitative language that was necessary for discussions of the energy involved in mental work did not fit the psychology of his day, and he recognized that he would have to wait a long time before progress in that direction might be made (James, 1907b).

As this leads one to expect, although James was a strong supporter, the mind-cure movement was not taken seriously by American academic or scientific psychologists. Eminently befitting James's practical, optimistic nature, he saw it as a typically American contribution to psychotherapy. When members of the medical profession saw the faith healers as competition, they introduced a bill in the Massachusetts State Legislature in 1898 that would require faith curers to become doctors of medicine. James knew that the required medical examinations would eliminate the movement, so he gave a speech before the Legislature opposing the bill, but to no avail. The medical profession got its way.

RELATIONSHIP TO TRADITIONAL PSYCHOLOGY

James tried to get American psychologists to be more sensitive to the provisional and hypothetical nature of the foundations of scientific psychology and to broaden their conception of humanity by seeing meaningful relationships among the data coming from a variey of sources. In the September, 1890 issue of the *American Journal of Psychology*, his letter to the editor asked for help in gathering data for a scientific investigation—a "census of hallucinations."

James's unrelenting emphasis on such phenomena and on the uniqueness and individuality of psychological facts and personal experience led to disputes with leading figures in American psychology about the subject matter and methods of psychology. The turn-of-the-century attitudes toward psychology held by academic psychologists differed from those of James. One might say it was one volition against many. James was well aware that the current thought in academic circles was against him and said, "I feel like a man who must set his back against an open door quickly if he does not wish to see it closed and locked" (James, 1902).

As this way of putting it suggests, James was not exempt from criticism. When his *Principles of Psychology* (1890) was published after 12 years in preparation, the old guard was anything but silent, and pronounced with confidence that the Jamesian propositions could hardly be taken seriously (Barzun, 1983). Although the volume was impressive in the range of its experimental findings and introspective depth, *Principles* was provoking. James used examples from history and the trivialities of everyday life. G. Stanley Hall called it "impressionistic," and Wundt referred to it as literature, not science—indictments that were somewhat flawed by the host of experimental data and the serious arguments provided by James. In any event, and regardless of criticism, the *Principles* was a smashing success. It was said that with the publication of the *Principles*, James became the recognized fountainhead of the most vigorous psychological thinking in the country (Angell, 1911).

In the *Principles of Psychology* and elsewhere, it is clear that *ambivalent* is the best word to use to characterize James's opinion of traditional psychological science. He respected the empirical method, but when the results of the empirical approach could not resolve an issue, then the traditional scientific method had to be seen as limited. Much of his argument singled out scientists who denounced faith and claimed that the scientific method was purely objective. He resented their condescending attitude toward subjects outside of science and suggested that such scientists failed to recognize their *own* faith in the exclusive verity of a materialistic world view that could not account for many human experiences. James insisted, as did Mach, that scientific language is man-made. For James, hypotheses are merely ways we have of talking, not a literal copy of reality. In some cases, certain religious interpretations should be tried.

Diplomatic but critical in his evaluations of the dominant psychologies of his day, James attacked particularly the associationists, whose reductionistic analysis he replaced with his "stream of consciousness." In his Presidential Address to the American Psychological Association in 1894, James continued his indictment of traditional psychology. He condemned laboratory work and reiterated his disagreement with the associationist position. He came out in favor of psychical research and announced that he had given up the materialistic position regarding consciousness that he had taken in the *Principles* (James, 1895). On the other hand, he denounced the "soul doctrines" of the transcendental philosophers who dabble in psychology.

James McKeen Cattell reacted negatively to James's address, taking particular exception to James's support of psychical research. In his rebuttal, James claimed that Cattell seemed to miss the essential point that psychical research "still remains baffling over a large part of its surface, for the evidence in innumerable cases can neither be made more perfect nor, on the other hand, be positively explained away . . . . [O]ne can only go by probabilities and improbabilities." It appears that a chief part of James's function was to protest in psychology and in life against artificial analyses and mechanical approaches to the study of human experience.

CONCLUSION

One does not have to agree with everything that James believed in to see that he made many fundamental contributions — contributions that were recognized as important by his colleagues and continue to be recognized today. A partial list includes: his account of space perception; with Lange, his revolutionary views of emotion; the inclusion of the investigation of instinct as an essential part of the study of the human mind; his conception of habit as the basic principle of mental organization; his use of materials drawn from the pathological side of mental life to illuminate the normal; his psychology of self, which included a version of what later became Maslow's concept of self-actualization; his treatment of memory in terms of stages that anticipated the currently popular information-processing model; his appreciation of the universal importance of inhibition in the organization of behavior — as well as his conscious and systematic struggle for the recognition of the vague, the transitory and the mystical (Angell, 1911).

As is true of his psychology and his personal philosophy, James's character eludes stereotyping. He had many selves, none independent of the others. His interest in the abnormal has sometimes been attributed to one aspect of his personal makeup. During one of his depressed periods, his mother wrote, "The trouble with him is that he must express every fluctuation of feeling, and especially every unfavorable symptom . . . . [H]is temperament is a morbidly hopeless one" (Perry, 1935). His morbidness was only one aspect of his fluctuating personality. He complained of distractions in his work but he could not have gotten along without them. An intellectual adventurer who enjoyed change, he reported in an article in *Mind*, after trying nitrous oxide gas, that the experience was comparable with the Hegelian identification of opposites (James, 1882). He experimented with mescal and entertained the possibility that yoga might be a methodological way of waking deeper levels of willpower to increase one's energy.

Although moody, rebellious, and pessimistic at times, James was also courteous, sympathetic, and charming. His restlessness is reflected in his changes of mood, his frequent changes in environment, and the diversity of his interests. He realized that he lived in a time of confusion in psychology, and in his sincere attempt to understand and resolve problems, he examined all positions. His refusal to assume one position and to defend it stubbornly was a quality unparalleled in the classical days of psychology. James did not compartmentalize his ideas nor did his thinking develop along a neatly arranged materialist-to-mystical scale. He entertained such a variety of conceptions concurrently that, to the casual reader, they would appear hopelessly contradictory and incompatible (Perry, 1935). The traditional chasms that other schools left unbridged were filled by James with a positive, experiential content by the inclusion of experiences of tendency, meaning, and relatedness, and his principles of pluralism and pragmatism opened up the possibility for human accomplishments and an alternative to the resignation and despair related to a deterministic view.

REFERENCES

Allen, G. W. (1967). *William James.* New York: Viking.

Angell, J. R. (1911).Editorial. *Psychological Review, 5,* 78–79.

Ayer, A. J. (1968). *The origins of pragmatism: Studies in the philosophy of Charles Sanders Peirce and William James.* San Francisco: Freeman, Cooper.

Barzun, J. (1983). *A stroll with William James.* Chicago: University of Chicago Press.

James, W. (1868). Review of Liébault, Moral Medication. *Nation,* July 16, 7, 50–52.

James W. (1873). Review of I. Ray, Contributions to mental pathology. *Atlantic Monthly, 31,* 748–750.

James, W. (1882). On some Hegelisms. *Mind, 7,* 186–208.

James, W. (1890). *The principles of psychology.* New York: Holt.

James, W. (1894a). Review of P. Janet, Histoire d'une idée fixe. *Psychological Review, 1,* 315–316.

James, W. (1894b). Review of J. Breuer and S. Freud, Über den psychischen Mechanismus hysterischer Phänomene. *Psychological Review, 1,* 199.

James, W. (1895). The knowing of things together. *Psychological Review, 2,* 105–124.

James, W. (1899). *Talks to teachers and students on some of life's ideals.* New York: Holt.

James, W. (1902). *The varieties of religious experience.* New York: Longmans, Green.

James, W. (1907a). A defense of pragmatism. *Popular Science Monthly, 70,* March–April, 193–206, 351–364.

James, W. (1907b). *Pragmatism: A new name for some old ways of thinking.* New York: Longmans, Green.

Le Clair, R. C. (1966). *The letters of William James and Theodore Flournoy.* Madison: University of Wisconsin Press.

Perry, R. B. (1935). *The thought and character of William James.* Boston: Little, Brown.

Ross, B. C. (1978). William James: A prime mover of the psychoanalytic movement in America. In G. E. Gifford (Ed.), *Psychoanalysis, psychotherapy,and the New England medical scene 1894–1944.* New York: Science Editions.

Shakow, D. (1978). The contributions of the Worcester State Hospital and post-Hall Clark University to psychoanalysis. In G. E. Gifford (Ed.), *Psychoanalysis, psychotherapy, and the New England medical scene 1894–1944.* New York: Science Editions.

Witmer, L. (1909). William James. *Psychological Clinic, 2,* 288–289.

Chapter 3

THE SPIRIT OF IVAN PETROVICH PAVLOV

Gregory A. Kimble

For the sake of the conversation to follow, please let me present academician Pavlov in a role that he would certainly reject, even for the light-hearted purposes of this occasion. Imagine that his ghost is an observer here at this convention, his presence motivated out of curiosity: has psychology managed to become a science since the 1920s, when he became interested in the problems of psychology, but was repelled by the kind of thinking that he found in the field? To help you get the spirit of his opinion, let us listen to the ghost of Pavlov speaking for himself.[1]

Regularly, from 1921 until the day I died, I held a series of laboratory meetings, known as my "Wednesdays." At these meetings I often spoke quite bluntly on many topics, including the psychologists. I had no respect for most of them. On one of those occasions I made remarks like these: I have gone back to the grudge that I had against the psychologists. At first I renounced them, then I became reconciled with them to a degree, but now the facts have turned me against them once more. They apparently want their subject to remain forever unexplained. How they love the mysterious! Everything that can be explained physiologically they reject (Pavlov, 1955, p. 554). It is clear to me that they jealously protect the behavior of animals and men from physiological explana-

---

[1]Much of the content of this chapter is almost quotation from Pavlov's *Selected Works* (1955). I gave up the use of exact quotations because there were too many expressions that were awkward.

*Photograph of Ivan Petrovich Pavlov courtesy of the National Library of Medicine, Bethesda, Maryland.

tions. They constantly ignore such explanations and do not try to apply any of them in an objective way (pp. 442–443).[2]

I suspect that this rejection of physiology was related to the fact that most psychologists prefer words to explanations. More than once, I criticized that kind of silliness; for example, now gentlemen, let us turn to the psychologists. They are, assuredly, experts at playing with the language but they fully disregard the facts. They amuse themselves with words, but they ignore reality. They are an exceptional type of thinking people. This is absolutely clear (pp. 571, 611).

This foolish search for explanation in vocabulary was the banner of the enemy I combatted in my lifelong struggle against the idealists. My approach was strictly materialistic, whereas the idea of the soul appeared to be ingrained in all of the psychologists. The trait was transparently obvious, even when they tried to hide it, behind expressions such as "dynamic organization" or something of the sort (p. 581). I am afraid that things have not improved much since my time. They may have gotten worse. I see that the American Psychological Association even has a Division, Number 46, that is just for psychologists who are mediums.[3] What a science!

Naturally I wonder. Does anything remain of the science I created more than 50 years ago? To find out, I will attend some of their meetings over the next few days and report back to you. Before I leave, however, perhaps I should review my life and contributions to remind you of the criteria I'll be using when I make these judgments.

BIOGRAPHY

I was born in the Russian town of Ryazan, about 200 kilometers south and slightly east of Moscow, on September 14, 1849, the son of a poor village priest. I learned to read by the age of 7 but I was seriously injured in a fall from a stone wall at about that age, and did not go to school until 4 years later.

Education

The first school I attended was the Ryazan church school. Upon graduation, I entered the Ryazan Ecclesiastical Seminary, expecting to

---

[2]From here on, I will not cite Pavlov's name or give the date, but only give the pages when I refer to Pavlov's *Selected Works.*.

[3]Obviously Professor Pavlov misunderstood the meaning of this division's name, "Division of Media Psychology."

follow my father's footsteps and become a priest. As I was entering my teens, in the 1860s, I became fascinated with science, as a result of reading some popular books on Darwin and physiology, and Sechenov's *Reflexes of the Brain*. This interest led me to leave the seminary and enter the University of St. Petersburg. I took advantage of an arrangement between the two institutions that made it possible for students to go to the university before completing their work in the seminary.

At the university, I was particularly impressed by Tsyon, a professor of physiology, who turned my interests toward research. Following graduation, in 1875, I continued my education at the Military–Medical Academy and studied for the MD degree, not to become a physician but to qualify myself for a career in physiology. At the academy, I served for 2 years as assistant to Professor Ustimovich and did the work on the circulatory system that formed the basis of several early publications and the dissertation that I submitted for my medical degree.

Professional Career

I received the MD degree in 1883 and spent 1884–1886 in Western Europe, working in the laboratories of Heidenhain at Breslau and Ludwig at Leipzig. Heidenhain was interested in studying digestion in the dog with the aid of an exteriorized section of the stomach. He had actually developed an operation to produce such a pouch, but he had not solved the problem of maintaining its nerve supply. Later, when I perfected the operation, the people in our laboratory referred to it as the Heidenhain–Pavlov pouch.

In 1890 I became professor of pharmacology at the Medical–Military Academy. One year later, I was invited to organize a department of physiology in the newly formed Institute of Experimental Medicine. In 1895 I was appointed to the chair of physiology and began the work on digestion for which I received the Nobel Prize in 1904. The first book-length report of this research, *The Work of the Digestive Glands*, was published in 1897. An English translation appeared in 1902.

RESEARCH ON DIGESTION

My experimental work on gastric secretions, with chronic physiological preparations, is traceable to the report by an American physician, of a patient who survived a gunshot wound that created an opening directly into the stomach, allowing observation of its reactions under various conditions. In 1842, the Russian, Bassov, and in 1843, the Frenchman, Blondlot, independently thought of creating such a fistula surgically in lower animals. Both performed the indicated operation on dogs, by opening the abdominal wall and inserting a metal tube directly into the stomach. The tube remained in place for a long time but, for the study of digestion, there were problems. Unless the animal had just eaten, little gastric juice came from the fistula. When larger volumes of the secretions could be obtained, they were mixed with food and difficult to analyze.

Eventually I found a way to solve these problems with the creation of the Heidenhain–Pavlov pouch—more commonly called the Pavlov pouch. To construct the pouch, approximately one-tenth of the stomach was surgically isolated, with nerve and blood supply intact, and formed into a miniature stomach with a fistula leading to the exterior of the body. The actions of this separate stomach exactly mirror the function of the rest of the organ but food does not reach it and the gastric secretions can be measured, uncontaminated by the presence of food. Because of its smaller size, of course, the pouch yields less gastric juice—only about one-tenth the amount secreted by the intact stomach.

In studies of dogs prepared in this way, we made a number of significant discoveries, all tied together by a fact that was basic in my later thinking about conditioned reflexes. Gastric secretions are adaptive; they meet the physiological needs of the animal in delicate and subtle ways: (a) The total amount of gastric juice secreted is proportional to the amount of food consumed. (b) There are variations in gastric secretions that depend upon the kind of food to be digested. (c) The rate of secretion is a decreasing function of time since eating. The amount of gastric juice is greatest just after eating, when the amount of food to be digested is large. After that, the secretion gradually decreases, as the amount of still-undigested food diminishes. (d) The control of the digestive mechanisms involves a "psychic" component that enhances their adaptive value in ways that I will describe later. You will recognize that these "psychic secretions" are the conditioned reflexes that I would study for the remainder of my life. Today, I am better remembered for that research than for the work that won the Nobel prize. Incidentally, the fact that I described some of these phenomena in *The Work of the Digestive Glands*, published in 1897, disproves the Americans' claim that the graduate student, Twitmeyer, discovered the phenomenon. He did not publish his dissertation until 1902.

STUDY OF THE HIGHER NERVOUS ACTIVITY

The main reason I shifted from gastric secretions to salivation when I began the study of conditioned reflexes was that, for such investigations, it was much easier to exteriorize a salivary gland than it was to make a Pavlov pouch. We performed this minor operation on dogs and studied the effects of delivering food, acid or sand into the dog's mouth. The presence of the psychic component in the reflex became immediately apparent. For example, one dog salivated when we merely displayed food or a familiar bottle of acid, or pretended to throw sand in his mouth.

At some point, I had the insight that these psychic reflexes reflect happenings in the dog's cerebral hemispheres rather than in the glands themselves, and that their study is the direct investigation of brain function. In *The Work of the Digestive Glands*, I relegated the concept of psychic reflex to the category of metaphor and introduced the term "conditional reflex" to express the idea that the reflex was contingent upon the presentation of the originally neutral stimulus. Unfortunately the English mistranslation, "conditioned reflex," which misses this essential point, was generally accepted. Whatever it was called, however, my science had become the science of "the higher nervous activity," an expression that the Soviets use to this day.

Temporary Connection

My earliest investigations led to the discovery, in their general form, of many of the most important principles of conditioning and to the outline of a neurophysiological theory that I will describe now. A conditioned reflex (CR) is formed by combining an indifferent conditioned stimulus (CS), say the flash of an electric bulb, with an unconditioned stimulus (US), for instance food, which produces the unconditioned reflex (UR) of salivation. In this experiment, the stimulation provided by the light goes from the retina to the visual center in the cerebral hemisphere and creates a focus of excitation there. Because the light is accompanied by the food, another stronger focus of excitation is produced in the nervous center corresponding to the US, and the weaker excitation, instigated by the CS, is diverted to the stronger one. With repeated pairings of the CS and the US, a path between the two centers is paved, and a *temporary connection*, a conditioned salivary reflex, is formed.

For a long time I believed that the connection was entirely in the cortex but, before long, I realized that it actually occurs at more than one neurological level. Subcortical pathways are always implicated and, in addition, the exact cortical locale of the highest connections depends on the kind of association. For example, connections involving the second signal system (language) occur in the frontal regions of the cortex. I reported some of the research that led to these conclusions at the International Congress of Psychology at New Haven in 1929.

Irradiation and Concentration

When the stimulation of the CS reaches the cerebral hemispheres, the excitation it produces there spreads out, or *irradiates*, and is attracted to the center of the US, forming the temporary connection. Once the connection has been elaborated, this process of irradiation plays a fundamental role in the functioning of the connection. For example, the irradiation of excitation from its cortical center allows the CS, presented all alone, to arouse the center corresponding to the US and elicit a response. Because of its dependence on irradiation, the strength of the conditioned reflex is a function of the physical intensity of the CS. The stronger the CS, the greater the irradiation and, therefore, the greater the strength of the conditioned connection.

After its initial irradiation, excitation returns to its point of origin and its residual effect is concentrated there. This process of *concentration* means that the conditional connection is specific to the cortical center of the CS involved in its establishment. Reactions to other stimuli are possible, however. When a stimulus similar to the CS is presented, it affects a center near to that of the CS. The excitation produced by the new stimulus irradiates to the center of the CS, arousing it and causing excitation there to irradiate, in turn. This indirectly–caused irradiation reaches the center of the UR and elicits a response. The strength of the arousal elicited in this fashion varies directly with the similarity of the eliciting stimulus to the CS. This explains the phenomenon of stimulus generalization and its associated gradient. Indeed, in those days I referred to generalization as irradiation. The processes of irradiation and concentration also apply to inhibition and have an important aftereffect. These are the topics that I turn to next.

Two Types of Inhibition

Inhibition is an essential component of the higher nervous activity but excitation and inhibition are so closely related that their effects are hard to disentangle. I often referred to them metaphorically as the Roman god, Janus, whose two faces looked simultaneously in opposite directions. They are inseparably linked, but they have opposite effects on reflexes. Excitation enhances reflexes; inhibition restrains them.

Almost from the beginning, I recognized two forms of inhibition. The first is *external inhibition*. It occurs, for example, when a novel (external) stimulus, presented just before or during a conditioning trial, prevents the occurrence of the CR. External inhibition occurs because arousal of the cortical center corresponding to this new stimulus attracts some of the excitation normally attracted to the center of the CS and, in that way, disrupts the CR.

The second type of inhibition, *internal inhibition*, develops whenever a CS is presented without a US, for example: (a) during extinction; (b) whenever the negative stimulus is presented in a discrimination-learning experiment; (c) in backward conditioning, where the CS follows the US; and (d) during the interval of delay in experiments when the time between CS and US is long. In this last case, the CS is nonreinforced during the first part of its duration.

Internal inhibition involves a temporary connection that is just as fragile as the connection of excitatory elements. Whereas the inhibition caused by withholding reinforcement destroys the excitatory connection, the delivery of reinforcement destroys the inhibitory one.

Mutual Induction

By the neural process called *induction*, both excitation and inhibition, leave the opposite states in their cortical centers after their arousal. Because of irradiation they also leave this opposite condition in nearby cortical regions. Thus, following their excitation, both the center corresponding to the CS and the centers that surround it are in an inhibitory state. Conversely, immediately following the inhibition of these centers, they are in a state of excitation. These processes of induction obviously add a great deal of complexity to my theory. They are very important, however, because they contribute to the adaptive value of conditioning, a point that I will come to in a moment.

Analysis and Synthesis

The cerebral hemispheres consist of a vastly complex collection of analyzers, corresponding to elements in the environment. These analyzers comprise a *cortical mosaic* that is constantly undergoing changes brought on by all the mechanisms just discussed. These mechanisms enable the organism to analyze events in the environment into their elements or to synthesize these elements to produce new combinations, depending on the requirements of the situation.

One of my complaints about the psychologists was that so many of them failed to understand that analysis is a fact of neural life. For example, when Karl S. Lashley argued for equipotentiality in the function in the brain, he drew the original, but quite inconceivable, conclusion that the most complex activities of the apparatus are effected without the participation of its local parts and chief connections; or, in other words, that the whole apparatus functions, somehow or other, independently of its components (p. 432).

The Gestalt psychologists were even worse than Lashley in their failure to appreciate the reality of analysis. They carried such holistic ideas to a totally absurd extreme. Since 1912, Gestalt psychology has endeavored to prove that any distinction in psychology between the elements and the whole is a misconception. That psychology invariably and exclusively deals with the study of the whole. But allow me, please, to ask this: How can anyone get to know the whole without breaking it up? Take, for example, the simplest machine. How can the principle of its working be understood, if it is not dismantled and if the interdependence of its parts is not considered? This is truly strange reasoning and it passes my comprehension (p. 572).

[This next point is both unkind and off the subject, but I think that I must make it]. The ringleader of this gang of intellectual hooligans was Wolfgang Köhler. Köhler tried to prove that apes are intelligent—that in this respect, unlike dogs, they are close to humans. What proof did he advance? His sole and fundamental, but peculiar, proof was this. When the ape is given the task of taking hold of fruit suspended at a certain height, and in order to accomplish this, it needs definite instruments, for example, a stick and some boxes, all its unsuccessful efforts to get the fruit are not proof of intelligence. These are simply trial and error. According to Köhler, the ape's intelligence is proved by the fact that it sits for a period without doing anything. In this view, the ape accomplishes some kind of intellectual work when it is sitting, and this proves its intelligence (p. 581). How absurd! How can a professor of Berlin University, not an old man living out his days but a young man in the prime of life, talk such nonsense? (p. 596). Now back to a more important subject, the adaptive significance of conditioning.

CONDITIONING IS ADAPTIVE

I realize now that I never understood the different schools of American psychology. I considered myself to be nearest to the behaviorists in outlook, although I criticized them because their neglect of the second signal system reduced the usefulness of that approach in the understanding of human behavior. I particularly admired Thorndike's studies of trial-and-error learning, which I thought of as belonging to the Behaviorist tradition. Now I know that Thorndike's laws of repetition and effect put him closer to the Functionalists than the Behaviorists. That is how I should have classified him and how I should have classified myself. For I believe, above all, that the higher nervous activity is adaptive.

However that may be, in their criticisms of Thorndike's work, the Gestalt psychologists found another way to reveal their limitations. In this case, the main offender was Kurt Koffka. [Koffka's diatribes were so full of nonsense that, once more, I am about to depart from the theme of these reminiscences. Please forgive me]. Discussing the problem of learning, Koffka based himself exclusively on the anthropoid studies of Köhler. He came to the conclusion that all learning consists in insight, and that Thorndike's claim that learning is by trial and error was simply a mistake on Thorndike's part, a misunderstanding of the meaning of the animal's behavior, you might say. Koffka thought that Thorndike's trial-and-error principle, if true, would have to mean that the elimination of unsuccessful movements and fixation of the successful ones must go forward without any participation on the part of the animal! How do you like that? You see how preposterous that deduction is! (p. 578). Now back again to the discussion of the adaptive value of the mechanisms of conditioning.

Unconditioned and Conditioned Reflexes are Adaptive

Most unconditioned reflexes allow the organism to make adjustments to critical occurrences in the environment. Such reflexes as salivation, blinking, and withdrawal from painful stimulation are important to survival. It is easy to see, however, that the survival value of unconditioned reflexes is limited in two ways: First, they only occur to very specific stimuli; their adaptive value cannot be general. Second, they only occur as responses to these stimuli. The reaction often is too late to be adaptive.

Conditioned reflexes correct both of these defects in the unconditioned reflex mechanism. First, they promote a more general form of adaptation because they can connect a reflex to any stimulus the organism can detect. Second, they solve the problem of timing because the very essence of conditioned reflexes is their anticipatory character. They permit the organism to foresee critical events and to react appropriately in advance. The fragility of the conditioned connection increases the subtlety of this adaptation. The easy making and unmaking of connections means that serviceable (reinforced) CRs remain with an organism whereas useless (unreinforced) CRs disappear.

I know now that my belief that conditioned connections can be established between a reflex and any stimulus whatsoever was too extreme. Later investigation would reveal that there are biological constraints on learning. Some connections are easy to condition; others are difficult, perhaps impossible. For example, research on taste aversions has shown that sickness is readily conditionable to tastes but not to visual and auditory stimulation. However, those demonstrations came long after I was dead.

Adaptive Value of Inhibition

One property that unconditioned and conditioned reflexes have in common is that they are automatic. Particularly in human beings, this is usually adaptive, because it allows the organism to respond to familiar stimuli without involvement of the second signal system. That system, then, is free to deal with more important projects. Such automatic reactions are sometimes maladaptive, however—on those occasions when the animal responds automatically instead of attending to an unfamiliar stimulus. External inhibition provides a way of disrupting automatic reflexes when something novel happens and the adaptive thing to do is to attend to this new event.

Internal inhibition has adaptive value of several sorts. It extinguishes useless CRs. It promotes the development of discriminations that inform the organism of the stimuli to react to and those not to react to. It serves a timing function, allowing the organism to deal adaptively with the long intervals that sometimes intervene between a signal (CS) and what is signalized (US). The inhibition of delay, established in the initial portions of such intervals, prevents the occurrence of a CR too far in advance of an appropriate stimulus. Finally, the inductive inhibition of the cortical cells immediately after their arousal prevents refiring of these cells, or lessens the intensity of firing. It protects them from damage by stimulation that is too frequent or too strong.

The idea that inhibition is adaptive has extremely general implications. For example, sleep is a widespread irradiation of inhibition that allows the cells of the cerebral cortex to rest and recover normal function. For such reasons I recommended sleep as therapy for nervous and mental disease.

INDIVIDUAL DIFFERENCES

At this point I would like to add a word on a topic that most psychologists proclaim to be important and then proceed to neglect—individual differences. Even in my early work on digestion, I was impressed by the great variation in the reactions of individual subjects. When I turned to the study of the higher nervous activity, I noted that there are also differences in the conditionability of animals. Some are positively indifferent and poor subjects. For success in the conditioning experiment, it was necessary to use impressionable and excitable animals. I also learned that one has to reckon with the understanding and cunning of the dog. It is important not to allow the animal to get the impression that it will be tricked or disappointed; otherwise the regularities in its behavior will disappear.

Later on, I developed a series of theories of these differences, always postulating that they result from variations in three fundamental dimensions of brain activity: (1) the absolute strengths of excitation and inhibition; (2) the balance between those two processes; and (3) their lability in a particular nervous system. Obviously these three dimensions provide for a great range of individuality among animals if one assumes that many gradations may exist on each dimension and that these values are less than perfectly correlated. In practice, however, I tended to limit my theorizing to a small number of types that I viewed as types of temperament.

From the beginning, I made a distinction between "temperament" and "character." I considered character to be the result of experience or upbringing, whereas temperament referred to the inborn strength, equilibrium, and lability of the nervous processes. The question whether a given trait is a reflection of character or temperament is an important topic for research, but most of the details remain to be discovered. At one time I had the hunch that cowardice in a dog is the expression of a temperament characterized by a weak or inhibitory nervous system, and that a brave dog's temperament reflects a strong or excitatory nervous system. This guess turned out to be wrong.

The evidence on this point came from a study in which the investigators divided puppies from two litters into two groups of four each. One group was confined from birth to cages. The other lived in a free environment. The results were that, after 2 years of these treatments, the dogs in the confined group were all cowardly, whereas the others were all brave. However, none of the dogs in either group was of a weak or inhibitory type when tested in conditioning experiments. These results meant that cowardice is a symptom, not of temperament, but of character (pp. 317–318).

The best known of my typologies gave neurological reality to Hippocrates's four categories of temperament: melancholic, choleric, phlegmatic, and sanguine. I described them in the following manner:

Melancholic—weak both in inhibitory and excitatory processes, so weak that equilibrium and mobility are irrelevant.

Choleric—strong but unequilibrated, excitatory processes being dominant.

Phlegmatic—strong and equilibrated with calm external behavior.
Sanguine—strong and equilibrated with lively external behavior.

You realize, of course, that this typology was tentative. I always regarded the development of an improved classification as an important matter for future theory and research, but physiology lost interest in such topics. Unfortunately, by default, they fell into the hands of the psychologists and psychiatrists who corrupted them. Possibly the worst offender was Ernst Kretschmer, whose classification obtained almost universal recognition, especially among psychiatrists. This system claims that mental disorders are inborn functions of our body type. The long, thin, cerebral physique is the basis for dementia praecox; the soft, round, visceral build is the foundation of the manic–depressive disorders. This theory implies that all human beings carry nervous and mental diseases in embryo. Such delusions must be regarded as mistaken and inadequate (p. 340).

HONORS AND LAST YEARS

Now it is Sunday, and it is almost time to give you my impressions of the quality of the psychology that I encountered at this convention. Before I offer my evaluation, however, I should finish the biography that I began much earlier in these rambling remarks.

Following the October Revolution of 1917, my (already comfortable) situation took a considerable turn for the better. Although I was critical of the revolutionists until the early 1930s, my international reputation as well as the nature of my teachings prevented reprisal. The Bolsheviks saw that the concept of the conditioned reflex implied the possibility of radically retraining an entire people. In 1921, in recognition of that implication of my work, the People's Commissars directed that steps be taken to create as soon as possible the most favorable conditions for safeguarding my research, to print a deluxe edition of my scientific work, to supply me and my wife with special rations equal in caloric value to two academic rations, to assure to us the perpetual use of our apartment and to furnish it and my laboratory with the maximum conveniences.

During the last years of my life I continued the work on conditioned reflexes and extended it to include instrumental behavior and problem solving in anthropoid apes. I made my peace with the Soviet government when Hitler came to power in Germany. In 1935, at the fifteenth International Physiological Congress, I was proclaimed the foremost physiologist of the world. I died of pneumonia on February 27, 1936, at the age of 87.

On February 29, 1936, just 2 days after my death, the Soviet government took immediate steps to preserve my memory. They issued a decree requiring that a monument be erected to my memory on one of the central squares in Leningrad, that the First Leningrad Medical Institute be renamed "The Pavlov Institute," that my collected works be published in Russian, French, English, and German, that my brain be kept in the Brain Institute in Moscow, that my laboratory and study be maintained as a museum, that my widow be given a pension of 1,000 rubles per month, and that the government furnish the expenses connected with my funeral and the perpetuation of my memory. I was buried on March 1, 1936, in Volkov cemetery beside the graves of Mendeleev and my son.

SALVAGING PSYCHOLOGY

Now, finally, after all this talk, let me give you my evaluation of contemporary psychology. As I said I would, I attended several of the meetings at this convention. My impressions come from that experience. Some of the research reported at what they called a "science weekend" seemed quite good but, elsewhere, there was nothing of much substance. I heard no mention of the science of the higher nervous activity. The contributions of Clark L. Hull, the American whose thinking was closest to my own, seem totally forgotten. More disturbing were the allegations that I heard, that modern psychology is guided in its theorizing by something that the neo-Gestalt psychologist, Edward C. Tolman, called a "cognitive map." You can imagine what I thought of that! In the end, I came away with the same old question. How did a science as important as psychology happen to fall into hands like these? Is there any hope of salvaging psychology as a science?

Perhaps there is. In addition to the papers on research, I listened in on several closet conversations in which the discussions were of politics. From what I heard at those meetings I gather that the thing to do, when you are dissatisfied with some aspect of psychology, is to submit a resolution to the council of Representatives. So I have written one, on the true purposes of psychology, which I hope will be adopted by the council. At first, I thought that I would have a problem getting recognized, for reasons of my ghostly status. But then I remembered Division Number 46, the division for psychologists who are also mediums. I have been trying, so far without success[4], to send a

---

[4]To be expected. What Pavlov could not have known is that Division 46 is a small division. It has no Representatives on Council.

telepathic communication to that division's Council Representatives, hoping that one of them will submit my resolution for me. I am proposing a change in the bylaws of the association, replacing Article I, *Objects*, with the following language. If we all concentrate together, perhaps the message will get through.

OBJECT

The principal object of the study of psychology is to disclose the laws of human psychical activity and to include psychology in the sphere of natural science. This mission includes the aim to elucidate the causes of human nervous and mental disorders, as well as the effects of drugs, so that we become able to repair the damaged mechanism of the human organism on the basis of an exact knowledge of it.

Psychology uses strictly physiological methods to learn the laws governing human mental activity, but with a special caution: it vigorously combats the animism and dualism of psychologists who deny the material foundation of the psychical processes.

This principle does not mean that psychology applies to man the laws of higher nervous activity observed in other animals, in a purely mechanical way. For, when evolution reached the stage of man, an extremely important addition, speech, was made to the mechanisms of the nervous activity. As a result, the peculiarities of the human nervous activity sharply distinguish man from other animals. It would be the height of presumption to regard these first steps of physiology as solving that supreme mechanism of human nature functions (pp. 643–647).

ACKNOWLEDGMENTS

This chapter, essentially verbatim, is the text of an invited address, delivered at the 1990 APA Convention, under the auspices of the Division of General Psychology.

REFERENCES

Pavlov, I. P. (1910). *The work of the digestive glands* (2nd ed.). (W.H. Thompson, Trans.). London: Griffin.
Pavlov, I. P. (1955). *Selected works*. K. Koshtoyants (Ed.). (S. Belsky, Trans.). Moscow: Foreign Languages Publishing House.

Chapter 4

FREUD: 3 CONTRIBUTIONS

Ernst G. Beier

The original title of this work was "Three Contributions to the Understanding of Man," but I have decided to change it, because of something that I am noticing here today: the astonishing similarity of men's and women's clothing. On looking around and seeing those resemblances, I realized at once that I should not have said "three contributions to the understanding of *man*," because the use of the word "man" for all humankind could be seen as prejudicial toward women. So permit me to correct my title to simply "three contributions." I will also try to curb my tendency to use sexist language throughout this presentation.

The observation that the men and women in the audience here look so much alike leads me to invite you to join me in some interesting lines of speculation. Apparently males and females no longer differ quite so much in their self-image as they used to. If this observation is correct, then my original formulation of men's and women's roles—that men are the proud but oversensitive possessor of a penis and that women are driven by their envy for men's defining part—was too simpleminded. The same conclusion seems to apply to my opinions about male and female creativity. Whereas, superficially, it seems true that women express their natural creativity by giving birth, and that men substitute art and war for their lack of natural creativity, those conclusions may be more fantasy than truth. It may well be, instead, that women have creative potentials that through the centuries have remained dormant—potentials that I failed to recognize, precisely because of their dormancy.

---

*Photograph by Max Halberstadt from THE LIFE AND WORKS OF SIGMUND FREUD, Vol. 3 by Ernest Jones. Copyright 1953, 1955, 1957 by Ernest Jones. Reprinted by permission of Basic Books, a division of HarperCollins Publishers Inc.

Women may, in fact, develop talents that my theory would find amazing and totally unexpected, once they are given the opportunity.

No doubt the same thing could be said for men, although I don't think that they ever can be trained to give birth. On the other hand, it seems that one of my students, Bruno Bettelheim, proclaimed that he had found in men the envy for symbolic wombs. If that is the case, that represents a bridge across the gender gap. On such grounds, I plan to revise my formulation as evidence permits. Actually, such revisions in my theorizing have already begun. In my earlier formulations, I used the term "castration anxiety" to refer to the little boy's fear of punishment for his sexual attraction to his mother. Today, however, I do not think of such anxiety as a specific male attribute. It is merely that the two words indicate the dread possessed by everyone, both male and female, of the loss of libidinal pleasures. Although the evidence is not all in, I am beginning to think that men and women may be pretty much alike, when their circumstances are the same. This change is in line with the many other changes that I've made in psychoanalytic theory upon the discovery of new facts.

A HISTORY OF CONTROVERSY

As some of you might recall, I was last in the United States at Clark University in 1909. On that occasion I got what you might call a mixed reception— probably not entirely due to the poor translations of my work done by my friend, Brill. At that time, America was even more governed by puritanism than it is now, and as a result, resisted some of the most daring tenets of psychoanalysis. Of course, this was not a great surprise to me; the University of Vienna had refused me the title of professor and only gave me the adjunct professor title, just because I had proclaimed that even children have sexual urges.

Responsibility for Incest

Speaking of sexual urges, I understand that there are those in many of the Western countries who hold me personally responsible for the prevalence of incest. These champions of the incest taboo claim that I shouldn't have changed my earlier formulations by stating that it is incestual desire as well as the incestual act that is associated with neurosis. My critics claim that I should have stuck with my original formulation that all neurotics have been victimized and molested in their youth. They feel that, if I had maintained the statement that all neurotics had been incestually molested, we would have less incest today.

While I am greatly honored by the supposition that a word of mine could have been so effective, I resent the implication that I lacked the courage to stand up for my beliefs. As far as courage is concerned, it probably took more of what you people call "guts" to say in the Victorian age that children have sexual urges than to claim that they were molested. However that may be, according to present estimates, there are more than 20 to 30 million individuals in the United States who are thought to have been molested and, although these figures are terrible, are these victims all neurotics? I have always been opposed to making patients out of people artificially by the stroke of a pen. However all of that may be, it seems virtually certain that one basis for the violent rejection of my views was that the formulation required acceptance of my concept of the Oedipus complex. And there we are dealing with violent feelings of love and hate and fear and anxiety, disregarding whether there is actual bloodshed.

Influence on Academic Psychology

In 1961 my daughter Anna came from England for a visit to Clark University. She observed that American psychology was so desperately preoccupied with pedantic research in an effort to establish its scientific credentials, that the mass of psychoanalytic literature was almost totally disregarded. Since then things have changed. Browsing through one of your major research libraries, I found that the index volumes of abstracts, each contain many thousands of references to psychoanalysis, reflecting altogether some 150,000 books, articles, and papers. Alas, as with most of the literature in psychology, they are left to gather dust now in the library. But, as you say, they have done their thing. It is with special excitement that I noticed, in the articles on information processing and retrieval, that modern psychologists have even rediscovered my concept of the Unconscious (with a capital U) and how it works. Paradoxical as it seems, the cognitive psychologists have rediscovered the fact that there are thought processes taking place even though the person has no awareness of them. I really don't mind that most of these researchers either are uninformed or are unwilling to give me credit for an early discovery of these phenomena. The fact that they have hit upon an idea that psychoanalysis had long ago is the important consideration.

Impacts on Everyday Life and Language

Although there are rises and declines in the popularity of psychoanalytic thought in the United States, I am pleased to observe that psychoanalytic ideas have had a great impact on many phases of everyday life.

Think of some of the words that have become part of the vocabulary of your language, such as repression, regression, psychosexual development, ego function, rationalization, defensive behavior, to mention just a few. I think that there are also deeper changes that have occurred in the Western nations that probably have to do with some of our earlier formulations. For example in the courts, judges nowadays not only deal with the crime committed, but also with the psychological history of the individual. The whole idea of rehabilitation is based on such an idea, the idea that people can be retrained so as to bring out the best of their life forces.

Relationships to Psychotherapy

The enormous spread of psychotherapy — which at first was only for the affluent, but is now drifting downward, even to the lowest classes, through official government centers — perhaps got its start in the discovery of the psychoanalytic talking treatment. I'm not claiming that psychoanalysis actually created the talking treatment. Obviously Socrates came before us, but the talking treatment, for people who suffer, was the key element of the psychoanalytic movement that soon spread, and came to dominate psychiatry.

I recall with some amusement how psychiatry, not quite knowing where it belongs in medicine, swayed back and forth between psychotherapy and somatotherapy in the early years of this century. At first the psychiatrists invented all sorts of ineffective electrical and chemical treatments for those who suffered from mental disorders. Then, in the competition with psychology and social work, most of the psychiatrists turned to mental treatments, and went whole hog for psychoanalysis. The Menninger Clinic was the hub of the psychoanalytic movement — or so it thought.

Even when psychoanalysis was in its heyday, a few of the psychiatrists continued doing lobotomies and using electric shock, often to the amazement and dismay of the other health-delivering professions. This preference for somatotherapy seems to be deeply ingrained in the makeup of psychiatrists. Today they are going back to chemical treatments, based upon new and monumental discoveries about the effects of mind-altering drugs, frequently those that had found earlier uses in primitive medicine. No doubt drugs do have an impact on individuals. But, alas, they also have significant side-effects — and although some of them will diminish symptoms of suffering, they will not restore a patient's dignity and well-being. Only psychoanalytic or a talking therapy can accomplish that.

In order for neurotic patients to recover from pain and discover a life of purpose, I believe that they must regain their continuity with their earliest experiences. Early imprinting (as you would say today) not only creates ego and superego, it also creates the conflicts that produce neurotic adjustments. An individual has to lift these early experiences into consciousness to mold a new life of purpose.

THREE CONTRIBUTIONS

Now that I have cleared my throat, I shall move on to the main theme of this address and talk about the three contributions that I think are the true bequest of psychoanalytic thought, particularly with regard to its impact on present-day culture.

Psychological Unity

The first major contribution of psychoanalysis is that it brought people closer together. Don't let that observation lead you to the false conclusion that I am a do-gooder. I am not. I started my career by analyzing brains in eels, and I didn't think very much of helping people at that time. Even now, I am usually most interested in how the various facets of personality hang together. Less frequently, I am interested in what interventions, from hypnosis to analytical interpretation, will bring the best results to suffering patients. But somehow the theory has helped to bring people together. It accomplished this unexpected feat by stressing that we are all pretty much alike. We all have significant sexual goals, trouble with controls, and internal conflicts and anxieties. At times we all behave without full comprehension of why we act as we do. All of us have irrational fears and hostilities that we often do not understand, and we all rationalize, project our weaknesses onto others, sublimate, and repress.

Even in hospitals for the incurably insane, as they used to be called, people are not so very different from the rest of us. They are just a little further gone. After all, we all indulge in our private psychoses, namely our dreams. I believe psychoanalytic theory helped us to discover that the distances among us aren't that large. We all come from similar genetic structures; most of us have brains, the ability to learn language, and opposing thumbs. We all have an unconscious, whether we want to admit it or not, and many prohibited wishes and thoughts. For centuries, people believed in the god-given virtues of the aristocracy, the powerful, and the rich. Today we know that rich people are just people who have made it, but people anyway. Surely psychoanalytic theory is not solely responsible for the recognition of the greater similarity among us, but it helped a lot.

Another way in which our group helped people to get closer together is in the following: Presently you have as many people serving as psychotherapists in your country as other nations have total populations. It has been said that the more psychotherapists you have, the more patients will develop. There are a number of factors at work that could turn the whole population into patients. I will discuss their operation more fully later, but when you have an unruly society, you place enormous responsibility on each person. Some cultures imposed rigid rules on their people and reduce the number of choices that are available to the individual. Such a reduction in alternatives for people reduces the anxiety of life. North American culture opts for freedom. Consequently your people have more different life-styles and there is more anxiety among you. With great stress you will also have a great need for relief systems. In your society, beyond the automobile, drugs (legal and illegal), the Wheel of Fortune, and Jeopardy, you developed psychotherapy as another relief system. Let us hope that this widespread use of psychotherapy will result in a better understanding of self as well as in greater sensitivity to others. Psychotherapy may just be the tool for breaking down the barriers among people.

The Importance of Childhood

A second major contribution of psychoanalytic thought is that we stressed the importance of early childhood experiences for later life. We not only studied in great detail early instinctual behavior of the infant, the ego and superego development of the young child, but also the psychosexual development of the child, which in its normal development results in identification with the significant adult. I take special pride in having suggested so far the only explanation for the diverse sexual attachments that adults exhibit. No other theory, and certainly not operant models, can explain why a man may get turned on when throwing hot, unpeeled potatoes at a woman. Strange as it may appear, the understanding of the psychosexual development of the child gives us a clue. It states that any outstanding pleasure or trauma in early childhood—be it a thought, a dream, or an actual experience—can become libidinized, that is, attached to the budding sexual pleasures. In turn, many of the sexual explorations of the child may result in fixation of the sexual instinct to an arousing stimulus, which, from child to child, will vary greatly. It is, however, the psychoanalytic emphasis on the significance of early childhood for later life that guided many investigators since then to do their research with children. I might add that this thought of finding a relationship between childhood and adult life, so obvious to all of us now, has only been the focus of research in very recent times.

Psychoanalytic theory emphasizes maturation more than learning in its treatment of individual development. It thinks of psychological development as an "unfolding" of potential, much as a flower unfolds. A flower does not learn to have its blossoms; it just develops them. In flowers this process of unfolding may be hindered by poor earth, by bad weather, by all sorts of influences. It is the same with human development. An individual's process of unfolding may be hampered by poverty, by a bad family situation, by the effects of a variety of other malignant environmental factors that interfere with growth.

Because of my emphasis on the impact of early experience, people who are philosophically minded sometimes call me a determinist, but my determinism is pretty soft. I firmly believe that present behavior patterns are determined by the past, but that by bringing these patterns into recognition they can be modified under the right circumstances. The end result is to give people the responsibility to formulate the good life for themselves. It is noteworthy that my theories were never accepted in Soviet Russia or in China, for that matter. The reason of course is that my theories gave people much greater freedom to determine their own lives than these countries would allow. The same, of course, is true for Islam.

Some modern theories of treatment carry the idea of personal freedom too far. They imply that, with the proper experience, all human beings have perfect freedom to grow and accomplish anything they want to, but I believe that this is an absurd idea. Returning to the metaphor of the flower: Every single flower in this world grows in its own spot. It has its own genetic roots. It obtains specific nourishment, it is uniquely subject to sun and rain, and it is exposed to particular predators and dangers. All of these forces will determine what the final flower will look like. Some environments produce strong and healthy flowers; others produce flowers that are weak and stunted. People, just as flowers, are limited by their personal situations in what they can become. No one is totally free. Freedom is an illusion, more accurately, a delusion. Although human beings can be taught to alter their lives, such teaching must not be based on the false belief that they are perfectly free. They are free within the constraints of their histories and situations.

Pleasure in the Symptom

The third major contribution of psychoanalysis—the first two were bringing people together and the recognition of the impact of early childhood experiences on later life—was our understanding that there is pleasure in the symptom. In psychoanalysis we recognized early on that no one gives up pleasure easily. No one willingly abandons a libidinal investment. Although this statement is pretty obvious, it became more complicated when we discovered that people find satisfaction in their problems. Patients take pleasure in their symptoms. That was new and much contested.

It has been called a "neurotic paradox" that people who come for psychoanalytic treatment, supposedly to be freed from problems, resist that very process and hold on to their problems with great manipulative skill and tenacity. The discovery that there is pleasure in the symptom not only explained that paradox—it also had an influence on the treatment process. In psychoanalysis, we always have to locate the origins of this resistance and help our patients discover what the pleasure is that they are getting from their problems—a difficult task, to say the least.

The explanation for this strange phenomenon is to be found in the childhood experiences that are shared by every one of us. We are all born helpless and go through several years of helplessness as we build up our ego skills and independence. Helplessness, however, is a trauma of great depth—a sense of wanting, a desperate feeling of need. In our period of helplessness, parents, brothers, sisters, and others respond to us in many different ways; with love and nurturance, with ridicule or pressure, with indulgence or indifference. We survive this traumatic period of our lives and, precisely because it was so traumatic, interpret the different responses we obtained as rewarding. Because the sense of helplessness was so intense, these responses are perceived as of great magnitude and imprinted very deeply. Whenever, as adults, we think we are confronted by severe and insurmountable problems, our unconscious reminds us of our earliest sense of helplessness and the often painful, yet "rewarding" life-preserving responses we obtained. In turn, we re-create the conditions under which we can obtain these very same reactions. As a result, they become repetitious, sometimes compulsively so. In actuality, these symptoms, that so frequently appear self-defeating, are simply formerly rewarded responses to a desperate sense of helplessness. There is pleasure in the symptom, but we often pay a heavy price to experience it.

Although the traumata that give rise to the pleasures that we derive from problems are an unpleasant aspect of growing up, the absence of such painful experiences could be disastrous. Psychologically, the worst condition under which a person can exist is indifference. As a result of such indifference, you can see here in the United States that children are very unruly; they do not appear to recognize authority. It seems to me that this must be because yours is a country of greater freedom than most. Tradition and authority do not play the same role as they do in other Western societies. Tradition and authority are based on a strong force in the home, usually the presence of a strong father. Without the presence of such a strong force in the home, discipline and what we call "castration anxiety" are minimized. This reduction of force in a home has as an immediate consequence that identification with authority figures is unlikely or even impossible. With little respect for authority, children become their own authorities. They are mostly governed by their id, which is a step toward narcissism. That itself is a terrible problem for the parents, who will never fail to tell you so. On the other hand, this very problem also gives pleasure and great benefit to society. It is this hidden benefit that makes people and societies tolerate problems.

With authority vested in the id, the individuals who comprise a culture have neither tradition nor history, and culture can go awry, as seems to many people to have happened in your country. They may be right. In my opinion, it is because of the sense of lack of structure that, during the last few elections, your population selected as their president a traditional father figure without, however, giving him the power and force to make significant changes. This fact betrays the existence of the hidden benefit that I have mentioned. There is pleasure in the symptom represented by a leaderless society and that pleasure may outweigh the pain and distaste for the problem. It is painful to live in an unruly society. It is painful not to have any control over the children. But it is pleasurable to feel free, to have a multitude of choices, to be unintimidated by authority figures like the police, to rebel against the government and destroy the symbols of its authority by burning flags, to reject religion and to commit childish acts of aggression against any deity one wishes to. Yes, there is a great sense of freedom in overcoming the boundaries of tradition. You feel young and energetic—and at times helpless.

SOCIAL RELEVANCE

As a way of moving toward an end to this discussion, I would like to relate the principles underlying these contributions to society at large. From reading *Totem and Taboo*, you might recall that I have the tendency to do just that.

Origins and Development of Democracy

In *Totem and Taboo*, I wondered how social rules came about in the early years of human existence. I suspected that, several millions years ago, when small hordes of people were roaming the land, these rules were set down by the most ferocious males in every horde and that these most ferocious males were apt to be the fathers. These rules were probably nonverbal because we suspect that they had no language. Members of these early hordes who did not obey the rules put forward by the fathers did not survive, and this helped perpetuate the rules.

There is reason to believe that the Cro-Magnon people experienced a mutation in the brain that made language possible, and this new talent gave them enormous power. Instead of attacking or defending with brute force against one another and the other hordes, they now could plan and divide labor. Within the horde the most ferocious man, the father, could no longer be quite so ferocious, because his sons were beginning to talk to each other, somehow communicating. In this way the sons would have discovered that, together, they were able to challenge the authority of their father.

If you permit me this speculation, this laid the foundation for democracy. According to this speculation, the beginnings of democracy came with the recognition by sons that, together, they were stronger than their father. If they so desired, they could kill their father, and as I suggested in *Totem and Taboo*, even eat him, even though they may have felt a primitive guilt about the deed. Now the rules were different.

I believed, and I still believe, that the first step in the evolution of democracy was this law of shared authority, made by sons against their fathers. The next step was the sons' belief that everyone else should have a part of this authority. One consequence of this new concept was that all women of the horde, who had been available to father and perhaps the strongest sons, instead of being available to all males, were now taboo to all of them, so that no one would touch a woman within the horde. This incest taboo resulted in various interesting practices. For example, women for breeding had to be stolen from other hordes.

Social Conflict

It seems to me that the problems that face the democracies of the Western world, and particularly the United States, were an inevitable result of the evolution of this earliest law. The demand of the sons for equality is at the heart of it. However, this demand is not now, and probably never will be, totally fulfilled. So far, every country that claims to follow the institution of democracy still has an underclass, "sons of a lesser god," if you permit my plagiarism. These underclasses that exist in all human societies, more in some and less in others, are the causes for rebellion, revolutions, terrorism, and war. Even the primitive guilt of having done away with the father has had noticeable consequences in democratic cultures. These include the puritanism and the rigid, sometimes inhuman, enforcement of rules that are so common there.

In my opinion, these problems are likely to continue, even though some of the excesses may be controlled. The history of any society determines to a large extent the values in its successor societies, just as we discovered that our personal history is determined by our earlier life. On an unconscious level we cling to tradition, even though we no longer know that it is tradition that influences our behavior and our motives. Today, values are materialistic, concerned with status, and, if possible, unlimited sexual freedom. Interestingly enough, these values are actually a reflection of the tradition of the aristocracy of the old countries, who were in a way rather narcissistic, thinking only of the now, of pleasures, and of property. But the fact is that very, very few of you would recognize—or admit to knowing it if you did—that the life-style that is so common now among millions of your citizens is in fact arrived at by identification with the aristocratic courts of yesteryear.

Psychotherapists as Jesters

Even your many psychotherapists are another instance of an unconscious tradition. Their situation is like that of the King's court jester, who was a friendly person who used humor for the purpose of giving very serious advice. The client in psychotherapy is like the King. The King could take or leave the jester's advice and did not have to give him credit when the advice was good. When the advice was bad, the King could not blame his court jester, but he could find himself another one. Kings were even known to have made up problems to have the pleasure of seeing their jesters solve them. So one might say that millions of your people now have found their own court jesters, their consultants whose advice they may choose to take or not take. Of course, there are always a few demigods and prophets among these consultants who claim to know it all, and who are not fun to work with. In all seriousness, though, the court jester of today, just as the one of yesteryear, plays a very significant role in helping people to look at options and make wiser choices.

Drug Abuse

A few comments on your drug problem. As some of you know, I smoked some 20 cigars a day and got used to it. Believe it or not, sometimes "a cigar is just a cigar" (Freud, 1940). Yes, I was also involved in the discovery of the anaesthetic effects of cocaine and I even tried it to see whether it would control human anguish. Because we did not know enough, one of my friends got habituated. Seeing his reactions, I came to the conclusion—that I passed on to Ferenczi—that, if taken to excess, cocaine can produce paranoid symptoms. The way I view the drug habit is that there are many disaffected people in the world today, who do not like their life-styles. Sexuality has worn thin for them. They don't just want another "high," they want to change their life-style altogether. Remember, there is pleasure in the symptom! People on heavy drugs often start dealing, which gives them libidinal pleasures in secrecy and danger. It gives them closeness with other users and street people, whereby they experience the libidinal satisfaction of renewing their lost "family ties." Some of the users engage in indiscriminate sex in which the unconscious satisfaction is the satisfaction of a desperate need not to commit themselves to any other person. With addiction to a drug, others become obnoxious, paranoid, or both, which means that they obtain libidinal gratification in isolating themselves. If your society really wants to help people to give up the drug problem, you will have to go much beyond it. You will have to deal with these secret pleasures in the symptoms and address the questions of family ties, loneliness, and commitment.

Other Notes on Relevance

As I mentioned early in this talk, our psychoanalytic group helped people to discover that they were not so very different from one another—that the worst impulses, fears, anxieties, and defense mechanisms that we all observe in other people are also present within ourselves. For that reason, I think it is not so easy any more to shut people out and call them different, strange, or crazy.

As a direct result of such a change in outlook, in the recent past you have eliminated a number of sick, criminal, or unpopular behaviors from your "no-no" list. The gay community is no longer "sick," even though that group may be far from popular acceptance. Abortion and adultery no longer are "civil crimes." Divorce is no longer keeping presidents out of the White House. Only very few of you will complain publicly when a Jew or a Black moves into your neighborhood. It is true that more recently you have voted for a government, and with it for a Supreme Court, which may set the ideals of humans living together in harmony and freedom back by some 30 years, but fortunately in your country, governments come and go, and so do Supreme Courts.

The most important item of this sort is that your mental hospitals have emptied. Patients are no longer labled as "incurably insane." Perhaps the hospitals have been overemptied, possibly because your government wants to save money—particularly on nonvoters—and you very often see these former patients in the streets, obviously still sick. But, then seeing them, even in this sad condition. may be bettter than locking them away and forgetting about them.

PROSPECTS FOR THE FUTURE

Permit me one last comment on my observations in America. When I was here in 1909, I felt that America was in a state of childhood. During the 1960s I believe that you went through your adolescence as a nation. Now I see the young adult, a country eager to maintain its useful ideals of freedom and power, but also awakening to the realities of constraints. There are impulses of wild action, but second thoughts for making the future secure. To help you along with this, you have an interesting two-party system, which has given you enormous stability among the nations of the world. You have one party representing your father that stands for conservatism and law and order; and another representing your mother that is more caring, even for the least of your sons and daughters, and more concerned with helping out.

So far, except during election years, your father and your mother get along reasonably well, so that actual differences between them are rather minute. The ship of state goes largely in one direction, whether father or mother has the tiller. It leaves the groups who see a need for radical changes without much of a political voice, unless they can mobilize millions of voters such as they were successful at doing in the Vietnamese war. The family is pretty well together. We shall see what happens when a fourth family arises, the European family, next to the American, Russian, and Chinese families. As I stated in *Civilization and its Discontents*, I can only hope that the mighty impulses for pleasure and destruction within each family can be contained, that interfamily fights which are erupting can be rationally negotiated, and that civilization will be spared. I am not too optimistic, but then it is better to work on a problem than to fool oneself and fiddle time away.

ACKNOWEDGMENT

Previous versions of this chapter were delivered as an address at the convention of the Rocky Mountain Psychological Association, in 1976, and at the American Psychological Association Convention in 1984.

REFERENCE

Freud, S. (1940).*Gesammelte Werke* London: Imago, Books I to XVIII.

Chapter 5

From "Paired Associates" to a Psychology of Self: The Intellectual Odyssey of Mary Whiton Calkins

Laurel Furumoto

The invention of the paired-associate technique for studying memory and the development of a system of self psychology stand out as Mary Whiton Calkins's (1863–1930) distinctive contributions to the discipline. As one ponders these achievements, a question arises. Why did this eminent early woman psychologist put aside the standard laboratory pursuits that had engrossed her at the outset of her career in the 1890s to promote a theory of self psychology, a task that occupied her for the remaining three decades of her life?

WHY A PSYCHOLOGY OF SELVES?

To begin, I think we can safely dispose of the hypothesis that her turn toward self psychology was part of the *Zeitgeist*. Calkins herself described the unpopularity of her stance in a 1915 paper titled "The Self in Scientific Psychology," in which she admitted that "The self-psychologist has still to explain the fact that a large number, perhaps a majority, of psychologists deny or ignore the self" (p. 520). In fact, historical accounts of trends in academic psychology during the decades that Calkins was enthusiastically endorsing self psychology indicate that she was most decidedly swimming against the ideological current.

For example, during the 1920s historian of psychology Franz Samelson (1985) notes that a shift in emphasis was occurring in academic

---

*Photograph of Mary Whiton Calkins courtesy of Wellesley College

psychology. In Samelson's view, this shift, popularly associated with Watsonian behaviorism, would deflect the science from a search for understanding to the goal of prediction and control. He concludes that by the late 1920s, Watson had convinced his colleagues that only behavior is available as an observable datum. While this still left major issues unresolved, such as which behavior should be observed (muscle twitches or some larger unit) and whether behavior was *the* subject matter or merely provides the data base for psychology, what was no longer an issue of debate was the goal of prediction and control— what remained controversial was only the *best* means to reach it.

Reflecting on the history of American academic psychology during the period of the 1890s through the 1920s, which coincides with Calkins's career in the field, Samelson observes, not without irony, that psychology started out, more or less, as the study of consciousness only to turn into the attempt to explain it away. He goes on to ask why, speculating that consciousness may have proved to be a source of resistance to the orderly change psychologists were attempting to create in the laboratory and even that it may have presented a potential threat that had to be neutralized.

As early as 1915, in Calkins's previously cited paper, she leveled criticism against this tendency of laboratory psychology to eradicate the conscious self:

> The remark may be hazarded that in view of the relative paucity of introspective studies and of their preoccupation with relatively impersonal experiences, and in view, also, of the directions given to introspecters and of the preconceptions on which these directions are based it is perhaps more surprising that the self has played any role at all in technical psychology than that many psychologists should fail to record its presence. (p. 524)

Clearly, Calkins was convinced that the reason academic psychologists were finding little if any evidence of the self in their research was precisely because they had arranged their experiments to exclude it.

How can we make sense of Calkins's adherence to the increasingly unpopular self psychology during the heyday of behaviorism? What was she trying to accomplish? And how did she come to this theoretical position in the first place?

Edna Heidbreder, well known for her work in systems and theories of psychology, addressed these questions in a 1972 paper on Calkins's self psychology, noting that

> Calkins first presented her self-psychology in 1900, having worked it out with the thoroughness and care appropriate to a proposed departure from

the classical (Wundtian and Titchenerian) system then dominant in American psychology. And though she kept developing her system throughout the remaining thirty years of her life, she did not in any essential way alter her initial position. It is safe to say that, insofar as her system was a paradigm, she *had* her paradigm in 1900. (p. 57)

What Calkins did do for her theory from 1900 on, according to Heidbreder, was to strengthen and to develop it including

clarifying it at points, modifying it occasionally, defending it against attack, and above all in extending its reach and exploiting its possibilities by meeting the challenges presented by the vigorous new systems that rose to prominence in the rapidly expanding and changing psychology of her day. (p. 57)

Heidbreder noted some similarities between Calkins's efforts at system building and Kuhn's description of the growth and development of a paradigm. One resemblance lay in the Kuhnian notion of what it means to adopt a paradigm. Calkins exemplified such an adoption in that she came to acquire something of a world view or a selective way of viewing her field. This is most clearly seen, as Heidbreder points out, in the sequence of papers in which Calkins contrasted her system to one after another of the rival systems of her day: structuralism, functionalism, behaviorism, hormic psychology, Gestalt psychology, and psychoanalysis. Her strategy in each case was to present her own system as capable of accommodating what was acceptable and important in the other and treating that part as indicating a trend toward some kind of self psychology.

Another way in which Heidbreder believed that Calkins's system fitted Kuhn's description of the development of a paradigm had to do with Kuhn's view that as a paradigm is increasingly used, and as those who use it find it satisfactory, the paradigm tends to be taken for granted, eventually becoming implicit, as if it required no defense or justification. Although Heidbreder maintains that Calkins never arrived at a point where she took her system fully for granted, Heidbreder nevertheless detected signs of increasing confidence in it in Calkins's successive writings.

Calkins's system most notably differed from Kuhn's account of the development of an accepted paradigm, Heidbreder claimed, in that it did not give rise to "normal science," Kuhn's term for the systematic, detailed, and highly technical research characteristic of a mature science. Her system of self psychology did not engage closely with active experimental investigation, although Heidbreder is careful to point out that this did not mean that Calkins disregarded or failed to use relevant, available experimental evidence. But in her own research and in that which she encouraged in her laboratory, no systematic program was conducted, no special procedures were devised, for the investigation of selves. Furthermore, in Heidbreder's view, the large volume of research that has been and continues to be produced on the psychology of personality seems not to have its roots in, nor to have been influenced by, Calkins's self psychology.

On the basis of various lines of evidence, Heidbreder concluded that it was highly unlikely that Calkins initially presented her system either because she found the classical system unsatisfactory from the standpoint of its *usefulness* in research, or because she regarded her own system as an improvement in that particular respect. Rather, Calkins's efforts on behalf of her self psychology, conducted exclusively at the theoretical level, were primarily concerned with reconceptualizing the subject matter of psychology.

Why did Calkins come to believe, as Heidbreder puts it, "that the conceptual geography of her field needed recharting?" (p. 63). Heidbreder suggests that Calkins became dissatisfied with the classical system because of its insistence that the empirical contents of psychology should be limited to elemental sensations, emotions, and images. Seeing this restriction of subject matter as the crux of Calkins's disagreement with the classical school, Heidbreder hypothesized that the problem arose for Calkins in the 1890s when she became convinced "that selves—persisting, complex, unitary, unique selves—are phenomenally, observably present in ordinary, conscious experience, and that they are therefore among the empirical facts with which psychology as a natural science must come to terms" (p. 63). Adopting this viewpoint led Calkins to regard the classical system as inadequate because it excluded from its subject matter psychological phenomena that she considered basic. Heidbreder maintains that accordingly Calkins came to see the classical experimental psychologists

> as out of touch—as deliberately and on principle out of touch—with important portions and aspects of that subject matter as it presents itself in ordinary experience: in ordinary experience as she herself observed it and as she believed, by checking with others, that they too observed it. (p. 63)

Heidbreder asserts that Calkins became convinced of the reality and importance of selves in everyday experience and that this formed the basis of her disagreement with the classical experimental psychologists. How and why she arrived at this conviction and why the classical experimental psychologists did not share her view were questions

Heidbreder did not address in her paper. One might expect to gain some insight into the answers to these questions by consulting the autobiographical chapter that Calkins (1930) wrote shortly before her death in 1930.

In this account, we do find Calkins attempting to trace the origin of the idea of "the self" in her work albeit not entirely successfully. As she confesses to her reader "I wish that I could recall more completely the sources of this personalistic doctrine of psychology" (p. 38). She credited her emphasis on the social nature of the self to the influence of James Baldwin and Josiah Royce. Calkins felt confident that her self doctrine must have been affected by William James's chapter on the stream of consciousness in *Principles of Psychology*, as well as by James Ward's article on psychology in the *Encyclopaedia Britannica*. Finally, she acknowledged the influence of Hugo Münsterberg on her conception of the double standpoint in psychology—the theory that every experience may be treated alike from the atomistic and from the self psychological standpoint, a position she was eventually to abandon in favor of a single-track self psychology.

Calkins's two textbooks of psychology highlight her transition from the dual to the single standpoint. In the earlier, titled *An Introduction to Psychology*, first published in 1901, psychology is conceived as a science of succeeding mental events *and* of the conscious self. In the later work first published in 1910 entitled *A First Book in Psychology*, the double treatment is dropped as Calkins explains in her preface "not because [she] doubt[ed] the validity of psychology as study of ideas, but because [she] question[ed] the significance and the adequacy, and deprecate[d] the abstractness, of the science thus conceived" (p. vii). She confides to the reader:

> This book has been written in the ever strengthening conviction that psychology is most naturally, consistently, and effectively treated as a study of conscious selves in relation to other selves and to external objects—in a word, to their environment, personal and impersonal. (p. vii)

The growth of that conviction is reflected in the prefaces to the three succeeding editions of the book. For example, in the preface to the third edition, published in 1912, Calkins announced three main goals prompting her to undertake the revision:

> [T]o emphasize the essentially social nature of the conscious self, to accentuate the fact that the study of the self, as thus conceived, involves a study of behavior, and finally to prune the book of expressions which lend themselves to interpretation in terms of an atomistic psychology. (p. ix)

In her autobiographical chapter, Calkins revealed that her psychological activities from the time that the fourth and last edition of *A First Book in Psychology* appeared in 1914 to the present, consisted "in attempts to elucidate, to enrich, and to defend self-psychology" (1930, p. 41). In harmony with this characterization, in the second half of her chapter, she turned from what she termed her "autobiographical outpouring" (p. 41) to set forth and to argue the essentials of a personalistic or self psychology. What were these essentials? To begin, she described her self psychology as a form of introspectionist psychology, opposed to those forms of behaviorism that denied self and consciousness. Next, Calkins distinguished between what she characterized as "two widely different types" (p. 43) of introspective psychology. One of these was the impersonal, which ignores the self, focusing instead, for example, on contents of consciousness or ideas. And the other was the personal which Calkins described as "the study of conscious, experiencing, functioning beings, that is, of persons or selves" (p. 44), the view to which she adhered. According to Calkins, there were two different forms of this personalistic conception of psychology: the strictly psychological and the biological. Allying herself with the strictly psychological school, she noted that the biological approach "studies . . . mind in body, or conscious organism, and conceives consciousness as one response among others" (p. 44). Calkins pointed out that the strictly psychological approach, by contrast, "teaches that the self has a body and is not in any sense, constituted by body" (p. 44).

Having thus carefully delineated her standpoint within psychology, she next proceeded to set down the basic tenets of her system. Self psychology had, Calkins explained, three fundamental concepts: "that of the self, that of the object, and that of the self's relation or attitude toward its object" (p. 45). "By self," she told her reader, she meant what we all mean when we use expressions such as "'I am ashamed of myself,' 'I approve of myself,' 'I appeal to you, yourself'" (p. 45). For Calkins, the "self," strictly speaking, was indefinable. In an earlier paper she presented the reasoning behind this claim: "to define is to assign the object to a given class and to distinguish it from other members of the class; and the self is *sui generis* and therefore incapable of definition" (1915, p. 495).

Although for Calkins the self could not be defined, it could be described. The list of properties she attributed to it varied somewhat over the three decades during which she was developing her system, but by 1930 it included the following five. The self was for Calkins, first of all "a totality, a one of many characters," secondly, "a unique being in the sense that I am I and you are you," thirdly "an identical being (I the adult self and my ten-year-old self are in a real sense the same self)," and yet also "a changing being (I the adult self differ from that ten-year-old)" (1930, p. 45). And finally, "the self is a being related in a distinctive fashion both to itself and its experiences and to environing objects personal and impersonal" (p. 45).

For Calkins the last characteristic in the list, the relation of the self to "objects," constituted "its consciousness of them" (p. 45). Maintaining that the self is conscious of objects, Calkins noted that she was using the term object in the "wide sense suggested by McDougall when he says that 'experiencing is an activity of some. . . subject who experiences something or somewhat'" (p. 46). For Calkins "this somewhat-which-is-experienced, whatever its nature, is the object," and objects were "marked off from each other in several different ways: as either personal or impersonal, and if impersonal as either physical or logical; and as either private or public" (p. 46).

Having described the properties of the self and having explained the sense in which she used the term object, Calkins turned next to an explication of the third and last basic concept of her self psychology: the self's relation to its objects. She saw these relations, which she termed "attitudes," as falling roughly into three groups. In the first group she put receptivity, activity, and compulsion. She believed the self to be always receptive and receptive in different ways: "for example, I receptively experience not only the fleecy whiteness of the clouds but also their charm (or pleasantness) and the contrast between the blue of the sky and the whiteness of the clouds" (p. 46). Besides being always receptive, Calkins believed the self to be often active, that activity taking one of two forms: wishing or willing. Finally Calkins thought that the self sometimes felt compelled "either by impersonal objects or by people" (p. 47), and she provided the following personal example: "I may experience my own impotence, in relation both to the wind, as it sweeps across Boston Common and to the imperious gesture of the traffic policeman" (p. 47).

Her second group of fundamental attitudes of the self to its objects contained the egocentric and the allocentric emphases, that is, the self stressing either itself or its environment including things or other selves. Calkins was careful to point out here that these attitudes were not mutually exclusive, "one may, at one and the same time, attend both to one's self and to one's object" (p. 47), and noted the attitude of sympathy as an especially important instance of this. Moving to the third group of attitudes, Calkins maintained that the self either individualizes "its objects as in emotion and will and, secondarily, in perceiving, imagining, and some forms of thinking; or it generalizes as in classification and conception" (p. 48).

Having enumerated her list of characters and attitudes of the self,

Calkins expressed concern that her reader might find the account "nonessential and dull" (p. 48). "Yet," she hastened to add, it was her belief that "anyone who, without bias, will study the material of psychology by the use of these categories will discover them for what they are—not impositions on experience but descriptions of it" (p. 48). And she confided to her reader her own experience in this regard: "With each year I live, with each book I read, with each observation I initiate or confirm, I am more deeply convinced that psychology should be conceived as the science of the self, or person, as related to its environment physical and social" (pp. 41–42).

Although it seems clear that Calkins by 1930 had a high degree of confidence regarding the correctness of her approach to psychology, the question of why she became so committed to conceptualizing the subject matter of psychology as conscious selves remains. I would like to suggest that clues to her embrace of this theoretical stance are more readily found in her life history than in her intellectual history and to turn to that life history next.

FAMILY BACKGROUND, EDUCATION AND CAREER

Mary Calkins was born in 1863, the eldest of five children, and grew up in Buffalo, New York, where her father was a Protestant minister. In 1881, the family moved to Newton, Massachusetts, a city about 12 miles west of Boston, where the Reverend Wolcott Calkins had accepted the pastorate of a Congregational church. Calkins's closeness to her family and especially to her mother Charlotte was a dominant theme throughout her life. This lifelong attachment to family was not unusual for a 19th-century American middle-class woman; rather, as recent scholarship in women's history tells us, it was the norm. Similarly, Calkins's devotion to her mother, which may strike the contemporary reader as somewhat odd, was typical for a woman of her day. Historian Carroll Smith-Rosenberg (1975) has characterized the mother–daughter relationship of the American middle class from the 1760s to the 1880s as intimate, observing that "the diaries and letters of both mothers and daughters attest to their closeness and mutual emotional dependency" and concluding that "the normal relationship between mother and daughter was one of sympathy and understanding" (p. 15).

Despite her strong familial attachment, Calkins left home in 1882 to attend Smith College in an era when higher education for women was still considered anexperiment. Colleges for women offering an education comparable to that of the established men's schools, such as Harvard, Princeton, and Yale, were not founded until after the Civil

War. Furthermore, in the first few decades of the existence of these colleges most people, men and women alike, were skeptical about the capacity of women to profit from a rigorous college course. Later, when women proved that they could indeed succeed and even excel in college studies, fears were raised that these pursuits would ruin their health, make them unfit for marriage, and stunt their reproductive capacities (Solomon, 1985).

All the evidence suggests that Calkins's parents were themselves strongly intellectually inclined and encouraged their sole surviving daughter's scholarly bent. Upon completion of her undergraduate studies at Smith, the whole Calkins family embarked on a European sojourn of more than a year, during which time Mary continued her study of languages and tutored her three younger brothers, who were preparing to enter Harvard. Returning to New England in September, 1887, Mary had plans to earn her livelihood by tutoring students in Greek. However, an unexpected opportunity arose to teach Greek at Wellesley College, a women's college located just a few miles from her family home in Newton. Calkins accepted the position and thus began a more than 40-year association with that institution, where she would spend her entire career.

After having been at Wellesley a little over a year, Calkins's talent as a teacher and her interest in philosophy prompted a faculty member in that department to recommend to the college president that Calkins be appointed to a newly created position in experimental psychology. The appointment was made contingent upon Calkins studying the subject for a year, an undertaking that required petitions and special arrangements since neither Clark University, where she was tutored by E. C. Sanford, nor Harvard, where she attended the seminars of William James and Josiah Royce, was willing to admit women as students at the time (Scarborough & Furumoto, 1987).

Upon her return to Wellesley in the autumn of 1891, Calkins established a psychological laboratory and introduced the new scientific psychology into the curriculum. Feeling the need for additional study, Calkins returned to Harvard a year later and worked in the psychological laboratory of Hugo Münsterberg for parts of the next 3 years. Although she completed all the requirements for the PhD, and in the spring of 1895 her Harvard professors enthusiastically recommended her for the degree, the institutional authorities refused to award it because she was a woman.

Publications by Calkins began to appear in the psychological literature as early as 1892. In that year, a paper on association, which was a product of the seminar she took with William James in the fall of 1890, found its way into print (1892b) as well as a paper that described the course in experimental psychology that Calkins had introduced at Wellesley College in the fall of 1891 (1892a). In 1893, she published the results of an investigation of dreaming that she had completed while she was a student of Sanford in the fall of 1890 (1893b) and the first paper reporting on research carried out in the Wellesley College laboratory (1893a).

The theoretical and experimental work on association that she carried out in Münsterberg's laboratory appeared in a series of three publications (1894a, 1896a, 1896b). It was in the course of this work, which would have formed the basis of her dissertation if the Harvard authorities had not refused to consider her as a candidate for the PhD, that Calkins invented what was later to be called the paired-associates technique. Investigating the influence of the factors of frequency, recency, and vividness on memory, Calkins showed her subjects a series of colors paired with numerals. Later, shown the colors alone, they were asked to recall the numbers with which the colors had originally been paired.

Calkins's basic finding was that frequency was a more influential factor in memory for color–numeral pairs than either recency or vividness. As she herself observed more than three decades after completing her study, what was "perhaps more significant than the results is the method" that she used (1930, p. 34). This conclusion was echoed in the 1960s by Herrnstein and Boring who recognized Calkins as "one of the first in this new field" of memory research and who credited her with having "created an experimental technique that is now called the method of paired-associates, which has survived to the present time" (1966, p. 530).

Throughout the 1890s, reports of research from the Wellesley College laboratory made their way into the psychological literature under Calkins's authorship (1894b, 1895a, 1895b, 1895c, 1896c, 1898, 1900). After 1900, although the stream of Calkins's publications continued unabated (four books, more than 50 papers, and numerous brief notes and reviews appeared between 1901 and 1930), her energies were no longer directed toward empirical investigations, but were focused instead solely on theoretical and philosophical work.

Calkins, as mentioned earlier, spent her entire career at Wellesley College, teaching, publishing prolifically in both psychology and philosophy, and achieving recognition in both fields. In 1905 she was the first woman to be elected president of the American Psychological Association and in 1918 was accorded the same recognition by the American Philosophical Association. Honorary degrees were bestowed on Calkins by Columbia University in 1909 and by her alma mater,

Smith, in 1910. In 1928 she was elected to honorary membership in the British Psychological Association.

This brief synopsis of her educational history and career, while an important feature of her life history, still does not shed light on why Calkins developed, around the turn of the century, such a passionate devotion to promoting psychology as a science of selves. One needs to look elsewhere, and I have come to believe that the key to this riddle lies in the particular institutional environment at Wellesley College during Calkins's tenure there.

A LITTLE WORLD UNDER ONE ROOF

Scholarship in women's history carried out within the past two decades has brought to our attention the prevalence and significance of female friendships among middle-class women in the 19th century. Smith-Rosenberg (1975) in a pathbreaking article on this topic, cited earlier in discussing the mother-daughter relationship, asserts that 18th- and 19th- century women routinely formed emotional ties with other women and that "such deeply felt, same-sex friendships were casually accepted in American society" (p. 1).

For educated women in the late 19th century who aspired to enter a profession, such relationships with other women became even more central because there was a strong societal norm that prohibited women from combining career and marriage. Wellesley College in the last quarter of the century, with its one-hundred-percent-single, all-female professoriate, was a microcosm in which female friendships flourished. A recent study of the early faculty at Wellesley by educational historian Patricia Palmieri (1983) provides a vivid portrayal of faculty life and the institutional atmosphere prevailing at the college in the late 19th and early 20th centuries. The social portrait emerging from her study is of a milieu dramatically different from that existing outside of women's colleges in male-dominated educational institutions of the day. Palmieri points out that Wellesley was unique among women's colleges in its commitment, from its founding date in 1875, to having women as presidents and a totally female faculty.

Wellesley's founders, Henry and Pauline Durant, had ambitions that went beyond simply establishing a college for women. Typical late-19th-century evangelical reformers, they envisioned Wellesley as a model community that would set a standard for the uplifting of women through higher education and consequently the uplifting of the entire society. Palmieri believes that Wellesley came to serve the Durants as both a sanctuary and a home. For them, as well as for its early faculty and students, it became a romantic refuge, sometimes described as "a little world under one roof." The most radical feature of the Durants' "Wellesley world" was, according to Palmieri, its dedication to the principle of women being educated by women. Wellesley was intended by its founders to be a "woman's university," the equivalent of Harvard, presided over and staffed entirely by women.

By 1910, fifty-three women who had been at Wellesley for more than 5 years were the senior members of the faculty. It is this group, to which Calkins belonged, that formed the basis of Palmieri's study. She notes that this group of academic women were "strikingly homogeneous in terms of social and geographic origins, upbringing, and sociocultural worldview" (p. 197). Most were born in New England, more than half were born between 1855 and 1865, and, as mentioned earlier, all were single. Almost all were children of professional, middle-class families in which both mothers and fathers provided their daughters with sponsorship and support. Other shared characteristics discerned by Palmieri in the Wellesley faculty were philosophical idealism, civic humanism, veneration of nature and, of course, extensive education, which tended to be a lifelong process.

In trying to explain what life was like in this community of academic women who had so much in common, Palmieri describes it as

> very much like an extended family. Its members, with shared backgrounds and tastes, shared visions of life and work, and often shared bonds of family or prior friendship, could hardly but produce an extraordinary community. In this milieu, no one was isolated, no one forgotten. (p. 203)

Palmieri observes that in contrast to our contemporary society where "occupational and private selves rarely meet, the academic women of Wellesley conjoined public and private spheres" and became "not merely professional associates but astoundingly good friends" (p. 203).

Life for these women was not idyllic, however. The college's financial base was slim during that era and faculty had heavy teaching loads and committee assignments. Some of the science faculty complained that they could conduct their research only at odd moments between teaching and committee work. And the close personal ties could cause conflict when a member of the community was given an opportunity for professional advancement outside of Wellesley.

Palmieri maintains that the life experience of the Wellesley faculty was very different from that of male academics of the period, in that the

> academic women did not shift their life courses away from the communal mentality as did many male professionals; nor did they single-

mindedly adhere to scientific rationalism, specialization, social science objectivity, or hierarchical associations in which vertical mobility took precedence over sisterhood. (pp. 209–210)

Of course, this loyalty to the Wellesley community was not simply a matter of choice. As Palmieri quite rightly adds, women were not invited to join the faculties of research universities or colleges, other than those for women, in that era.

Nevertheless, the fact remains that the Wellesley faculty did not conform to the model of the modern academic professional described by Bledstein (1976) as an individual who feels no personal attachment to her or his institution, valuing academic mobility over loyalty. On the contrary, Palmieri contends that "the Wellesley group of academics defined themselves intellectually and socially in a local, particularistic, face-to-face community rather than a bureaucratic, professional society" (p. 210).

The experience of the Wellesley faculty stands in striking contrast to the academic milieu of, for example, Johns Hopkins University, during the same period. Hawkins (1960) has written of the unbreachable gulf that existed between isolated specialized researchers there, and of how extremely difficult the men found it to get to know fellow faculty members. One senior member of the faculty at Johns Hopkins pictured the situation thus: "We only get glimpses of what is going forward in the minds and hearts of our colleagues. We are like trains moving on parallel tracks. We catch sight of some face, some form that appeals to us and it is gone" (p. 237). How different from Wellesley where, as Palmieri describes it, "the academic women wrought a world which touched every woman in every aspect of her life, and gave each a sense of belonging to an all-purposive, all-embracing whole" (p. 211).

CONCLUSION

Returning to the question of why Mary Whiton Calkins became so intensely committed to conceiving the subject matter of psychology as the self—and more specifically, interacting social selves—once one appreciates the Wellesley context of her era, it seems almost embarrass-ingly obvious. From the time she entered the Wellesley community in 1887 until her death in 1930, her personal and professional life was closely intertwined with those of her Wellesley friends and colleagues. Although trained in the mainstream academic laboratory psychology of the 1890s by her male professors at Harvard and Clark, she soon thereafter came to question the atomistic, impersonal conception of the subject matter characteristic of this approach, and still later rejected it outright. As Heidbreder (1972) put it, Calkins came to see "the classical experimental psychologists as out of touch . . . with important portions of . . . [the] subject matter [of psychology] as it presents itself in ordinary experience as she herself observed it and as she believed, by checking with others, that they too observed it" (p. 63). It is worth noting here that these classical experimental psychologists were over-whelmingly male psychologists in bureaucratic university environ-ments, whose experience as isolated specialists was vastly different from that of Calkins. It should come as no great surprise then that the alternative to the classical experimental view espoused by Calkins concerned itself with something of the utmost significance to her and to the other women with whom she shared her Wellesley world, namely the reality and importance of selves in everyday experience.

AUTHOR'S RELATIONSHIP

Mary Calkins was first brought to my attention in a graduate level history of psychology seminar at Harvard University taught by R. J. Herrnstein in the early 1960s. In addition to pointing out that it was Calkins, rather than Müller and Pilzecker, who invented the paired-associate technique for studying memory, Herrnstein also had some-thing to say about Calkins's experience at Harvard: namely, that she had completed all the requirements for a doctoral degree there which the university refused to grant because she was a woman and that, in turn, she refused to accept a Radcliffe PhD offered instead as the woman's version of the Harvard PhD.

Since I was a student in the operant conditioning wing of the psychology department, Herrnstein also came to serve as my disserta-tion adviser. When the time came for me to begin a job search, he suggested that nearby Wellesley College, an institution dedicated to providing a liberal arts education for women, might be just the right place for me. As it happened, the one experimental psychologist in the Wellesley department was about to leave for another job, and I was hired to replace him. In the fall of 1967, I found myself in the psychology laboratory that Mary Calkins had founded approximately three quarters of a century earlier. It was not literally the same laboratory; the original had gone up in flames in the spring of 1914, along with the rest of College Hall, the main building on the campus in that era. Subse-quently, the psychological laboratory had existed in a number of temporary, makeshift sites, before it found a more permanent place in the 1930s in a new building it shared with chemistry and physics.

Once at Wellesley, I became interested in learning more about my predecessor. The college archives contained disappointingly little personal material on Calkins; most of what was there consisted of reprints of her numerous publications in psychology and philosophy. A junior leave in the 1970–1971 academic year gave me the opportunity to expand my search for material that might shed more light on Calkins's personal life and led me eventually to several members of the Calkins family. Wives of two of her brothers and one of her nephews were especially helpful and generous in providing access to family papers that gave me tantalizing glimpses of Mary Calkins the person. Unfortunately for me and for posterity, the hurricane of 1938 flooded the basement of the Newton, Massachusetts, home of Calkins's youngest brother, where her personal papers had been put in storage after her death in 1930. Most of the contents of the basement were badly water damaged and judged unsalvageable, including the bulk of Calkins's papers.

It has now been almost two decades since I experienced the disappointment of learning that most of Calkins's personal papers were destroyed by an act of God. In the interim, I have continued to gather information about her, gleaning it from published sources as well as from various archival collections, and I have written several pieces on her life and career. Yet an uncomfortable gap remains, blocking a goal that in all likelihood will never be realized, the opportunity to get behind the public persona to behold the private self of Mary Whiton Calkins.

REFERENCES

Bledstein, B. J. (1976). *The culture of professionalism: The middle class and the development of higher education in America*. New York: Norton.

Calkins, M. W. (1892a). Experimental psychology at Wellesley College. *American Journal of Psychology, 5*, 260–271.

Calkins, M. W. (1892b). A suggested classification of cases of association. *Philosophical Review, 1*, 389–402.

Calkins, M. W. (1893a). A statistical study of pseudo-chromesthesia and of mental forms. *American Journal of Psychology, 5*, 439–464.

Calkins, M. W. (1893b). Statistics of dreams. *American Journal of Psychology, 5*, 311–343.

Calkins, M. W. (1894a). Association. *Psychological Review, 1*, 476–483.

Calkins, M. W. (1894b). Wellesley College psychological studies: A study of the mathematical consciousness. *Educational Review, 8*, 269–283.

Calkins, M. W. (1895a). Minor studies from the psychological laboratory of Wellesley College: Synaesthesia. *American Journal of Psychology, 7*, 90–107.

Calkins, M. W. (1895b). Wellesley College psychological studies. *Pedagogical Seminary, 3*, 319–341.

Calkins, M. W. (1895c). Wellesley College psychological studies. *Psychological Review, 2*, 363–368.

Calkins, M. W. (1896a). Association. An essay analytic and experimental. *Psychological*

Review Monograph (Suppl. 2), viii, 56.

Calkins, M. W. (1896b). Association. *Psychological Review, 3,* 32–49.

Calkins, M. W. (1896c). Community of ideas of men and women. *Psychological Review, 3,* 426–430.

Calkins, M. W. (1898). Short studies in memory and association from the Wellesley laboratory. *Psychological Review, 5,* 451–463.

Calkins, M. W. (1900). Wellesley College psychological studies: An attempted experiment in psychological aesthetics. *Psychological Review, 7,* 580–591.

Calkins, M. W. (1901). *An introduction to psychology.* New York: Macmillan.

Calkins, M. W. (1910). *A first book in psychology.* New York: Macmillan.

Calkins, M. W. (1912). *A first book in psychology* (3rd ed.). New York: Macmillan.

Calkins, M. W. (1915). The self in scientific psychology. *American Journal of Psychology, 26,* 495–524.

Calkins, M. W. (1930). Mary Whiton Calkins. In C. Murchison (Ed.), *A history of psychology in autobiography.* (Vol. 1, pp. 31–62). Worcester, MA: Clark University Press.

Hawkins, H. (1960). *Pioneer: A history of the Johns Hopkins University, 1874–1889.* Ithaca, NY: Cornell University Press.

Heidbreder, E. (1972). Mary Whiton Calkins: A discussion. *Journal of the History of the Behavioral Sciences, 8,* 56–68.

Herrnstein, R. J., & Boring, E. G. (Eds.). (1966). *A source book in the history of psychology.* Cambridge, MA: Harvard University Press.

Palmieri, P. A. (1983). Here was fellowship: A social portrait of academic women at Wellesley College, 1895–1920. *History of Education Quarterly, 23,* 195–214.

Samelson, F. (1985). Organizing for the kingdom of behavior: Academic battles and organizational policies in the twenties. *Journal of the History of the Behavioral Sciences, 21,* 33–47.

Scarborough, E., & Furumoto, L. (1987). *Untold lives: The first generation of American women psychologists.* New York: Columbia University Press.

Smith-Rosenberg, C. (1975). The female world of love and ritual. *Signs, 1,* 1–29.

Solomon, B. M. (1985). *In the company of educated women.* New Haven, CT: Yale University Press.

Chapter 6

The Intrepid Joseph Jastrow

Arthur L. Blumenthal

On September 28, 1988, psychologists trained at the University of Wisconsin returned to their alma mater in Madison to launch a 3-day celebration of the Wisconsin psychology department's centenary. Fifty years earlier, in 1938, a similar jubilation took place in Madison to mark the first half-century of the Wisconsin department. On that evening in 1938, Wisconsin's two most notable psychological pioneers were present to speak at a banquet. One was Joseph Jastrow, the department's founder, then retired and living in the East. It was to be his last visit to Wisconsin. The other speaker was Jastrow's former graduate student, a man of radically different outlook, Clark L. Hull, who had resigned his Wisconsin teaching position a few years earlier to accept a position at Yale. The two men had clashed and had written disparagingly of each other's views and styles.

The Wisconsin department has, of course, modeled itself more in the image of the neobehaviorist, Hull, than in that of the antibehaviorist, Jastrow, who remained a man of the 19th century in mannerisms, language, and ideas. The life and works of Hull, so well known, are pored over again and again by historians of this field. The Wisconsin centenary of 1988 created an occasion for the rediscovery of the life, times, and prolific works of the earlier pioneer, Jastrow, now mostly unknown to writers of texts on the history of psychology.

---

*Photograph of Joseph Jastrow courtesy of the Archives of the History of Psychology, Akron, Ohio

LOCATING JASTROW

That process of rediscovery began when Wisconsin's Professor William Epstein called me in advance of the 1988 meeting to ask whether I might be interested in investigating and interpreting the unusually long history of the Wisconsin department, and then in reporting on it to the centenary celebration in Madison. Indeed I was interested. Such an assignment was bound to involve exciting detective work and, as it turned out, some discoveries of historical treasures and skeletons in closets. It led this detective into snares of historical mysteries, to nagging, enigmatic clues, and to trails barely visible beneath the dust of time. Leads and tips stretched from coast to coast, archive to archive, retirement home to retirement home, and attic to attic. Here's an example of the excitement this kind of research offers:

After rumors surfaced concerning the existence of a collection of Jastrow papers, and after some months of frustrated searching, I stumbled on a faded footnote in an old Wisconsin state historical magazine in an article on the lively social life Jastrow had brought to that campus. The footnote cited "The Jastrow papers," which were, it claimed, deposited in Duke University's Archives. Jastrow had, as far as I know, never visited Duke. When his closest surviving relative, a nephew named Jastrow Levin, was located in Baltimore, I learned from that 80-year-old gentleman that an aggressive Duke librarian had simply expressed more interest in taking care of Jastrow's papers than had the Wisconsin librarian. Therefore the family decided to give Joseph's things to Duke. Duke probably was alerted to this opportunity because Jastrow's death in 1944 was reported in a long article on the *New York Times* obituary page. And that was because he had become something of a media celebrity in that city near the end of his life.

An immediate call to the Duke library produced nothing. No Jastrow papers. But one sublibrarian remarked that Duke also maintained a rare manuscripts library. Another call brought the reply that several large boxes with the name "Jastrow" on them were located in that library. Then came a further report: No one had been there to study those papers since they were deposited in 1944. After the time necessary for a short plane ride and long taxi ride, I opened those boxes, and for the first time a serious unraveling of Jastrow's life began, barely in time for the centennial meeting in Madison.

THE PERSONAL BACKGROUND

Joseph's father, Marcus Jastrow, was one of the leading Rabbis, Talmudic scholars, and Jewish educators in America at the turn of the century, and he was also distinguished by an heroic past of fighting for human rights in mid-19th- century Poland. I doubt that you could find an encyclopedia of Jewish history that lacks a summary of the life of Marcus Jastrow. This charismatic family patriarch had been an effective crusader for social and moral causes both within and outside of the Jewish community. He had groomed his two sons (Joseph and Morris) for the rabbinate, raising them in a literate, articulate, and socially aware environment. Both sons, however, eventually fell into conflict with their distinguished and strong-willed father. Both left the congregation Rodeph Shalom in Philadelphia to devote their lives to the academic world. Morris received a PhD in semitic languages from Leipzig and went on to a distinguished academic career at the University of Pennsylvania. Joseph strayed further and abandoned his father's religion altogether. That religion, however, never left him. Throughout his life he was dogged by antisemitism which, according to some accounts (e.g., Roback, 1964), retarded his career. But, until the letters that I uncovered in the Duke Library came to light, those accounts remain largely in the limbo of hearsay. In the Duke letters, however, it is very clear that Jastrow was the focus of some ugly antisemitic barbs. These came in retaliation to some personal attacks that he had initiated on people. His sometimes abrasive character, and especially his pronounced arrogance, is still remembered by a few oldtimers in Madison. It must have been partly responsible for the trail of conflict he left in the historical record everywhere.

Beside that negative image, however, I found a counterimage built of flattering reminiscences. For example, here are a few lines from a letter by a patient at the Austen Riggs Foundation in Massachusetts, where Jastrow was also a patient at the end of his life, suffering one of his recurring depressions. The conditions leading to this final depressive episode were these: A few months earlier, Jastrow's only child, an adopted son, was lost to the war in Europe. Jastrow had been a widower since 1926, and he seemed not particularly close to his three sisters, one of whom was in a mental hospital. His brother, Morris, had died early. His passions for Miss Elsie Junghans, his private secretary in the 1930s, who had provoked a gush of romantic poetry from the old professor, were left sadly unfulfilled. Even in that depth of depression, Jastrow inspired the following glowing admiration in a letter sent from one J. H. Preston to a niece of Jastrow's on January 28, 1944:

> I was at Stockbridge during the summer and found Dr. Jastrow the most interesting and stimulating person there. . . . He was such a kind, noble and truly great human being. . . . In the last note I got from him he said: "My downs seem more constant than my ups.". . . I was deeply fond of

your uncle, though I knew him only in the last half-year of his long and distinguished life. He was a prince of men, and I shall remember him always. (Preston, 1944)

The sentiments of university administrators toward Jastrow over the earlier several decades were, invariably, 180 degrees the opposite of Mr. Preston's reminiscences. And therein lies a bitter story, which unfolds in part in what follows here.

But let us first catch a bit more of Jastrow's earlier, happier years, before his depressing and nearly suicidal tangles with bankers and university administrators. While in graduate school at Johns Hopkins, Jastrow roomed and boarded in Baltimore in the home of the Rabbi Benjamin Szold who had no fewer than eight daughters. (It is my sense that these were Jastrow's happiest years.) Some of the Szold girls later wrote of Jastrow because he had constantly entertained them in the 1880s by using them as subjects in psychological experiments, which they regarded as greatly amusing. Jastrow maintained a lifelong correspondence with one of the Szold daughters (Henrietta), who sometimes spurned his attention, referring to him as "a godless Darwinian" (Jastrow, 1884). Henrietta matured into one of the great women of this century. She was to be the founder of the Hadassah Society and, as a courageous Zionist and underground operative in the 1930s and 1940s, became a heroine of Israel honored to this day. The Henrietta Szold archives in Jerusalem contain some of the Jastrow letters. As soon as he was offered his first gainful employment from Wisconsin, at the age of 23, Joseph married Henrietta's sister, Rachel.

DISCIPLINARY ROOTS

Jastrow's education in psychology began as auspiciously as any centered entirely in the United States could have been in the late 19th century. He received the first doctorate from the first formally organized PhD program in psychology in this country, G. Stanley Hall's graduate psychology program at Johns Hopkins, which existed for only a few years in the mid-1880s. As a graduate student in 1884, Jastrow coauthored an important article on psychophysics with C. S. Peirce, who was at Hopkins as a lecturer and who was the first to encourage Jastrow to take up the new experimental psychology. Peirce gave Jastrow a lifelong reverence for logic, for which Jastrow was later criticized when it dominated his approach as a popular media psychologist and a writer of self-help literature. Mental health was, in that later work, represented as the acquisition of the ability to think logically.

Jastrow's doctoral dissertation on psychophysics was widely cited, and still is cited and described in present-day psychophysics literature (for instance the book by psychophysicist Lawrence Marks, 1978). Five years after the dissertation, Jastrow already had 25 publications. With the possible exception of Cattell, Jastrow is cited more often than any other American psychologist in William James's *Principles of Psychology*. Soon after arriving at Wisconsin, Jastrow (1890) surveyed and summarized, in a long monograph, the results of experimental psychology's first systematic research program of interlocking progressive studies, namely the early mental chronometry research program that began a generation earlier with Wundt. At about the same time, he invented the "automatograph," a scientific-instrument version of the Ouija board. It was designed to study distinctions between voluntary and involuntary behavior. For instance, the automatic writing sometimes produced with hypnosis might be assessed for its essential characteristics with this instrument. With piles of squiggly records of unconscious hand movements, Jastrow claimed to have found important and revealing patterns.

Jastrow's only apparent academic shortcoming, in those early years, was that he lacked a degree from a European university, perhaps a considerable weakness in the American university of the 1880s. In 1889, however, he accompanied William James to the first International Congress of Psychology in Paris. They were the only two American academics in attendance, and this was the beginning of Jastrow's relationship with James, whom he always praised and whose writing style he tried to emulate. Jastrow apparently refrained, judiciously, from criticizing James's final turn to spiritualism, an interest that Jastrow quickly attacked when it appeared in others. The relationship to James sometimes seemed to me to be that of Jastrow's tugging at James's coattails, with hat in hand, asking for financial help, advice on dealing with administrators, or opinions on the psychological issues of the day (see Jastrow's letters to James, Harvard Archives). Jastrow had also been a reader of the fiction of William James's brother, Henry, and had attempted to write fiction in the Henry Jamesian style, though none of it was published (two short stories, Duke Library). Both Jastrow and William James spent summers vacationing near each other on the coast of Maine. On those occasions, both were under the care of the same physician for recurring depression.

In the 1890s, Jastrow introduced hypnosis research at Wisconsin and for years thereafter taught a medical hypnosis course in the university's medical school. He eventually turned that course over to Hull. The institutional context and intellectual atmosphere was thus prepared for Hull's unusually precise and quantitative studies of hypnosis (Hull, 1933). These studies reflected all the rigor soon to be displayed in the elaborate learning theory that Hull developed after his move to Yale.

Jastrow's hypnosis research is a good place to begin the account of his interests because, as well as any other work, it locates him in the modern history of psychological ideas. Hypnosis reflects quite well the major theme in his writings and his life. That was the distinction between voluntary and involuntary behavior and, connected with it, the problem of self-control and self-deception. It was expressed in the concluding paragraph of his doctoral dissertation (1886), which concerned, in one part, the subject of threshold psychophysics and the finding that subliminal stimuli may influence psychophysical judgments. The idea that subliminal stimuli may subtly shape our mental processes was his theme for years thereafter.

The same theme is the topic of Jastrow's 1906 book, *The Subconscious*, concerning dissociations of mental processes, slips, lapses, suggestibility, daydreams, levels of attention, voluntary-involuntary distinctions, subliminal perception, and multiple personality. Typical of his style, the book is unsystematic and rambling. It contains more literary allusions than systematic data. But today's authority in research on slips and lapses of action, James Reason of Manchester England, informs me that he is an avid fan of Jastrow and reads his books (Reason, 1989). And John Kihlstrom, now at Arizona, well known for hypnosis research, also writes that he is a reader of Jastrow on that topic (Kihlstrom, 1988).

A few years earlier, Jastrow's (1901b) book, *Fact and Fable in Psychology*, had been his first commercial success, and is the one that is probably best remembered today. Reprinted in 1972, it is a collection of essays built on the same pattern of interests that were developed later in *The Subconscious*.

Jastrow's interest in self-control and its deflections or failures is also a connecting thread that runs through his long obsession to expose the frauds and fakery of mind reading, telepathy, feats of magic, spiritism, and religious cults. As I now see it, he continued to write and rewrite on those themes for the rest of his life. They also underlie his explanations of mental illness. They underlie his commercially successful popular writings and radio broadcasts on self-help psychology, which were his sole occupation in the 1930s near the end of his life.

THE CAREER AT WISCONSIN

In 1888, two years after receiving the PhD degree and after 2 years of searching for a position, Jastrow was hired as "professor of experimental and comparative psychology" by the young science- and engineering-oriented University of Wisconsin. The laboratory he then constructed at Madison soon received international recognition when a French science-journalist, Henri Varigny (1894), described it in an article entitled "La laboratoire de Madison," which was published in the prestigious *Revue Scientifique*. Jastrow, however, seemed always to have regarded himself more as a broad renaissance man rather than a mere laboratory researcher. Though hired to import the new scientific psychology, which he did, he preferred his self-anointed role as bearer of culture-in-general to the crude frontier people of Wisconsin. In fact, a few years after his arrival at Wisconsin he was forced into bankruptcy as a consequence of building a "palace of culture," stocked with fine arts, cultural events, and a lavish office for himself, on the edge of the Wisconsin campus.

Jastrow's financial difficulties at Wisconsin, keeping him in debt to friends and relatives for many years (see the Duke papers), stemmed partly from the university's refusal ever to give him a substantial salary increase. It must be noted that the Wisconsin president, Thomas Chamberlain, who hired Jastrow was replaced shortly by Charles Adams, formerly president of Cornell, and the man who had refused to give Jastrow a position at Cornell 2 years earlier, preferring to hire no one and to delay the founding of the Cornell psychology lab rather than hire Jastrow. It was Adams, with his punishing, ironhanded, autocratic ways, an administrator tangled in numerous faculty conflicts both at Cornell and Wisconsin, who always refused to increase Jastrow's salary. As the pain of that circumstance grew, Jastrow gradually withdrew to activity outside of his university position.

At the turn of the century, Jastrow became perhaps the most forceful critic of the emerging pattern of the administration of universities in the United States, comparing it unfavorably with university administration in other countries. His studies of "the administrative peril in education" were in fact the product of detailed research and historical studies (Jastrow, 1912). He worked closely with James McKeen Cattell on this project when Cattell was embroiled in similar conflicts at Columbia. Jastrow helped found the American Association of University Professors with the hope that it would be a radical reformist organization that would foment faculty strikes and shut down those universities ruled by "despots" representing business interests external to the community of scholars.

One important change in the style of publication of the new psychology came from Jastrow's influence on the form of journal articles. In the *American Journal of Psychology*, in a series of articles during 1890–1892, he initiated the printing of "Minor studies from the Wisconsin psychology laboratory." When Harvard, Yale, Cornell, and other American universities formally established psychology programs (several years after Wisconsin's), they adopted that same procedure of Jastrow's of publishing shorter, briefer accounts of laboratory work. In contrast to the longer essays dominating early psychology journals, these short articles first stated a simple problem, described a research method, then findings and data analysis, then a conclusion, all in a few pages. Such "minor studies" usually appeared in fine print in the back pages of journals in the 1890s but then emerged as the standard form of research publishing for articles throughout the psychology journals in the 20th century.

One especially important contribution to the American public's recognition of psychology came from Jastrow's organization and administration of the psychology pavilion at the World's Fair (the Columbian Exposition) at Chicago in 1893. He arranged for the import and display, for the first time to a large American audience, of the best of the world's "new scientific" psychology. It involved mostly the European artifacts of the new science—representations of the best of early work, laboratories, and instrumentation. He used the facilities of the fair to collect a massive amount of psychophysical and reaction time data on thousands of subjects who passed through the pavilion. The whole project was patterned after Galton's slightly earlier and similar work in England. It was at this site that Jastrow met the young Hellen Keller and gave her the first systematic tests of her abilities. The amount of effort that Jastrow had to devote to all of this organization and administration was enormous. Yet Wisconsin had refused to release him from his classes that year, and he was forced to run back and forth between Madison and Chicago for the duration of the fair. By 1894 he was ill, exhausted, and broke.

Finally, under the weight of these difficulties, Jastrow buckled and caved in, and landed in his first serious depression in 1894–1895. That forced a leave from teaching and required extended medical care. In 1894, a Chicago newspaper reported these events under the heading: "Famous mind doctor loses his own" (Duke Library). It can be seen in his writings that at about this time, or near the turn of the century, he lost and never regained his early enthusiasm for experimental psychology. But before that change, he had published experimental work in perception, memory, mental testing, psychophysics, and suggestibility.

There were only six psychological doctoral dissertations during Jastrow's years on the Wisconsin faculty. All were interesting and good studies in their time. Hull's 1918 dissertation on concept formation using Chinese characters is still well known (Hull, 1920). (Some of Hull's original materials for that dissertation were, by the way, found with the

Jastrow papers at Duke.) Years ago when I was a graduate student, and long before I had heard of Jastrow, I began studying the early history of experimental psycholinguistics. I then stumbled upon the first doctoral dissertation completed under Jastrow's direction: J. R. Quantz's *Problems in the Psychology of Reading* (1897) which developed the techniques necessary for studying the eye–voice span that occurs when people read aloud and that appears to reflect a short-term memory or buffer storage in mental processes (Blumenthal, 1970). The other dissertations were those of Wilmot Lane, *The Psychology and Physiology of Fatigue* (1899), Isaac Ash, *Fatigue Effects on Control* (1914), Elizabeth Seaberg, *Recognition of Complex Visual Impressions* (1919), and Andrew Weaver, *Experimental Studies of Vocal Expression* (1923).

ALIENATION AND SURVIVAL

After the turn of the century and after travels in Europe and the Middle East, Jastrow grew obsessed with building something best described as an ornate Islamic mosque on the top of his palace of culture in Madison. Still there and still containing elegant materials imported from the middle East, it is located in a very large attic in what remains of his old palace of culture. Jastrow used this exotic sanctuary as a place in which to escape the tensions of his world to remain secluded for periods of meditation, or, as G. Stanley Hall wrote in a letter to him, "whatever you do in that place" (Wisconsin Archives). A scant few of Jastrow's more prestigious acquaintances (including Hall) were invited to see it. Through some considerable negotiations, I was afforded that opportunity. It still is, even in its dilapidated condition, an electrifying thing to behold. My first discovery there, for instance, was that the frayed wiring of the ornate Islamic lamps is still live, and I found myself frightfully close to electrocution. After he abandoned it in the mid-1920s, Jastrow's palace, named "The Altruia" on the ornamental letterhead of his stationery, was used as a boarding house and sorority house. Now it is in the hands of a tightly knit radical religious community. The present occupants should cause the old professor to roll in his grave because he had waged a personal war against religious cults his entire life. I could not help marveling at the old pictures of the once ornately decorated rooms, thinking that the house would have made an exquisite bordello. It is worth noting that a good part of early Wisconsin psychology instruction took place in that exotic setting.

Along with the architectural projects surrounding his palace in Madison, Jastrow's interests in the arts, always strong, began to expand, and he began serious art collecting and the teaching of aesthetic theory.

After the turn of the century, his interest in experimental psychology had clearly lapsed. When American academic psychology unfolded in its own unique way in the first quarter of this century, Jastrow was left behind, and was left shaken by what he saw as a disastrous turn in the newer efforts to redefine psychology. He applied himself with acid pen to the popular press. He published diatribes against behaviorism and against the imported cultish followers of Freud in many of the popular magazines of his day. In contrast to his writings about Watson, however, he always honored Freud as possessing a great mind—though misusing it. He perceived both of those movements as evolving into quasireligious cults—again his usual theme of attack.

By this time, Jastrow had easy access to the popular press, for as a result of the early financial failure, he had become a traveling psychologist-entertainer on the commercial lecture circuit of the day. When examining the artifacts surviving from that activity, it appeared to me that Jastrow had almost assumed the life of a vaudevillian. Advertisements for, and reviews of, his popular lectures are found in the newspapers of the day across the country (Duke Library). Ironically, his academic lectures back in Madison were considered dull and "windbag." Yet on the lecture circuit he proved himself a popular entertainer. (William James, by the way, had the same problem as a lecturer at Harvard while extremely effective as an after-dinner speaker with non-Harvard audiences.) Jastrow the entertainer thus dug himself out of his financial hole.

Jastrow taught his last course at Wisconsin in 1925. Rachel finally died in New York of a long and painful illness in 1926. For more than a decade, they had divided their lives between the east coast and Madison, and now he found it too difficult emotionally to return to Wisconsin. His writing during this period, mostly concerning the subjects of "character and temperament," may have been his least successful. He had withdrawn more and more from things at Wisconsin. Hull had effectively taken over the department even before he finished his dissertation under Jastrow in 1918.

It is interesting how Hull, this one stellar student of Jastrow's, so disliked Jastrow's writing and speaking style. One can easily see how Hull suffered through the hours of listening to Jastrow's long and windy phrases. Scores for both men on the early *Strong Vocational Interest Test* were preserved years ago by D. P. Campbell (1965). This comparison helps explain why the two men did not mix: Hull scored high on Chemist, Physicist, Physician, and Mathematician; Jastrow was high on Architect, Musician, Artist, and Author–Journalist.

Anyone writing about Jastrow must address his Victorian style. I've commended some of his writings to colleagues, who later came back to me with a bearing of pain and perplexity, making me realize that I should have said more to prepare them for what they were about to read (though others were delighted by what they read). Here is an excerpt from one of the more ornate Jastrowisms. It is from his presidential address to the American Psychological Association in 1900. Early in the talk, after an already profuse quantity of prologue, he said that the intention of his remarks would be to

> create a mood for a stroll along the shores of psychological waters, with the stroller's privilege of lingering to note what catches his eye and his interest, to watch the procession of the waves and the deposits which they roll up at one's feet, to follow the retreating rush of the waters, to note the action of the tide and the shifting of the sands, and with it all the building of permanent deposits and the shaping of continents. Or, if we prefer to cruise in the waters themselves, we may sail with interest as our compass, and follow a course not too rigidly set. Yet he who cruises to advantage must neither drift nor go as the wind listeth, but follow the invitations of shore and bay, keeping in mind, yet not too consciously, the headlands and reefs, touch at harbor and port, and be not unmindful of the attractions of home and the fireside. In some such way I shall attempt to cruise in and out among the currents and the undercurrents of contemporary psychology. (Psychological Review, 1901a, p. 4)

Jastrow then continued to splash and slosh through the major issues of psychology in that day.

But let me point this out before anyone scoffs at his style: Some recent library research has revealed to me that the Harvard English department, in the 1960s, put one of Jastrow's books on library reserve as required reading for Harvard English majors. The book was *Wish and Wisdom* (1937; reprinted by Dover Press in 1962). In the preface, Jastrow states his purpose as follows: "My theme concerns the life of reason, and the emotional encroachments, intrusions, distortions, and perversions that illustrate its course and endanger its sanity."

Fortunately for him, Jastrow's retirement was an emotional, if not intellectual, rebirth. He spent the first year of this new life in 1926 as a professional writer and the guest of an old family friend in Boston. There he hired a young assistant to run back and forth between his study and the Harvard Library for books and citations. That assistant was the young Frank Geldard, destined to become the leading name in sensory psychology years later. In Geldard's autobiography you find a very positive description of Jastrow. It is in the same category of positive praise as those comments I quoted earlier from the observer of Jastrow at Austen Riggs. Also in that Boston year, Jastrow was active in organizing the collection of funds for the defense in the infamous Sacco and Vanzetti trial.

From 1927 to 1932, Jastrow was a lecturer at the New School in New York. During the next decade, he wrote eight books, the best known being *The House that Freud Built*. In 1935, he published one of his sharpest and best-worded essays in the *American Scholar*, in which he argues passionately that psychology as a science had recently failed, but he held on to the faith that there is nothing inherent in the subject that should make it fail. Nevertheless, 1935 appeared to him to be the threshold of an advancing dark age for theoretical psychology.

For many years Jastrow wrote a syndicated column entitled "Keeping Mentally Fit," which eventually appeared in 150 different newspapers. From 1935 to 1938, he had an NBC radio program, also about keeping mentally fit. Near the end his life, he became even more of a social and moral critic. He left an unfinished manuscript of a book titled *Hitler: Mask and Myth* (Wisconsin Historical Archives). He was honored with a special plaque commemorating his accomplishments and writings at the New York World's Fair at the end of the decade.

Thus, the rabbi's wayward son finally found himself in a pulpit, as a sermonizing crusader, as his father had been, yet with a congregation likely much larger than any his father ever dreamed of.

REFERENCES

Blumenthal, A. (1970). *Language and psychology: Historical aspects of psycholinguistics.* New York: Wiley.

Campbell, D. P. (1965). The vocational interests of American Psychological Assocation presidents. *American Psychologist, 20,* 636–644.

Hull, C. (1920).Quantitative aspects of the evolution of concepts: An experimental study. *Psychological Monographs, 28* (Whole No. 123).

Hull, C. (1933). *Hypnosis and suggestibility.* New York: Appleton-Century.

Jastrow, J. (1884). Letter to Henrietta Szold, Wisconsin Historical Archives, Jastrow papers, Madison.

Jastrow, J. (1886). *Perception of space by disparate senses,* doctoral dissertation, Johns Hopkins University, Baltimore. (Published in *Mind, 2,* 1886.)

Jastrow, J. (1890). *Time relations of mental phenomena.* New York: Hodges.

Jastrow, J. (1901a). Some currents and undercurrents in psychology. *Psychological Review, 8,* 1–26.

Jastrow, J. (1901b). *Fact and fable in psychology.* New York: Houghton Mifflin.

Jastrow, J. (1906). *The subconscious.* New York: Houghton Mifflin.

Jastrow, J. (1912). The administrative peril in education. *Popular Science Monthly,* November, 315–348.

Jastrow, J. (1935). Has psychology failed? *American Scholar, 4,* 261–269.

Jastrow, J. & Peirce, C. S. (1884). On small differences in sensation. *Memoirs of the National Academy of Science, 3.*

Kihlstrom, J.(1988). Letter to A. Blumenthal, Sarah Lawrence College.

Marks, L. (1978). *The unity of the senses*. New York: Academic Press.

Preston, J. H.(1944). Letter to Mrs. Hutchison, Duke University, Durham, N.C., Rare Manuscripts Library, Jastrow papers.

Quantz, J. O. (1897). Problems in the psychology of reading. *Psychological Review, Monograph Supplement*, No. 5.

Reason, J. (1989). Letter to A. Blumenthal, Sarah Lawrence College.

Roback, A. (1964). *A history of American psychology*, (2nd ed.). New York: Library Publishers.

Varigny, H. (1894). La laboratoire de Madison. *Revue Scientifique*, 1, 624–629.

Chapter 7

E.B. Titchener on Scientific Psychology and Technology

Rand B. Evans

The main content of this chapter takes the form of a lecture that Titchener might have given and says nothing about Titchener as a person. A few introductory observations on the character of the man seem necessary, however, because the Titchener that most psychologists "know" is a caricature. The real person has been lost among the stories that surround his memory. These stories present Titchener as a chronic cigar smoker and a sexist. They have him lecturing in his Oxford robes, expressing a dogmatic certainty about the truths of psychology, and patronizing colleagues and students who failed to understand him. As with all such stories, these contain a grain of truth but there is more exaggerataion. My forthcoming biography, *E. B. Titchener: The Structured Mind*, attempts to get behind these fictions. In these few paragraphs available to me here, I can only offer a glimpse of what the man was really like.

Titchener's was an overpowering personality. He seemed bigger that life and often overwhelmed his students and colleagues by sheer strength of character. Much of this impact derived from the view that he projected of what a professor and scholar should be. One part of this image was that of the German *Gelehrter*, the scholar–professor, of whom Wundt was probably the model. The other part was that of the 19th-century "English Gentleman," an individual who is supremely confident in thought and action. Paraphrasing what Titchener is alleged

---

*Photograph of Edward B. Titchener courtesy of the Archives of the History of Psychology, Akron, Ohio

once to have said, "If you're an English Gentleman, you can turn a handspring in the street and, when you're on your feet again, you're still an English Gentleman. If you worry about what the neighbors think, you probably won't turn the handspring." This model of the professor's role was not familiar to Americans. Put forward with Titchener's enormous confidence and his deep commitment to scholarship, it led to frequent misunderstandings.

The only thing that was important to Titchener in science was the truth of nature as revealed by direct experience and the logic of the scientific system. Ideas that did not meet these criteria came in for criticism that could be harsh. Titchener was more than willing to call someone's brainchild an idiot if it fell short of his standards. Although he rarely received such frankness in return, Titchener prized those who were willing to give it to him.

One point of wide misunderstanding is of Titchener's view of the role of women in science. Many psychologists regard Titchener as a misogynist because he excluded women from the meetings of "Experimentalists," formally, the Society of Experimental Psychologists. Titchener had founded the society on the model of an Oxford smoking club. He invited a group of experimental psychologists to get together once a year to smoke and discuss their work in perfect frankness, without the artificial restrictions of polite society. None of this seemed appropriate for ladies.

By present standards, such an attitude is absurd, but such was not the case in the late 19th century, when men and women typically separated, even after a dinner party, for separate conversation and, in the case of men, smoking. Actually Titchener took women into his graduate program at Cornell at a time when Harvard and Columbia would not. More women completed their PhD degrees with him than with any other male psychologist of his generation. About half of his PhDs were women. Titchener also favored hiring women for academic positions when they were the best candidates for a job. In one case he did so, even over the objection of the dean. His only complaint about his women PhDs was that so many of them married and did not go into academic settings, thus wasting their potential. Thus, contrary to the popular opinion, Titchener's attitude toward women was supportive. Trapped by the social norms existing in his time, Titchener did exclude women from the meetings of the Experimentalists but this is something quite different from misogyny.

FORMAL PRESENTATION

The talk to follow is a collage of the words of E. B. Titchener, assembled from a transcription of Titchener's speech to the Clark University

Conference on Psychology in 1909 (Titchener, 1910), a paper published in a popular magazine (Titchener, 1914) and two letters to the psychiatrist Adolf Meyer (Leys & Evans, 1990; Titchener, 1909, 1918). The few transitional phrases interjected by the author are set off by brackets.

[I have been asked to speak to you today on scientific psychology and its relation to applied psychology. This matter is one] upon which agreement is hardly to be expected. For agreement implies in the first instance, a common point of view; and my own standpoint, which is that of pure science, or the desire for knowledge without regard to utility, is in all likelihood shared only by a small minority of this audience. Moreover, agreement within the domain of pure science presupposes a certain measure of progress, a platform of assured results; and to that point, perhaps experimental psychology has not yet attained. Nevertheless, while I anticipate that you will reject my conclusion, I trust that you will also remember the general attitude and point of view from which it is derived.

The Rise of Applied Psychology

If, then, one were asked to sum up, in a sentence, the trend of psychology during the past 10 years, one's reply would be: Psychology has leaned, very definitely, toward application. And if the questioner were thereupon to look for proof of this statement, he would find it confirmed not only by the range and variety of current practical work, but also and more particularly by the incursion into the field of practice of men whose training and previous interests might naturally have held them aloof.

The diversion into practical channels of the energy which would otherwise have been expended in the service of the laboratory must be regarded as a definite loss to pure science; and it is from the standpoint of pure science that I am now speaking. You will reply, perhaps, that there are compensating advantages. Application will discover new problems, which must be referred back for solution to the experimentalist. I recognize the advantages; but I do not think that they offset the loss. Every one, for instance, who has followed the history of science, knows that successful application is but a very imperfect measure of the validity of a theory; material improvement may go astonishingly far under the guidance of some scientific hypothesis which later generations roundly pronounce erroneous, and which shows, indeed, but a glimmer of the later found truth.

That is the situation, as it appears from my point of view; others will see it differently. It is, in any case, a situation that must be accepted.

Science and Technology

Psychology has, of recent years, been exhorted to be practical, praised for its willingness to be practical, blamed for its unwillingness to be practical. "A kind of psychology which is needed is that of every-day people." "Psychology is ceasing to be a purely academic science and is now willing to study questions dealing with every-day life." "Psychology as it is being taught and investigated deals with matters of no concern, or of too abstract a nature, for practise." "The normal psychologist has been forced out of his academic reserve." A psychology is needed "which is aimed at practical ends," "a psychology which works and lives rather than a psychology easy to teach or easy to write," a psychology of a "matter-of-fact-type," which adopts "the commonsense attitude," a psychology whose problems "really go at the causal relationships vital to the student, vital to any layman who wants to know what psychology is and does, vital to the physician," in a word, a truly "dynamic" psychology. The demand, as these few quotations show, far exceeds the supply; exhortation and blame are more strongly in evidence than encouragement and praise.

[I believe that] hostilities are in the main kept up through the neglect of a very elementary distinction, the distinction of Science and Technology. . . . [I]f the distinction is regarded, there may be an end of railing accusation and a new birth of what theory and practise both alike require—serious and well-weighed criticism.

We are still told, in textbooks and scientific addresses, that the various sciences represent various departments of knowledge. The territory of science, that is to say, is conceived of as parceled out among the separate sciences, very much as a continent is mapped out into a number of adjoining countries. If the tale of the sciences were complete, the whole map would be variously colored; since, however, there are "gaps" in our knowledge, the map shows blank spaces, unexplored regions to which the methods of science have not yet attained.

Points of View

What in fact differentiates science from science is . . . something that we may term objectively point of view and subjectively attitude. Giving up the figure of the map, one might conceive of the world of experience as contained in a great circle, and of scientific men as viewing this world from various stations upon the periphery. There are then, in theory, as many possible sciences as there are distinguishable points of view about the circle. Every science seeks to view the whole world of experience from its particular station; and every science deals, from that station again, with identically the same subject matter, namely, with human experience. The separate sciences, are, therefore, not at all like countries on a map; they are rather like the successive chapters of a book which discusses a complex topic from various points of view. In this sense, they overlap; they are mutually complementary; no one of them in truth exhausts experience or completely describes the common subject matter, though each one, if ideally complete, would exhaust some aspect of experience.

It is, then, from some such figure as that of the circle and the men around it that a classification of the sciences must start.

The Scientific Point of View.   We are bound to characterize more closely the scientific attitude, or the scientific point of view. Human experience may be brought together in other than scientific ways; and while we still need not seek for formal definition or final classification, we must try at least to differentiate science from the appreciating discipline and from what we have called technology. We must find distinguishing adjectives for the attitude itself, for the method which it implies, and for the problem which it discovers.

The history of science leaves no doubt of the answer to be given to this threefold question. The attitude of science, to begin with that, is before all things a disinterested attitude: Witness the rise and growth of astronomy, chemistry, and physiology. Until mankind has learned to take experience in serious earnest "for its own sake," to subordinate personal ends to the pursuit of truth, there is no science, but only something which at its worst is quackery and pseudoscience, at its best common sense and rule of thumb. Conversely, so soon as a man starts out to examine some aspect of experience as if it were for itself important and knowledge of it were intrinsically desirable, so soon does the germ of a science appear. For the race, the learning of this lesson was difficult enough; and so, in large, the negative form of the adjective—disinterested—may be justified; science sets aside the oldest and what we might consider the most natural interests of man. For the individual, on the other hand, a positive term would be more suitable.

The scientific attitude, then, is disinterested; the point of view of science is one that shall reveal the unvarnished fact; so much we are plainly taught by the history of science. We gather from the same source that the method of science is observation. All the "facts" of science are gained by a disinterested observation; sometimes, by an unaided observation; more often, since the conditions are complex, by the roundabout way—which is still observation—of experiment and measurement. We need not pause to illustrate, or to cite the authorities; the conclusion is generally accepted; and every piece of apparatus in our laboratories shows as an instrument for the control or the extension or the refinement of observation.

It is, perhaps, less apparent that all the problems of science may be summed up in the single problem of analysis; that the task which lies before the man of science, in his character as scientific, is always the analysis—under which is included, of course, that synthesis which is a test of analysis—of some complex object or complex situation. The reduction of a compound to its elements, the differentiation of factors, the establishment of correlations among their components of a given whole, these are the things that the scientific investigator find himself doing. True, we shrink a little from running all men of science into the same mold; we individualize them; we think of Newton as wielding "the ponderous instrument of synthesis," of Darwin as "working in true Baconian principles, and without any theory collecting facts on a wholesale scale." We are right in thus individualizing; for not only is the man of science something more than a scientific machine, but science itself is also (as we are to see in a moment) something more than what we have so far made it out to be. The witness of history is nevertheless, straightforward enough; what Newton and Darwin, as scientific men, had before all things to do was to analyze, and to analyze again, and again to analyze. To be scientifically active is disinterestedly to apply the method of observation to the task of analysis.

Meaning of science. Our three adjectives are thus given: disinterested, observational, analytical. Taken together they characterize the scientific attitude with sufficient accuracy for the purposes of this talk. They do not, however, cover the full meaning of "science" as that word is ordinarily used and understood. When we speak of science, we mean, not an assemblage of observed facts, the direct results of analysis, but rather an organized and systematized body of knowledge, a closed and self-contained whole. That every science, every transcription of the world from a scientific point of view, should yield a system, as if there were of necessity some immanent principle of order which the facts illustrate and to which they conform, is of course an assumption, and an assumption that we might find curious were it not so familiar. Originating perhaps in physics, supported by the belief in the general uniformity of nature, and favored by the tendency to regard the sciences as departments of knowledge, and therefore as concerned with divisions of the cosmic mechanism, it has been accepted, more or less consciously, by biology and psychology. Whether the acceptance is wise, and whether economy of thought may not be paid for too dearly, are questions beside our immediate point. What we have to note is this: That to systematize the facts of science, by any principle immanent or external, is to bring logic to bear upon them, to arrange them in the light of those logical laws which the experience of the race has tested and found secure, and which therefore form the stock in trade of a beginning theory of knowledge. We proceed, says Bacon, "by observing or by meditating on facts"; "to the formation of a science," writes Whewell, "two things are requisite—Facts and Ideas; observation of Things without, and an inward effort of Thought"; and Huxley demands for a science "scientific observation" and "scientific reasoning." Science, that is to say, in the meaning of a scientific system, is the outcome of scientific activity ordered by logic.

Science, therefore may mean two things, scientific activity and the scientific system; and this twofold meaning is a fertile source of confusion. There is always the danger, for instance, that logic, which is a good servant, become the master, as it does when Pearson tells us that the goal of science is "nothing short of a complete interpretation of the universe" (Pearson, 1892). Science, as scientific activity, aims at no goal; even the phrase "pursuit of truth," useful and inevitable as it may be, may also be misleading; science is, in strictness, only self-directed on an endless task. So the result of scientific activity is not an interpretation, in any pregnant sense of that term, but only a transcription of the world of human experience as it appears from a certain point of view. Science, in Pearson's formula, thus stands for the system of sciences; and the system in turn is made to stand, not only for the outcome of scientific activity as worked over by an accepted theory of knowledge, but also for a special theory of knowledge under which the outcome of scientific activity has, to Pearson's satisfaction, been subsumed; logic has become the master. The same logic is, nonetheless, an indispensable servant.

We may sum up these paragraphs in the statement that science is defined by its point of view. The scientific man looks out upon experience from a certain standpoint; sees and can see his world only under one aspect; and by this attitude, which he has taken up toward experience, is limited to a particular type of method and to a particular type of problem. To invite him from his "academic reserve," or to demand that he interest himself in "practical ends," is simply to bid him cease from scientific activity. The scientific man, again, is logical, just as the historian or the jurist is logical; but logic is not science; and within science the facts of observation take precedence, and logical methods are secondary. To say that science leads to, or suggests, some general "interpretation" of things, is to say what may or may not be true; but the saying, in either case, transcends science itself and changes the man of science into the philosopher. It must, indeed, be acknowledged that science, despite the immensity of its scope and the multitudinous variety of its subject matter, confines its followers within relatively narrow limits; the shadow of the three adjectives [point of view, disinterested, analysis] is always upon them; and it is just because science is narrower than life that the man of science, unless he be of a certain temperament, is tempted to transgress the limits, and to betake himself in the long run to philosophy—or to spiritism.

Technological point of view.   Against science now stands what we have called technology. In a certain restricted meaning, this term, which we have so far employed without comment, is familiar enough; the greatly extended meaning which it is here to receive must be justified by the sequel. The word is used henceforth to cover, in the broadest way, the activities that are ordinarily and misleadingly referred to as "applied science"; such things, that is to say, as engineering and medicine, all their branches; such things as scientific agriculture, and domestic science, and school hygiene, and industrial chemistry, and eugenics. All these disciplines have a common character, by which they are set off from science; for, if science is defined by its point of view, technology (in the new and wider sense) is defined by its end or goal. Technology thus has its own narrowness; it is held down to the pursuit of some particular practical end; but this narrowness is different from the limitation of science. The technologist may change his point of view as often as he likes; he will use any method that promises to be serviceable; he will attack any problem that rises in his path. The result is that a "system" of technology is likely to appear to the man of science as a mixed medley of more or less unrelated knowledge, and that a pure science is likely to appear to the technologist as an example of finespun and quite needless consistency. A textbook of engineering will range from sections on pure mathematics and pure mechanics to practical directions for the setting-up of instruments and the reading of indicator cards; and a system of medicine, in the same way, will skip from theory to practice and from practice back again to theory within the boundaries of a single paragraph. The authors are entirely in the right; their readers are physicians and engineers, and not physiologists and physicists; their subject matter is held together and unified by a practical aim, and not by an initial point of view; it is unfair to judge them by the standards of science. A textbook of physics or of physiology, on the other hand is — as we have seen — a transcription of the world of experience from a particular standpoint, which is deliberately adopted at the outset and deliberately maintained to the end; no item of experience that is not visible from this standpoint can properly get in to it; and it is unfair to judge it by the needs and aims of a technology. All human activities have their limitations, and if the technologist is less clearly conscious of the restriction laid upon him by his practical end, and the man of science feels more keenly the narrowing of his universe by the scientific point of view — the rule is certainly not without exceptions; but we may grant the tendency — that is due partly to the greater outward diversity of the technological career, and partly to the more rigorous training in logic that scientific investigation affords and demands. The technologist never, to be sure, handles experience in its totality, but he deals with individual cases, and so comes nearer to the concrete than his scientific colleague; and he may, moreover, change from the practical to the scientific or the appreciative attitude without any great fear of leaving his last; his interests are thus diversified. The man of science, constantly applying the principles of logic, and constantly on his guard against the encroachment of logical theory upon the facts of observation, is forced to be self-critical, and so comes nearer to a true perspective.

Relation of Science and Technology.   Different, however, as science and technology may be, they are also closely related. Technology draws on other than scientific sources; it draws upon common sense, upon existing technologies, upon prescientific practise; but it draws continually upon science: science, in its turn, if furthered by technology. The pursuit of a practical end often reveals some defect of theoretical knowledge; and the repairing of this defect, itself a contribution to science, may perform more than it promised, may in fact open up some wholly new field of scientific enquiry. That is the nature of the relation; and at first sight the advantage seems to lie with technology; for if the technologist needs the aid of science, he also appears capable of supplying for himself the science that he needs; he has only, for a little while, to shift his attitude, and the science is forthcoming. Where, then, would be the loss if pure science, with its "unreal" and "abstract" concerns, went by the board and we all became practical together?

In answer to this question there are two things to be said. We must remember, in the first place, that every technology is limited by its end. When a technological need suggests a problem in pure science, the suggestion bears directly upon the need out of which it arises, and upon that need only; when the need is satisfied, there is no further sanction, within the technology, for purely scientific work. If, in other words, the progress of science were made dependent on the progress of technology, and theory were never invoked save for the sake of practise—if such a state of things were conceivable—then our scientific knowledge would perforce remain scrappy and partial, so scrappy and so partial that a halt would ultimately be called to the advance of technology itself. An all-embracing technology, starting out with things as they are today, would no doubt be able to maintain itself for a relatively long time; theory is, in general, so far ahead of practice that, though science now stopped short, technological advance would long be possible. It is this fact, of course, which gives a plausible coloring to the demand that science leave its heights and come down among "everyday people," and that the man of science, instead of adding to his store of observed facts, use his scientific capital for "practical" and "vital" purposes. Sooner or later, however, the capital would be exhausted; sooner or later, progress would slow down to stagnation; the needs of technology, occasional needs of a circumscribed activity, would not suffice in the long run for the advancement of science. And then there is the other side of the shield! Technology, we said, draws from many sources, but is continually drawing upon science; each separate technology, we may here add, upon many sciences. Now if any indication from the history of human achievement is secure, it is surely this: that there is nothing in science so abstract, or so remote from matter of fact, or so indifferent to common sense, that it may not, some day or other, prove of service to a technology; and since this is the case, it is really to be the interest even of the most practical man that scientific activity would be conserved and encouraged.

A second consideration brings us by a different road to the same conclusion. The close relationship that we have shown to hold between science and technology is the relationship that holds in a scientific age, at a time when science has won recognition, is cultivated internationally, is widely popularized. In such an age, it is nature, as it is also the best policy, for technology to draw upon science. Technological activity, however, is a very complicated affair; and it may be doubted whether technology, if left wholly to itself, would turn instinctively even to the best scientific systems available; still more that it would supply for itself, by arduous and unaccustomed work, the knowledge that those systems fail to furnish. The tendency would rather be (and this is no dispraise to the technologist, who may never lose sight of his practical end) to fall back upon past science, upon science that was already more or less familiar, or to extend technological activity by purely technological means. Indeed, this tendency may be observed at the present day. The leader of a reform movement in psychiatry, which has found critics and adherents over the whole civilized world, expressly bases his teaching upon psychology; but the psychology which he has in part adopted, in part worked out anew — and which he appears to find entirely adequate to his technological needs — is in essentials the psychology of a past generation.

The moral of such things is surely plain: that the technologist, for the very sake of his technology, needs the stimulus, the criticism and the assistance, of the man of science. Practical work tends, always and everywhere, to become routine work; routine tends toward conservatism, toward the defence of the old and the avoidance of the new; and conservatism ensures social stability. But if our ideal of society is a progressive equilibration, rather than the mere inertia of routine, then the conservatism of practical work must be tempered by the radicalism of science.

It is difficult in writing upon a disputed question, not to give the impression that one is trying to disparage one's opponents. Yet the writer has no desire, despite the many hard things that technologists have said of the science with which he is most nearly concerned, to attempt any sort of disparagement of technology. Science and technology are, first of all, different. Science is defined by its point of view; the man of science takes his stand at the handle of the fan, and looks out along the sticks to an undefined periphery. Technology is defined by its practical end; the technologist, moving over the periphery, chooses and shapes the sticks which are to meet at the pivot that he has always held in view.

It follows from this primary difference that no technology is properly characterized as the application of a special science. Every technology is itself a special discipline, indebted (to be sure) to many sciences and to many other sources than science, but adding matter and method of its own, and rounding up all that it handles into a single whole. It is therefore no more in order to speak today, say, of an "applied psychology," than it would be to call engineering by its older name of "applied mechanics"; and the sooner we recognize that, in this particular sense, technology is independent of science, that the technologist lives and moves in a world of his own, has his own problems and methods, is charged with a special message to his generation, the sooner shall we exchange our present bickering for the harmony that we desire.

Science and technology are, in the second place, closely related; the nature of the relationship has been sketched in preceding paragraphs. If we look at this relation from without, from the side of maintenance and material aids, then the advantage lies with technology, and science is the beneficiary. The scientific man, accordingly, should rejoice at every technological advance, seeing that it ensures by just so much the material future of science "How many men," asked Kepler in the old time, "how many men would be able to make astronomy their business, if men did not cherish the hope to read the future in the skies?" And, with change of terms, the story is told again of us moderns. If contrariwise, we look at the relation from within, then, as this paper has tried to show, technology appears as a beneficiary of science. The technologist should accordingly rejoice at every scientific advance, seeing that it means just so much more of observed fact which he may someday utilize in his practice. To slight the "leisure-class problems of true science" in the supposed interest of activities which "earn their bread in terms of usefulness for the questions of life" is really to mistake that interest, and to wound technology in the house of its friends.

Lastly, science and technology are alike in their free recourse to the established laws and approved methods of logic. Science is, on the whole, more rigorous than technology in this logical regard; not through

any superior virtue in the man of science, but simply because the
technologist, in the nature of the case is a logical opportunist, working
for results and toward a practical end, and therefore content to work in
a logical twilight so long as results are forthcoming and progress can be
reported. That the technologist would, on occasion, betray impatience
with the stricter canons of scientific procedure is only natural. That the
student of science should stir in his own defence must also be expected:
How great, after all, are the benefits that science has conferred upon
humanity! What we may hope for is that men of intelligence and sound
training, after they have been distributed by temperament or circumstance to scientific and technological activities, may still so far keep in
touch that each understands the other's limitations and sympathizes
with the other's ideals.

We must admit that practice and theory interlock and help each other.
There were bridges built before there was a mathematical physics. But
bridge building helped toward pure physics; and very certainly mathematical physics has helped the bridge builder. There were cures made
and operations performed before there was a science of physiology; but
certainly pure physiology has been of aid to medicine. Demons were
exorcised, and David played the harp before Saul, when there was no
science of psychology. But by all analogy the working-out of a science of
psychology should advance psychiatry. It seems indeed, if we look at
the history of science, as if there were no great advance possible in the
applied field until some group of men had devoted themselves to pure
science, to the apparently useless and remote, to interests that lie as far
as we can be from application. When pure science has been studied,
then—even, so to say, against the will of the men who have given
themselves to it—we invariably find a great progress in application.

SUMMARY AND CREDO

[I will close by summarizing my own credo in brief form, taken from the
point of view of scientific, experimental psychology].

(1) I think that Science deals with existential experience from the
three methodologically different points of view of physics, biology,
psychology. The Fact, a matter of direct acquaintance-with, I regard as
scientifically ultimate. The System of science I take to be built of nothing
more than facts and logic. Hence I consider science to be independent of
Philosophy. Any philosophical system, on the other hand, must, if it is
to satisfy, take account in equal measure of the three scientific systems.
Hence Philosophy is not independent of Science.

(2) Outside of science I find that men recognize Values. Apparently
these values are taken by these men to be no less ultimate for axiological

systems than facts are for science; and apparently there are different classes of values (as in science there are three classes of facts) which appear from methodologically different points of view. I am ready to accept these conclusions, and the resulting systems of values. I regard all such value-systems as independent of Philosophy. Any satisfactory philosophy, however, must take account, in equal measure, of the various value-disciplines. Hence philosophy is not independent of Axiology.

(3) Beside Science and Axiology I find mixed aggregates of knowledge and precept, held together by a Purpose, which I call collectively Technologies. There seem to be technologies roughly correlated with value-disciplines, as there certainly are technologies roughly correlated with sciences. I am concerned primarily with those that correlate with sciences. The interrelations are extremely complex. Common to all such technologies, however, – for the obvious reason that they aim to "get things done," is an ultimate recourse to physical energies. The physical technologies work directly with energy; the "biological" technologies work at one logical remove, and the "psychological" technologies work at two logical removes, from physical energetics. Misunderstanding on this point is, I believe, responsible for the controversy of mechanism versus vitalism in biology, and of parallelism versus interactionism in psychology. I can thus understand how those controversies arose, and why they survive. Personally, I regard them as transcended.

(4) Philosophy begins, I think, as the great universal technology of Common Sense, the Art of Living. I regard the Aristotelian system as typical; it is at once a cyclopedia and a sublimation of Common Sense. Facts and Values were at first undifferentiated within this vast technology. As they have become differentiated, the various philosophical systems have naturally tried to cover and include them. But a satisfactory philosophy must take account of all the sciences, of all the value-disciplines, and of all the technologies: not in detail, but nevertheless adequately, so that there is no loose end left over. It must both legitimate distinctions and transcend them.

I cannot assure myself that this task has as yet been satisfactorily performed, or even that the existing systems promise its satisfactory performance. Hence I cannot as yet commit myself to any existing philosophical system.

(5) All this scaffolding I have worked out in the interest of my scientific work within Psychology. When I began to "profess" psychology, I found that I did not know what a science was, or in what sense psychology was a science, or how a science was related to its "applications." The greatest obstacle to my thinking on these and cognate questions has been (in myself and in others) what I have called "muddle," a lack of strict usage following on strict definition, and the presence of vague fringes of implication never made explicit. I am not

sure that the clearest thinking will ever be adequate to the universe; but I am very sure that muddy thinking cannot be. And sad experience has taught me that my own training and that of many of my contemporaries did not insist on clear thinking. So I am trying to be so far clear as that those who read me later on will be able to accept or reject with full understanding of what it is they are accepting or rejecting. No doubt, the attempt is aimed too high: Let us call it rather an ideal.

(6) I hope, as I suppose we all do, that something of my constructive work will stand the test of time; and when a man crosses my field, I am very happy to match logics with him and to test my own ideas by his. But I have changed so much that I can't feel antagonistic to a difference of opinion, and I certainly have never tried to proselytise. The synthesis that I look forward to will take, I believe, some centuries to accomplish, and meantime I would let every man go his own way, checked only by the logic of his critics.

PERSONAL COMMENTARY

When I was asked to reconstruct this lecture by E. B. Titchener, I selected the topic of the relationship between scientific psychology and applied psychology rather than one on Titchener's systematic position, structuralism, because I believe that Titchener's lasting contribution to American psychological thought was his championing of psychology as science and of the laboratory as the primary source of data for psychological research. There were others in America and elsewhere who supported the same things, of course, but none so effectively as E. B. Titchener.

In this regard, the excerpt from Titchener's Clark University speech is particularly significant. He was chosen to speak at that conference, the conference at which Sigmund Freud, Carl Jung, and other psychoanalysts were formally introduced to America, because Titchener was to represent the interests of scientific, experimental psychology against the growing tide of applied and theoretical psychologies (see Evans & Koelsch, 1985). That he did with sufficient gusto, that Freud reportedly greeted him after that talk as *der Gegner*, the adversary.

Titchener's goal was for a truly independent, scientific psychology and for that scientific psychology to be centered on the laboratory. When Titchener refers to "psychology" in most of his writings, he is presupposing the meaning of scientific, experimental psychology. It is easy to see Titchener as an opponent to applied psychology. He was not opposed to applications of psychology, only to the applied, or technological aspects of psychology being mixed uncritically with scientific psychology. What Titchener was attempting to do was to establish scientific psychology as one of the fundamental sciences, along with physics and biology. For that to be possible, psychology had to be a "pure" science, equivalent to physics and biology but it had to be clearly independent from them. The rise of applied psychology, intermingling with scientific psychology, threatened the first of these requirements.

Titchener believed that applications of psychology should be developed in other departments outside of psychology. The applications of psychological facts for education were best found in colleges of education. Educational psychology belonged to education; medical psychology to medicine, legal psychology to law, business psychology to business. Even in 1909, however, Titchener assumed in the opening lines of his talk that most of his audience held views that favored application rather than science.

Titchener did not succeed in separating applied from scientific psychology. Because of that he also did not succeed in gaining for psychology the status of a basic science. When we look around today at the way modern psychology is regarded by our scientific colleagues and the hodgepodge it has become, we we can only wonder how things might have been different if Titchener's model of psychology as a fundamental science had been followed.

Titchener did succeed, however, in establishing the laboratory as the center of the psychological enterprise, both as central in the educational preparation of psychologists and of the scientific enterprise itself.

ACKNOWLEDGMENT

This chapter was prepared, in part, with the aid of National Science Foundation Grant No. SES 8319882.

REFERENCES

Evans, R. B. & Koelsch, W. A. (1985). Psychoanalysis arrives in America: The 1909 psychology conference at Clark University. *American Psychologist, 40*, 942–948.

Leys, R. & Evans, R. B. (1990). Defining American psychology: The correspondence between Adolf Meyer and E.B. Titchener. Baltimore: Johns Hopkins University Press.

Pearson, K.(1892) *The grammar of science.* London: Dent (1937 printing).

Titchener, E. B. (1909). Letter to Adolf Meyer, September 19. In Adolf Meyer Papers, Chesney Medical Archives, Johns Hopkins University, Baltimore.

Titchener, E. B. (1910). The past decade in experimental psychology. *American Journal of Psychology, 21*, 404–421.

Titchener, E. B. (1914). Psychology: Science or technology? *Popular Science Monthly,* January, 40–51.

Titchener, E. B. (1918). Letter to Adolf Meyer, November 17. In Adolf Meyer Papers, Chesney Medical Archives, Johns Hopkins University, Baltimore.

Chapter 8

Continuity for Women: Ethel Puffer's Struggle

Elizabeth Scarborough

I want to discuss Ethel Puffer as a pioneer in two fields: psychology and women's studies. These represented for her two distinct, sequential career ventures – and the reason that these ventures were so separated, both in subject matter and in time, is central to understanding the situation of early women psychologists, and of early women professionals in general.

But first let me ask: How many of you had even heard of Ethel Puffer before seeing her name in the APA program? If you do not recognize her, that is really not surprising. Although she was one of the earliest accomplished women in psychology, until 1986 you would not have found her name in publications on the history of psychology. In fact, when the program for this meeting was distributed, my dean, a psychologist who had taught the history of psychology course and is characteristically very direct, called me up to ask "So who the hell is Ethel Puffer?"

Puffer is better known in the context of her other career. Her work is discussed in some detail by Betty Friedan (1986) in *The Second Stage*. And, in *The Grand Revolution: A History of Feminist Designs for American Homes, Neighborhoods, and Cities* (1981), Dolores Hayden (a professor of urban planning) devotes an entire chapter to Puffer and her campaign to legitimize the career goals of women. In each of these books, however, Ethel Puffer is called Ethel Puffer Howes. I believe that in the addition of the new surname, acquired when she married, we find the clue to the

---

*Photograph of Ethel Puffer courtesy of Smith College Archives, Smith College

disparity between the two phases of her professional work, to her obscurity in the history of psychology, and to the motivation for her struggle, throughout the latter part of her life, with the crucial problem faced by women of her generation: the necessity to choose between motherhood and serious professional work. Puffer saw that problem as an issue of *continuity*.

Let me state Puffer's position by quoting from an article she wrote in 1925 for the *Smith Alumnae Quarterly* (Howes, 1925). She was then 53 and on the threshold of her second career:

> "The Good Life" for woman must be a true integration of her emotional or family life and her continuous intellectual interest. . . . Increasingly college-trained women have realized a certain dislocation between the emprise of their intellectual undertakings, and the normal life of marriage and motherhood which claimed them. The more sharply focussed their intellectual aims, the more completely did these seem in marriage to come to a dead end. At the worst, the professional interest was either pursued ruthlessly, to the exclusion, or the neglect, of family life, or dropped completely for it; at the best, an adjustment was made between the family and the intensive individual or professional interests, which was felt as more or less temporary, questionable, or needing apology. So that, as marriage and motherhood were understood even by the ablest women as debarring from any intensive or professional activity, and as their woman's heritage was certainly not to be foregone, the result was to give a certain unreality and lack of continuity to the intellectual aims and efforts of the college itself. (p. 1)

Puffer believed that, for the educated woman, real happiness and fulfillment required finding some way to combine family life and intellectual activity. She was not alone in this; it was a burning issue in her time—and need I say it?—an issue that has not yet been satisfactorily resolved for hosts of women today. Nor was she alone in experiencing on an intensely personal level, the wrenching discontinuity that occurred when marriage required an early, forced retirement from academic positions.

I have chosen to talk about Puffer not only because she was an active pioneer in two career fields, but also because she stands as a good prototype of a subgroup of psychology's first women: those who married and thereby relinquished their most obvious career opportunities. When Laurel Furumoto and I examined the lives of these women for our book *Untold Lives: The First Generation of American Women Psychologists* (Scarborough & Furumoto, 1987), we found that none of the early women psychologists who married continued to pursue professional interests to the neglect of family life, the "worst case scenario," given in the aforementioned quotation (Howes, 1925). A few did completely abandon their professional roles in favor of family life; more, however, made the kind of adjustments Puffer herself eventually advocated. Puffer stands out from that group, though, because although her activity was an effort to find a resolution in her own life and family, she was, in that struggle, directly addressing the problem as it affected other women as well.

I'm getting ahead of myself. I want here to do two things: first, to establish Puffer's credentials as an accomplished and promising psychologist by describing her preparation and early work, and second, to give attention to Puffer's efforts to promote continuity for women. She was a pioneer in each of these spheres, and examining the issues involved gives us some insight into the social and cultural history of early 20th-century American psychology.

BIOGRAPHICAL SKETCH

Let me begin with a biographical context: Ethel Dench Puffer, whose years were 1872 to 1950, was the eldest of four daughters. Her family lived in Framingham, Massachusetts, where her father was a railroad station master and her mother, before marriage, had taught at the Framingham Academy. This closely knit family valued and supported education and expanded opportunities for women. All of the daughters graduated from Smith College, and two of them (including Ethel) earned doctoral degrees. Ethel graduated from college just before her 19th birthday in 1891. The next year she taught at the high school in Keene, New Hampshire. She then returned to Smith to teach mathematics for 3 years.

In the summer of 1895, Puffer traveled to Germany for advanced study, her strongest interest being in esthetics. This was at a time when psychology was just emerging as an independent science, separate from philosophy. Applying the scientific method to aesthetics, a topic that had an established position in philosophy, was a major step in this development. Puffer contributed to the transition and became one of the pioneers in the psychology of art with her thesis under Hugo Münsterberg, a student of Wundt. Later, this thesis, "Symmetry in Painting," became the basis for her doctoral dissertation at Harvard. After working with Münsterberg for a year, Puffer returned with him to the United States, when William James brought Münsterberg to Harvard as head of the psychological laboratory. She completed her dissertation with him in 1898. In 1905 she published a book on her research in aesthetics, *The Psychology of Beauty* (Puffer, 1905).

During the 10 years after completing her doctorate, Puffer held academic positions in the Boston area, at Simmons and Wellesley colleges, while concurrently serving as Münsterberg's laboratory assistant at Harvard. She was also being courted by Benjamin Howes, a man a few years younger than she, whom she had apparently met while she was teaching in Keene and he was a high school student there. He had gone on to receive an engineering degree from Massachusetts Institute of Technology and continued to spend time in the Boston area. Following their marriage in 1908, the couple first lived in New York City, and then moved about as his work dictated. By 1915 they were settled in Scarsdale, New York, where their 2 children were born when Ethel was in her mid-40s. During World War I, she helped organize the Woman's Land Army, a program to mobilize women's labor to replace on farms the men who were away at war. She also played a leadership role in the National College Equal Suffrage League. In the early 1920s she began writing articles and collecting data on "women's interests," seeking ways to combine women's emotional and intellectual fulfillment. Based on this work, she organized at Smith College the Institute for the Coordination of Women's Interests and served as its director.

Benjamin Howes became a well-known specialist in the construction field. In the 1930s, the couple moved to Washington, DC, where he served in the Federal Emergency Relief Administration, was a senior engineer and chief of the Resettlement Administration, and later chief of the U.S. Housing Authority and Federal Public Housing Administration. While they were in Washington, Ethel Puffer Howes (then in her 70s) was active in civic affairs, particularly those having to do with economic planning. The couple left Washington in the late 1940s to live with their son in Connecticut, where she died shortly after her 78th birthday. Benjamin Howes survived her by 18 months. (See also Scarborough & Furumoto, 1987, chap. 3.)

STUDY IN GERMANY

Ethel Puffer's decision to pursue graduate study abroad was a bold one—especially so for a late-19th-century woman. The attitude of European institutions toward women's higher education was no less inhospitable than in the United States, but it was to Europe that serious young scholars flocked, especially those intrigued by psychology. A substantial packet of letters to her mother from Germany (now in the Morgan–Howes papers at the Schlesinger Library of Radcliffe College) gives a very personal glimpse of the situation faced by a young woman who attempted to gain an educational experience comparable with that of the American men who were seeking training with the leaders of the new discipline of psychology.

In Berlin, Ethel experienced a rich social life in the company of a group of highly cultured people: Americans, British, Russians, and others. She enjoyed the usual sight-seeing activities and took special pleasure in the excellent concerts and art galleries. Her major purpose, however, was to study psychology. For a woman to gain admission to courses at the University of Berlin, it was necessary to petition the university author-ities as well as to seek permission directly from individual professors, by calling on them at home. The task of gaining admittance was therefore a formidable undertaking for a newcomer. Puffer succeeded, however, and began attending lectures in October, 1895. As the only woman present she reported to her mother that she was "much scared" on the first day. Some of the students, however, had been alerted by a young German who lived at her boarding house and took a protective attitude toward her—"the students stared, of course, but were nice enough" (October 27, 1895).

Because her chief interest was in esthetics, one of Puffer's classes was with Carl Stumpf, well known for his work on tonal fusion. Stumpf recommended that she attend the lectures of Max Dessoir, who was working out a theory of aesthetics. Puffer wrote: "The room is jammed—there are only benches with desks before them, and I don't much enjoy being so crowded, the only woman, so I have persuaded [a woman friend] to come too. . ." (November 2, 1895). After that class, her conversation with another student about William James's psychology was overheard by a young Canadian who was in Berlin for postdoctoral study after receiving a PhD from Harvard University a few months earlier. He introduced himself and indicated that he knew Hugo Münsterberg, who had just returned from Harvard to the University of Freiburg. This was indeed a fortunate encounter, for Puffer knew of Münsterberg and was much interested in his work.

With a letter of introduction from her new friend, Puffer traveled to Freiburg in March of 1896 and met the Münsterbergs at their home on a Sunday. They attended an afternoon concert and, while having coffee later, the professor shifted "from a polite hospitality to real interest" in her career and offered to direct her study himself and let her work in his private laboratory, though he had usually refrained from such intimate contact with students. She wrote her mother, "I was tempted to fall on his neck on the spot, but Prudence plucked me by the sleeve." Puffer was elated to have, as she put it, "one of the three or four best men in Germany personally interested in me, and ready to further my aims socially and intellectually. . . . [H]e personally offered his wife's aid in making things pleasant for me; and to know a German University faculty really well is certainly something to wish for" (March 29, 1896).

So Puffer quit Berlin and took advantage of an unexpected event, as she was later to do on other occasions, blending opportunity with an eager reaching out for new experiences. Within 2 months she was in Freiburg, attending Münsterberg's lectures. The class was large and included several American students, although she reported that there were "no ladies, and of course I came in for a good deal of staring—but I am accustomed to that" (May 4, 1896).

During the fall of 1896 Puffer followed a regular schedule. In the mornings she worked at the Münsterbergs' home, sorting and measuring pictures for symmetry, the topic of her thesis. Afternoons were spent in Münsterberg's laboratory, followed by tea with Mrs. Münsterberg and the children. In the evenings she attended lectures: Münsterberg's on ethics; Grosse's on the science of art; and Rickert's seminar on esthetic theory. But there were also social events. After one dinner party with a particularly cosmopolitan group she commented: "It is amusing after all to feel oneself—a lone unaccomplished American, by virtue of the real goods one has, at least a match for these worldly wise Philistines" (December 5, 1896).

Puffer spent Christmas with the Münsterbergs and, during that time, she read to Münsterberg a paper she was working on. He complimented her profusely, which was unusual for him, and then said, "Yes, you will do something!" (December 31, 1896). Shortly afterward it was announced that Münsterberg would be going back to Cambridge to join the Harvard faculty permanently. So Puffer sailed home with them.

CAREER IN PSYCHOLOGY

During the 1897/1898 academic year, Puffer worked with Münsterberg at Harvard while registered as a Radcliffe College graduate student. She held the American fellowship granted by the Association of Collegiate Alumnae (now the American Association of University Women). In recommending her for the award, Münsterberg wrote that, based on earlier experience during his temporary appointment at Harvard, when he had taught large classes of women at Radcliffe,

Miss Puffer is the only woman I ever met who reaches in every respect the talents and methods of Miss Calkins (who passed such a brilliant examination for the Ph.D. degree at Harvard University). . . .I have never met in America a woman with whom I connect so serious a hope for the

progress of psychology and philosophy and for the highest interests of
pedagogical life in America. (cited in Helmer, n.d., p. 9)

That reference to Mary Calkins makes this a good time to consider a
comparison between Calkins and Puffer (see Laurel Furumoto's chapter
on Calkins in this book). There's a certain justice, it seems to me, in
combining Furumoto's fine study of the unique aspects of Calkins's
career with an examination of Puffer's. Furumoto makes the case that
Calkins's emphasis on the self in her theoretical psychology might be
linked to her life situation: She lived and worked in a stable, supportive
community of women academics. By contrast, Puffer's career was
characterized by variability and by attention to the practical. Calkins is
well known (at least well known "for a woman"), whereas Puffer is not.
Yet these two women came from similar backgrounds, both graduated
from Smith College, both received training at Harvard under Münsterberg, and both were considered to have exceptional potential for making
outstanding contributions to psychology. What accounts for the difference, then, in their careers and subsequent status in psychology? I
believe that the difference can be attributed to the fact that Ethel Puffer
received and accepted a proposal for marriage and took on the responsibilities of motherhood, whereas Calkins followed the life of a single
woman, living at home with her parents and teaching at a women's
college.

There is every reason to believe that Puffer was as committed to her
intellectual calling as was Calkins. Indeed, Puffer doggedly pursued
every avenue available to continue developing her interests. It was she,
for instance, who forced the issue of the granting of the PhD to women
who did graduate study at Harvard, though enrolled as students at
Radcliffe College.

In the early 1890s, Radcliffe instruction was provided by Harvard
faculty who repeated their lectures separately for the women students
(and thereby supplemented their incomes with separate pay!). In 1895 a
few Harvard courses, mainly at the graduate level, were opened to
qualified Radcliffe women, but the women were not eligible to receive
degrees upon the completion of doctoral-level work. Therefore, when
Puffer completed her dissertation and her oral defense in 1898, she
received not a diploma, but a three-page typewritten statement signed
by her seven examiners (including William James, George Santayana,
and Hugo Münsterberg). The quasicertificate attested that they had
administered an "oral examination of the same nature as would have
been given by the Division [of Philosophy] to a candidate for the degree
of Doctor of Philosophy in Harvard University" and that they had
"unanimously found her unusually well qualified for that degree." In an

accompanying letter to her Josiah Royce, head of the division and an early APA president, seemed to be apologizing that the faculty were "limited to an informal and unofficial action of [that] sort" (May 23, 1898, in Faculty files, Smith College Archives).

Three years later, Puffer and others had become convinced that the Harvard authorities could not be persuaded to grant the degree to women, so she requested that Radcliffe College consider granting the PhD to her and those other women who were also qualified by doctoral level work completed at Harvard. In 1902, she and another woman received the first doctorates granted by Radcliffe under Harvard's oversight. In that instance too, Puffer was a pioneer, forcing the resolution of a nagging issue, unsatisfactory though the resolution was to many whom it concerned. (Mary Calkins, one of the four eligible women, declined the degree on the ground that she had never been a *Radcliffe* student.)

The same sort of subterfuge was used to disguise Puffer's postdoctoral work as a faculty member at Harvard. She was listed as holding the position of assistant in psychology at Radcliffe from 1898 to 1907, but she was actually an assistant to Münsterberg, who was head of the Harvard psychological laboratory. A newspaper article stated that her name was not printed in the Harvard catalog for fear that it would "create a dangerous precedent" (n.d., in Faculty files, Smith College Archives). "Dangerous" also was the idea that a married woman should hold an academic position anywhere, so with her decision to marry in 1908, Puffer relinquished the possibility of academic employment. And thus her career—as a psychologist—came to an early and abrupt end, 10 years after she had completed her training at Harvard.

A SECOND CAREER

By the time she married, Puffer had known Benjamin Howes for a good many years. One wonders if she delayed marriage because she knew it would disrupt the professional work to which she was deeply committed. However that may be, she did not slip quietly into domesticity. In the early years of her marriage, she continued to write and to submit articles to the popular press, a practice begun some time earlier, probably at the suggestion of Münsterberg, who also was active in writing for a general audience.

Although marriage, mothering, and her active volunteer work were emotionally satisfying for Ethel Puffer Howes, she still yearned for something more—something to give expression to her intellectual interests. In 1922, the year she turned 50, Ethel Howes went public with her concerns in two essays printed in the *Atlantic Monthly*. These foreshadowed the work she would undertake a few years later and signaled her entrance into her second career. In her first article, "Accepting the Universe," she presented the predicament faced by educated women: the "persistent vicious alternative, marriage *or* career—full personal life *versus* the way of achievement" that made women "still unable to bring their performance up to the level of their acknowledged abilities" (Howes, 1922a, p. 444). She described, as she would put it later, "the existence of a deep-lying . . . intrinsic self-contradiction in the life of the well-trained woman" (Howes, 1922b, p. 731). Such a woman felt a strong urge to use her training in productive work (that is, in a career). At the same time, if she were married and a mother (as Howes assumed most would want to be), she would inevitably be "drawn from [the] systematic activity [required by a career] to the paramount interest of her children and her home life" (p. 731).

The two roles, career woman and mother, were in Ethel Howes's thinking mutually exclusive, because each required a person to be constantly "on call" and simultaneously devoted to both of them. At the conclusion of the first article, Howes proposed a Kantian solution: rather than "accepting the universe" women should rise above it! Since it was impossible to combine a normal career and motherhood, women should accommodate by altering their conception of a career. She asked, "Why not deny, erase, transcend the whole notion of a career, with its connotations of competition, success, rewards, honors, titles?" (Howes, 1922a, p. 458).

Notice that Ethel Howes was asserting that it was important for a woman to use her intellectual talents, even though that might mean foregoing the acknowledgments that men expect to receive. She was suggesting substituting intrinsic satisfaction for extrinsic recognition, a compromise she thought necessary for a married woman. Notice also that she did not propose adjusting the requirements of domesticity and mothering. (Although these may be disturbing thoughts in our time, one should remember that we're dealing here with history, not with contemporary gender politics.)

In her follow-up article, "Continuity for Women," Howes discussed her solution more fully. She rejected the then-popular "home-use" theory, which advised women to be satisfied by applying their learned skills within the circle of the family, thereby transforming homemaking into a "career." Instead, she suggested supplanting the notion of "career woman" with the idea of the "contributing professional." Her concept was modeled on the well-known case of the contributing editor of a journal, whose concern is not full editorial duty, rank, or emoluments but rather editorial quality alone. She suggested that women might find professional satisfaction in "creative scholarship" (that was her term; it reminds one of our current usage of "creative financing," "creative scheduling," and the like). At any rate, she felt that a woman would not be "falling short of her professional ideals in contracting the scope, or modifying the type, of her work" (Howes, 1922b, p. 736). She did acknowledge that implementing the "conception of the 'contributing professional'" would require "wide changes in public opinion, in the actual mechanics of the professions, and in women's education for the professions" (p. 736).

For the next several years, Ethel Howes worked to establish a firm base for her ideas and to put them into practice. I maintain that this constituted a *second* career for her because, although it involved full-time, paid professional work, the activity neither depended on nor developed directly from her training and experience in psychology. It could have been done by a woman trained in any of the scholarly disciplines. I believe, however, it would not have been done with such intensity except by a woman who was also married and who had experienced the frustration of not being able to use her training in a productive way. There is evidence for that assertion in material that I turn to now.

FROM IDEAS TO PRACTICAL ACTION

Following the *Atlantic Monthly* essays, Howes published a series of articles in *Woman's Home Companion* on questions related to women's interests and needs. She made a survey of several projects across the country that were attempting through cooperative means, such as communal kitchens and laundries, to alleviate the burden of house-keeping chores so that women might give attention to other interests. At this point, Howes was beginning to acknowledge that perhaps some adjustment in the way family life was conducted might be necessary. This led her to propose to the president of Smith College, whom she knew well because she had maintained close ties with her alma mater, that an institute be founded at the college to study and develop the status of women.

A 3-year grant was received from the Laura Spelman Rockefeller Memorial Fund for what came to be called the Institute for the Coordination of Women's Interests (see Hayden, 1981, chap. 12). The institute began functioning in 1925 with Howes as director of a competent staff and oversight resting in the hands of a special committee appointed by the Smith College Trustees. This committee was chaired by Mary van Kleeck, a recently appointed Smith alumna trustee and director of the Department of Industrial Studies at the Russell Sage Foundation. In an informal letter to the president, telling him that the funds would be made available, Lawrence Frank of the Rockefeller Foundation stressed the importance of conducting "the type of inquiry suggested by Mrs. Howes" and expressed his hope that the committee would not wish to change the application. He noted his admiration for the purpose of the enterprise and said "the notion of an exploration and inquiry appeared very refreshing in contrast to the usual formal investigations and academic dissertations! We need, I think, more of discovery and invention than proof, in this field of inquiry" (Lawrence K. Frank to William A. Neilson, June 20, 1925, ICWI Records, Smith College Archives).

During the 3 years that Ethel Howes served as director of the institute, her children were of school age. To accommodate their needs, she worked a flexible-time schedule, typically spending 3 or 4 days a week with her family at their home near New York City, then traveling by train to Northampton for a shortened professional workweek after having arranged for such things as what the children would wear to school, how they would spend their afternoons, and what they would eat for dinner during her absence. She was not entirely comfortable with the arrangement, but it was a way of coordinating her own interests and serving a larger need. Fifty years later her son, Ben Jr., reported: "We had a housekeeper during this period to care for me and my sister . . . . I believe my mother felt that she thereby demonstrated that such an arrangement was feasible. I would agree" (cited in Russell, 1977, p. 37).

The institute was intended to conduct survey research on how women were attempting to combine intellectual interests with family life and also to set up experimental demonstration projects for addressing the issue. Several studies were conducted and a number of projects were undertaken. The most enduring of these were the Smith College day and nursery demonstration schools, which were set up to operate very much like the cooperative day-care centers we know today, with parents sharing responsibilities in the planning of the programs and mothers assisting in the actual day-to-day activities. Howes's vision began to expand, however, during the period of the grant, and concurrently, it appears, the conception of the Trustees Committee became more limited. She had written earlier that education would be required to change the social conditions of the professions and the ideas of women themselves and had become convinced that the greatest need of the college woman was to find a "philosophy of life" and ways of managing to meet all her primary interests—intellectual as well as social and emotional. The grant proposal had focused on the college-educated housewife, but Howes was, after all, a former college instructor and was working on a college campus. Now she became convinced that college women should begin to confront the realities of their future lives and prepare for those through directed study while they were still college students. She was intensely interested in developing and spreading a philosophical theory of women's education, thereby fulfilling the potential that Münsterberg had identified in her 30 years earlier.

During the third year of the grant, when it looked as though the Rockefeller Foundation support would not be continued despite a proposal for a 2-year extension, Howes developed a syllabus for what she called a "woman's orientation course." It was to be taught by Howes through the Smith College Sociology Department, to juniors and seniors. The central concept of the course was the principle of individuality and continuity in work, the only principle that would "resolve inhibitions and free [young women] from those internal conflicts which spell defeat in marriage and in work" (*Progress of the Institute*, 1929). That principle was to be presented as emerging in the history of women, as a group and as individuals, from the genetic point of view and from the orientations of mental hygiene and social ethics. The outline for the course was very similar to those now employed in introductory women's studies courses. It was offered in the summer of 1928, along with other courses to be included in a summer institute on women's coordination issues, but an insufficient number of students registered so it "didn't fly." It appeared in the 1929–1930 list of course offerings, but in 1931 the trustees voted to abandon the course.

Nor was the grant renewed. Though Mary van Kleeck, chair of the Trustees' Committee, wholeheartedly supported Howes's ideas, there was difficulty in communicating them to the foundation officers. A more basic reason for nonrenewal may have been opposition to the whole project on the part of Smith College faculty (Hayden, 1981). Howes alienated single career women by her contention that women typically seek emotional fulfillment in marriage and motherhood. She offended educators by insisting that

> the serious higher education or professional training of women . . . is literally founded on self-deception; a solemn farce in which all the actors consent to ignore the fact that the most natural, necessary, and valuable of human relations will in all probability soon ring down the final curtain. (Howes, cited in Hayden, 1981, p. 276)

Further, the Smith faculty saw the emphasis on "coordination" as opening the door to home economics and the other applied sciences, which many at the women's colleges abhorred because these subjects appeared to threaten the excellence in the liberal arts tradition that they had worked so hard to achieve. Years later, Lawrence Frank wrote that faculty resistance was the reason the institute ended and that the faculty rejected it because of its "unintellectual and unacademic concerns" (cited in Hayden, 1981, p. 277). This despite the fact that Howes was directly proposing further work on the philosophy and psychology of women's status and educational needs!

The faculty was not so negative about other aspects of the institute's work. The nursery school quickly became successful, and just prior to the third year's operation, the Smith College Trustees moved to appropriate the program by shifting responsibility for its operation to the Department of Education. That precipitated a situation that illustrates in a poignant way the very conflict Howes had been trying to get people to take seriously: a woman's conflict between the demands of career and motherhood.

COORDINATING ONE WOMAN'S INTERESTS

I want to conclude this presentation with a description of some of the happenings in those traumatic times, based on records in the Smith College Archives. The trustees met in June of 1927. Howes was then in Washington with her family. She sent anxious letters to Smith College President Neilson and van Kleeck, describing what she perceived as the trustees' negative attitude toward the institute. Howes was determined to protect the integrity of the nursery school operation, based as it was on an active parents' organization, and wrote that the parents "wished to cooperate with the college in allowing the educational observations and experiments on their children" but only on the condition that the institute and their appointed teacher remain in full authority and supervision (Howes to William A. Neilson, July 6, 1927, ICWI Records, Smith College Archives). She was unable, however, to address the problem as vigorously as she might have wished. In one instance that summer, her secretary replied to a letter from the president, saying "Mrs. Howes . . . would be acknowledging it herself, but her little boy has been very sick with an infected knee and she has consequently had a great deal of care. They are taking Bennie to the hospital this week and hope that the results will not be too serious" (Esther H. Stocks to William A. Neilson, July 30, 1927, ICWI Records, Smith College Archives).

Then in the fall there was a great rush to prepare a document for the Trustees' meeting that would adequately interpret the purposes of the institute and elicit their support. Van Kleeck and Howes corresponded frantically by mail to perfect the report in time for distribution first to the special committee. Again Howes's secretary in Northampton wrote for her, this time to van Kleeck:

> Your special delivery letter just missed Mrs. Howes who left on the eight o'clock train this morning [Friday] wondering why she had not heard from you. I have wired her about your suggestions. Of course it will be impossible to get the reports out by tomorrow since she isn't here to make the revisions but we shall make every effort to get them off by Monday. Perhaps you will want to call Mrs. Howes in Scarsdale. . . (Stocks to Mary van Kleeck, October 14, 1927, ICWI Records, Smith College Archives)

It appears that Howes rushed back to Northampton because on Monday she wrote van Kleeck: "The reports after a strenuous day in Scarsdale, were mailed late Saturday afternoon but I believe just missing the last mail out, so that they actually departed only Sunday night. . . .I can make any arrangements here that you desire: I am staying up now through the week" (Howes to Mary van Kleeck, October 17, 1927, ICWI Records, Smith College Archives). Van Kleeck responded on Tuesday that she would arrive in Northampton early Friday and suggested that the committee might wish to confer with Howes sometime on Saturday, if she planned to be in Northampton then. Howes wrote back on Wednesday that she would be very glad to stay over for possible consultation on Saturday, as she was very eager to do anything to further any plans for the future. Thus the professional demands gave way in one instance because of a child's illness; time with family was compromised in another; and Ethel Puffer Howes demonstrated during those months, as so often she had done before, the tradeoffs that were necessary to live the life of a "coordinating woman."

In closing, Ethel Puffer represents those early women psychologists who were barred, because of marriage, from normal careers in psychology. This, of course, can be seen in a very negative light. She also represents, however, the ingenuity and sense of purpose those women demonstrated as they moved later in their lives into innovative types of professional activity, drawing on their early training but applying it in areas outside what was then defined as "psychology." We need to explore more systematically what all of this meant for the evolution of psychology and the status of women in our field. Perhaps another time.

ACKNOWLEDGMENTS

This chapter is based on an invited address, delivered at the 1987 annual convention of the American Psychological Association.

The ideas and information used here depend heavily on my collaborative work with Laurel Furumoto, to whom, as always, I express my deep appreciation. Others who deserve recognition include Professor Judy Jolley Mohraz, Amelie Russell, and Leslie Mayers, all of whom have provided scholarship on Ethel Puffer Howes's work. Appreciation is due also to the Schlesinger Library, Radcliffe College (Cambridge, MA) and to Smith College Archives (Northampton, MA) for permission to use their collections. At the Schlesinger, materials cited here are located in the Morgan-Howes Papers; at Smith, relevant items are in the Faculty files and the Institute for the Coordination of Women's Interests Records.

REFERENCES

Friedan, B. (1987). *The second stage.* New York: Summit Books.
Hayden, D. (1981). *The grand revolution: A history of feminist designs for American homes, neighborhoods, and cities.* Cambridge, MA: MIT Press.
Helmer, B. B. (n.d.). *Association of Collegiate Alumnae: Report of Committee on Fellowships.* In ACA papers, Schlesinger Library, Radcliffe College, Cambridge, MA.
Howes, E. P. (1922a). "Accepting the universe." *Atlantic Monthly, 129,* 444–453.
Howes, E. P. (1922b). Continuity for women. *Atlantic Monthly, 130,* 731–739.
Howes, E. P. (1925). The Institute for the Coordination of Women's Interests. *Smith Alumnae Quarterly, 17,* 1–5.
Progress of the Institute. (1929). Unpublished report in Institute for the Coordination of Women's Interests Records, Smith College Archives, Northampton, MA.
Puffer, E. D. (1905). *The psychology of beauty.* Boston: Houghton Mifflin.
Russell, A. (1977). *A matter of compromise: Institute for the Coordination of Women's Interests.* Unpublished manuscript.
Scarborough, E., & Furumoto, L. (1987). *Untold lives: The first generation of American women psychologists.* New York: Columbia University Press.

Harvey Carr

Chapter 9

Harvey Carr and Chicago Functionalism:
A Simulated Interview

Ernest R. Hilgard

The main reason that I selected Professor Carr for my "interview" was that he had followed James Rowland Angell as head of the Chicago department, as an exponent of functionalism that I had always found congenial. I had known Angell well as the president of Yale during my time there.

I also knew several of Carr's admiring students and disciples well, including: Edward S. Robinson, a professor at Yale during my graduate years and later a colleague, who had a great influence upon me; Florence Richardson Robinson, his energetic psychologist wife; John A. McGeoch and his first wife Grace, also a psychologist; and Arthur W. Melton, a fellow graduate student at Yale (actually a McGeoch student before taking his PhD with Robinson at Yale).

I visited with Harvey Carr only once, in his office in the old, remodeled building of the University of Chicago's Department of Psychology. I had a pleasant interview, as expected, but not the imagined interview reported in this chapter.

INTRODUCTORY REMARKS

I propose to give an account of Harvey Carr's functionalism in his own words as published in his writing. In order to do so I have arranged my

---

*Photograph of Harvey A. Carr courtesy of the Archives of the History of Psychology, Akron, Ohio

talk as an interview with him in 1940, shortly after his retirement. Imagine that the interview is being held in Carr's home in a small town away from Chicago, where he moved upon retirement. I believe it will be clear when I am asking him questions and when he is replying. The questions are mine but, except for a few transitional statements, Carr's substantive replies are direct quotes from his writings. Only incidental transitional statements have been added to support the interview style. I am presenting his remarks without comments of my own upon them. In the text to follow, H = Hilgard; C = Carr.

H: Professor Carr, I believe you are now enjoying your retirement.
C: Yes, I retired away from the city 2 years ago in 1938, and here I don't spend my time worrying about psychology's unfinished business.
H: But I suppose you won't object to reflecting on psychology as you interpreted it during your many years at the University of Chicago?
C: Not at all. I wrote down my views, and I didn't have to change my views very much between my books and articles. I find it easy to state where I stood in my two textbooks, the *Psychology*, which was published in 1925, and the *Introduction to Space Perception* of 1935, which seems only yesterday. Then, of course, I stated my position in my chapter on "Functionalism" in Murchison's *Psychologies of 1930 (1931)*, and wrote a short autobiography in Vol. 3 of the Murchison series on psychologists in 1936.

ORIGINS OF FUNCTIONALISM

H: O.K. Let's touch briefly on those from whom you picked up your functionalism. I know that you studied at DePauw and got as far as the master's degree from the University of Colorado, but I believe we are more interested in your Chicago days. What was your first year like there, back in 1902?
C: Psychology and education were in the Department of Philosophy. The fellows were distributed among the three fields, and I found to my keen disappointment that I had been assigned to Education. I had courses in education and in the history of philosophy, but I was most pleased that I was permitted to take a year's work in experimental psychology. Before coming to Chicago, I had heard much of Dewey, but nothing of the other men in the department. On reaching Chicago, I heard that experimental psychology was taught by an assistant professor—a young man by the name of Angell.
H: What was Angell like?
C: On the opening day I appeared early so as to have time to locate the laboratory in the maze of Gothic architecture. Imagine my surprise in encountering a small, weatherbeaten, dilapidated, frame structure that had evidently been discarded as unfit for human habitation. I joined a couple of graduate students seated on the front steps and was told that the professor

had not yet arrived. Shortly there appeared a young man with an erect posture, a jaunty walk, a semiquizzical smile, and a hat slightly atilt over one eye. He entered the building and was mentally labeled as another graduate student not socially inclined.

On entering the building, I found my "graduate student" at the lecturer's desk ready for business. Apparently erudition was associated in my mind with age and some degree of pompous dignity. There was nothing to do but make the best of the situation, but I felt much better at the end of the hour, and in a couple of weeks, in common with the other students, I found myself being completely sold on the instructor.

It is difficult to characterize this versatile and engaging personality from the standpoint of the students—especially during the period when he was devoting his whole time and energy to the work of the laboratory. There was the keen and incisive intellect, the judicial attitude toward controversial questions, the delightful idiosyncrasies of manner and expression, the bubbling humor, which ran the gamut from good-natured levity to brilliant wit, and the free and easy flow of choice diction, which always seemed so well adapted to the illumination of the topic under discussion. Finally, there was the penchant for long and involved sentences—in the middle of which we would find ourselves in breathless suspense wondering how it would be possible for a mere mortal to extricate himself from the bewildering maze of clauses with due conformity to the rules of syntax and grammar. We often compared notes and were forced to admit that the feat was always achieved—and usually in some unexpected manner. With the beginning of research our relations became more intimate and informal. We found him to be intensely human, stimulating, encouraging, and genuinely interested in our intellectual and scientific development—an interest that continued to manifest itself long after we left the laboratory. Our general reaction was one of admiration, respect, and genuine affection. Due to his influence, the students were a friendly and cooperative group, the laboratory morale was excellent, and there were times when we were even disposed to take some pride in the drabness of our surroundings.

H: Who were the other teachers?

C: At the end of the first year, Dewey left the university, psychology was made a separate department with Angell as head, and Watson was appointed as an instructor. My fellowship was tranferred to psychology, and I felt that the promised land was near at hand. I had heard of Watson the first year but did not meet him. In my capacity as handyman around the laboratory, there was much contact thereafter. My first reaction was one of slight reserve and suspicion—the basis for which I have never been able to fathom. This initial attitude did not long survive the influence of his genial and friendly spirit, and there soon developed an intellectual and scientific comradeship that persisted many years.

I admired his tremendous energy and enthusiasm in both work and play, his irrepressible spirits, his intellectual candor and honesty, and his scorn of verbal camouflage and intellectual pussyfooting. He seemed to be wholly oblivious to the distinction between instructor and student, and regarded us as partners and coworkers in his scientific endeavors. This attitude was an expression of his nature, and it materially strengthened our initiative, confidence, and self-reliance without exerting an inflationary effect upon the ego.

I was thus inducted into the mysteries of animal experimentation, and Watson in turn heartily cooperated in my early experiments in space perception. Watson influenced me in many intangible ways, and his subsequent loss to psychology was a matter of personal regret.

EARLY CAREER

H: You left for a while—when did you come back to teach at the university?

C: I got my degree in 1905 and taught in a high school and normal school before returning to Chicago to take Watson's place when he left in 1908.

That summer the department moved into its present quarters—a remodeled, three-story, double apartment building, and the old laboratory was retained for animal work. The contrast was so great that our new surroundings seemed almost palatial, and they served our needs fairly well until we encountered the postwar influx of students.

I taught the various courses in experimental psychology, and continued the work with animals that Watson had started. The work in learning was extended with the rapid development of this field, and finally a course in space perception was added. The early years were largely devoted to more adequate preparation, and in time there was the supervision of the thesis projects as I became established with the students. Life once more was enjoyable and alluring.

H: Now that you have completed a successful career as a longtime department head with 130 doctorates conferred, how well were your initial expectations satisfied?

C: I had entered the field of experimental psychology with considerable faith, but little knowledge and an open mind. To what extent were my expectations realized? Quite early in my career, I became impressed with the limitations of the experimental method in the field of human psychology. By experimental, I refer to the usual laboratory practice of eliciting certain modes of activity under specified conditions. Any thoroughgoing and extensive control of human activity is a difficult matter. The difficulty of eliciting a genuine fear in a laboratory situation may be mentioned. Industrial psychologists have encountered similar trouble in reproducing genuine test situations. The control of the environment and the entire activity of the subject for an extensive period requisite to the solution of many problems—genetic problems especially—is wholly impossible. The use of drugs is limited, and vivisection is out of the question. This limitation has been responsible in times past for the great interest in "Nature's experiments," and for the extensive use of animals in recent years. Psychologists have turned to animals for the same reason as did physiologists—the inability to experiment with man.

H: How did the difficulty of experimenting with human subjects affect your views?

C: I do not think that the experimental method—in the usual sense of that term—is the only scientific method. I am an experimentalist, and expect to remain one, partly because of my training in that technique, but mainly because this mode of attack is so well adapted to those fields which happened to elicit and retain my interest. Are we not all too prone to over-estimate the relative importance of our own problems and techniques? We talk much about the desirability of studying basic and fundamental problems, without defining the terms, and I suspect that we all secretly cherish the belief that we are engaged upon such a task. Perhaps all problems are really basic, at least to something else, and if this attributive characteristic is a quantitative variable—to use the present scientific jargon—I sometimes wonder if the most basic problems will not of necessity be the last to yield to a solution. Too much specialization seems to be conducive to a loss of perspective and a judicial temper, and yet a catholic attitude is supposed to be one of the essential characteristics of the scientific spirit.

CHARACTERIZING FUNCTIONALISM

H: You are often said to represent functionalism in psychology. Would you care to characterize functionalism as a system of psychology?

C: Even the early writers agreed "that functionalism refers primarily to the dominant modern American type of psychology as contrasted with the structuralism or existentialism of Wundt and Titchener."[1]

I doubt if Angell would limit the term exclusively to American psychologists. I am inclined to think that he would classify Stout, for example, as a functionalist, while Titchener refers to him as an act psychologist. Perhaps the distinction between a functional and an act psychology is not as clear-cut and definite as Titchener assumes, or perhaps the two psychologies are not mutually exclusive and the same person may legitimately be assigned to both classes.

These minor differences will be ignored, and, for the present, we shall use the term functionalism to refer to the American empirical movement that rebelled against the proposed limitations of the structural or existential school of Titchener and his disciples. I shall adopt the caution of Angell and refrain from adding to Titchener's list of functional psychologists, as I fear

---

[1]Because of the different meaning assigned to existentialism today, hereafter where Carr used existentialism to refer to Titchener, it is called structuralism.

that some might be rudely surprised, if not insulted, at being labeled a functionalist. Functional psychology is not to be identified with that of Angell or the Chicago group of psychologists. There is no functional psychology; rather there are many functional psychologies. In speaking of functionalism, we are dealing with a group of psychologies that differ from each other in many particulars, but which exhibit certain common characteristics in virtue of which they are labeled functionalistic.

H: Can you summarize the common characteristics that distinguished the many functional psychologies from the structuralism of Wundt and Titchener?

C: Functionalism, according to Angell (1907), differs from structuralism in three respects:

(1) Structuralism deals with the whats or contents of consciousness, and it attempts to describe these in terms of their analytical elements. Functionalism does the same thing, but it refuses to confine itself to this limited program. It proposes to deal also with the whys and hows of these contents, and to study them in their relation to the context of which they are a part.

(2) This context in its widest and most inclusive sense is the biological process of adjustment. Functionalism regards mental processes as means by which the organism adapts itself to its environment so as to satisfy its biological needs. Mental events are thus studied from the standpoint of their relation to the environmental world and to the ensuing reaction of the organism to that world. Functional psychology is thus practical and utilitarian in spirit and interest. Functionalism studies the uses and utilities of conscious processes, and it is naturally interested in developing the various applied fields—educational psychology, industrial psychology, abnormal psychology, mental hygiene, and so on.

(3) Functional psychology insistently attempts to translate mental process into physiological process and, conversely, it is interested in discovering and stating the organic concomitants and correlates of the conscious processes. Such a program is obviously incumbent upon any dualistic psychology, which regards mental processes as means of adjustment to the environmental world. A functionalist can accept any one of the various conceptions of nature of the mind–body dualism with the single exception of that of epiphenomenalism.

H: Some people get into disputes over the term "function."

C: Ruckmick (1913) canvassed 15 modern American and English texts, and carefully studied the meaning of the term function whenever used. He found that all usages of the word could be grouped in two classes, and that the same author might use the term in both senses.

(1) In the first usage the term function is equivalent to mental activity. All mental activities such as seeing, hearing, perceiving, conceiving, imagining, recalling, are termed functions. Mental functions and mental acts are thus synonymous expressions.

(2) The term function was also employed to denote service or use for some end, as when an author speaks of the function of a word when it is used as a symbol for an object.

With both usages mentioned by Ruckmick, the term function, in my opinion, is used in the same way as it is in mathematics. When a mathematician says that X is a function of Y, he is asserting that the term X stands in a contingent relation to Y without specifying as to the further nature of that relation. Psychologists, in my opinion, use the term function whenever they are dealing with a contingent relation irrespective of whether that relation is also one of act and structure, cause and effect, or means and end. A contingent relation and a functional relation are synonymous expressions.

H: Do you think of functionalism as finding nothing positive in structuralism?

C: Most functional psychologists are accustomed to incorporate a considerable amount of [structuralist data] in their texts. They object to the proposed limitations of this program, and insist upon the inclusion of other data.

(1) Functional psychology chooses mental acts, such as seeing, tasting, conceiving, and willing, as its objects of study, rather than bare contents.

(2) It thus includes the phenomena of meaning and of functional relationships within its subject matter.

(3) Some functional psychologists, I am inclined to think, would object to limiting their scientific task to that of mere description.

(4) Functional psychologists, insofar as they do describe, insist upon the necessity as well as upon the right of describing an object—be it a content or a mental act—in terms of its relations to other objects, as well as in terms of its analytical components.

(5) They have also continually insisted that a description even of contents in terms of their analytical constituents must embrace other components than elemental contents if the description is to be adequate and complete. I have heard that this latter proposition has been lately rediscovered by the [Gestalt psychologists], and hence I shall add by way of illustration a quotation from an article published by Stratton in 1909:

"Is the nature of a mental compound accurately seized, after all, when we have told of its constituents, even in their right proportion? . . . And yet nothing, it seems to me, could well be farther from the truth. For the original mental fact which we would describe has, in most instances, what we might call architectural features, and its nature and quality consists not only in the character of its materials, but in the manner of their union or arrangement.

"Any analysis that names merely the ingredients may therefore miss the full truth; it may note no difference in compounds that actually are different. The safe and reliable description of the more complex mental facts accordingly requires that our idea of analysis be revised to include an attention to the architectural features of such phenomena, including of course their manner of change. Or if we prefer to let analysis mean what it has ordinarily meant, then only when analysis is supplemented by an account of the form of the process or object is there any guarantee that the description will be faithful to all the fulness of reality."

H: Another criticism of functionalism is that it tends to speak of purposes and so becomes teleological, with the goal serving as a cause of events leading to it.

C: When implications are involved, the statements may not imply any particular kind of explanation—let alone an illegitimate one, such as that of design. The "purpose" psychologist does assume more or less explicitly the existence of innate conscious purposes to explain the origin of adaptive behavior, but in my opinion the great majority of functional psychologists do not do so either implicitly or explicitly.

However, there can be no objection to statements that are explanatorily suggestive, if these telic relations can be legitimately explained. The usual explanation of the adaptive character of our acquired reactions is that of the law of effect, which accounts for the selection and elimination of acts on the basis of their consequents. The law does not attempt to explain the origin of these acts, any more than does the theory of natural selection purport to account for the origin of mutants. The law merely accounts for the fixation of the adaptive acts and the elimination of the nonadaptive ones, and thus accounts for the direction of mental development. Neither does the law of effect violate the temporal requirements of a cause-and-effect relation, for many of the effective consequents occur during the performance of the act, and besides the law assumes that these consequents merely affect the subsequent performance of the act.

We would thus conclude that telic concepts can be legitimately retained in a science so long as it confines itself to factual statements of these relations and explains these facts in a legitimate manner.

THE "FATE" OF FUNCTIONALISM

H: What would you say has happened to functionalism?
C: What happened to the functionalist movement? Did it evolve and disappear in the process of development, or does it still persist in modified form? In my opinion, American empiricism has undergone two major developments since the time of which we speak.

Dynamic psychology represents a further development of the implications of the biological point of view. Functionalism had assumed that mental acts grow out of and minister to the biological needs and impulses of the organism.

According to this conception, the organic background of needs and desires operates to motivate and direct the whole course of mental development, but this fact was more or less taken for granted, or at least the influence of these factors was not sufficiently emphasized. In their emphasis upon drives and motivation, dynamic psychologists [such as Robert Woodworth] have been attempting to portray these factors in a manner that is more commensurate with their importance.

Behaviorism, to a considerable extent at least, was an attempt to avoid the difficulties inherent in a dualistic position. The radical behaviorists solved the problem by either denying or ignoring the fact of consciousness, while the moderate behaviorists are prone to talk in monistic terms of the behavior of a psychophysical or a psychobiological organism.

The functionalistic movement has thus undergone considerable development. Did functionalism disappear with this development, or are these later developments functionalistic in character? The answer depends on the definition of functionalism adopted. Functionalism and structuralism represent two opposing points of view toward the subject matter of psychology, and this subject matter, at the time of this controversy, was conscious processes dualistically conceived. If functionalism, however, is to be defined solely in terms of its point of view without any regard to what it studies, then the various behaviorisms are functional psychologies.

SUBJECT MATTER OF PSYCHOLOGY

H: I believe that you defined the subject matter of psychology in your *Psychology* text as including mental activity and conduct.

C: Psychology is primarily concerned with the study of mental activity. This term is the generic name for such activities as perception, memory, imagination, reasoning, feelings, judgment, and will. The essential features of these various activities can hardly be characterized by a single term, for the mind does various things from time to time. Stated in comprehensive terms, we may say that mental activity is concerned with the acquisition, fixation, retention, organization, and evaluation of experiences, and their subsequent utilization in the guidance of conduct. The type of conduct that reflects mental activity may be termed adaptive or adjustive behavior.

Functional View of Adaptation

H: You referred to adaptive acts. Maybe you can explain further.

C: Organisms are necessarily active because they are alive and are continually being subjected to sensory stimulations. An adaptive act involves a motivating stimulus, a sensory situation, and a response that alters that situation in a way that satisfies the motivating conditions.

A motive is a relatively persistent stimulus that dominates the behavior of an individual until he or she reacts in such a manner as no longer to be affected by it. Likewise an adaptive response is one that is aroused by a motive and that frees the individual from the dominance of that stimulus. Hunger, thirst, sex, pain, and extremes of temperature are some of the more important and fundamental human motives. The insistent and dominating character of these stimuli is readily apparent. The interjection of such stimuli disturbs and disrupts our activity until their demands are satisfied. The fundamental motives are often called "organic needs" because their satisfaction is essential to the continued welfare and existence of the organism. These motives are sometimes referred to as the "drives" or mainsprings to human action, a term that erroneously implies that an individual would cease to act at all without the existence of motives. Motives are not essential to activity; rather they must be regarded as the directive forces that determine what we do, for necessarily we must react in a manner that is adapted to satisfy these conditions if we are to continue to exist. It is these motives that largely determine the direction of our mental and social development. The character of our civilization and social organization would be profoundly altered, if humans were suddenly freed from the necessity of satisfying their hunger and sexual motives.

H: You have mentioned the maintaining or motivating stimuli. What roles do other stimuli play in the adaptive act?

C: All adaptive responses thus consist of a rather complex coordination of sensory and motor elements. All sensory stimuli exert some effect upon the act and practically the entire musculature of the body is either directly or indirectly involved in its execution. Even the simplest type of adaptive response involves a serial organization of elements. The act excites new sensory stimuli while achieving its objective, and these sensory factors are in turn incorporated into the act and modify its subsequent development. Some adaptive responses are serially quite complex, and may contain a number of minor adaptive elements. All activities that are essential to the satisfaction of a motive are constituent elements of the adaptive response, and it is this complete act that is the unit of behavior.

Association

H: Adaptive acts lead to learning, I know, but you haven't said anything about the role of associations.

C: Any two items of experience are said to be associated whenever they are organized in a stimulus and response relation, that is, when the presence of one will stimulate or arouse the other. Any adaptive activity may be regarded as an associated sequence of analytical elements, for any part of this act is a stimulus to that which follows, and conversely any part is a response to that which preceded. Learning may now be defined as a process of establishing such associative connections, of organizing the items of experience into larger functional units.

H: Would you comment on the laws of association?

C: There are two explanatory laws of association—contiguity and assimilation. These laws purport to state the conditions under which these associative connections are established. The law of contiguity may be stated as follows: Whenever two mental events are experienced together or in immediate succession, they thereby become so related that thereafter the presence of one will tend to arouse the other. However, these conditions must be frequently repeated in order to establish any very effective connection between the two acts.

An effective and enduring association will be established only between those mental events that are experienced together with some degree of frequency. Roughly speaking, we may say that there are three general conditions that determine the character of our associations:

(1)   Every organism must necessarily acquire in the manner we have just described a system of perceptual–motor associations that are adapted to the satisfaction of its motivating needs and appetites. The nature of these associations will vary with the type of organism and the character of its environment.

(2)   As we have previously noted, all aspects of a sensory situation exert some influence upon and hence become associated with the organism's reaction to that situation. In other words, all objects that are frequently experienced together must necessarily become indirectly connected in virtue of the fact that they are associated with the same response. All natural conjunctions and sequences of objects and events must necessarily become associated with each other in time. For example, every individual must necessarily acquire a system of topographical associations. An association will be established between the sight of a person and the sound of his voice. The flash of lightning will be associated with the sound of thunder, and the appearance of heavy clouds will naturally suggest the thought of rain.

(3)   Certain associations are also imposed upon us by society. For example, a certain prescribed system of associations is imposed upon a child when it is taught to read and write. In fact, society imposes a given set of associations upon the members of each new generation just in so far as it attempts to guide the character of their mental development.

Habitual Behavior

H: Are associations the same as habits?

C: An established system of associations is said to function in an automatic and habitual manner. Acts differ in their habitual strength. The more habitual an act, the greater is the ease and facility and the accuracy with which it is performed. All aspects of the behavior situation exert some effect upon the performance of an act. Many of these stimuli tend to inhibit, distort, and disrupt the act, and prevent the attainment of its objective. All novel circumstances are likely to induce some such effect. A rat that learns a maze in one situation usually makes a number of errors when it is required to run that maze under different environmental conditions. A college teacher may acquire the ability to lecture to students with precision, ease, and confidence, and yet be unable to deliver the same lecture with any degree of readiness and precision to a strange audience. The more habitual an act, the more readily and accurately it can be performed in novel surroundings. Habit thus firmly welds the constituent parts of an act together, gives it greater coherence, and isolates it from the distractive influences of novel surroundings. The more habitual an act, the more easily it will be excited, the more likely it is to be repeated from time to time in an identical fashion, and the more likely it is to attain its objective without error. We may thus speak of our thoroughly engrained or stable habits as opposed to those of a more plastic and flexible character.

THE FUNCTIONALISTS ON PERCEPTION

H: Because functionalists lay so much stress on learning, as in maze experiments and nonsense syllable learning, do they neglect perception?

C: You should know better. My doctoral dissertation was on perception, and I supervised five dissertations in the area. It is true that there were 29 in learning, but I retained my interest and my last book was an extensive one on space perception.

H: What is unique about a functionalist's view of perception?

C: Perception may be defined as the cognition of a present object in relation to some act of adjustment. An act of perception involves a stimulating situation, a preliminary attentive adjustment toward it, and the arousal of its meaning or significance for what we are doing or in reference to some contemplated mode of reaction . . . . According to our definition, a perceptual object does not necessarily involve the presence of an objective material stimulus. For example, a negative after-image can be perceived. The apprehension of any constituent item of experience as a potential object toward which we can react is an act of perception.

H: One quarrel between functionalists and structuralists was over the problem of meaning. How do you handle meaning?

C: External objects do not intrinsically possess meaning. Rather they are endowed with meaning by the percipient organism, and the amount and character of the significance that they attain is a function of the individual's experience. The meaning of objects is thus a matter of growth and development. This fact is illustrated by the character of a child's definitions, for a definition of an object is a statement of its meaning. All objects thus acquire in the course of time a variety of potential meanings, but relatively few of these are ever aroused in any given situation. The meaning that is aroused by any object is largely a function of the varying circumstances in which it is perceived.

H: Your perception book was entitled *An Introduction to Space Perception*.

C: I taught space perception for a number of years, and became convinced that an introductory textbook was needed.

H: I notice that the largest number of pages devoted to a single experiment was assigned to the experiment of Stratton (1897), on the effects of reversing the visual field by wearing distorting lenses. You cited it first as an illustration of the spatial cooperation of the senses.

C: I liked the experiment because it showed, first, that the normal cooperation of the senses could be disrupted for a certain period of time by means of the optical devices. There were visual–auditory discrepancies, visual–somaesthetic discrepancies, visual–memorial discrepancies, and adaptive disabilities.

However, Stratton also studied the course of readjustment. The experiment proves that the spatial agreement of the senses is a matter of their functional coordination. Since the normal coordination, representing a lifetime of experience, may be disrupted and a new mode of successful cooperation be readily acquired, it is evident that the perfection of the normal coordination during early childhood is easily within the bounds of possibility.

H: Does this mean that you have concluded that empiricism wins out over nativism in space perception?

C: That issue is not resolved in that simple fashion. The extensive character of the visual field is undoubtedly innate and given. It follows that the perceptible size and shape of objects, insofar as they are dependent on these attributes of the retinal image, are also innately given. Perceptible size is dependent on some of the distance factors, but we know little of the nature of these relations. Its relation to such factors as binocular disparity, and convergence and accommodation is probably innately conditioned in part. It is generally assumed that dependence of the perceptible size and shape upon pattern is empirical in origin. The nature of their relation to retinal position is a matter of opinion. The retinal theory implies an innate relation, while both conceptions are possible for the distance theory.

The usual discussions of the native or empirical nature of space are wholly futile. Each particular must be studied separately, and the relative importance of the two factors probably varies with the relation. When viewed in this analytical manner, the inadequacy of our knowledge for a final decision is quite apparent. Furthermore the importance of this problem for space perception has been considerably exaggerated.

THINKING AND REASONING

H: Let's turn to the problems of thinking and reasoning. How do you treat ideas?

C: There are three kinds of ideas: memory, imagination, and conception. One can remember, imagine, and conceive of things. These thoughts can also be distinguished in terms of their objective reference. A person remembers some previous experience of one's own in the way in which it occurred. One imagines objects that have not been encountered in actual experience, but which are hypothetical or prospective objects of experience, which may or may not be encountered in the future. One may thus imagine some actual object not yet experienced, some nonexistential object that may be constructed as a new machine or a new style of dress, or some fantastical object like a cat with horns. Memorial and imaginary objects thus differ in their temporal reference. Objects of memory belong to the past, while imaginary objects can be experienced only in the future. Memorial objects are familiar and actual things, while imaginary objects represent some novel or hypothetical item of true experience. A personal reference characterizes both. In memory, subjects think of some item of their previous personal experience, while in imagination they represent to themselves the probable nature of a hypothetical or prospective experience.

H: You have spoken of memory and imagination. What about conception?

C: Conceptual objects are abstract and general as opposed to the concrete and particular character of perceptual, memorial, and imaginary things. An abstraction is some item or group of items that are apprehended apart from the concrete relations that obtained in actual experience. One can conceive of size and shape as independent of each other; a rectangle as conceived has no definite size. One can think of the pitch of a tone as distinct from intensity and any positional or temporal relation to other items of experience.

All sorts and degrees of abstraction are possible. Objects may be abstractd from their *spatial* relations. Objects may be abstracted from their *temporal* and *personal* relations. Conceptual objects consist of single items or groups of items which have been abstracted from past experience. Objects may be conceived which transcend the limitations of concrete experience. Nonexistence, infinity, and the fourth dimension are conceptual objects, but they can be neither perceived or imagined.

H: Do you specify the function of ideas?

C: An idea, like a perception, is a dynamic as well as a cognitive process. Any idea is a stimulus to a great variety of potential responses. Thought serves much the same purpose in adaptive conduct as does perception.

(1) Objects of thought may constitute the end or goal of conduct.

(2) We also think of and act in reference to objects as a means of attaining other ends.

(3) Finally, ideas may represent movements and their consequences.

H: Is reasoning a special way in which ideas are used?

C: Reasoning may be defined as the process of solving problems by means of ideas, or as a rational or ideational method of acquiring or learning a new adjustment.

H: How does reason compare with the motor method, which some others have called trial-and-error, although I believe you do not use that expression?

C: For the purpose of a preliminary analysis, reasoning may be contrasted with the motor method of learning, since a human being may employ either method in the solution of a perceptual problem.

The thought of an act will arouse that act whenever such behavior is regarded as relevant to the situation of the moment. After performing the act, subjects may discover that their judgment of its adaptive character was erroneous, and the ideational quest for a solution is then continued until the subjects discover an act they believe to be appropriate and this belief is verified by the successful performance of that act.

The two methods of adjustment are identical in most respects. Most involve a motivating problematical situation, a variable, persistent, and analytical mode of attack that is continued until the solution is more or less accidentally discovered, and a series of repeated trials to perfect and fixate the correct response. In both cases the problem is solved in terms of previous experiences acquired in dealing with similar situations. The motor method involves a series of overt responses to a perceptual situation, while reasoning is primarily characterized by the fact that it employs ideas as substitutes for or representatives of those movements or percepts.

Reasoning is subject to some serious limitations, and in these cases a person is compelled to rely upon the motor method for a solution. Contrary to popular opinion, the motor method is distinctly serviceable and is quite extensively employed in human adjustments.

PSYCHOLOGY OF MOOD

H: We haven't discussed the affective life. Have you something to say about moods?

C: Moods are variously aroused. They often develop from some previous emotional state. A strong fit of anger may finally subside into a sullen, irritable, and resentful mood, cheerfulness and gaiety may be the product of an emotion of joy, while a gloomy and melancholic attitude may find its origin in a previous attack of grief. Moods may also be aroused by nonemotional mental conditions. Success is conducive to a cheerful, buoyant, and optimistic mental attitude, while any signal failure is likely to induce a gloomy, melancholic, or resentful attitude toward the world. Moods may also arise from overwork, mental fatigue, monotony, undue excitement, and excessive worry.

H: What is their adaptive significance?

C: Moods do not merely tinge or color mental events; they also exert an influence upon the character of our thoughts and actions. Obviously, a despondent and melancholic individual will react to a social situation in a manner entirely different from that of a person who is in a happy and cheerful frame of mind. Any particular mood must necessarily acquire during the course of experience a great variety of ideational associations, and hence the continued presence of that mood will naturally exert an influence upon the sequence of ideas.

The phenomena of moods thus illustrate very nicely the mutual dependence and interaction of the mental and the bodily activities. On the one hand, the course of mental events is often shaped by moods of a physiological origin.

Likewise, any mental situation that is responsible for a prolonged attack of gloom and despondency must have exerted a depressing effect upon the vital operations, while all situations that arouse a buoyant and cheerful mental attitude exert a stimulating and tonic effect upon the vital processes.

H: Critics tended sometimes to refer to functionalism as an applied psychology. You haven't said much in particular about this.

C: As an experimentalist, I don't think of my work as applied any more than that of any other experimenter who is curious about mental activity. You will note, however, that I had a chapter on the measurement of ability in my textbook, and to some people that sounds very applied. Tests are, of course, used in industrial psychology, and I encouraged Kornhauser and Kingsbury in our own department to go ahead with their work on *Psychological Tests in Business* (1924).

The field of psychology is generally divided into a number of special branches, such as comparative, genetic, abnormal, general, individual, social, religious, educational, and applied. Psychology is interested in mental operations wherever found and irrespective of their peculiar character or complexity.

H: Thank you, Professor Carr. I think that you have clarified your standpoint very well.

REFERENCES

Angell, J. R. (1907). The province of functional psychology. *Psychological Review, 14,* 61–91.

Carr, H. A. (1925). *Psychology: A study of mental activity.* New York: Longmans, Green.

Carr, H. A. (1931). Functionalism. In C. Murchison (Ed.), *Psychologies of 1930.* Worcester, MA: Clark University Press.

Carr, H. A. (1935). *An introduction to space perception.* New York: Longmans, Green.

Kornhauser, A. W., & Kingsbury, F. A. (1924). *Psychological tests in business.* Chicago: University of Chicago Press.

Ruckmick, C. A. (1913). The use of the term "function" in English textbooks of psychology. *American Journal of Psychology, 24,* 99–123.

Stratton, G. M. (1897). Vision without inversion of the retinal image. *Psychological Review, 4,* 341–360, 463–481

Stratton, G. M. (1909). Toward the correction of some rival methods in psychology. *Psychological Review, 16,* 67–84.

Chapter 10

Edward L. Thorndike:
A Professional and Personal
Appreciation

Robert L. Thorndike

When I was born my father was already 36, and by the time I had much
awareness of his professional activities he was well into his 40s. I have
vague memories of his commuting to Washington during the first world
war on war work, but most of my memories postdate that war. So any
personal knowledge is only of the latter half of his career when he was
already a substantial figure, in the eyes both of psychology and of his
bathroom scales. I must rely on printed sources and family legends for
his early days.

   I remember my mother's telling about the first year of her married life,
when the New York City apartment was shared with four active
monkeys. She claimed that this was prophetic of the four of us who
came on the scene over a span of 16 years. I remember the tale, probably
apocryphal, of the cat that escaped from its cage and went up into the
rafters of Schermerhorn Hall at Columbia with my father in hot pursuit.
The fate of the cat is better not reported.

   My older brother has told me that he knew my father as a contentious,
combative, and subtle tennis player. But by the time that I remember
him, his tennis was still sneaky but largely stationary. He is pictured in
Geraldine Joncich-Clifford's biography as quite a feisty and contentious
young man, challenging the psychological establishment of that time,
but my memory is of a gentle, retiring person who avoided contention
and conflict and who felt that controversy was unproductive, who

---

*Photograph of Edward L. Thorndike courtesy of the Archives of the History of
Psychology, Akron, Ohio

would rarely respond to critical attacks but would rather get on with collecting more data.

Though he appeared in his writings and in reactions to them as a Connectionist, he was not by temperament a systematist but rather an empiricist, a conductor of investigations and an analyzer of data. His approach to learning was an outgrowth of 19th-century associationism tempered by the microneurology of the turn of the century. He was impressed by the emerging picture of the neuron with its multi-branching dendrites, implying a multitude of neural pathways, but he did not presume to delve into neurology and the details of the central nervous system, and it remained, in large part, a "black box" whose operations he accepted as reported to him. Ultimately, he defined a "connection" at the behavioral level as the probability of making some specific response to a particular stimulus situation.

QUANTITATIVE ORIENTATION

My father's orientation was basically quantitative and is epitomized by his statement in the 1918 *National Society for the Study of Education Yearbook* that "Whatever exists, exists in some amount. To know it thoroughly involves knowing its quantity as well as its quality." And I would think that you would find that his full statement there constitutes a worthwhile agenda for quantitative programs in psychology and education even today. I suspect that he would have been willing to supplement "amount" by "degree," accepting intensity as well as number as a legitimate quantification. Much of his professional career was devoted to designing operations that would make these amounts manifest and gathering and analyzing data based on those operations.

But his training in mathematics was quite meager and there is little in his early training and background that would forecast a strongly quantitative orientation. His undergraduate major field was literature. As an undergraduate, he wrote a play, though I found no evidence that it was ever produced. Even when he went to Harvard for graduate work, it was still with the expectation of becoming a teacher of English. William James converted him to psychology, but James was no quantifier. It was only as a doctoral student at Columbia that my father got exposed to statistics and became a devout convert to quantitative methods. The completeness of his movement into this new phase can be seen by his publication in 1904 of his *Introduction to a Theory of Mental Measurement*, a volume that became the psychometric and statistical bible for a generation of graduate students in education and, to some extent, psychology.

My father never had a course in calculus or advanced algebra and was quite conscious of his mathematical limitations. As a consequence, the quantitative procedures that he applied tended to be relatively simple and intuitive. But he undertook the measurement of everything from educational achievement through human wants and interests to the quality of cities. Data analysis was a different sort of undertaking when my father did much of his work. Most members of the audience can remember the olden days when you did not have access to a digital computer, and some can remember when there were no electronic hand calculators, but mighty few will remember a time when there were no electrically driven desk calculators. However, back around 1900, even hand cranked desk calculators were rare.

My father started his labors of data analysis at a time when mechanical aids to calculation were largely nonexistent. And he had very little faith in his own ability to use mechanical devices of any kind. I never knew him during his lifetime to use either a calculator or a typewriter. His manuscripts were written out in longhand for a secretary to type, and his only aid in computation was a huge volume entitled *Krelle's Rechen-tafel*, which provided the products and quotients of all numbers up to 1,000. He wore out several of these during a busy lifetime, saving the covers to serve as backing for the sheets on which he wrote his manuscripts. Parenthetically, he encouraged all of his children to get a solid mathematical grounding, with the result that my two brothers both took doctorates in physics and my sister one in mathematics. Thus, I became the only intellectually disreputable member of the family.

PSYCHOLOGY OF THE SCHOOL SUBJECTS

I can't remember when I first realized that my father was a psychologist. I knew that he worked at Teachers College, carried his bag over there each morning, and disappeared into the inner recesses, but I was primarily conscious that he wrote arithmetic textbooks since some of my contemporaries gave me a hard time about them. "So your father wrote those blankety blank arithmetic books with all the problems that we had to work out." As a matter of fact, almost my first personal involvement with his work was in preparing the answer key for his algebra text. I was paid to do all of the problems and provide the answers. I'm not sure that my accuracy was at a level that made the product very helpful, but I got paid just the same.

For perhaps 20 years, a course in the psychology of the school subjects was one of my father's major instructional responsibilities. He applied a certain amount of formal psychology and a considerably larger dose of shrewd common sense to rationalizing instruction in a wide range of fields. For example, in the case of arithmetic, he pointed out that previous texts had given vastly more practice to the very easy task of 2 + 2 than they had to more difficult tasks such as 7 + 8. With problems, he urged that they be realistic ones such as a child might meet rather than the absurd puzzles of the sort that had tended to appear in texts at that time. He pointed out that if the problems were to test *arithmetic* they shouldn't present undue reading burdens and generally shouldn't include irrelevant data. Incidentally, one of the joys of my youth was a book that had been given to him entitled *A Boy's Own Arithmetic*, a wonderful caricature of the problems in arithmetic texts of that day. I quote a typical problem.

> Benjamin, a beagle aged 9 months and weighing 28 pounds, was owned by Samantha Smithers, a spinster, age and weight not reported, living in East Greenbush. Benjamin was kept tied up so that he could not chase rabbits, but every time that a rabbit came within Benjamin's ken he barked for 7½ minutes. He used up 53 calories for each 10 minutes of barking time. How many dog biscuits, each containing 78 calories, would be required to maintain Benjamin's weight if he was excited by an average of 17 rabbits a day?

He especially railed against those problems in which one would have to know the answer in order to be able to phrase the problem. By way of illustration:

> A pizza will serve exactly 6 children. Miss Jones's class can just finish up 4 pizzas. How many children are in Miss Jones's class?

This is hardly how one would go about determining class size!

Those were precalculator days when most people did their calculations by hand, and if computational skills were to have personal or commercial value one had to come out with the correct answer a high proportion of the time. Applying binomial expansions, he showed that with 95% or even 98% correctness in single numerical operations, one would rarely arrive at the correct answer in a series of numerical operations such as multiplying two 3-place numbers or adding up a grocery bill—and one's errors would frequently even frustrate efforts to check a result because one wouldn't even get the same wrong answer twice in succession. For this reason, he emphasized the need for a very sure mastery of the basic numerical skills.

WORD COUNTS AND THE DICTIONARY

In the field of language learning, he recognized early that if teaching was to be functional and effective the teacher and the preparer of textual materials needed to know what words would be encountered by the child in reading and in speech. This led to the counting, laboriously and by hand, of the occurrence of different words in some millions of running words of text (Thorndike & Lorge,1944), and the preparation of a sequence of *Teachers' Workbooks* based on these counts. In my youth, practically every other book that I picked up to read had words underlined. Early on, my father had committed to memory the thousand or so most common words whose relative frequency had been quickly established and which no longer needed to be counted, and he underlined the others. Another of my early ways of earning spending money consisted of transcribing and tallying these underlined words.

Perhaps the most significant of my father's contributions to improving educational materials, and one from which many of you will have benefited, was his revolutionizing of children's dictionaries. In my childhood a school dictionary was produced by simply abbreviating an adult dictionary, eliminating some words and condensing the definitions of others. There was little consideration of the fact that shorter, telegraphic definitions tended to be harder for a child, or that the words used in definitions needed to be easier than the word defined. My favorite illustration of this, which I have quoted many times, is a definition of a bear as "a carnivorous, plantigrade quadruped," a definition that would surely be helpful to an elementary school child who did not know what a bear was!

The Thorndike, and subsequently Thorndike–Barnhart, dictionaries were based on a number of principles designed to make them useful for a teacher or a child. For example, first, any word should be defined by the use of simpler words. Second, the commonest words should not be defined at all, but should merely be used in illustrative sentences: "An elephant is a *big* animal. New York is a *big* city." Third, there should be many carefully selected sentences focusing on the meaning of the word. Fourth, there should be many pictures clearly illustrating the object or the element being defined. Fifth, the definitions of multi-meaning words should be given starting with the most common or frequent usage, rather than being organized by parts of speech. And there were other principles that I won't go into at this time. In large part, these changes have been assimilated by other producers of dictionaries for children's use, but after 50 years, I am happy to say, the Thorndike–Barnhart series still occupies a dominant place.

ANIMAL LEARNING

Of course, where my father originally made a name for himself was with his work on animal intelligence. Those studies of cats, dogs, chicks, and subsequently of monkeys, getting out of and into puzzle boxes were his first research—his dissertation in 1898 and a subsequent publication in 1902. He would have liked to have studied children, but the Harvard community of 100 years ago was not very sympathetic to having its children experimented on and at that time he had none of his own. The idea that you could experiment systematically with animals and that this could illuminate not merely comparative psychology but psychology in general was a new and radical one at the time. That it was a fruitful idea is seen in the rich literature of experimental work on animal learning and all aspects of animal behavior that has developed since. However, my father was not well suited by temperament for experimentation on animals and soon deserted it for other more congenial fields, returning to it only once briefly some 30 years later.

MEASUREMENT OF ACHIEVEMENT AND INTELLIGENCE

Well before he got involved with educational materials, my father was convinced that the possibility of effective research on instruction and the improvement of instruction depended on having standard measures of the outcomes of that instruction. At the beginning of this century, there were no objective instruments available for measuring the outcomes of teaching or the progress of an individual student. At Teachers College, through his own work and that of his students, there were developed a varied array of tests, crude by present standards but an enormous advance over what had gone before, by which educational progress could be measured.

My first full-time involvement in my father's activities came during the year between high school and college. At 15 I was judged a bit young and immature to go away to college so I spent the year employed by him and working in the big office that housed his Institute of Educational Research at Teachers College. It was, incidentally, one of the most instructive years in my educational career. The projects that were under way at the institute that year exemplified three of my father's main lines of research interest and effort. In the first place, work was progressing on the final stages of the analyses that led to the publication of *The Measurement of Intelligence* (Thorndike, Bergman, Cobb, & Woodyard, 1926). This was the culmination of my father's long-term interest in and work on intelligence and individual differences that had first reached publication in 1905 in correlational studies of pairs of twins, one of the earliest studies of that sort, and perhaps the earliest. That interest had been expressed through work during World War I on the selection of Army and Air Corps personnel, and led shortly after that to the publication of a series of forms of the *IER Intelligence Examination for High School Graduates*, used in college admission at Columbia, Stanford, and other selective colleges for a number of years prior to the appearance of the *CEEB Scholastic Aptitude Test*.

The Measurement of Intelligence represented a systematic attempt to establish a ratio scale of intellectual development, that is, one with a true zero and equal units. The final product was the *Intelligence Scale CAVD*. This had several properties. First, it presented a specifically delimited definition of intelligence: completion, arithmetic, vocabulary, directions. Second, the unit in which ability was expressed was based on normal deviates within an unselected group of a specific age. Third, as Thurstone had proposed at about the same time, comparison of the means and variabilities of adjacent age groups was used as a way to reduce the data from those different groups to a common size of unit and common reference point. Fourthly, the judgments of a pool of experts were used to extend the scale down to absolute zero. Tasks were judged in pairs, ranging from the easiest that could actually be administered to children to one that was conceived to be an absolute minimum. If I remember correctly, this was "When a vile tasting substance is placed in the mouth, spits it out." Items were scaled by the percentage of overlapping in the judgments. This, incidentally, was in contrast to the procedure that was used at about the same time by Thurstone, who based his estimate of absolute zero on extrapolation of the apparently linear relationship between the means and variances of scores. When one reaches zero variability, one has presumably reached zero intelligence.

Here, as in other publications, Thorndike emphasized the multidimensionality of intelligence. He spoke of abstract, mechanical, and social or executive intelligence. Incidentally, his own pattern of abilities serves to document the difference. In abstract intelligence, he was unquestionably in the top fraction of a percent of the population, while in mechanical intelligence he was a slow learner. He never learned to drive a car; I never saw him fix any device; and if you look at pictures of the equipment that he used in his original animal experiments you realize that they would have shamed Rube Goldberg. I feel less sure about a judgment on social intelligence. He was not a sociable person, but he was reasonably successful in managing his institute and committees that he served on, so I guess that on that dimension he was at least average.

My father viewed individual differences in intelligence as a reflection of the different number of neural connections operating in different persons. The observed correlation between scores on different types of tasks was viewed as due to the overlap in the connections involved in each. He rejected Spearman's "g", which Spearman conceived of as some type of mental energy. He didn't quarrel with the data, but found more congenial as an explanation the sampling conception as set forth by Godfrey Thompson at Edinburgh University. The correlations were thought of as due to the proportion of connections shared by the two tasks.

A CONNECTIONIST VIEW OF LEARNING

The second program of research under way during the year that I spent at the institute was an extensive series of studies of human learning that were later reported in a little book entitled *Human Learning* (1931), and in somewhat tedious detail in *The Fundamentals of Learning* (1932). Though my father's reputation was originally established through his research on animal learning, he did not get involved in systematic research on the principles of human learning until the 1920s.

As a connectionist, he viewed learning as the strengthening or weakening of connections. A connection was not explicitly defined except in stochastic terms as the probability of a specific response to a specific situation. Strengthening of a connection was evidenced by an increase in the probability and weakening by a decrease. This notion of a connection led to the use in much of his work in the 1920s of an experimental paradigm with certain distinctive properties. First, because of the probabilistic nature of strength, one needed to be able to study a large number of similar connections in order to get an estimate of any change in the probabilities. Secondly, one needed to start with initially low and presumably specifiable probabilities, which typically involved weak and rather arbitrary associations. A typical design presented a specific number of alternatives for response, such as pressing some one of a set of five keys. Thirdly, one pooled the results over many specific connections in order to permit an estimate of the impact of a particular treatment on the probability.

The treatments were spoken of as (1) occurrence of a situation, (2) occurrence of a connection with no outcome, (3) reward and (4) punishment. Reward, which would be more congenially spoken of these days as reinforcement, was in most experiments simply the experimenter saying "right," though sometimes it included a material reward as well as the purely symbolic one. Punishment usually meant that the experimenter said "wrong." I cannot remember now when any of the experiment series involved a more severe penalty.

Merely the occurrence of a situation, with no clear connection, appeared to produce little or no change in response probabilities. A prototype of this design involved having a blindfolded subject draw a line of a specified length – 3 inches, 4 inches, 5 inches – but never giving information on the length of the line that had been produced. Under these circumstances, there appeared to be no systematic change in either the mean length or the variability of the lines drawn.

The type of connection studied could be illustrated by having the subject respond with a number from 1 to 5 when a stimulus word such as "potato" was spoken by the experimenter. If this led to no outcome, the change in probability was very modest. The probability of saying "5" the next time "potato" was encountered (if "5" had been said before) was higher than chance, but only slightly so. A response followed by a reward was clearly strengthened in the sense that the probability of repeating that response was noticeably increased. It also appeared that the strengthening spilled over a little bit to the connection that occurred before and the one that followed the rewarded one—a phenomenon called *spread of effect*—and this was interpreted as showing a direct biological effect of the reward. The amount of the reward appeared to be irrelevant, and, in fact, an unexpectedly large reward was in some cases disruptive of learning rather than especially effective.

The studies indicated that one learned, though rather slowly, even when one did not know what element in a complex situation was being rewarded. This is exemplified by one series in which I was directly involved. I was sent out at the beginning of December to get four copies of every different Christmas card that I could find in New York City. These became the raw material through which it was possible to reward some subtle element that appeared in a number of different cards. The element that I remember was whether the design had gold in it. If a choice was rewarded, as by the experimenter saying, "Yes, I like that one too," subjects came increasingly to select those cards that had gold in the design without knowing that this was the basis for their choice, but it was a slow and devious improvement. This was a little like some of the Skinnerian enterprises in which a pigeon is rewarded for turning around in circles or some other behavior that appears completely unrelated to the final goal behavior of getting food.[1]

TRUNCATING THE LAW OF EFFECT

Perhaps the most surprising outcome of this program of learning studies, so far as my father was concerned, was the finding that in this

---

[1]The claim that such learning occurs without awareness led to a great deal of research during the 1950s. Most of the results were negative. Careful questioning revealed that, although subjects could not verbalize the exact contingency, they were aware that the experimenter was responding positively to *something* that they did. They often developed "correlated hypotheses" about the behavior that was rewarded and, on such bases, responded positively at an above-chance level (for a summary, see C. W. Eriksen (1962), *Behavior and awareness*, Durham, NC: Duke University Press).

experimental paradigm punishment had little or no weakening effect. As a matter of fact, the strengthening from a connection occurring appeared to more than offset any weakening from the connection leading to punishment. It was concluded that any effect of punishment depends on what it then and there leads the individuals to do. If the individuals can at that point immediately do something else and be rewarded for it, they learn, but the learning has been due solely to the reward and not to the prior punishment.

I am not sure how much he realized the extent to which the results that he obtained were dependent on the properties of the paradigm that he was working with—the weak and often arbitrary connections that he was reinforcing. I believe that one of the legitimate bases for criticism of the studies was this rather special setting in which the effects were manifested. However, I suspect that he would have felt that even at higher levels of thinking the cumulative effect of reinforcements and rewards provides the foundation on which productive thinking and higher level intellectual activities are built.

BRIEFLY BACK TO ANIMAL LEARNING

My final involvement in my father's learning research came in the summer between college and graduate school. At that time he made his brief return to work with animals, again with chickens, and I, serving as the experimenter, got a firsthand exposure to some of the harsh realities of animal experimentation. I don't know how familiar the reader is with coccidiosis in chickens. It was a problem that considerably depleted our experimental population. It was further depleted by the family dog.

Basically, he applied the same paradigm as that used in many of the experiments with human beings, a multiple-choice task with no initial cue to indicate the correct response. Several different versions of the apparatus were built by a professional carpenter, so they were a little more elegant than the devices used in his early research, and presumably provided distinctive cues for a chick. In each there were several alleyways, and if the chick entered the correct one it was rewarded by release to a pen with food and the company of other chicks. Punishment for a wrong choice consisted of being penned up in the alley and then put back in the starting box. The findings were again that with reward the chick was more likely to choose the alley that it had entered before, but that with punishment there was no tendency subsequently to choose some other alley. One fact that I observed, but that never got into the published results, was that with punishment a chick became more and more reluctant to enter *any* alley. I would sit there and wait and wait, and would finally have to record the trial as "no response." So I suppose that if you were a Skinnerian you could say that the punishment *did* suppress the operant though it did not redirect the respondent behavior of the chickens.

TESTING FOR VOCATIONAL GUIDANCE

The third major thrust under way during the year that I worked at the institute was what came to be called "The Guidance Study." The results from this were first published in 1934 as *Prediction of Vocational Success*. The study serves as one more illustration of my father's compulsion to seek firm data as a basis for policy decisions, in this case a concern about the fruitfulness of guidance testing. This was, so far as I know, the first largescale longitudinal study of ability tests and school records as predictors of later vocational performance, though Terman's study of intellectually gifted children got under way at about the same time.

In 1922, age 14 or the eighth grade seemed the appropriate level at which to test a group for later follow-up, since many would not stay in school much beyond that age and grade. A test battery was developed comprised of (1) a measure getting at abstract intelligence, (2) a set of tests to appraise simple clerical skills, and (3) a mechanical assembly test developed by Stenquist, different for boys and girls, that required the putting together of 10 or so simple devices such as a bicycle bell. The battery of tests was administered to some 2,500 boys and girls in a number of schools in New York City. All available information was transcribed from their school records, and the follow-up was set in motion. The hunt was in full cry during the year 1926–1927 when I was at the institute. Only those of you who have lived in a big city such as New York will have any idea of what a program of detective work the follow-up involved. Back then, the first of October was traditionally moving day, and a large segment of the experimental population moved to new addresses – often to avoid the bill collector and with the objective of not being found. The girls got married and changed their names as well as their addresses. I remember vivid descriptions by my late colleague, Irving Lorge, of his exploits in tracking down some of the more devious cases.

In spite of all hazards, some 90% of the cases were followed for 9 years and periodic reports obtained of their educational and work histories. Composite indexes were formed: one for educational progress, one for type of employment and earnings, and one for job satisfaction. The results were, by and large, rather discouraging as to the prospects for productive vocational guidance. Jobs had been classed as being primarily mechanical, primarily clerical, and mixed. Only for the clerical did any semblance of correlation with the test results appear, and even these correlations were only in the mid-20s. As I looked back to refresh my memory of my father's tables of correlations, I found them strangely prognostic of those that I found in my own *10,000 Careers* study 25 years later, where 6% of some 15,000 correlations were significant at the .05 level (R. Thorndike & Hagen,1959).

In contrast to vocational prediction, educational prediction was, of course, fairly successful. Correlations with school success were of moderate size, and those who managed at least to reach college were a full standard deviation above the average for the whole group. The record cards from the guidance study were still in the files of the institute when I inherited its direction from Lorge after his death in 1960. Various abortive attempts had been made to re-establish contact with members of the group later in life. I had hoped at one point to be able to use social security numbers, and to make contact through the Social Security Administration, but it turned out not to be possible. Social Security is extremely jealous of the confidentiality of its records, and reasonably so. But I still drool slightly when I think of those 60-year-old records that might be tied to the complete vocational lives of the survivors who would now be in their 70s.

IN CONCLUSION

I have spoken mainly of those aspects of my father's career to which I was closest and in which I had some involvement. There are a number of others that I might have delved into. There were his studies of transfer of training, both experimental studies of involving special intensive practice with specific tasks and correlational studies of the transfer from particular school subjects to general intellectual ability. These confirmed his conviction that one should teach things that are worth learning for their own sake and not those whose only value would lie in some mental discipline or hoped-for transfer to something else. There were his studies of adult learning, indicating that with appropriate motivation adults in their 40s could learn new things about as well as those in their 20s. There were his studies of mental fatigue and of the effect upon learning of such physical conditions as ventilation; his studies of wants, interests, and attitudes of persons of different ages. He studied not only individuals, but also communities, applying quantitative methods to the evaluation of cities and the determination of what made them good places in which to live. This involved what I suspect was one of the earliest uses in psychology of what tends now to be called "structural equations," the techniques of path coefficients devised by Sewell Wright. There was his ambitious, if only partly successful, attempt to extend psychological methods and thinking to a wide range of social problems in *Human Nature and the Social Order* (1940).

His 50 books and more than 400 articles, many of which I cannot claim to have read, cover a broad spectrum with no single, continuing focus. He himself wrote, a little apologetically, in the brief sketch that he prepared for Murchison's *History of Psychology in Autobiography*, that he never had any one dominant and continuing theme in his professional career. Rather, he took whatever came his way that seemed to need doing and devoted himself wholeheartedly to it.

By and large, his work and his family were his life. Last weekend I was talking to my older daughter, who was about 7 when my father died, about her memories of him. Her picture was of someone who spent most of his time in his study with his feet up on the desk and a cigarette in his mouth, but who was always ready to blow smoke rings for her entertainment or to make her a hat or paper boats out of a newspaper. And this epitomizes perhaps as well as anything his interests and values. He was not actively involved in politics or in religion or in social life. He was in some ways the original workaholic, reading the *Encyclopaedia Britannica* in bed to locate good passages for reading comprehension tests, not, I think, because he was driven to it but because he would rather be getting or analyzing data than most anything else. In spite of ill health, he continued to work on the sorts of problems in which the data could be brought to him, as, for example, the correlational analysis of traits as estimated from biographies, up to the last months of his life. This used to amaze me, but it seems less strange when I realize that at the time of his death he was almost exactly the same age as I am today. When one's work has been a congenial focus for one's life, one doesn't easily drop it, and I suspect that I shall be grinding out test items and doing simple-minded factor analyses until I fade away.

REFERENCES

Joncich, G. (1968). *The sane positivist: A biography of Edward L. Thorndike.* Middletown, CT: Wesleyan University Press.

Thorndike, E. L. (1904). *Introduction to the theory of mental measurement.* New York: Science Press (Cattell's).

Thorndike, E. L. (1931). *Human learning.* New York: Appleton-Century-Crofts.

Thorndike, E. L. (1932). *The fundamentals of learning.* New York: Teachers College, Columbia University Press.

Thorndike, E. L. (1934). *Prediction of vocational success.* New York: Teachers College, Columbia University Press.

Thorndike, E. L. (1940). *Human nature and the social order.* New York: Macmillan.

Thorndike, E. L., Bergman, E. O., Cobb, M. V., & Woodyard, E. (1926). *The measurement of intelligence.* New York: Teachers College, Columbia University Press.

Thorndike, E. L., & Lorge, I. (1944). *Teacher's wordbook of 30,000 words.* New York: Columbia University Press.

Thorndike, R. L., & Hagen, E. (1959). *10,000 careers.* New York: Wiley.

Chapter 11

C. G. Jung:
The Man and His Work,
Then and Now

Irving E. Alexander

The invitation to participate in this effort to tie present-day psychology to its history through the study of its pioneers triggered a moment of soul searching in me. I was flattered to be asked to reflect on the work of so prominent a figure as Carl Jung, but I also had misgivings. I am not a "Jungian" and I wondered whether I had the appropriate credentials for the task. But then I remembered an interview with Jung, filmed in the closing years of his life, in which he made the comment, with a wry smile, that he was not a Jungian.[1] That helped remove that obstacle.

The suggested format for the presentation, to assume the identity of the central figure, also gave me pause. I could easily envisage the image of Jung in a Jehovah-like pose, towering over me and thundering, "Nobody speaks for Jung but Jung himself." The image was reinforced by a story that Barbara Hannah, one of Jung's disciples and his biographer (Hannah, 1976), was fond of telling. Her first presentation in Jung's seminar met with such strong criticism from Jung that it took her 10 years to venture such an effort again.[2]

The recollection of Jung's concept of introversion, as elaborated by Shapiro and myself (1975), was a more important impediment to my adopting Jung's identity. People living in the introverted mode naturally

---

*Photograph of Carl G. Jung courtesy of the Archives of the History of Psychology, Akron, Ohio

[1]The memory is probably of an interview with Jung, filmed for the BBC by Laurens van der Post.

[2]The story was told in a seminar given by Hannah, which I attended while on a sabbatical leave, in 1955–1956, at the Jung Institute, Zurich.

and automatically put distance between themselves and others that cannot be overcome without the threat of the loss of ego boundaries. It is not easy for me to try to be someone else.

Finally, a related barrier to accepting the role of Jung was that I could not escape the realization that anything that I would say would be thinly veiled projection and I felt uncomfortable with the concept of presenting my own thoughts as though they were the thoughts of Jung.

After all these ruminations my decision—to accept the task but not the role—was based largely on curiosity about what would emerge from my 35 years of thought about the man and his work. In one sense I had begun this task some years ago, in a psychobiographical exploration of Jung's relationship to Sigmund Freud (Alexander, 1982). In what follows, I shall tread an intertwined path between Jung's life and work in reflecting on his contributions. Because of its importance, I shall place major emphasis on the period between 1909 and 1922, which includes Jung's break with Freud, and its sequelae.

THE EARLY YEARS

Jung was born in 1875, in Switzerland, to a Protestant minister and his wife who shortly thereafter moved to the rural environs of Basel. Jung grew up there, left largely to his own devices, the child of a marriage that he identified as difficult. Jung described his father as dogmatic, but reliable and trustworthy. He saw his mother as having two dispositions, one somewhat unstable, mystical and clairvoyant, the other practical, mundane and directed. Jung identified with his mother's mystical side, which he called her number two. Later on he referred to his own makeup similarly.

During these early years, Jung suffered from various ailments, some of which may have had a psychosomatic base. He was ill attuned to the demands of school and had difficulty with interpersonal relationships. Although I have chosen not to follow the usual path of analyzing Jung's early experiences and memories as a guide to understanding his personality, I do wish to describe the incident at age 12 that Jung (1961) himself believed opened the path to an existence free of neurotic symptoms. He describes being attacked unexpectedly by a schoolmate, striking his head while falling, and being dazed by the experience. He then goes on to say, "I was only half unconscious, but I remained lying there a few moments longer than was strictly necessary, chiefly in order to avenge myself on my assailant" (p. 30). Immediately following, Jung used this accident as an excuse to avoid school. He also developed fainting spells that kept him home-bound for several months.

Jung's recognition of the pathological quality of such behavior came when he heard his father respond to a friend's inquiry about Jung's health with great concern about the darkness of his future. Jung then reports how forcefully the reality issues struck him. At that moment, he recognized that the path that he was on was self-defeating. He faced up to his fears and, by dint of will, overcame his strong neurotic symptoms. From then on, Jung's work in school improved and he became a superior student. He ultimately decided to follow a career in medicine. For this purpose he entered the University of Basel, in the spring of 1895, barely a year before his father died. He finished 5 years later.

In 1961, after reviewing the successful confrontation with his symptoms, Jung described his subsequent recognition of the significance of that episode:

> Gradually the recollection of how it had all come about returned to me, and I saw clearly how I myself had arranged this whole disgraceful situation. That was why I had never been seriously angry with the schoolmate who pushed me over. I knew that he had been put up to it, so to speak, and that the whole affair was a diabolical plot on my part. I knew, too, that this was never going to happen to me again. I had a feeling of rage against myself, and at the same time was ashamed of myself. (p. 32).

From this description the following threads emerge, which I think are important ones in Jung's life. First, the external stimulus for the distress, the unwarranted aggression of the other, is bypassed and his focus goes to the resolution of an internal problem instead. Second, the distressing affects identified, although not quite in appropriate context, are anger, rage, shame, and humiliation. These are emotions that might easily result from the aggressive action of another but in this case they do not. They enter awareness only when they result from an intrapersonal conflict. Third, the displaced external conflict is then fought out in a confrontation with self, which leads to the antidote to all ills—work. These are threads that we shall see revealed again.

EARLY YEARS IN PSYCHIATRY: JUNG'S
SELF-OTHER PROBLEM

When, in December 1900, Jung took up his first post as assistant at the Burghölzli, Zurich's mental hospital, he was 25, largely without research experience and only recently drawn to psychiatry. Although he identifies the source of this new interest as Krafft-Ebing's text, read earlier that year in preparation for the state medical exams, we know that he had this interest as early as 1898 when, following a series of unexplained occult-like events at home, he began a 2-year observation of séances held by a young relative of his who exhibited attributes of dual personality. A report of these observations, submitted as a doctoral thesis in 1900, became Jung's first publication in 1902 (Jung, 1970a). It seems likely that the reading of Krafft-Ebing's text made it clear that psychiatry would allow him to pursue the mysteries of mind, a calling to which he had been attracted for many years without recognition of its appropriate designation.

Jung devoted 1901 to learning the basic tools of his new trade in typical frenzied, medical school fashion. It took him 6 months to devour the contents of 50 years of the *Allgemeine Zeitschrift für Psychiatrie*. The lessons were well learned and by 1902 he already published a complete case history of an hysterical attack in an accused incarcerated person in the *Journal for Psychology and Neurology* (Jung, 1961, Chaps. 3, 4). This tremendous capacity for work, unusual observational abilities, and the talent rapidly to translate his thoughts into written communications were conspicuous features of Jung's scholarly career. More than 90 bibliographical entries, including several books and monographs, dozens of clinical papers, a major series of empirical research reports, and numerous reviews of the significant publications in his field appeared during the 10 years following his first publication.

But let us return to the beginning psychiatrist and review his early work, its content, the messages intended, its impact in its time, and its probable lasting value. The association studies stimulated by Eugen Bleuler, his chief at the Burghölzli, had as their real goal the understanding of dementia praecox. Bleuler was centrally concerned with the everpresent problem of psychiatric diagnosis and more specifically with the etiology, prognosis, and possible therapy of dementia praecox. Having adopted the association methodology as a tool, he sought an agent to gather the necessary data to hone that tool for use in answering his questions. Such a person he found in Jung. No matter how they were initiated, however, all that emerged in these ensuing 10 years bore the stamp of Jung's own thinking.

The background that guided Jung's participation in this project is given in the opening paragraph of his first paper in this series, *The Associations of Normal Subjects* (Jung, 1918/1969, p. 8). It specifically describes Bleuler's influence, including the task he set for Jung and his collaborator, Riklin. Jung makes it obvious that he embarked upon this journey to do the necessary scientific work so that his chief could continue with greater precision the investigation of his central concerns, the psychoses. That this was only part of the story, a clear reflection of

Jung's lifelong need to pursue his own path no matter what his momentary allegiances demanded, is suggested by a statement of Bleuler in the introduction. After indicating that Jung's studies had opened the possibilities of answering many diagnostic questions, he says (p. 6), "But this does not exhaust the results. By ingenious interpretations, which can be readily proved correct, Jung and Riklin have shown that the unconscious mechanisms are accessible to this method far more extensively than we dared hope." This aspect of the research did not stem from Bleuler's concerns; it was a continuation of the work that started with Jung's dissertation subject. He was still searching for the key to the "world behind the world" that he had observed in his young relative. He thought he found it, in the analysis of controlled associations, as a unified core of ideas in the unconscious, accompanied by excessive or inappropriate affect—a complex. That this insight would attract him to Freudian theory goes without saying. What is important to see is that Jung was already embarked on a path of his own. He did not discover this path through the assignment by Bleuler nor by his reading of Freud's work.

Why then, if Jung was destined to follow his own path, did he embark intensively on Bleuler's journey and then Freud's? One clue stems from aspects of Jung's personality that were recognized by others but probably hidden from his self-awareness until later in life. At various times and by various people he was described as arrogant, vain, ambitious, status seeking, competitive, and even untrustworthy. The fact that these designations occur alongside others such as humble, caring, undefensive, even saintly, will give some sense of the complexity that is reflected in Jung's No. 1 and No. 2 personalities. He was clearly the possessor of both sets of attributes, but it was the power of his ambition and competitiveness, part of his No. 1, that made those alliances to mentors so attractive.

Frequently in *Memories, Dreams, Reflections* (1961) Jung refers to his attitudes toward ambition and competition. He indicates that he enjoyed success during his gymnasium days, but that it came at too heavy an internal price. He says that, even though he succeeded in reaching the top of the class, his pleasure was spoiled by the envy of his classmates. "I hated all competition" he writes, "and if someone played a game too competitively, I turned my back on the game" (p. 43). Jung was ambitious but he could not deal with the interpersonal consequences of recognized achievement, aggression toward others, and hostility from them.

At another point Jung is recalling his medical student days, circa age 25, his choice of psychiatry as a specialty, and the consequent disappointment of his teacher and his friends. He tells us that he came out at the top of his final examinations, tripped up only by an unexpected error in a subject matter in which he excelled. He then says, "Had it not been for this I would have had the highest mark in the examination." Jung's thoughts then take him to the following:

As it was, another candidate received the same number of points as I did. He was a lone wolf, with a personality quite opaque to me and suspiciously banal. It was impossible to talk to him about anything except "shop." He reacted to everything with an enigmatic smile, which reminded me of the Greek statues at Aegina. He had an air of superiority, and yet underneath it he seemed embarrassed and never quite fitted into any situation. Or was it a *kind of stupidity*? I could never make him out. The only definite thing about him was the impression he gave of almost *monomaniacal ambition* which precluded interest in anything but sheer facts. A few years afterward he became schizophrenic. I mention this as a characteristic example of *parallelism of events*. My first book was on the psychology of dementia praecox (schizophrenia), and in it my personality with its bias or "personal equation" responded to this "disease of the personality." I maintained that psychiatry, in the broadest sense, is a dialogue between the sick psyche and the psyche of the doctor, which is presumed to be "normal." It is a coming to terms between the sick personality and that of the therapist, both in principle equally subjective. My aim was to show that delusions and hallucinations were not just specific symptoms of mental disease but also had a human meaning. (p. 110)

This fascinating aside, written almost 60 years later, seems almost dream-like, filled with gaps and non sequiturs. Unreal or not, however, we can see that what Jung abhors in the other is his ambition, his monomaniacal persistence to achieve, and his arrogant disregard of others, attributes that others saw in Jung, to which he seemed oblivious in himself. This memory may well have served to protect Jung from the consequences that he feared would follow if he allowed himself to be solely directed from either of his two sides. If he pursued his place in the world as his No. 1, he would be haunted by internal pressures produced by envy from others and aggression toward others. If, on the other hand, he withdrew into himself, he feared being overwhelmed or lost in unconscious material. A conflict of this sort could easily lead to the balancing of opposites as an ideal solution.

EARLY WORK AND ITS IMPACT

The three major products of Jung's first decade of work were *The Psychology of Dementia Praecox* (Jung, 1972), *Studies in Word Association* (published as separates from 1904 on) and *Symbols of Transformation*, sometimes translated as *The Psychology of the Unconscious* (1916/1949). Although dealing with disparate subject matters on the surface, the underlying theme in all of the work relates to the orderliness and meaning of the products that emanate from *undirected* thought, such as the fantasies of psychotic people, and the creative imaginings of an ordinary person. In this respect Jung was very much in the tradition established by Freud in the study of hysteria and in the examination of the meaning of dreams. Jung, however, went further in extending the power of unconscious (undirected) processes to the development of dementia praecox, emphasizing the psychological origin of the disorder, a position not shared in psychiatry then and of limited popularity in psychiatry now. Additionally, Jung's work enlarged the scope of imagery to be studied as a key to the understanding of personality and psychopathology. Appropriate content now embraced any form of undirected thought as well as dreams. The mode of interpretation broadened from the uniquely personal or idiosyncratic to that which could be learned from common thinking as reflected in symbols and myths.

If we ask whether these early contributions have stood the test of time, the response would have to be strongly affirmative. The methodology for examining unconscious processes still flourishes in a variety of ways, from personality assessment, to police detection aids, to literary criticism, and even to the understanding of history. The idea that there are psychogenic factors in the development of the psychoses led, after a long period of time, to the psychological treatment of psychotic states, a development that was initially impeded by Freud's dictum that the psychoses do not respond to psychological intervention, and later slowed by the development of electrical, surgical, and pharmacological therapeutic aids.

If one asks what impact the work had in its own time, the answer would also be resoundingly positive. Less than 5 years after his medical degree, Jung was a senior staff member and director of a research laboratory in one of the most prestigious psychiatric facilities in Europe and he held an academic appointment in the university. Within the next 5 years he was awarded an honorary degree from a foreign university (Clark), and was elected to serve as the first president of the International Psychoanalytic Association. Not yet 35, Jung seemed destined to fulfill whatever worldly ambitions he harbored. What then conspired to interrupt this triumphant march?

DISSOLUTION OF THE RELATIONSHIP WITH FREUD AND ITS AFTERMATH

As is often true in life, multiple forces were involved, some objective, some subjective, some realistic, some neurotic, some highly personal, some seemingly transpersonal. Jung described this confluence of forces in *Psychology of the Unconscious* (1916/1949). This work, an analysis of the written fantasies of a young woman, Miss Miller, expands the concept of libido beyond sexuality to more general motives, and treats incest as having a meaning related to the more general issues of union and separation. Such a treatment indicated his dissatisfaction with the limitations of psychoanalytic conceptualizations, but it also brought on a return of the neurotic problem that grew out of his relationship to Freud. Jung knew that the publication of these ideas would bring that relationship to an end. From his own reports of his childhood, one can deduce the conflict. Reliability and safety were afforded by the father, and separation from the father figure implied the loss of these supports. On the other hand, maintenance of protection by the father meant cessation of growth and a reliance on dogma.

One can easily see this struggle in Jung's situation at the time. Jung clearly cast Freud in a parental role, a parent who demanded loyalty to his particular ideas. Jung's No. 1 personality enjoyed the gratification afforded by his allegiance to Freud: He clearly was the second in command, the heir apparent. This comfort came, however, at a cost to the needs of his No. 2 side. The conflict was of such intensity and had such profound manifestations that Jung knew, at some level, that it had to come to resolution. Later on, after the return from the trip to America with Freud, Jung recalled those days as ones during which his dreams increased in symbolic and archaic material. His attempts to understand the unconscious processes through reading in mythology and mysticism led to increased feelings of confusion.

The *Psychology of the Unconscious* speaks to separation and its consequences. After quoting a poem by Hölderlin, Jung interprets:

> This recognition, that man must sacrifice the retrogressive longing (the incestuous libido) before the 'heavenly ones' tear away the sacrifice, and at the same time the entire libido, came too late to the poet . . . . This sacrifice is best accomplished, as is shown by the most obvious meaning [of the poem], through a complete devotion to life, in which all the libido bound up in familial bonds must be brought outside into human contact. For it is necessary for the well-being of the adult individual, who in his childhood was merely an atom revolving in a rotary system, to become himself the centre of a new system. (1916/1949, pp. 453–454)

Jung winds up this discourse with the recommendation of a remedy for the threat of this retrogressive longing. "The best liberation is through *regular work*" (Jung, 1916/1949, p. 455), a solution that he had discovered at age 12.

What I am intimating here is that Jung's need for separation was powerful, and included a need for separation from the father figure and separation from the ambitious search for status and position directed by his No. 1 extraversive side. The neglect of these needs threatened his mental well being. Why he could not act easily on these needs we shall shortly see. The publication of this work did in fact hasten the ending of Jung's relationship with Freud and his embarking on the solitary path that he followed for almost all of a half-century.

Jung's work up to this point had centered on the importance of unconscious processes, decoding their meaning, and understanding their dynamics. The direction in the *Psychology of the Unconscious*, using mythology, theology, literature, and mysticism as interpretive sources, was a new one. No longer was the problem simply to discover what consciousness repressed, but how to bring to awareness the vast store of experience already contained in the unconscious and reflected in undirected imagery. Jung became aware of the possibility that the structural properties and dynamic operations of mind were already known, and were told in the more esoteric imaginal productions of societies, their symbols, rituals, mythology, folk and fairy tales, and mystical speculations. Explicating the statics and dynamics of mind as he conceived it eventually became the central task.

For the next decade (1912–1922), Jung was in a position analogous to that of Freud between 1890 and 1900, a period of splendid isolation, from which a number of important works emerged, including the first part of the *Two Essays on Analytical Psychology* (1953) and *Psychological Types* (1971). The break with Freud cut him off from a great many of his "in-the-world duties," including the editing of journals and the presidency of the International Psychoanalytic Association. It is reported that his psychiatric practice declined. By this time, Jung had already resigned from the Burghölzli and the university. He retained contact with only a limited number of his Swiss psychiatric colleagues. He himself comments on how difficult a time this was for him, how his dream material and fantasies increased in complexity, threatening to overwhelm him. He describes this period as a "confrontation with the unconscious" (Jung, 1961, Chap. 6).

To illustrate the kind of personal material that Jung reveals about this period in his life, I should like to describe for you a dream that Jung (1961, p. 180) had in December, 1913, just 2 months after writing his final letter to Freud, in a correspondence that had been continuous since 1906. In that letter Jung resigned one of his editorial responsibilities because he had heard that Freud doubted his *bona fides* (McGuire, 1974, p. 550). The dream is important because of what it reveals about Jung's struggle at that time, and its resolution in his work. It is also reminiscent in several ways of his intrapersonal encounter at age 12.

I was with an unknown brown-skinned man, a savage, in a lonely, rocky mountain landscape. It was before dawn; the eastern sky was already bright, and the stars fading. Then I heard Siegfried's horn sounding over the mountains and I knew that we had to kill him. We were armed with rifles and lay in wait for him on a narrow path over the rocks.

Then Siegfried appeared high upon the crest of the mountain, in the first ray of the rising sun. On a chariot made of the bones of the dead he drove at furious speed down the precipitous slope. When he turned a corner, we shot at him, and he plunged down, struck dead.

Filled with disgust and remorse for having destroyed something so good and beautiful, I turned to flee, impelled by the fear that murder might be discovered. But a tremendous downfall of rain began and I knew that it would wipe out all traces of the deed. I had escaped the danger of discovery; life could go on, but an unbearable feeling of guilt remained.

When Jung awoke from the dream he could not understand its meaning and was plagued with the thought that if he could not decipher its message he must shoot himself. Relief came with the recognition of the layered symbolic meaning of the content of the dream. Siegfried represented the German nation and its people, and their need to impose their will on others. He also saw that Siegfried was a symbol of his own worldly, ambitious, power side. He decided that he had to kill this side of himself in order to continue to grow and develop. As you may recall, this theme had already emerged in his reminiscences about the year 1900, some 13 years earlier, in both his loathing for ambitious people and the calling to attention of the inevitable consequences of ambition, interpersonal alienation and schizophrenia. The necessity of following his own path was an important message that can easily be gleaned from the content of the dream. This is the lesson that Jung said he took away from the dream and it served to relieve his great distress.

One cannot help but wonder why the break with Freud produced such inner upheaval in Jung. On the surface he felt as though he had done nothing improper because Freud was the intolerant one who could not stand anyone else's independence of thought.[3] Jung was a man of means by this time who could not have been concerned about loss of income. His accomplishments in the world were also considerable. What then might have produced this internal unrest?

One possibility is that although Jung was aware on some level of the

---

[3]One can infer this from the letter from Jung to Freud (McGuire,1974, pp. 534–535) written 1 year to the day before Jung's Siegfried dream. In it he berates Freud openly (a marked change in Jung's usual correspondence demeanor) for taking unfair advantage of his "pupils," treating them as patients. Jung clearly lays the blame on Freud for what has happened to change their relationship.

need to separate from Freud, he was unaware of the hostility he bore toward Freud for forcing him out of the favored position in the analytic community and the loss of status that went with it. It is one thing to separate, quite another to be cast out. The latter is frequently followed by humiliation, an affect that I think Jung found particularly intolerable. Through the analysis of the Siegfried dream, Jung came to recognize the importance of abandoning the ambitious status-seeking path, an internal and abstract solution. What he perhaps missed in the dream were the immediate interpersonal referents, his repressed anger toward Freud, and his role in the dissolution of the relationship.

The conscious attitude that Jung expressed about the ending of the relationship with Freud was that he, Jung, was the victim, aggressed against unjustly by a power-exercising colleague. If we invoke the Jungian view of dreams as compensation for one-sided conscious attitudes, the conjectured meaning appears in bold relief. The dream content reveals Jung's anger and wish to slay Siegfried [with little distortion, "Sig Freud," a possibility recognized by Samuel Rosenberg, in his book, *Why Freud Fainted* (1978)].

Corroborating evidence for the conjoint anger and wish not to give up his position may also be gleaned from an examination of the correspondence between Freud and Jung, from December, 1912, to its effective end in October 1913, two months before the dream appeared (McGuire, 1974, pp. 534–550). After his angry diatribe in the letter of December 18, 1912 (see Footnote 3), Jung came back, in succeeding letters, to a softer and more reconciliatory position, even after Freud expressed his wish to discontinue any personal aspect to their relationship. In that last year of active correspondence, Jung wrote some 22 missives, while Freud wrote 9. The last two, which are missing, were dated February, 1913. Jung continued to write for almost 8 months without reply. Previously, Freud had been the more frequent and persistent correspondent.

RETURN OF THE SCRIPT: INTERNAL CONFRONTATION AND WORK

The consequences of the psychological resolutions revealed by the dream are evident in the *Two Essays* (1953) and *Psychological Types* (1971). In the first, one can see what from then on became Jung's major attitude toward psychoanalysis. He did not oppose it, he subsumed it. It was not wrong, just limited. It was a one-sided view, whose opposite was the Adlerian position. Both were parts of a larger framework envisioned by Jung but not yet worked out in detail. On the personal level, this position could be translated into the thought that one did not really have to slay authority in order to survive. One need only to see it in perspective, as one element in a duality not to be feared but understood.

The whole idea of benefiting from that which you fear, that which is largely unknown to you but to which you are intimately attached, that which has the power to overwhelm you, is given at the close of the first edition of the *Two Essays*, in a small section entitled, *General Remarks on the Therapeutic Approach to the Unconscious*. This section seemed particularly autobiographical and perhaps indicative of what Jung was experiencing in the years surrounding the separation, the fear that the individual path could lead to being lost in the unconscious, an underlying theme in the analysis of the Miller fantasies.

After pointing out the dangers inherent in exploring the unconscious, especially when neurotic symptoms are present, he goes on (Jung, 1953, pp. 112–114) with words that seem applicable to himself:

> But the neurotic cases are not by a long way the most dangerous. There are cases of people apparently quite normal, showing no especial neurotic symptoms — *they may themselves be doctors and educators* [emphasis added] — priding themselves on their normality, models of good upbringing, with exceptionally normal views and habits of life, yet whose normality is an artificial compensation *for a latent psychosis* [emphasis added]. They themselves suspect nothing of this condition. Their suspicions may perhaps find only an indirect expression in the fact that they are particularly interested in psychology and psychiatry, and are attracted to these things as a moth to the light. But since the analytical technique activates the unconscious and brings it to the fore, in these cases the healthful compensation is destroyed, the unconscious breaks forth in the form of uncontrollable fantasies and overwrought states, which may in certain circumstances lead to mental disorder and possibly even to suicide.

After further explication of hidden negative possibilities in the unconscious, Jung continues,

> It would be wrong, however, to dwell only on the unfavorable side of the unconscious. In all ordinary cases the unconscious is unfavorable or dangerous only because we are not at one with it and therefore in opposition to it. A negative attitude to the unconscious, or its splitting off, is detrimental insofar as the dynamics of the unconscious are identical with instinctual energy. Disalliance with the unconscious is synonymous with loss of instinct and rootlessness.

> If we can successfully develop the function which I have called transcendent, the disharmony ceases and we can then enjoy the favorable side of the unconscious. The unconscious then gives us all the encouragement and help that a bountiful nature can shower upon man. It holds possibil-

ities which are locked away from the conscious mind, for it has at its disposal all subliminal psychic contents, all these things which have been forgotten or overlooked, as well as the wisdom and experience of uncounted centuries which are laid down in its archetypal origins.

These rich paragraphs contain much of what emerged as Jungian psychology after 40 additional years of intense, scholarly elaboration. However, from the personal point of view, what we can clearly see is a resolution to rely most on an intrapsychic path, where human relationships will assume an importance secondary to that of internal psychological experience.

What I am trying to draw together from these bits and pieces of historical data is that, in 1913, Jung lived through the deep difficulty of separation from the internalized father image, first slaying him, and later incorporating him as a positive but lesser figure. It was evident by 1916, when the early sections of the "two essays" were finished, that Jung had moved from the angry, fearful position of the Oedipal son to the more independent and benign role of the leader and father. I hesitate to say Oedipal father because he certainly gave no evidence from then on of the classic fear postulated by Freud and demonstrated in his life, namely that of displacement.[4] In fact, for a long time afterward Jung worked alone, much as a father without a family or a leader without a tribe.

THE PROGRESS OF THE WORK IN OUTLINE

The "two essays" clearly marked both the freedom of Jung from his allegiance to psychoanalysis and the freedom to explore the essence of those things that had originally attracted him to psychoanalysis, his fascination with the concept of duality in nature and the dynamic products resulting from the interplay of opposites. The emphasis on duality, formally introduced in the *Psychology of the Unconscious* (1916/1949) received a variety of expressions in the two essays. Perhaps the most direct and important of these expressions was the delineation of the attitudinal types, introversion and extraversion, which was a first step toward Jung's theory of types. The book, *Psychological Types* (Jung, 1971) presents a clear delineation of this typology, probably his closest point of articulation with American psychology both then and now.

The year 1944 marked a turning point in Jung's life. At age 69 he

---

[4]This difference between Freud and Jung is reflected in their attitudes toward their work and is attributed to the differences in their relationship to their mothers (Alexander, 1982).

suffered a massive heart attack and hovered between life and death for weeks. What he experienced during that time he describes vividly in *Memories, Dreams, Reflections* (1961, Chap. 10). The outcome of this was to follow even more stringently his own inner directions. Important manuscripts were produced. The major ones were *Mysterium Conjunctionis*, begun long before the attack and finished in 1955 (1970b), *Aion* (1968), and *Answer to Job* (1969). In these, he returns to earlier themes and their resolution, duality, separation and union, good and evil as contained in the concept of god, the individuation process and its outcome, selfhood. Unlike the previous periods of work when fundamental issues of mental life were liberally interspersed with real-world problems of psychopathology, psychotherapy, and cultural change, problems more connected with the outer world, we see instead, a man being almost totally directed by his inner life.

IMPACT OF JUNG'S WORK

Jung died in 1961, at a time when his ideas were beginning to receive a hearing, both in psychology and in the larger world, that they had never previously enjoyed. Until the end of World War II, Jung's major impact had been on a very limited group of followers, mainly psychotherapists and a restricted segment of the European intellectual community, mostly interested in the esoteric, symbolic, and cultural aspects of Jung's work. In more general circles he was referred to as a dissenting student of Freud and the originator of some ideas about introversion and extraversion. What then served to bring Jung's name and his work to the fore?

One factor seems to have been the tremendous growth in mental health interest in the wake of the devastation produced by World War II. In our country this led to the rapid development of mental health specialties, including clinical psychology, and their attendant training needs. The study of personality theory and its application to the psychotherapeutic process were a fundamental aspect of the training programs that were developed to meet these needs. There was no question, then, that Jungian ideas would receive a much more extended hearing.

The development of these training programs was inhibited by the limited opportunities for training in psychotherapy available to psychologists, partly because of the restrictions placed on nonmedical personnel by psychoanalytic training institutes in America. Thus, after the opening of the Jung Institute in Zurich in 1948, a sizable contingent of foreign professionals, including many Americans, were attracted there to study

Jungian theory. One result of this trend was an increased number of Jungian training centers in the United States, with a resulting increase in the dissemination of Jungian ideas.

A second and I believe extremely important factor resulted from cultural changes that took place throughout the world beginning in the late 1950s. I refer here to the increased interest in inner imaginal processes experienced through the use of consciousness expanding or hallucinogenic drugs. The step to an interest in Jungian ideas is an obvious one.

A third factor, not completely independent of the second, relates to Jung's continual concern with the problem of religion as it is represented in the psychology of the individual. There were clearly points of articulation between various aspects of modern Protestant theology and Jungian notions of individuation. Thus, people struggling with the relationship of God to man, in the personal rather than in the dogmatic sense, were likely to find their way to an interest in Jung's ideas.

FUTURE PROSPECTS

Having traced some aspects of its development and history, it is not unreasonable to raise the question of the future of Jungian psychology. I see this as a complex question of which the answer resides only in small part in the explanatory power of the ideas. What one tends to get from global, seminal thinkers like Jung is a direction, a path, a fundamental set of concepts. When such ideas increase in attractiveness, this reflects the increments of power that occur as their limits are extended to include new realms. These avenues are not usually traversed by the innovators. They are usually left for others to explore. Thus, not only must the ideas contain intrinsic merit; they must also attract people who will investigate their value, and not simply accept them uncritically.

The Jungian movement has not attracted such people in great numbers. Consequently, I see the present moment as a transitional time for Jung's ideas. Whether they will turn out to be among the great ideas in the history of human thought or be consigned to the category of esoteric speculation, I do not know. Too many uncertainties remain.

Some things do seem clear, however. Jung was an unusual man with a fertile intellect. He contributed much to the study of personality. His connections to modern efforts are legion: his recognition of the importance of imagery, and the concept of its script-like aspects; his emphasis on the study of the entire life span, and to the problems of the second half of life; his attention to various aspects of the psychotherapeutic relationship that do not stem solely from transference; his broad perspective on the nature of dream material. These are but a few of the ways in which his more general influence may be detected.

Lest one come away from this discussion feeling that I have either glorified his achievements or paid insufficient attention to his shortcomings, let me close by reminding you of one of his lifelong insights—one that began in childhood with his forbidden image of God dropping a turd on the church and demolishing it (Jung, 1961, p. 39)—and ended some 70 years later with the publication of his book, *Answer to Job* (Jung, 1969). He was convinced of the dual nature of God, good and evil, the dual nature of man, and I am convinced of the dual nature of Jung. He was led to emphasize his relationship to his introverted, abstract, imaginal side, not infrequently at the expense of his touch with the real world, the world of people and relationships. Even at the end of his life, he expressed a density about the meaning of his encounters with others, in comparison to the clarity he felt about the meaning of inner, imaginal events (Jung, 1961, p. 95). It was a price that he had to pay.

ACKNOWLEDGMENT

A more extensive version of this article appears in Alexander (1990).

REFERENCES

Alexander, I. E. (1982). The Freud–Jung relationship: The other side of Oedipus and countertransference. Some implications for psychoanalytic theory and psychotherapy. *American Psychologist, 37,* 1009–1018.

Alexander, I. E. (1990). *Personology: Method and content in personality assessment and psychobiography.* Durham, NC: Duke University Press.

Hannah, B. (1976). *Jung, his life and work.* New York: Putnam.

Jung, C. G. (1916/1949). *Psychology of the unconscious* (B. M. Hinkle, Trans.). *New York: Dodd, Mead.*

Jung, C. G. (1918/1969). *Studies in word-association* (N. D. Eder, Trans.). London: Routledge & Kegan Paul.

Jung, C. G. (1953). Two essays on analytical psychology. In H. Read, M. Fordham, & G. Adler (Eds.), *The collected works of C. G. Jung* (Vol. 7). (R. F. C. Hull, Trans.). Princeton, NJ: Princeton University Press.

Jung, C. G. (1961). *Memories, dreams, reflections.* New York: Pantheon.

Jung, C. G. (1968). Aion. In H. Read, M. Fordham, & G. Adler (Eds.), *The collected works of C. G. Jung* (Vol. 9, II). (R. F. C. Hull, Trans.). Princeton, NJ: Princeton University Press.

Jung, C. G. (1969). Psychology and religion; also, Answer to Job. In H. Read, M. Fordham, & G. Adler (Eds.), *The collected works of C. G. Jung* (Vol 11). (R. F. C. Hull, Trans.). Princeton, NJ: Princeton University Press.

Jung, C. G. (1970a). On the psychology and pathology of so-called occult phenomena. In H. Read, M. Fordham, & G. Adler (Eds.), *The collected works of C. G. Jung* (Vol. 1). (R. F. C. Hull, Trans.). Princeton, NJ: Princeton University Press.

Jung, C. G. (1970b). Mysterium conjunctionis. In H. Read, M. Fordham, & G. Adler (Eds.), *The collected works of C. G. Jung* (Vol. 14). (R. F. C. Hull, Trans.). Princeton, NJ: Princeton University Press.

Jung, C. G. (1971). Psychological types. In H. Read, M. Fordham, G. Adler, & W. McGuire (Eds.), *The collected works of C. G. Jung* (Vol. 6). (R. F. C. Hull, Trans.). Princeton, NJ: Princeton University Press.

Jung, C. G. (1972). the psychology of dementia praecox. In H. Read, M. Fordham, & G. Adler (Eds.), *The collected works of C. G. Jung* (Vol. 3). (R. F. C. Hull, Trans.). Princeton, NJ: Princeton University Press.

McGuire, W. (Ed.). (1974). *The Freud–Jung letters.* (R. Manheim & R. F. C. Hull, Trans.). Princeton, NJ: Princeton University Press.

Rosenberg, S. (1978). *Why Freud fainted.* Indianapolis: Bobbs-Merrill.

Shapiro, K., & Alexander, I. (1975). *The experience of introversion.* Durham, NC: Duke University Press.

Chapter 12

Perspectives on John B. Watson

Charles L. Brewer

In 1956, Gustav Bergmann claimed that, second only to Sigmund Freud, John B. Watson was the most influential shaper of psychological thought in the first half of the 20th century. In 1957, the American Psychological Association cited Watson for spawning a revolution in modern psychology and providing new directions for fruitful research. Some psychologists agree that these accolades are not exaggerated. Watson's signal contributions to scientific psychology and to the movement of behaviorism are well known, and I shall not repeat them here. Instead, I shall mention some less familiar things about Watson that might help us better understand the man and his career.

BEGINNINGS

John Broadus Watson was born in the small village of Travelers Rest near Greenville, South Carolina, on January 9, 1878. His parents were Pickens Butler Watson and Emma Kesiah (Roe) Watson. Most of Watson's family members were devout believers in fundamental religion and his grandfather helped to establish one of the many Baptist churches in the area. In fact, Watson was named for John Albert Broadus, a Baptist minister in Greenville, who rose to national prominence as a theologian and educator. As a youngster, Watson was called Broadus and not John B.

*Photograph of John B. Watson courtesy of Charles Brewer

In a short autobiographical sketch published in 1936, Watson wrote that his earliest academic memories concerned the district schools in the picturesque hamlets of Reedy River, White Horse, and Travelers Rest. From the age of 6, he trudged to one or another of these places to attend a rural school. He was using tools, half-soling shoes, and milking cows when he was 9, and was a pretty good carpenter at 12. This manual skill never lost its charm for him and years later he built a 10-room house from blueprints and then added a garage and a barn.

Watson was the fourth of six children in a dirt-poor family, but his mother had high hopes for her offspring. When he was 12, she moved the family from Travelers Rest to Greenville because the schools were much better than the small, rural schools. He was arrested twice: once for what he called "nigger fighting," which was a favorite after-school activity, and once for "shooting off firearms inside the city limits."

FURMAN UNIVERSITY

In 1894, at the age of 16, Watson entered Furman University, a Southern Baptist school, where he remained for 5 years. He worked for 2 years as an assistant in the chemistry department to help defray his college expenses. Although he joined the Kappa Alpha fraternity, Watson was not very sociable and had few friends at Furman, one notable exception being Professor George Buist of the chemistry department. Watson's Furman transcript lists the following courses: six in mathematics; four each in philosophy and Greek; three each in English, Bible, German, and physics; two each in French, psychology, and geology; and one each in chemistry, economics, Latin, mechanics, and sociology. His academic marks were satisfactory but not distinguished; some of his lowest marks were in psychology. Watson recalled that he was the only student who passed the final Greek exam during his senior year but did so only because he crammed all night—fortified with a quart of Coca-Cola syrup. In those days, Coca-Cola had a spot of cocaine in it, so that late-night cramming session could have been very interesting. (I wonder if Watson knew about state-dependent learning.) He liked his philosophy and psychology courses, and singled out Weber's *History of Philosophy*, Davis's *Elements of Psychology*, and collateral reading in Wundt as being memorable.

Watson also mentioned Professor Gordon B. Moore, a philosopher and cleric who taught psychology courses, as being especially important in stimulating his intellectual development and heading him into psychology. Moore was a stern taskmaster who told the class that any student who turned in a paper "backward"[1] would flunk the course. During his senior year, for some strange reason, Watson handed in his final paper backward. Moore flunked him and he had to stay at Furman for another year, at the end of which he received a master's degree rather than a bachelor's degree.

In 1950, a group of psychology students at Furman dedicated the first isssue of their *Journal* to "John Broadus Watson, scholar, educator, and leader in practical application of psychology, as a token of esteem and admiration." When he heard of their kind gesture, Watson wrote them a letter, which I will refer to more than once in this chapter. In this letter Watson (then 72 years old) remembered the influence of G. B. Moore:

> I have a very warm spot in my heart for Furman. Probably any time during my five years there they would have sold me for a plugged nickel (and rightly). But Prof. G. B. Moore really gave me inspiration. He delivered a sermon at the Greenville Baptist Church—probably the only sermon I ever listened to. The title was "Lift Me Up, Lift Me Up." There wasn't much religion in it—it was rather the whole theory of evolution in blank verse.

Moore was later fired from Furman for his liberal religious views.

Watson recalled that his frustrating years at Furman set him against colleges. His main complaint was that college ignores students' vocational slants and coddles them too much. He concluded that until colleges start teaching about practical living, they will be tolerated as safe havens for boys and girls—an interlude between childhood and adult life in the real world.

During his senior year, Watson fell in love with Mary Brunson, a student at Greenville Woman's College (which, because of financial troubles, merged with the all-male Furman University in 1932). Mary gave Broadus little encouragement, which probably wounded his pride. The thought has crossed my mind that this rejection might account for Watson's single-mindedness and assiduity later in graduate school, but he probably would not cite this as an example of the sublimation of sexual desires.

The Watson file at Furman University contains some interesting observations on Watson's personal makeup. Ben Geer, a Furman professor, called him a nonconformist in college and in later life and said that he explored theories and ideas for their sensationalism. Geer mentioned that Broadus's brother Edward was a deeply religious man who married in Greenville and moved to Gaffney, South Carolina,

---

[1]This is Watson's (1936) expression. Probably he meant "with the pages backward" but that is not certain.

where he ran a hardware store for many years. The woman that brother Edward married was Isabelle Manly, daughter of a former president of Furman, for whom one of the residence halls is named. Geer remembered Broadus as a brilliant but somewhat lazy and insolent student—a bit heavy but handsome—who thought too highly of himself and was more interested in his own ideas than in people.

THE YOUNG TEACHER

Watson graduated from Furman in 1899. Because of limited finances, he took jobs teaching, in the summer session at a rural school in nearby Pickens County, South Carolina, and at the now-defunct Batesburg Institute during the following schoolyear. Watson received $25 per month for teaching, plus free lodging, meals, and laundry provided by parents of various students on a weekly basis, as he moved from one home to another in the community. Such a migratory status for teachers was common in those days.

Ben Field, a retired educator who was 86 years old when I interviewed him in 1975, had been a student in Watson's fourth-grade class in the summer of 1899. Watson lived in Field's home for at least 2 weeks that summer. Field shared some recollections of Watson. He said that Watson's mother was a kind, Christian woman whose life centered around the Reedy River Baptist Church, but that his father was a genuine reprobate. The father ran a "groundhog" (itinerant) sawmill several miles from home during the week and mostly ate, slept, and drank whiskey all weekend. After that summer, the Fields visited the Watsons' home on numerous occasions, but Broadus's father was never there.

Field recalled that Watson was never much interested in the Pickens County "beauty queens" his own age. Rather, he enjoyed the company of younger children or, perhaps even more, of his animals. Field concluded that Watson was altogether a perfect gentleman—very quiet and reserved.

Ralph Hawkins, Watson's first cousin who lived in Greenville, described a tragic incident from their youth. Hawkins's brother, Hampton, and Watson were good friends. They were preparing to make a trip together in 1899 and hired a livery-stable rig to take them to bid farewell to a young woman named Maude Cely. Because there had been a recent "Negro uprising," Broadus told Hampton to take his pistol. As Hampton was loading it, the derringer slipped out of his hand. He accidentally shot himself and died 3 days later. Hawkins also mentioned that on Broadus's infrequent visits to Greenville thereafter he seemed to have "grown big in his ideas."

Watson's outspoken atheism repelled many in Greenville. The mother of Hampton Hawkins declared that she had rather have her boy dead than for him to be an atheist like Broadus. Ironically, somewhere along the line, Watson's mother extracted from him a vow that he would become a Baptist minister, perhaps hoping that he would carry on the tradition of his namesake. But Broadus was never as religious as his brother Edward and, following their mother's death in 1900, he gave little thought to the ministry, Baptist or otherwise. In fact, Watson's name was dropped from the roll of the First Baptist Church in Greenville on December 20, 1908, because of the length of time since there had been any communication from him.

THE UNIVERSITY OF CHICAGO

After a year of teaching at the Batesburg Institute, and a few weeks after his mother died, Watson began to think seriously about continuing his education in graduate school. At that time he was more interested in philosophy than psychology and considered two universities, Princeton and Chicago. Learning that Princeton required a reading knowledge of Greek and Latin, he decided to go to the University of Chicago, where he arrived in 1900 with $50 in his pocket and no other financial resources.

At Chicago, Watson was ambitious but broke. To earn money, he worked as a janitor, a waiter, and a caretaker for Professor H. H. Donaldson's laboratory rats. His studies were concentrated in philosophy, neurology, physiology, and experimental psychology. He took philosophy courses with A. W. Moore and John Dewey, but Watson claimed that he never understood anything that Dewey said. After 3 years and two summers, in 1903, Watson received his PhD degree in experimental psychology (magna cum laude, Phi Beta Kappa), his research being directed jointly by James Rowland Angell and H. H. Donaldson. Watson is said to have been the youngest person to earn a PhD at the University of Chicago up to that time: he was 25. After receiving his degree, Watson stayed on at Chicago, which was then an intellectual hotbed filled with academic hotheads. He served first as Angell's assistant and later as a regular member of the faculty.

In 1904, Watson married—for the second time—Mary Amelia Ickes, who had been a student in one of his classes at Chicago. According to family legend (Buckley, 1989), Mary had developed a crush on her professor and during one long exam wrote a love poem in her copybook instead of answers to the test questions. When Watson insisted on taking the paper at the end of the quiz, Mary blushed, handed him the paper, and ran from the room. The literary effort must have had its desired effect. But the courtship that ensued was hardly blissful. (p. 9)

Mary was the sister of Harold Ickes, who later became Secretary of the Interior in Franklin Delano Roosevelt's cabinet. Harold openly and vehemently opposed his sister's marriage to Watson whom he considered to be a contemptible megalomaniac. His opposition was so violent that Watson later claimed that he had feared for Mary's physical safety. However that may be, partly out of chivalry, and partly

to indulge his penchant for melodrama . . . he and Mary were secretly wed on December 26, 1903. . . .But the marriage. . .was kept secret, and when Harold Ickes decided to remove his sister from college and send her to an aunt in the East, Mary was forced to comply with her brother's demands. (p. 50)

While she was gone, Watson broke off an affair with a former lover who tried to win him back. After that "Watson sent for Mary, and they were publicly married in the fall of 1904. Watson confessed everything to his bride, even though he realized that the situation did not provide 'a very good foundation for marriage'" (p. 50). The marriage never was a happy one.

In spite of its inauspicious beginnings, this marriage produced two children, Mary (nicknamed Polly) and John. Polly's daughter, by the way, is a well-known actress who has performed in Shakespeare plays, on Broadway, in movies, and on television. Her performance in the series, "Goodnight, Beantown," got good reviews and a nomination for an Emmy Award in 1983. She gained visibility by doing a series of offbeat television commercials for Polaroid cameras with James Garner and by hosting a CBS morning television show. In 1990, she began appearing in "WIOU," a television series on CBS, and published *Breaking the Silence*, a book about her troubles and triumphs (Hartley & Commire, 1990). This grandaughter of John B. Watson is Mariette Hartley.

Watson's work at Chicago went well but did not receive the support that he thought it deserved. With two small children, the Watsons seemed always to be living from hand to mouth. Perhaps because of his precarious financial situation, Watson used his increasing professional reputation to attract offers from other universities.

THE JOHNS HOPKINS UNIVERSITY

In the fall of 1908, at the age of 30, Watson accepted a position as professor and director of the psychological laboratory at Johns Hopkins University, almost doubling his salary. At Hopkins, he renewed acquaintance with James Mark Baldwin, another native of South Carolina. Watson had earlier spent an unpaid research leave at Hopkins working with William Howell to perfect a procedure for performing surgery on animals.

Since coming from Princeton in 1903, Baldwin had supervised an impressive rejuvenation of psychology at Hopkins. Not long after Watson arrived, however, Baldwin left unexpectedly. In the summer of 1908, Baldwin was involved in a delicate situation after being caught during a police raid on a Baltimore bordello. At the time, Baldwin gave a fictitious name and later succeeded in having his case dropped without fanfare. When the mayor of Baltimore nominated Baldwin for a position on the school board in the spring of 1909, however, the tawdry details came to light in the form of insinuations in the local newspapers. To avoid an all-out scandal, Baldwin was forced to resign from Hopkins at the age of 48.

Baldwin's abrupt departure shifted responsibility for psychology at Hopkins and for editing the *Psychological Review* to Watson. Except for these unusual circumstances, such important duties would probably not have come to one so young, not even to John B. Watson. In his letter to the Furman psychology students that I mentioned earlier, Watson recalled that episode for them:

So there is a new magazine—JOURNAL OF PSYCHOLOGY-FURMAN UNIVERSITY PSYCHOLOGY CLUB! I congratulate the founders and the editors and wish them luck. They will have fun and some grief.

A few weeks after I began work at Johns Hopkins, Prof. James Mark Baldwin came into my office and said, "I am resigning and leaving now for the University of Mexico. You are the new editor of the *Psychological Review*." I was aghast. The *Psychological Review* was the official organ of the American Psychological Association. I was about as well prepared to undertake this work as I was to swim the English Channel. More manuscripts poured in on us than we could publish. I must have made a lot of enemies by refusing many articles, some possibly quite as good as those accepted. But the magazine prospered. Prospered to such an extent that it was thought best to add the *Journal of Experimental Psychology*.

Professor H. C. Warren of Princeton University became interested in these publications. He bought the *Review*, the *Journal*, and *Psychological Mono-*

graphs. I believe Dr. Baldwin sold out his holdings for $5,500. It was a godsend to us at Hopkins to have the financial end of the journals taken care of. Prof. Warren took over the editorship of the *Review* and I of the *Journal.*

Watson's work at Hopkins flourished. His research and writing, especially "Psychology as the Behaviorist Views It," published in the *Psychological Review* in 1913, made him a powerful but controversial pioneer in behaviorism. In addition to editing the *Psychological Review,* he was the founding editor of the *Journal of Experimental Psychology* in 1915. In the same year he served as president of the American Psychological Association at the age of 37.

Watson's prodigious work at Hopkins was interrupted by World War I, when he was ordered to active military duty on September 20, 1917. Serving in the Signal Corps, he went to England to give tests to aviators. On one occasion, he was almost court-martialed for expressing opinions that were not shared by his superiors. Watson's reactions to the military were characteristically sardonic. He said that his army experience was a nightmare and that the American officers were nincompoops. Nevertheless, he attained the rank of major before his honorable discharge on November 30, 1919.

Watson's reputation soared still higher with the publication of *Psychology from the Standpoint of a Behaviorist.* In an obvious attempt to encourage him to stay at Hopkins, President Frank J. Goodnow offered to raise Watson's salary and wrote a cordial letter supporting his work. The irony of Goodnow's kind words would soon become ominously prophetic.

DIVORCE AND AFTERMATH

Watson's professional prestige was skyrocketing but his personal life was a different matter. Watson had begun research on the development of emotions in young children. One of his research assistants was named Rosalie Rayner, who graduated from Vassar College in 1919 and was a member of a prominent Baltimore family. Watson and Rayner's relationship extended beyond their study of emotions in the laboratory. The marriage between Watson and Mary Ickes — always tempestuous — ended formally with a much-publicized divorce in 1920. Watson then married Rosalie Rayner; he was 42 and she was 21. After many discussions and much correspondence with the administrative officials at Hopkins about his scandalous situation, Watson was asked to resign; and, as James Mark Baldwin had done before him, he did.

Career in Advertising

Watson was so devastated by his treatment at Hopkins and so hurt that his colleagues did not come to his defense, that he was on the verge of a breakdown. The academic world was closed to him. He had a new wife and considerable financial obligations from his divorce settlement, but no job and no promising prospects. He moved to New York City and took a job with the J. Walter Thompson advertising agency. Trying to determine what motivates people to buy certain products, he studied the marketing of rubber boots in Mississippi, did some door-to-door selling, and worked as a clerk at Macy's in New York. His approach to advertising impressed his superiors and he became a vice-president of the company in 1924. He left J. Walter Thompson in 1935 and served as an advertising executive at the William Esty Company until his retirement in 1945 at the age of 67. He was the prototypical entrepreneur with a luxurious office and a handsome salary. Along the way, he lectured at the New School for Social Research and published numerous articles in popular magazines, but nothing in the psychological journals. In his letter to the Furman students, Watson wrote about his getting out of academic publishing this way:

> One of the questions I am most often asked is, WHY DID YOU QUIT WRITING? The real answer is I had nothing more to say. In advertising work, I had no laboratory and no ready reference library. Under such conditions one dries up. I turned then to "popular" magazine writing and for a long time I averaged about one article per month. Since these articles paid anywhere from $750 to $1,500 each, I became quite cocky. I never had one turned down.

> Then I decided to give the magazine reading public a "good" article. I put time and study on this and called it WHY I DON'T COMMIT SUICIDE. Not a single magazine would touch it. I still have the manuscript. I have no real answer as to why it was turned down. I amuse myself with the thought that the article was submitted just about the time Mr. Roosevelt had made democracy safe for himself, the non-voting population of the South, and for Mr. Stalin and his Communists. Maybe the title poured salt on open wounds.

> But isn't it a good thought to quit writing when you have nothing to say? If this were the irrevocable rule, think what we would have been spared from the pens of G. B. Shaw, Einstein, Freud, Kipling, et cetera. Death seems our only sure protector.

Despite the light perspective that is implicit in this passage, Watson never forgave the academic community, which he thought had betrayed him. Perhaps he would be reassured if he could know that he is now considered to be one of the important pioneers in modern advertising.

Life-style

The Watsons lived on a beautiful estate, called Whippoorwill Farm, in Westport, Connecticut. Watson enjoyed speeding around Long Island Sound in his 200-horsepower boat at full throttle. He was fond of pound cake, farming, riding, and bourbon. He enjoyed reading western novels and detective stories, and playing bridge with a few friends. In all, he was a strong and handsome man—rugged and dashing—but a polished gentleman in social situations.

Some people have speculated that Watson's physical attractiveness and engaging personality made him almost irresistible to many women. In fact, he often had a coterie of young and beautiful women at his side. One story about this aspect of his life ended with the comment that Watson was never involved in any love triangle but in a romantic polyhedron of indeterminable dimensionality.

Watson and Rosalie had two sons, William Rayner Watson (called Billy), born in 1921, and James Broadus Watson (called Jim), born in 1924. One might wonder if the combination of their sons' first names into "William James" was fortuitous. Considering the esteem in which Watson held that important American philosopher and psychologist, I suspect that it was not a chance occurrence.

Unfortunately, Rosalie became seriously ill, her condition deteriorated, and she died in 1935 at the age of 35. Watson's son Jim says that his father never completely recovered from Rosalie's death. After she died, Watson lost much of his panache. He sold his Westport estate in the early 1950s and moved to a small farm in Woodbury, Connecticut, where he spent his last years.

A SON'S REMINISCENCES

As part of a 1981 symposium at the annual meeting of the American Psychological Association in Los Angeles, Jim Watson, the second son of John B. and Rosalie Rayner Watson, made the following revealing comments about his father and what it was like being reared by the author of *Psychological Care of Infant and Child*:

> Based on published information such as the debate with McDougall, it would be hard to come to any other conclusion than [that] in his unbridled enthusiasm for behaviorism, my father was arrogant or, at best, not

inhibited by conventional modesty—perhaps he had to be a rebel to rock the world's psychological boat. But in real life, at least as I knew him, he was a much different person—one, incidentally, of considerable contradiction. Despite his reputation as more of an evangelist for behaviorism than a scientist, he was shy and conservative . . . and he was a considerate human being. He had a vocabulary second only to Webster, but he used more four-letter words than a mule skinner. He had all of the he-man attributes of Ernest Hemingway, but limited his hunting prowess to clay pigeons on the skeet range. He drove a high-powered boat with abandon, but he was scared to death of driving a car, and, in fact, never learned to do so. In his presence, one felt an aura of genuine warmth, but as an individual he was hopelessly unable to communicate or demonstrate any affection—I am not sure if that was the cause or the effect of his theories of behaviorism.

Both dad and mother, although she died when I was still a child, rigorously pursued the foundation teachings of behaviorism. Frankly, I think that a better end product would have resulted if the process of growing up had been [tempered] with some measure of affection—it certainly would have made growing up less like a business proposition where one is judged by bottom-line performance. It is my hope that the teachings of his disciples and others who have followed him have tempered the emotionally spartan upbringing that he espoused. His behavioristic theories on child development unquestionably have value in terms of life's preparation through the setting of standards and developing an understanding of the parameters of acceptable and responsible behavior, but they could have been much improved if one were permitted to mix in a big helping of parental affection. I believe to do so would provide a better psychological foundation for all of us who, at one time or another in life, are ultimately put to the test of weathering the emotional storms that often topple people because of the frail egos and low levels of self-esteem, which usually result from a childhood diet that lacks a deeper sense of human connection.

Later on, in the spring of 1989, Jim Watson provided an additional set of what he called "rambling recollections" about his father, specifically for inclusion in this presentation:

Dad was a handsome fellow. His hair turned white when he was a young man. His voice was very quiet, rather deep, and touched with a southern accent. Although he talked quietly, he did not speak in a monotone. He never raised his voice. If he were angry, which was not very often, you would never know it by the way he talked. He had an enormous vocabulary—scholarly but practical. He had a large number of four-letter swear words that he used regularly. Interestingly, he used swear words to tease and not as expletives. I don't think many people felt that he was vulgar when he used them.

Dad was always impeccably dressed. He had all his clothes made at Tripler's and his shoes were made in England. His business attire was always blue; his suits were blue, his shirts were blue, and his ties were blue. He usually had his initials on his shirts. . . . When he was in the country, he dressed the model Maine woodsman. All of his country clothes came from L. L. Bean. He wore wash pants, Bean canoe shoes or rubber-bottom boots, and Pendleton shirts, never tucked in—always loose. He never wore a hat except when he thought one was required in the business setting. I have seen some earlier pictures of him in Europe when he had a hat, but he hated hats. He was criticized, however, by people like Bill Esty at the Esty advertising agency for not wearing hats.

Dad was a smoker—only smoked about half a pack a day—but never inhaled. He smoked Lucky Strikes all his life until he joined the William Esty Company. They handled the account for Camel cigarettes, and he switched because of the need for brand loyalty. He only smoked the first quarter of a cigarette. As far as I know, it was a lifelong habit, but it seemed to be more affected smoking than addictive smoking.

Dad wore big black or dark hornrimmed glasses—very round. He was nearsighted and when he was doing close work, such as carpentry or reading, he would push his glasses up on his forehead. When he was pensive, he would put his right thumbnail against the very small gap in his front upper teeth and cock his head down just a little. You could often find him in this posture. Incidentally, he was very fastidious about his personal cleanliness, including his nails, which were always clean and clipped. (He did his own manicuring.) He was always clean shaven—never knew a morning when he didn't shave.

Dad was inclined to be somewhat overweight. He always boasted that his college weight was 176 pounds. But I know that during the latter part of his life, at any rate, he got up to 210 or 215. He talked a lot about dieting but didn't do much of it. He loved southern food and often did much of his own cooking: baked biscuits, cooked beans, and made preserves. He ate a wide variety of foods but he drank only bourbon whiskey—and that straight. He drank a lot, but I rarely saw him under the influence of liquor to the extent that it was evident—only when he was depressed. He drank a lot of coffee—always black. He always cooled his coffee by dribbling spoonfuls of it through the air and then he would put the spoon back into the cup.

Dad went to bed at about 11 o'clock at night, but he slept a lot between dinner and the time he went to bed. He always got up about 4:00 or 4:30 in the morning. I think he did that even in his younger years; he used to talk about it as his laboratory hours.

He was a quiet, soft-spoken man with a very good sense of humor. He liked to tell dirty jokes, but he wasn't raucous. He was a good communicator when he wished to talk, but he didn't talk very much. He was not one you could engage in much of a dialogue. He was only a fair listener, and he carried around with him a number of firmly fixed ideas about life and the world in general. He shared enough of them to let you know how he felt, but he never bothered to get into detailed conversations. . . .

I have no doubt that he was arrogant professionally and, as nearly as I can determine, defended his theories and beliefs rigidly and dogmatically. But I didn't see those characteristics in him firsthand. He was in the twilight years of his scientific career when I was born.

Dad was disciplined, punctual, straightforward, and charitable. He couldn't stand any kind of cruelty or arrogance. He had a habit of walking away from things that he didn't like, as a method of disengaging himself. He wasn't rude about it—he always had something else to do, like go check on the animals, or go check in the kitchen, or go to the bathroom.

He liked all kinds of sports: boxing, riding, skeet shooting, and fishing, but he was not much on baseball or football. He was a great carpenter and loved to garden—grow his own vegetables. He loved animals of all sorts—sometimes I think more than people. We always had dogs, cats, cows, sheep, horses, and chickens on the farm. He was a consummate weekend farmer.

Dad was an atheist in the truest sense. He was staunchly Republican and very conservative. He despised politics and politicians.

He was big on the ladies and he loved to flirt. I think the flirtations were primarily fishing expeditions. If he got something on the hook, he knew what do to with it, but he was not a womanizer.

He much preferred the quiet country life but it was mother who always pushed him to go to parties, take trips to Europe, invite company in—and all the other social activities. He was good about going to them—he didn't protest too much—but he really didn't like to initiate them. In his later years, he had a lot of company at the farm on weekends, but most of the visitors were old friends of mother's. It may sound silly, but he always seemed to strive for simplicity in his life. Later on, after we sold the farm in Westport and he moved up to the country at Woodbury, Connecticut, he much preferred to use the outhouse rather than the inside plumbing. He often said that he'd prefer to use kerosene lamps than electricity and the fireplace rather than central heat. He was just tired of complexity in his life.

CONCLUSION

Watson's alma mater awarded him an honorary degree in 1919, not long before his widely publicized divorce and second marriage. The citation read in part: "Graduates of Furman University have become eminent in many fields, and the institution always delights to honor her sons who have proved themselves worthy to wear the laurels she can bestow." I chuckle to think of the embarrassment, or even horror, the university officials must have experienced when the front-page stories about Watson's affair with his graduate student at Hopkins appeared in so many newspapers. One elderly Greenville matron remarked that Watson denied his heredity and his heritage. She probably had no idea how accurately her statement reflected Watson's own views on the relative importance of heredity and environment.

In his declining years, Watson regained a modicum of his lost academic respectability. The citation in 1957 from the American Psychological Association mentioned earlier is a mark of his improving situation. Such recognition came grudgingly. Many people still resented his earlier "fall from grace" and his stunning success in the business world. There were those for whom the concept of behaviorism was so offensive that they rejected its founder. Also, some people thought that his popular writing smacked of hucksterism.

With passing time, however, Watson seems, increasingly, to receive due credit for his contributions. He is one of the most important figures in the history of psychology. He insisted that psychology must be a rigorous, scientific study of overt and measurable behavior. He totally rejected the speculative and mentalistic psychology of his day and promoted his own behavioristic alternative with a religious fervor. He was a vigorous and formidable proponent, who inflamed many adversaries. Admitting that he overstated his case, Watson seemed delighted by the polemical protests from his critics. Although many of his primary emphases have been discarded as simplistic, few people have had such a profound impact on our intellectual and scientific history. John Broadus Watson died in New York City on September 25, 1958, at the age of 80. He would be quietly amused that we are still talking about him.

PERSONAL REFLECTIONS: CHARLES L. BREWER

When I joined the faculty at Furman University in 1967, I was surprised to learn that John B. Watson's alma mater had virtually ignored the "father of behaviorism" since awarding him an honorary degree in 1919. I was perplexed and irritated when some members of the Greenville Historical Society were reluctant to talk about Watson because of his outspoken atheism and his "fall from grace" almost 50 years earlier. Had I moved to the buckle on the bible belt? Without answering that question, I resolved to restore some honor to Watson "in his own country."

When the Alumni Association solicited nominations for its Hall of Fame, the psychologists in my department were galvanized into action. Gathering information to support Watson's nomination was my first serious attempt to learn about his life and career. Our campaign was successful; Watson was inducted as a charter member of the Furman University Hall of Fame in a special ceremony on October 30, 1970. His photograph is displayed in a permanent gallery, which includes other luminaries, such as the Nobel-prize winning physicist Charles H. Townes. Fascinated by the research for this project, I began interviewing Watson's relatives and other people in the area who knew something about him.

An invitation to present a 12-minute talk on "John B. Watson: A Product of Furman University" at the Atlanta meeting of the Southern Society for Philosophy and Psychology in April 1976 forced me to organize my information. I had barely enough material to fill the allotted time, but the audience's reaction spurred me to learn more.

During the last 10 years, Watson has been singularly honored by his undergraduate college and his native state. In April 1979, Furman University sponsored a 2-day celebration of the centennial of Watson's birth. The guest lecturers were James V. McConnell, Fred S. Keller, and B. F. Skinner. Furman spared no expense in staging this festival, which was attended by more than 2,000 persons from 20 states. Among the honored guests were many of Watson's relatives, including his son Jim, who lives in Palos Verdes Estates, California. As another tribute, our laboratory was officially named The John B. Watson Laboratory of Psychology.

By Governor Richard W. Riley's formal declaration, Watson was inducted into the South Carolina Hall of Science and Technology in a special ceremony at Furman University in May 1984. Watson's son Jim and Jim's son Scott were among the dignitaries who attended. In connection with this occasion, the South Carolina Department of Archives and History erected a commemorative marker on U. S. Highway 276 near Watson's birthplace in the village of Travelers Rest, which is located about eight miles northwest of the city of Greenville, not far from Furman's present campus. Driving past this marker on trips to and from my office at Furman, I almost always smile.

ACKNOWLEDGMENTS

Many people have contributed to my work on Watson. The following persons shared their research in progress: L. J. Borstelmann, Jack

Demarest, Donald Dewsbury, Ben Harris, Robert Klein, Robert Prytula, Franz Samelson, J. N. Watson, George Windholz, and Everett Wyers. Horsley Gantt, Mary Cover Jones, and Curt Richter provided recollections of Watson. Ruth Lieb, Watson's longtime secretary, sent several photographs and other documents. Tom Roe and Carroll Smith supplied genealogical details; Glen Clayton helped to arrange and conduct interviews. Mary Wyche Burgess, Kerry Buckley, and Cedric Larson were especially generous in sharing information from their extensive research.

Several Furman administrators have encouraged my work with words and money: Gordon Blackwell, Frank Bonner, John Crabtree, and John Johns. Colleagues in the psychology department have cooperated in untold ways and helped to clarify my thinking and writing about Watson; special thanks to John Batson, Gil Einstein, and Lib Nanney, our indefatigable secretary.

Finally, and most important, my work yielded an unexpected personal reward—a friendship with Jim and Jackie Watson and their family. These charming and gracious people shared much private information about my pioneer. They also enriched my life, for which I am grateful.

REFERENCES

Bergmann, G. (1956). The contributions of John B. Watson. *Psychological Review, 63,* 265–276.

Buckley, K. W. (1989). *Mechanical man: John Broadus Watson and the beginnings of behaviorism.* New York: Guilford Press.

Hartley, M., & Commire, A. (1990). *Breaking the silence.* New York: Putnam.

Watson, James B. (1981, August). Untitled remarks. In C. L. Brewer (Chair), *John B. Watson's life, times, and work.* Symposium conducted at the annual meeting of the American Psychological Association, Los Angeles.

Watson, John B. (1936). John Broadus Watson. In C. Murchison (Ed.), *A history of psychology in autobiography* (Vol. 3, pp. 271–281). Worcester, MA: Clark University Press.

Chapter 13

Max Wertheimer: Modern Cognitive Psychology and the Gestalt Problem

Michael Wertheimer

I realize zat much has chanched in psychology, und in American society, since I left zis vorld in 1943. But my son, even if his facial hair is ze reverse of my own (vy ze funny-looking partial beart? Vy not a proper valrus moustache?), my son tells me zat if anyone is to take Gestalt ideas seriously today, zen zey must be restated in vords zat people today can understant. Chargon chanches. So now I vould, srough ze somevat imperfect understanding zat my son has bos of classical Gestalt seory proper und especially of modern cognitive psychology, like to share vis you my perspective on vat role Gestalt ideas have played, do play, und should play in vat is now called cognitive psychology. I vill try to say somesing about modern cognitive psychology, somesing about vat ze Gestalt problem is, und somesing about how ze two may or may not fit togezer. To try to make the presentation appropriate to today, I will make an effort to avoid sexist usage in my talk, and will also try to use a modern American accent, rather than my mode of speech long ago.

AUTOBIOGRAPHY

But before I engage in this exercise, perhaps I should tell you a little about myself. It is a long time since I entered a different stage of

---

*Photograph of Max Wertheimer courtesy of the Archives of the History of Psychology, Akron, Ohio

existence, and not every psychologist today is familiar with the Gestalt approach. I was born April 15, 1880, in Prague, now Czechoslovakia, but then part of Austria–Hungary. My father was the director of a successful business college in downtown Prague, and my mother was a lady who was well versed in central European literature, art and culture and an accomplished violinist. My older brother, Walter, was groomed to take over the Wertheimer business college, but died while he was still in his 20s.

My early education was in private schools in Prague, and I attended Charles University in the same city, studying a broad range of subjects from philosophy and art through law. Among my more influential teachers there was Christian von Ehrenfels, who suggested that the psychology of the 1880s, a systematic elementistic Wundtian psychology, had neglected an important element: the element of Gestaltqualitäten or "whole qualities," characteristics such as a melody or as squareness that must be added to the elements (the tones or lines) that make up a perceptual whole. Eventually I left Prague for the University of Berlin to study philosophy and psychology with such outstanding professors as Carl Stumpf. I completed my PhD in Würzburg in 1904 with Oswald Külpe and Karl Marbe, working on a word-association technique for the detection of guilt in criminal proceedings.

During the next few years I engaged in a variety of projects in several different settings: further work on the detection of guilt, more explorations of the word-association method, and studies of patients suffering from aphasia. In 1910, intrigued with the phenomenon of apparent motion (such as in today's cinema), I began a set of experiments that culminated in a paper in 1912, which many consider to have launched the Gestalt school. The experiments, for which my friends Kurt Koffka and Wolfgang Köhler served as observers, showed that the phenomenon of perceived movement (when two visual patterns are successively exposed at appropriate temporal and spatial intervals) cannot be derived from the summation of the sensations or perceptions of the two patterns. The quality of the entire experience, the motion, cannot be derived from the qualities of the two "component elements," the two stationary patterns. Indeed, it was soon clear to Köhler, Koffka and myself that this principle holds widely throughout psychology and even throughout nature: dynamic, integrated wholes (or *Gestalten*) are usually not the sum totals of their constituent parts or elements. Rather, characteristics of natural wholes determine the nature, role, and function of their constituent parts, and parts of a genuine Gestalt are far from indifferent to each other.

This general principle first occurred to me in the context of music and the psychology of thinking. My interest in the psychology of thinking also generated conceptions of problem solving and creative thought on which I worked from about 1912 until I finished a book, *Productive Thinking*, shortly before my death (1982). It is this phase of Gestalt theory on which I will concentrate my remarks today. The psychology of productive thinking, as much as the psychology of music, perception, personality, and social phenomena, provides rich examples of the need for a precise, rigorous, and experimental holism. That is what Gestalt theory is about.

To finish my own story, I worked in Berlin for a number of years and then was called to the chair in philosophy and psychology at the University of Frankfurt in 1929. I had married a young student of mine, Anna Caro, in 1923, and we had three children in rapid succession: Valentin (who became a lawyer) in 1925, Michael (who became a psychology professor) in 1927, and Lise (who also became a psychology professor) in 1928. By 1933 the political situation in Germany had deteriorated to such an extent that it became clear we should leave. My Jewish ancestry posed a danger to the welfare of my family. So we left for Czechoslovakia early in 1933, and came to the United States that September; I taught at the New School for Social Research in New York from then until my sudden death in 1943.

Returning to my main theme here today, I will share some thoughts on modern cognitive psychology, some on what a Gestalt approach entails, and then some on the extent to which the two may or may not fit together.

PRODUCTIVE THINKING REVISITED

Let me start by paraphrasing and quoting from a preface that my son, with two colleagues who are experts in cognitive psychology, Anders Ericsson and Peter G. Polson, prepared for the 1982 reissue of my book, *Productive Thinking*. I must confess that a few of the things in that preface surprise me a little. Perhaps my son should have been more careful not to agree with certain assertions in it; or he should have rephrased some of the statements to make them more accurate and precise.

The Impact of *Productive Thinking*

Ericsson, Polson and Wertheimer kindly suggest (1982, pp. xiff.) that *Productive Thinking* "was seminal for the period in which it was written, generated much research during the intervening decades, and continues to present relevant challenges to the cognitive psychologist—

indeed to any thoughtful human being—of the 1980's." They point out that I was lecturing on the major themes, and on many of the examples of productive thinking, in the book, before 1920; the book had a long gestation. It was written in the context of the prevailing theoretical paradigms of that time, derived from Wundtian elementism, British associationism, and American behaviorism, all of which assumed that rigorous experimental work on the acquisition of simple associations or stimulus–response connections would lead to a complete understanding of all human conduct, complex as well as simple. While such paradigms probably can account fairly well for *reproductive* thinking, my book showed that they cannot account for *productive* thinking, that is, for true understanding of conceptual problems and relationships.

For several decades, my colleagues and I (e.g., Duncker, Katona, Koffka, Köhler) demonstrated the necessity of considering integrated mental structures, with organized subparts whose characteristics are determined by their place, role and function in these structures, if one is fully to understand cognition in general and problem solving in particular. Ericsson et. al, suggest that this work, together with the work of Bartlett (1932), Polya (1945) and others, yielded detailed descriptions of examples of problem solving and thinking whose scientific explication requires analysis of complex mental structures and processes. They generously assert that these demonstrations are the bedrock on which modern theories of such complex cognitive processes as remembering, problem solving, and thinking have been constructed.

The Emergence of the Information-Processing Paradigm

The authors claim that there was little progress in the development of the understanding of such phenomena between the early 1940s and the late 1950s, because the conceptual tools were lacking for building theories about complex mental structures and about processes that can operate on these structures to produce intelligent behavior. But this changed with the publication of Chomsky's (1957) work on transformational grammar and especially of Newell, Shaw, and Simon's (1958) description of a computer program that could solve problems in propositional logic, and of their General Problem Solver (1962). Such developments, they assert, demonstrated that mental structures, including goals and the processes that generate and manipulate them, can be described with complete rigor. This, incidentally, is one of the places where I think my son may have been a bit careless: do these programs really describe the processes that *generate* and *manipulate* mental structures and goals? Manipulate, maybe, but generate, probably not. I will return to such questions later. At any rate, the coauthors of the preface point out that General Problem Solver successfully simulates the steps taken by college students in solving elementary problems in logic. It generates goals and subgoals (or "ends"), they say, in order to select the next step (or "means") in moving toward the solution for a problem, and they assert, perhaps somewhat incautiously, that these goals and other processes are in some respects similar to the structures and processes that were described earlier by various members of the Gestalt school.

Newell and Simon (1972) and Simon (1978) have detailed the information-processing paradigm for problem solving. This widely accepted model describes problem solving as a "goal-directed search" among a variety of possible solutions within a specified "problem space." Such a model does a reasonably good job of simulating the problem-solving efforts of people who have little knowledge about or experience with attempting to solve puzzles, especially with the means–ends analysis that is such an ingenious part of the General Problem Solver. But explanations based on such goal-directed search mechanisms cannot describe how experts in a domain go about solving a problem in the area of their expertise.

Reproductive Thinking, Schemas, and Insight

So, much of this simulation remains closer to what I have called "blind" or senseless reproductive thinking than to truly insightful productive thinking. If one is to retain this general model, the theoretical conceptualization of understanding itself must be much further developed and refined. Cognitive psychologists have indeed been grappling during the last decade with the processes and structures underlying understanding in a number of different domains, and have suggested that complex abstract knowledge structures, such as schemata, scripts, or frames, can account for text comprehension and many other cognitive processes.

Several analyses of the role of understanding in problem solving are based on work in linguistics and in artificial intelligence. Current models assume that successful comprehension involves the construction of an appropriate mental representation of a problem, using processes and knowledge structures that are somehow organized into one or more relevant schemata. In this usage, a "schema" is a complex knowledge structure that represents three things: (1) the goals that can be satisfied by execution of the operations contained in the schema, (2) the conditions under which the schema can be applied, including the prerequisites for the successful execution of the schema's procedures, and (3) the knowledge structures and processes that are involved in the achievement of the schema's goals. A relatively low-level schema may represent the steps required to solve a very specific problem, the kind of structure involved in blind mechanical or reproductive thinking. More meaningful learning, Ericsson, Polson and Wertheimer point out, requires at a minimum the generalization of an existing lower-level schema; "insight" is then characterized as the discovery of the applicability of an existing schema to a novel situation.

Our triumvirate next make the insightful observation that (p. xv) "modern workers have as yet very little understanding of such discovery processes." They mention that Anderson, Greeno, Kline, and Neves (1981), in attempting to describe a possible mechanism for schema generalization, suggest that becoming an expert in a domain requires the acquisition of a large number of "general" schemata. But (p. xv) "how these schemas are integrated so as to yield understanding and insight. . .is still far from clear." I am tempted to add that it is also far from clear how a computer program could know which one of a large number of "general schemas" will be reasonable to try on a particular new problem. I believe that this is one of the major shortcomings of modern cognitive psychology, and will return to this issue later.

Ericsson, Polson, and Wertheimer elaborate on this point by summarizing Greeno's (1977) analysis of the relationship between the outcomes of what they call "such an understanding process" and successful problem solving. This kind of "understanding process" yields a successful solution if three criteria are met: (1) the representation corresponds to the actual structure of the problem (I might add that this is the crux of the issue); (2) the representation is well integrated in the sense that all of its components are appropriately interconnected; and (3) the representation is well integrated with the problem solver's other knowledge. The authors observe that representations that work do have precisely these properties. But they add (p. xv) that "the processes that generate genuinely productive thinking (i.e., that yield representations which can in fact be used successfully in problem solving) still remain elusive." A blind or mechanical application of schema-generalization is not apt to be productive; the restructuring and insight emphasized in my book are still missing in the contemporary models. That is the conclusion of which I hope to convince you by the end of my talk.

BASIC FEATURES OF GESTALT THEORY

Let me next remind you of some essential aspects of the Gestalt approach. I will begin with some quotations and paraphrases from a chapter that my son wrote on the Gestalt theory of learning a few years ago (1980). Parts of this chapter, it seems to me, *do* demonstrate a reasonably good grasp of what Gestalt psychology is about. Maybe there is hope for him yet.

How about the most basic concept: What is a Gestalt? It is an articulated whole, a system, within which the constituent parts are in dynamic interrelation with one another and with the whole, an integrated totality within which each part and subpart has the place, role, and function required for it by the nature of the whole. It is the antithesis of a sum, or of a bundle, or of a tree diagram or of a flow chart whose component parts happen to be connected. The structure of a Gestalt is such that alteration of one part inevitably also produces changes in other parts and in the whole itself; parts of a Gestalt structure are not isolated components that are indifferent to one another. A slight displacement of one playing card in a house of cards may make the entire structure come tumbling down. A break at one tiny point in a soap bubble produces an instant and dramatic change in the entire whole. In a Gestalt, the nature of the whole and of its constituent parts are all integrated. The characteristics of the whole determine the characteristics of each part and its function in the whole, and the characteristics of various parts are mutually interdependent.

The Nature of the Learning Process

Gestalt theory holds that a mechanical, associative, inert image of the psyche does not do justice to the richness, creativity, and intricately organized nature of mental processes and events. At the core of genuine learning is understanding, insight, catching on. Associative hookups are empty caricatures of real learning which, instead, is characterized by getting to the heart of an issue, by being true to the specific nature and structure of the material being learned, and by the satisfying experience of understanding something that previously made no sense—the "Aha!" experience of genuine insight. Typically, learning is a process of going from a situation in which something does not make sense to a state in which the previously unknown or incomprehensible now is clear, is understood, and can be coped with readily. Let me give you a little example. Long ago we hired a new immigrant to help with housework in our house in a suburb of New York City. She soon learned to answer the phone, too. One day the phone rang, and I heard her answer, "Yes. . . yes. . . it sure is," and then hang up. Moments later it rang again, and the same sequence occurred. When it happened a third time, "Yes. . . yes. . . it sure is," and she hung up, I couldn't contain my curiosity. I asked her what the calling party had said. She told me "Is this the Wertheimer residence?, so I answered yes; then he asked whether Professor Wertheimer is at home, and I said yes; then he said 'Long distance from Washington.' And I said it sure is."

The transition from not making sense to making sense is what learning is all about. Learning has occurred when the learner has understood, has developed insight into the actual nature of the problem situation, and can act in ways that show that the relevant features of the task have indeed been grasped. If understanding has occurred, it is only a minor step, one that presents little difficulty, to transfer the learning to a new situation to which it also applies. Thus one test of whether learning has really happened is to check whether what has been learned will generalize to a related task—if all that has transpired is sheer memorizing or blind associating, the learner will be unable to recognize the similarity between a task that has already been mastered and a new one which, while superficially quite different, requires the same insight to solve it that also worked in the earlier task.

Problem Solving, Representations, and Reorganization

Problem solving requires development of a reasonable, appropriately organized, representation of the problem domain. This can mean going from a chaotic perception of the information provided to an organized, clear, and integrated conception of it; or it can mean reorganizing an erroneous conception of the problem into one that works. Many a problem is such that the first time people encounter it, they have no idea how to go about solving it, and the problem may, indeed, initially appear quite incomprehensible or opaque. Solution becomes possible only when the central features of the problem are clearly recognized, and paths to a possible approach emerge. Irrelevant features must be stripped away, core features must become salient, and a representation must be developed that veridically reflects how various parts of the problem fit together; relations among parts, and between parts and whole, must be understood. To repeat, the test of understanding is whether the insight that has been acquired can be transferred to other problem situations that are structurally similar but which differ in superficial detail.

Problem solving, then, typically involves reorganization. It involves developing a representation that does justice to the relevant aspects of the problem domain. Further, an insightful approach to problem solving avoids stupid errors of a kind that might occur with a blind or mechanical approach. What is learned can be transferred insightfully to appropriate new situations; senseless transfers to situations in which they could not work are never attempted.

The Höffding Step

This process of appropriate transfer is one aspect of a phenomenon that Gestalt theorists called the Höffding step, after the Danish philosopher-psychologist Harald Höffding who identified it late in the 19th century. How do you know that a particular strategy might work in a particular situation? More generally, how do you recognize a new situation as one that, in some form or another, you have encountered before? For example, how do you know that a person you meet at a party is someone you met before? Höffding suggested that *similarity* is the crucial determinant of recognition. When you meet someone for the first time, this experience (call it *A*) sets up a trace in your long-term memory store (call it *a*). Later you run across this same person again, producing the experience *A'*. How is it possible for you to recognize the person as someone you have seen before? Obviously, the new experience, *A'*, must somehow make contact with the memory trace, *a*, that was set down during the first encounter, *A*. But the only way that *A'* can make contact with *a* is through their *similarity*. Comparably, transfer of a solution for a familiar problem (*a*) to a new problem (*A'*) can occur only if the solver is capable of seeing the similarity between the two. Recognition of this similarity is the crucial step, the Höffding step, that makes transfer possible. It is a step that requires insight into the applicability of the old solution approach to the new problem. The crucial step in insight or understanding is knowing what solution strategy to try; thereafter, application of the strategy is relatively trivial.

From Above Down Rather than From Below Up: Analysis and Synthesis

One more point about classical Gestalt theory before going on to the question of the extent to which modern cognitive psychology encompasses or solves the Gestalt problem. This point concerns the ancient logical distinction between analysis and synthesis. Gestalt theorists have always favored analysis over synthesis. Rival approaches advocated that one should start with the elements, and try to understand how their combination yields the whole. This is the synthetic approach, and over the centuries it has been proposed with a wide variety of elements: simple ideas, sensory attributes, stimuli and responses, reflexes, concepts, nodes in a semantic net, and, now, switches in microcomputers. By contrast, the Gestalt approach admonishes that analysis should proceed from above down rather than from below up; this strategy recognizes the primacy of the whole and its decisive role in articulating its parts. To do justice to the integrated, articulated, and dynamic nature of a whole, it is essential to start at the level of the whole and to work down to its constituent parts, rather than attempt to ascend to the level of the Gestalt characteristics of the whole by beginning with elements that are presumed to make it up.

GESTALT IDEAS IN "MODERN" DRESS?

Let me now speak to the question of the extent to which modern cognitive psychology reflects some of these older Gestalt concerns, before going on to the more crucial question of the extent to which modern cognitive psychology speaks to the major Gestalt problem of meaning, understanding, reorganization, and insight, the core of what Gestalt theory considered characteristic of genuine thinking. A superficial glance at recent literature may yield the impression that, quite aside from some influence of Gestalt thought on contemporary work in perception, cognitive psychology today incorporates at least three major Gestalt ideas: part–whole relations, top–down processing, and insight. But a closer look shows that this impression is illusory. The specifically Gestalt aspect of these ideas has disappeared.

Part–Whole Relations

In modern cognitive psychology, the part-whole issue is not how the whole determines the nature of the parts, nor how parts are integrated so as to perform the functions that the nature of the whole requires them to perform. Rather, it is the distinction between a whole system or program or sum and its subsystems or subroutines or subsums. In modern cognitive psychology, to exaggerate a bit, two quarters and a silver dollar could make up a whole of $1.50, the parts of which are the silver dollar and the two quarters. From the Gestalt point of view, such inert sums are not a Gestalt within which there are meaningful parts: they are mere conglomerates without any of the dynamic attributes of a genuine Gestalt. Similarly, a complex microcomputer program with various subroutines that can be plugged into it is not a whole with meaningful parts in the Gestalt sense because adding these components together does not yield a transsummative whole with parts. Only if there is top–down determination of the characteristics of the parts is it reasonable, from the Gestalt point of view, to speak of part–whole relationships.

"Top-Down" and "Bottom-Up" Processing

The use of the phrase "top–down" in modern cognitive psychology is also different from its use in Gestalt theory. A few minutes ago I emphasized the advantage of analysis over synthesis. That is what Gestalt theory meant by going from above down rather than from below up. But this is different from the comparison between "theory-driven" and "data-driven" strategies in problem solving or learning, as referred to in modern cognitive psychology by the terms "top–down" and "bottom–up"; whether you start with a rule or with a concrete instance of a rule has nothing to do with whether you are going from a whole to one of its parts or from a part to its superordinate whole. The similarity between "from above down" and "top-down proccessing," then, is purely verbal; it ends there; the meanings of the two phrases really have nothing in common.

Insight

How about the fate of the Gestalt concept of "insight" itself in the context of the information-processing models that dominate modern cognitive psychology? It is not fully integrated into these models. In fact it tends to be rather badly distorted and misunderstood, as is demonstrated by a series of studies by Weisberg and his colleagues (e.g., Weisberg, 1980)[1]. Weisberg tried to explain subjects' performances on traditional "insight" problems from an information-processing viewpoint, and claimed that Gestalt ideas of "insight" and of "fixation" are neither necessary nor useful in accounting for problem-solving behavior. Weisberg argues that Gestalt theorists claim that the puzzles they studied initially pose difficulties because subjects are fixated on unwarranted assumptions about the problems and that this fixation interferes with the insight needed to solve the problems; if the source of fixation is removed, the solution should occur suddenly. To solve an insight problem, one must view the problem in a new, restructured way, which does not depend on past experience. "The term insight," writes Weisberg (1980, p. 288), "is sometimes taken to mean that one solves such problems by 'seeing into' the structure of the problem in a flash of illumination. Supposedly, this insight enables one to produce a truly

---

[1] This account of Weisberg's studies is paraphrased from a fine paper by Mark Schlager for a graduate seminar at the University of Colorado.

creative solution, one which is relatively independent of past experience."

Weisberg then tries to debunk the ideas of insight and fixation by demonstrating that subjects achieve "insightful" solutions simply by using their past experience, that lack of insightful solutions is not due to fixation, and that even when the assumption that presumably caused the fixation is removed, the problem does not become easy to solve. His findings with several different problems lead him to the conclusion that insight problems are difficult because the instructions call forth obvious "solutions" that fail to solve the problem. The subjects cannot immediately see that these solutions will not work, and sometimes the correct solution is not obvious even after the erroneous solutions are abandoned. Weisberg concludes that in solving such problems, subjects develop a representation based on past experience and on the information provided in the problem. In constructing this representation, subjects retrieve from memory only information that is relevant to the nature of the problem, and if the problem cannot be solved directly, the subject modifies the way in which the information is conceived by forming a new representation; solutions achieved with this new representation can then be transferred to other new problems, as long as they are similar.

Do these findings and conclusions demolish the tenability of the Gestalt concepts of "fixation" (functional fixedness) and of insight? No. Classical Gestalt theory drew many of the same conclusions as Weisberg himself. Köhler (1929), for instance, characterized insight as including an understanding of the "why" and "how" of a phenomenon; "there is no mere sequence of indifferent events, connected indirectly. Each phase of what happens grows out of its predecessors, depending upon their concrete nature" (p. 390). A situation is experienced without insight if none of its states depends on, or determines, another. Köhler also suggests that automatic processes cannot be considered insightful because only the result is experienced, not its "why" and "how." Insightful behavior is goal-directed behavior in which each state is related meaningfully to the preceding ones and to the next ones, in accord with an accurate representation (or model, if you like) of the whole sequence. Partial insights, as described, for example, by Duncker (1945), are part of the eventual development of the appropriate representation. Köhler refers neither to sudden illumination nor to total independence from prior experience. But *Productive Thinking* (1982, pp. 170–171) does characterize the restructuring of a problem as a "sudden radical transformation from a first to a second view," and suggests that blind behavior may be due to sticking to a certain view out of habit. A problem is described there as a structurally incomplete situation (S1), a structurally complete situation (S2) and the steps or operations involved in changing S1 into S2. The particular concrete nature and structural features of S1 lead one to perform the particular operations necessary to satisfy the concrete requirements of S2. This process typically occurs gradually, rather than all at once. The understanding process (p. 240) does not involve merely the given parts and their transformations. It works with structurally relevant material that is selected from past experience. But the information recalled from past experience is not, of course, simply thrown together. Only information which is consistent with changing S1 to S2 is used, and only in accordance with the requirements of S2.

Perhaps the point need not be further belabored. The results of Weisberg's studies, and indeed his own interpretations, are fully consistent with the classic Gestalt view of insight.

COGNITIVE PSYCHOLOGY AND THE PROBLEM OF UNDERSTANDING

But let me, finally, get to the main point of my talk. Does modern cognitive psychology succeed in solving what I have been calling the Gestalt problem, the problem of meaning, of understanding, of insight? I would like first to acknowledge some of the brilliant achievements of modern cognitive science, both in artificial intelligence and in information processing. Programs with artificial intelligence, of course, work in ways that are very different from how people, even people with extraordinary intelligence, actually think; their intent is not to simulate human thought but rather to come to optimal decisions. They do better than most human experts in such tasks as finding oil, predicting the weather, making accurate medical diagnoses, detecting hostile missiles, and playing chess with their prodigious perfect memory, their brute force search, and occasionally the ingenious heuristics built into them. As for information-processing models, some have been constructed that do a fine job of simulating how people actually go about solving problems, especially problems in domains with which they are not familiar. Programs exist that accurately simulate the solution efforts, including fine-grain aspects such as patterns of errors, of students working on such puzzles as the water-jar problems (e.g., Atwood, Masson, & Polson, 1980), the cannibals and missionaries (or, as it is now called, the Hobbits and Orcs) river-crossing problems (e.g., Jeffries, Polson, Razran, & Atwood, 1977), the towers of Hanoi (e.g., Ernst & Newell, 1969) and even the geometrical task of proving the equality of vertical angles that is discussed in Chapter 3 of *Productive Thinking* (Greeno, 1982).

The Cognitive Psychology Strategy

Products of work in cognitive science, then, can generate solutions to highly circumscribed problems better than most people can, and can generate patterns of solution efforts that are indistinguishable from the patterns generated by people confronted by the same problem. How do they do this? Both kinds of programs use a *representation* of a problem, and systematic *search* through the problem domain for a solution[2]. Problems have been described as a set of world states along with a set of operators whose execution transforms these states into others. For example, in chess, the world states are board positions of the chess pieces at any point in the game and the set of operators is legal moves for the pieces. This "problem space" can be represented as a graph whose nodes represent world states and whose links represent transformations from one state to another. Given this representation, the process of problem solving consists of a search through the problem space, that is, finding a path from the start node to the node in the graph that represents the goal to be reached. The problem space can be traversed in three ways: blind search, evaluation functions, and heuristic search. Blind search is a brute force method in which each path is explored until the goal is found. A solution is assured, but the time and expense required can be enormous. Evaluation functions allow the graph to be pared to a more manageable size through the elimination of branches. For example, if a fatal move is found somewhere on a branch, the entire branch is avoided. Various kinds of heuristic search all involve some type of shortcut that reduces the time and expense required to search the problem space but does not ensure that the goal will be found (much less an optimal path to it). Means/ends analysis is a search heuristic in which the space is searched backwards, that is, from goal to start state. Essentially, the present state and the goal state are compared, differences are noted, and a table of connections is consulted to find the operator(s) that can reduce the differences.

Shortcomings of a "General Problem Solver"

This is the basic approach of the pioneer General Problem Solver (Newell, Shaw and Simon, 1962), and of many similar programs that

---

[2]This and the next three paragraphs are paraphrased or quoted from another fine paper, by Denise Dellarosa, for the same graduate seminar.

have been written or described since. Such an approach has several shortcomings, some of which have already been mentioned. First, while means/ends analysis adequately describes the problem-solving activity of novices, it does *not* satisfactorily describe that of experts. The primary difference between novice and expert approaches to problem solving appears to be the degree of complexity or richness of the problem representation generated (Greeno, 1977). Problem representations generated by experts are usually well integrated and coherent, and contain much domain-specific knowledge. Representations generated by novices, by contrast, tend to be loosely integrated, and dominated by information given in the problem description itself.

The second shortcoming is related to the first. As Halasz (1982) points out, problems usually modeled using this approach (e.g., the towers of Hanoi) are ones in which the role of prior knowledge is trivial or unnecessary. As a result, the whole emphasis of problem solving is on finding strategies for *searching* through the problem space quickly and efficiently. But more naturalistic problem solving, such as natural language understanding or trouble shooting, is a knowledge-intensive activity; a significant amount of domain-specific knowledge must be represented and used in solving problems in these domains.

Basically, models are a way of representing the mental state associated with insight. An insightful state can be viewed as a model in which entities necessary for problem solution and their relevant properties are represented in correct relations to one another. Indeed, once the correct relations are "seen" (i.e., represented), the necessary solution path should simply run off. A good model will represent only information that is necessary to problem solution. If a problem is particularly difficult, *knowing which information is necessary for its solution* and which is irrelevant is a non-trivial problem in itself. This is at the heart of what I have called the Gestalt problem. Also at its heart is that choosing the correct model with which to represent the known domain is anything but a trivial choice; guidelines for matching models to tasks have not yet been forthcoming.

Blind Rigidity vs. Meaning and Understanding

Models like the General Problem Solver, then, describe how problems are solved *once they are understood*. The problems must be fed to such programs with all the relevant information already extracted, and organized in an insightful way. No program exists that can set up a problem in a form in which a computer can solve it; formulating a problem in a meaningful way requires extensive well-organized relevant knowledge. General Problem Solver and other programs like it are, then, elegant but blind models of the search procedures *once the problem has been understood.* As Newell (1983) admits, even the best current expert programs and systems are all "shallow"; they don't know what they know and why they know it.

Where, then, are meaning, understanding, insight, in the computer models that make up the bulk of modern cognitive psychology? Let's start with meaning. As everyone who has interacted with a computer knows, computers are excruciatingly literal: the rigor that is necessary in interacting with a computer has, as a corollary, rigor mortis. That is why computer translations from one language to another so frequently result in gibberish; context determines meaning in exquisite ways in natural language, ways that would require an enormous computer memory even to specify, for example, the possible connotative and denotative meanings of the spoken English word, "well." Flexibility in specification of a concept or idea is not one of a computer's strengths. Further, I don't know of any computer with a sense of humor. Could a program generate the following brief *Reader's Digest* filler? "Ahhh, the jet age. Breakfast in Paris; dinner in Hong Kong; luggage in Peoria." Meaning in computers is hopelessly, rigidly, and unimaginatively literal. They have no imagination, no creativity.

CONCLUSION

Where is the insight and understanding in a computer model? Nowhere. Among other things, the Höffding step is missing. The process of mapping the real world into the computer is not something the computer can perform. All the computer can do is stay within the map itself, not translate from the map back to the real world. It cannot generate appropriate representations, and know when it has one and when it doesn't have one. Insight and understanding are *presupposed* by the program; they are prior to the program. The organizing, the thinking, the understanding, the reorganizing are all in the *programmer*, not in the program. Let's face it, what the computer and the program can do is trivial in comparison with what the programmer must do in coming up with the "right" representation. Representation and search in a computer program are the final product of an insightful thinking process, and include no insight or thought themselves. How do you know in which domain a problem is? The computer doesn't; the programmer does. How do you know what program to call up for a particular purpose? That takes understanding, and the Höffding step, on the part of the programmer. How do you know what representation to construct or to use for a particular situation? That takes understanding, and must be built into the program. How do you know what information to feed into the computer, and in what form? That requires understanding of what is relevant, and of the computer's literal dictionary. How do you know when you have actually found what you were looking for, the solution? That takes understanding of the similarity of what is required by the problem and of the particular relevant aspects of the solution itself: again the Höffding step.

To summarize, computers don't have ideas, only strings of symbols that map precisely onto what is already in their memory or can be processed by them; if the exact wording happens to be wrong, the computer is helpless. It cannot map symbols onto their real-world meanings. Indeed, computers can't even decode meaningful words: A 3-year-old child can recognize the word "cat" when it is said by 10 different people, even by strangers, but at least so far no computer can. Worse, computers can't recognize concepts, only particular literal strings of symbols. Computers can't recognize principles, nor can they tell you which principles apply in a particular case. What it all comes down to is that computers do not understand; no computer can go from not understanding to understanding. Computers may be excellent for blind (or even partly directed) literal search through the particular domain you happen to have coded into their potentially enormous memory, and for blind operations on information stored in them, but they have no understanding either of the meanings of the symbols they contain and manipulate or of the structure of any problem (no insight). All of the requisite thinking, insight, and understanding go into the writing of the program; once the program is running, neither the computer nor the program nor the combination of hardware and software *thinks*: all the thinking has been done beforehand, and was used in constructing the program.

Does, then, modern cognitive psychology do justice to the Gestalt problem of insight and understanding? It is true that some contemporary psychologists are valiantly trying to deal with the issue of where appropriate and relevant representations and operations come from, but no computer models have anything to say about this core issue. So from the perspective of the book *Productive Thinking*, the answer is an unequivocal no. Computers can certainly be *productive*, but none of them is capable of *thinking*. It's not that the modern information-processing approaches are *wrong* as such; they simply don't speak to the issue of insight. They have bypassed it completely. So the basic Gestalt problem remains as unsolved — and as crucial — as it was before modern cognitive psychology came on the scene.

ACKNOWLEDGMENTS

Based on an invited lecture, part of a series on *Seven Psychologies Revisited*, presented at the annual convention of the American Psychological Association, Anaheim, California, August 26, 1983. An edited version of this address appeared under the title "A Gestalt perspective on computer simulations of cognitive processes," in *Computers in Human Behavior*, 1985, *1*, 19–33.

REFERENCES

Anderson, J. R., Greeno, J. G., Kline, P. J., & Neves, D. M. (1981). Acquisition of problem-solving skills. In J. R. Anderson, (Ed.), *Cognitive skills and their acquisition.* Hillsdale, NJ: Lawrence Erlbaum Associates.

Atwood, M. E., Masson, M. E. J,. & Polson, P. G. (1980). Further explorations with a process model for water jug problems. *Memory and Cognition, 8,* 182–192.

Bartlett, F.C. (1932). *Remembering: A study in experimental and social psychology.* Cambridge, England: Cambridge University Press.

Chomsky, N. (1957). *Syntactic structures.* The Hague: Mouton.

Duncker, K. (1945). On problem solving. *Psychological Monographs, 58,* Whole No. 270.

Ericsson, A., Polson, P. G., & Wertheimer, M. (1982). Preface to the Phoenix edition. In M. Wertheimer (Ed.), *Productive thinking* (pp. xi–xvii). Chicago: University of Chicago Press.

Ernst, G. W., & Newell, A. (1969). *GPS: A case study in generality and problem solving.* New York: Academic Press.

Greeno, J. G. (1977). Process of understanding in problem solving. In N.J. Castellan, D. B. Pisoni, & G. R. Potts (Eds.), *Cognitive theory* (Vol. 2). Hillsdale, NJ: Lawrence Erlbaum Associates.

Greeno, J. G. (1982). *Forms of understanding in mathematical problem solving.* Technical Report No. UPITT/LRDC/ONR/APS–10, University of Pittsburgh, August, 1982.

Halasz, F. (1982). *Trouble shooting: Problem solving in a knowledge-intensive domain.* Palo Alto, CA: Applied Information Processing Project, Xerox Palo Alto Research Center, Memo No. 172.

Jeffries, R., Polson, P. G., Razran, L., & Atwood, M. E . (1977). A process model for missionaries–cannibals and other river crossing problems. *Cognitive Psychology, 9,* 412–440.

Köhler, W. (1929). *Gestalt psychology.* New York: Liveright.

Newell, A. (1983). *The next problems for artificial intelligence.* Lecture held at the University of Colorado, Boulder, April 25.

Newell, A., Shaw, J. C., & Simon, H. A. (1958). Elements of a theory of human problem solving. *Psychological Review, 65,* 151–166.

Newell, A., Shaw, J. C., & Simon, H. A. (1962). The process of creative thinking. In H. E. Gruber, G. Terrell, & M. Wertheimer (Eds.), *Contemporary approaches to creative thinking.* New York: Atherton.

Newell, A., & Simon, H. G. (1972). *Human problem solving.* Englewood Cliffs, NJ: Prentice-Hall.

Polya, G. (1945). *How to solve it*. Princeton, NJ: Princeton University Press.

Simon, H. A. (1978). Information-processing theory of human problem solving. In W.K. Estes (Ed.),*Handbook of learning and cognitive processes, Vol. 5: Human information processing*. Hillsdale, NJ: Lawrence Erlbaum Associates.

Weisberg, R. W. (1980). *Memory, thought, and behavior*. New York: Oxford University Press.

Wertheimer, M. (1980). Gestalt theory of learning. In G. M. Gazda, & R. J. Corsini (Eds.), *Theories of learning: A comparative approach*. Itasca, IL: Peacock.

Wertheimer, M. (1982). *Productive thinking*. (Enlarged ed.; Phoenix ed.). Chicago: University of Chicago Press.

Chapter 14

Psychology from the Standpoint of a Mechanist: An Appreciation of Clark L. Hull

Gregory A. Kimble

As you read this chapter, you should imagine yourself in New Haven in the spring of 1952. Ruth Hays, Clark L. Hull's secretary, has just brought you into Hull's office and introduced you as a group of psychologists visiting the Institute of Human Relations at Yale. Because of his infirmity, Hull is seated, with his foot up on a stool and his cane leaning against his chair. On a table at his elbow is a stacked set of gray, cloth-bound notebooks.

BACKGROUND

Good Morning. It is a great pleasure to welcome you all to the institute. I gather that you want to hear about my previous work and my plans for the future. I will be glad to discuss these things with you. Miss Hays will protect us from interruptions for the next hour or so.

As you know, Garry Boring has just come out with the fourth volume of the *History of Psychology in Autobiography*. I am in it. So are Richard M. Elliott, who edited my books for the Century Psychology Series, L. L. Thurstone, whose scaling methods I have been using to quantify reaction potential, and Edward Chace Tolman, my strongest competitor in the field of learning theory. Rereading my own biography, I wish now that I had done it differently. I failed to communicate a good many

*Photograph of Clark L. Hull courtesy of the Archives of the History of Psychology, Akron, Ohio

things that would help people understand me better. I especially failed to get across the most important ambition of my life—to produce a mechanistic analysis of the higher mental processes. This was to be my magnum opus. But so far it has not been completed.

I am old now, and I doubt that the time remains for me to do the job myself. If I had put some of my ideas into the autobiography, some younger man might have picked them up and carried on with the work. With this thought in mind, I have been going through these notebooks— my idea books, I call them. There are 27 altogether, that I have been keeping for 50 years. You haven't really asked me to, but I would like to share with you some of the memories that this review brought back to me.

BEGINNINGS

I began these notebooks in the autumn of 1902 when I went away from home for the first time, to attend high school in West Saginaw, Michigan. I was 18 then and in the 10th grade. No, I was not retarded. In fact, I had already had a brief career as a schoolteacher. But I am getting ahead of the story. It is better to take things up in order.

I was born in 1884 in a log cabin near Akron, New York. My father was a farmer, a giant of a man with an ugly temper. He usually became profane when angry. My mother was a contrast. She was a gentle person who had married my father when she was 15. She had had some schooling and was able to read better than my father, who had very little education. She helped him to improve his reading after they were married.

When I was 3 or 4, the family moved to Michigan. I went to a one-room school until I was 16. An ambitious teacher had given me some special work in algebra and geography so that I passed the teacher's examination at 17. This gave me the credential to teach in a one-room school myself for a year. During that year, two things happened that made me realize that I should further my education.

The first thing will occur to you at once. It quickly turned out that even students in that backwoods school brought up questions that I couldn't answer. The second thing was that I got religion and then lost it. I and several other youngsters were "converted" by a group of Bible-thumping Methodist revivalists. But this new religiosity was short-lived with me. I soon began to develop doubts.

Perhaps this reaction was a biological inevitability in my case. My first paternal ancestor to come to this country was a heretical Church of England clergyman who settled in Massachusetts in 1635. Not many of his descendants were religious. My grandfather was one of the few pious ones, a Deacon in the Baptist Church. But my father professed no religion at all. I myself went to church on Sunday, as a youth, and took an intellectual interest in theology. But I was never a devout Christian. In fact, my opinions so verged on atheism that at one point I considered myself qualified to become a minister in the Unitarian Church, which I saw as a free-thinking, essentially godless enterprise.

To get back to my story, however, the importance of my brief encounter with religion was that I soon realized that I lacked the knowledge to argue for the doubts I could only feel. It was on these bases that I gave up my career in teaching, returned to high school and, as I mentioned before, began to keep my idea books (Ammons, 1962).

WHY THE IDEA BOOKS?

In my autobiography I say that I kept these notebooks as an aid to memory and to getting my thoughts in order. But they didn't begin that way. My first entry refers to the notebooks as "a daily record of the events which transpire under my observation." It goes on to express the ambition that "I may someday rise to a position among men where I can look back with pride at the time when I was an obscure choreboy. This will serve to more clearly preserve the memory of my doings and the thoughts and desires which animated my being." I was 18 when I wrote that.

Later on, when I was 32, I saw the value of the notebooks differently. Then I wrote, "When I get old, and my mind gets still and I am no longer able to conjure up new notions and points of departure, I may turn again to these notes and find them still warm and intimate in my hand. I shall thus preserve my youth, or at least the most valuable trait of it, to my years of greatest ability to criticize theories. Thus I shall have, in my later years, the chief advantages of youth while largely escaping its weaknesses."

As you can see, some of the content of these notebooks is fairly personal, and I think appropriate for my own eyes only. I can remember only one time when I thought that the materials on a page were so revealing that it should be torn from a notebook, but what remains would tell people more about C. L. Hull than they really ought to know. The *entire* content of these notebooks certainly never should be made public.

THE TWIG IS BENT

After a year in West Saginaw, I transferred to the academy associated with Alma College in Alma, Michigan, where I was later to go to school for a while. At the academy, the most important event in my intellectual life occurred. This was the study of geometry, which gave me a concept of deducing new relationships from established premises. At one time, I even tried to use the geometrical method to prove some heretical religious propositions. I never got far with this project, however, probably because I had decided to become a mining engineer. The abstract side of geometry would not be very relevant for such ambitions, and there was little to keep me at it. But the germ of an idea had been planted. Later on in my life, I would become famous for the use of what we called the "hypothetico-deductive method." Now I think that an earlier expression of mine, "logical empiricism," is more accurate. But, however that may be, the method is the method I originally came to appreciate in the study of geometry.

Germs of ideas are one thing. Real germs are something else and two of them got to me not too much later. First I caught typhoid fever and almost died from some contaminated food they served at a college dinner. This left me amnesic for the events that happened in the month before the illness and with a very bad memory for details and names that I have to this day. I am sure that this is one thing that kept me at these notebooks.

The second germ was poliomyelitis, which I caught after 2 years at Alma College, still intending to become a mining engineer. I was left with one leg so badly paralyzed that I could manage to locomote only with the aid of a steel brace that I designed myself and had constructed at a local blacksmith shop. By then, I had developed a feel for equipment that has continued to play an important part in my life.

It was at that time that I decided to change my career plans and prepare for a calling that would require less physical activity than mineral engineering. I ended up choosing psychology. By way of preparation, I worked my way through all 1,400 pages of William James's *Principles of Psychology*.

Those bouts of illness made me very much aware of my own mortality. I have always worried that I may not have the time to complete the important projects that I have planned for myself, and from time to time, set down in the pages of my idea books. Back then, of course, I did not see things quite so starkly, and only looked forward to completing my work in my newly chosen field of scientific psychology.

But my education had to be postponed again. Still too weak to be away from home on my own, I got a teaching position in my old school, where I taught the 7th, 8th, 9th, and 10th grades for 2 years. After that, still with poor health, little money, no definite future, and a new wife,

Bertha Iutzi, I left to finish my undergraduate work in Ann Arbor at the University of Michigan.

The freedom at the University of Michigan was a sharp contrast to the narrow religious perspective at Alma College, and I flourished in the new atmosphere. I took a course in logic under Dr. Sellars and once more made good use of my skill with tools. I designed and constructed a logic machine, which consisted of concentric metal plates. One could set up all the syllogisms and logical fallacies on this machine, and just inspection would reveal all of the implications of these logical relationships. More important for the future was that I developed an interest in the evolution of concepts. The theme for my magnum opus had been established.

GRADUATE SCHOOL AT WISCONSIN

I graduated from the University of Michigan with my savings gone, and I had to take a 1-year teaching job at the Normal School in Richmond, Kentucky. They paid me $75 a month to teach psychology and other subjects. During that year I tried to get a graduate fellowship at Yale or Cornell, but both schools turned me down. Eventually I got an appointment at Wisconsin as a teaching assistant to Professor Joseph Jastrow. It was my job to attend Jastrow's lectures, take roll and run recitation sections for the students. Jastrow had a remarkable verbal fluency. Sometimes he would lecture for a full 5 minutes, in perfectly good sentences, and hardly say anything. Naturally, the students had trouble getting anything out of those lectures, and I had trouble finding anything to cover in the quiz sections. When the students complained about Jastrow's lectures, I would just tell them that "Professor Jastrow has a genius of a kind, but it is not of the pedagogical variety."

Although I continued on with Jastrow and did some work on three-dimensional depth perception, I spent most of my 4 years as a graduate student on my dissertation, which was concerned with the evolution of concepts. I had the idea for this work before I came to Wisconsin and had constructed the apparatus for the study. The plan I had devised was to use the methods of Ebbinghaus to study concept formation. In order to do this, I made an automatic memory machine. It consisted of a drum fashioned from a discarded tomato juice can, fitted with wooden ends, through which I ran a metal axle which connected the drum to a frame. The drum advanced in a stepwise fashion, driven by a coarse escapement wheel activated by a system of weights and a pendulum, something like that of a grandfather clock. In those days, a person with a little initiative and a few hand tools could create a perfectly satisfactory psychology laboratory in the wilderness.

As everyone knows, the concepts I studied (Hull, 1920) were those represented in Chinese ideographs. Professor Shepard at Michigan had given me a Chinese–English dictionary, which contained all of the common characters in that curious language. With a little practice, I got so I could copy them quite well and did so to produce the materials for the subjects to master in my research.

The task of the subjects in my experiment was to learn to identify 12 different concepts that could be recognized by a common stroke, called a radical, running through a family of characters. I gave each of these families a nonsense name and the subjects were required to learn to call each example of the concept by this name.

Thinking back, I suppose that it is an important indication of the times that it never occurred to me to give these concepts anything other than nonsense names. Today I am sure that we would use the English

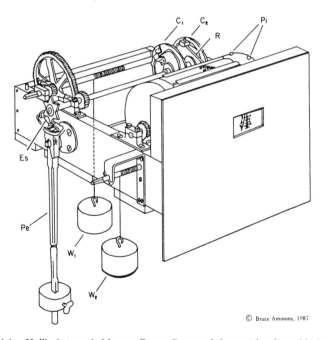

© Bruce Ammons, 1987

FIG. 14.1. *Hull's Automatic Memory Drum.* **Pe**, pendulum with adjustable bob. **Es**, escapement. **C1** and **C2**, interchangeable cams controlling rate of movement of the drum. **R**, rod controlling a secondary escapement, not shown. **Pi**, pins that allow the drum to move in steps that are 1/12 its circumference. **W1** and **W2**, weights that drive the clockwork and the drum separately. (From *Psychology from the Standpoint of a Mechanist: The Early Life and Work of Clark L. Hull*, by Bruce Ammons. Unpublished Doctoral Dissertation. 1987. Duke University)

translations or at least the Chinese words for the concepts. But in those days, we were so obsessed with the notion of experimental control that we did some things that now seem pretty strange.

In my experiment, I used the method of prompting and had the subjects learn a set of individual examples to criterion. Once they had mastered one list, I put 12 new characters, each with one of the same radicals, on the drum and had the subjects learn them by the same method. Eventually they were able to identify all of the radicals and even draw them. It seemed to me in those days that the method had great potential for the objective study of the higher mental processes. It was then, at the age of 30, that a definite plan took form in my mind, to produce a major work that would present a theory of mental operations anchored in experimental data.

COMMITMENT TO MECHANISM

Looking back on the dissertation, it now seems to me that the main idea that persisted in my theorizing was that concepts evolve gradually and that such gradual mastery must be characteristic of all mental operations. Later on, my equation for the growth of habit ($_sH_R$) expressed this notion formally. However that may be, my major project had to be postponed. I was soon to join the faculty at the University of Wisconsin. My first appointment and my first research were in the area of applied psychology. I did one study that showed the bad effects of smoking on steadiness and memory. Later on, I published a book that I now view as one of my major contributions to psychology, *Aptitude Testing*, which came out in 1928.

During that period I continued to exercise my knack for the construction of mechanical apparatus. I invented and built a machine to do correlation coefficients, something I had to do because of a terrible tendency on my part to make errors when I carried out the calculations by hand. At the same time, I got the idea that machines like this might make it possible to do universal vocational guidance automatically. *Actuarial prediction* would have been a good name for the process, if I had happened to think of it.

The greatest significance of this feeling of mine for machinery is that, to this day, it controls my way of looking at psychological processes. For me, the human being is a machine, a queer and complex one, but a machine nonetheless, which requires no ghostly operator to run it. I have always thought that the best way to understand the functions of this machine would be to build a robot that would simulate these functions. If, for example, you want to understand intelligent behavior,

create a machine that has artificial intelligence. Then you would understand it. I had given some thought to how such a machine would work
and what some of its fundamental principles would be, even when I was
working on my dissertation.

One of these fundamental principles would be that every stimulus
spreads all over the body, but in varying amounts. Probably the
stimulation would be too feeble in most places to have an effect. But
some synapses might produce vague and random responses. It occurred
to me that, if I were designing this machine, I would build into it a
tendency for these movements to continue if the stimulus were noxious—until the noxious stimulus disappeared—but to cease if it were
satisfying. In this way the machine could be made to turn off annoying
stimuli and preserve satisfying ones, much as Thorndike's law of effect
insists that it should.

The various parts of the machine would have to be autonomous to a
certain extent, but also subject to certain hierarchies of control by one
part over another. In a vague way it seemed to me that this control
relates to what we call habit. The more I studied the matter the more I
became impressed with the probable importance of a very fluid principle
of habit-hierarchies or stimulus–response hierarchies. This would be a
mechanism by which certain generalized habits, or dispositions, could
act as selecting agents and evoke and control other habits. It struck me
more than once back then that if I could discover this mechanism I could
found a new school of psychology, a school that would be far superior
to Watsonian behaviorism, which had not even appreciated the problem, much less solved it.

As you can imagine, such mechanistic thinking was not universally
appreciated in those days. There was a great deal of interest in
mysticism and the occult. I remember once, soon after I went to
Wisconsin, some friends and I went to a séance, conducted by a
medium, Miss Park, and some mercenary associates of hers, who took
up a collection after the show was over. It was very crudely done and,
besides that, they shamed us into putting all of our money (a dollar or
so) into the collection plate. But it was worth it! Among us we got Miss
Park to call up from the dead and speak to us four people who were
actually living.

On another occasion, I am afraid I made myself quite unpopular by
overt expression of my preference for mechanistic interpretations. Hans
Driesch (who should have stuck to biology, where he made giant
contributions) gave a public talk on paranormal phenomena at Wisconsin. The interest of the people in Madison was so great that by the time
I got there the only seat I could find was an iron chair in the rear of the
auditorium. I must say that I was impressed with Driesch's way with an

audience. He held them spellbound and had them utterly convinced. The only questions from the audience afterward were such as to elicit additional undocumented descriptions of precognition and poltergeists—until I couldn't stand it anymore. So I stood up (a noisy performance, with my brace clanging against the leg of the metal chair) and inquired of Professor Driesch why it was that, when these miraculous happenings occurred, a scientist was never present—only poets, philosophers and others who are not competent to make objective observations. I don't remember how or whether he answered, but it became clear later on that such questions had no effect on Driesch's opinions. In 1929 he published a totally nonsensical theory of entelechy, an all knowing superior mind that allegedly controls the universe. I took him to task for that superstition in *Principles of Behavior*, which was published in 1943.

It has always seemed to me that Gestalt psychology is also in the camp of the mystics. At first I was intrigued by the work of the Gestaltists, and I tried to find a way to go to Giessen, Germany, to spend some time with Koffka. That didn't work out, so being the director of a laboratory by now, I brought Koffka to Wisconsin for a time. We never hit it off, probably because I rejected everything *gestaltisch* too vigorously. Obviously the organization of mental life is a problem, and I don't know that my concepts of habit-family hierarchy and afferent neural interaction are solutions. But Gestalt psychology obscures too much with its subjectivity.

This brings me to Tolman. It is clear enough, as Spence points out in the second edition of Moss's *Comparative Psychology*, that our theories are more similar than they are different. Both are examples of the intervening variable approach and the independent variables and concepts that we use are very much alike. In recent years, with my development of the theory of incentive motivation, even our treatments of the functions of reinforcement have become more similar. We do not agree on the role of reinforcers in the establishment of habits (which Tolman insists on calling expectancies) or on the question of what is learned, but those are the only important disagreements—except for one thing, general intellectual style. Tolman lapses into the subjective and anthropomorphic too often for my taste. If you will promise to keep this to yourselves, I will tell you a personal story that will give you a glimpse of how I react to that sort of thing.

The students in my laboratory, here at Yale, read Tolman's (1938) presidential address to the APA before I did and came to tell me about it. They said that Tolman came right out and admitted that in his future animal work he planned to try to imagine how he would feel and what he would do, if he were the rat in one of his maze experiments. Do you know what I said? This is why we have to keep this to ourselves; I said, "I'll bet the Gestalt son of a bitch can do it, too."

FUNCTIONALISM NOT BEHAVIORISM

Since I have always been so opposed to the subjective and so much of a mechanist, I probably need to explain two things about my career. The first is that I am *not* a behaviorist. Although I am often called a behaviorist, sometimes even by myself, I am not a behaviorist in the Watsonian sense of that term. If you remember my 1929 paper in the *Psychological Review*, you will realize that what I really am is a functionalist, a Darwinian functionalist, you might say. I always try to understand the adaptive value of a bit of behavior or how it functions for the survival of the organism.

In the 1929 paper I tried to show in several different ways that the survival value of the conditioned reflex results from the delicate balance between the excitatory and inhibitory properties of the conditioning mechanism. For example, the excitatory aspect of conditioning is indiscriminate. It leads the organism to respond to situations with just a few of the components of a biologically significant situation. Because situations never repeat themselves exactly, this tendency is adaptive. If it did not exist previous experience would be useless and learning could never occur. But the tendency is also maladaptive because it could lead to responses in situations containing too few components of the important situation. Experimental extinction puts an adaptive damper on the process.

In a very similar way, stimulus generalization (which I was still calling *irradiation*) leads to the adaptive tendency to respond to situations resembling important ones, but simultaneously to a maladaptive tendency to overgeneralize. Differential inhibition keeps such reactions in check and narrows the range of generalization.

Quite a different problem with conditioned excitation is that the process leaves the organism with no way of dealing with patterns of stimulation. This is an important lack. For, as William James once said, "It is one thing to step on a man's foot and then apologize, but quite another to apologize and then step on his foot." Although the mechanism is not very efficient, the process of conditioned inhibition allows the organism to cope with patterning.

Finally, the tendency for conditioned responses to move forward in time is adaptive, because this makes it possible for the organism to react to situations before they eventuate in moments of crisis. But the tendency also leads to the premature appearance of responses before they are required. Inhibition of delay provides the corrective mechanism by forcing a postponement of the response.

In all of these ways the conditioned reflex, with its opposed excitatory and inhibitory phases, stands revealed as an automatic trial-and-error mechanism that mediates (blindly but beautifully) the functional adjustment of the organism to its environment.

I am also not a Watsonian behaviorist in another sense. Watson was naïve and worse. If he had really understood the interpretation of psychological concepts that Tolman was trying to explain to him as early as 1920, he would not have been so quick to brand everything he failed to understand as subjective and discard it. As Carroll Pratt (1939) said later, the trouble with Watson was that he threw the baby out with the bath, the baby being everything interesting in our field, the bath being everything that appeared to be subjective.

HYPNOSIS AND SUGGESTIBILITY

The other thing that may seem odd in the career of a mechanist is that I got involved with hypnosis, surely one of the least objective of all psychological phenomena. My plan, of course, was to produce an objective account of hypnosis, and I think that my book, *Hypnosis and Suggestibility*, published in 1933, comes close to doing that. I have always had mixed feelings about that work. I see it now as the second of my important contributions. The first was the book on aptitude testing. And it did get me a job at Yale. But it also distracted me for 6 years when I might have been working on my magnum opus, the book on the mechanisms of mental life.

I have always been a great one for making lists of the things that I had to do, or might do, or wanted to do. The day before I returned home from West Saginaw for Christmas, after my first semester away, I made a list of 20 things I had to do before I left. That was in 1902. In 1927 I had a list of almost 100 possible research projects on hypnosis. For a while I thought I would publish the plans for these projects under the title of "One Hundred Research Projects in Experimental Hypnosis" or possibly the more modest title, "Ninety-nine Projects in Experimental Hypnosis." In any event, I spent most of the next 6 years on the topic, first at Wisconsin and then at Yale. Perhaps if I hadn't had that list I would have spent my time on other projects that I now think would have been more important.

As you may have heard, the hypnosis project came to an embarrassing end after I had moved to Yale. First, I was hassled by the medics who saw hypnosis as somehow their private enterprise. Then Yale was

sued by one of my female subjects who brought charges that were pretty
bizarre, given my cane and brace. But in spite of that, Yale paid $100,000
to buy her silence, and I was required to give up work on hypnosis.

THE INSTITUTE OF HUMAN RELATIONS

In 1929 I had torn myself away from the associations of 15 years to make
a new start in my scientific life in New Haven. I came here attracted by
the prestige of Yale and the better opportunities to do basic research, in
the interdisciplinary *Institute of Human Relations*. I brought with me a
plan to complete three major projects—to finish the book on hypnosis,
to pick up my earlier interest in aptitude testing and develop the
methods of automatic vocational guidance and to get to work on my
magnum opus, the book on the mechanisms of mental life. The first of
these projects was completed, the second was dropped. The third so far
is incomplete. It may never be finished. I am now 66 years old. I once
assumed that after 50 years a man's creative possibilities are practically
exhausted. In my case, thank God (if there be one), it was not so. By
1929, when I was already 45, I began to see that the conditioned reflex
might be the key to the problem of producing an objective account of the
higher mental processes. By the time I was 50, I had moved this idea
forward to the point where it would become the basis for my very most
important contribution to science. The situation at Yale was an important plus in this regard.

I had no formal teaching duties at Yale but, by 1936, in order to keep
contact with the younger men, I was running an informal seminar on
Monday nights. For the first time in the history of the institute there was
a truly interdisciplinary program going on. In that seminar we explored
topics that ranged from the question of why horses urinate in concert to
the viability of a Marxist society and the scientific status of psychoanalysis. Sometimes as many as 60 or 70 people attended. Someone took
notes. At first it was Hobart Mowrer. I had Miss Hays mimeograph the
proceedings, which were distributed widely until 1943, when the
publication of *Principles of Behavior* made the notes less useful.

PRINCIPLES OF BEHAVIOR

This was an exciting period in my life. Some of us applied my
developing principles to verbal learning and produced the *Mathematico-
Deductive Theory of Rote Learning* (Hull et al., 1940), the third of my four
best contributions. Others extended the theory to the phenomena of

frustration and aggression (Dollard et al., 1939). And Miller and Dollard (1941) applied it to social learning and imitation — three major books, all of them between 1939 and 1941.

During that same period, plans for a book that I was calling *A Behavior Primer* developed rapidly. It had become clear that I could not move on to my magnum opus until the essential theory was worked out at the most elementary level. I began to see in those days that the great need in psychology was for a basic set of principles, like Newton's *Principia*. My ambition for the *Behavior Primer* was to create such a basic theory. The mails between New Haven and Iowa City, where Spence had gone, were very busy for the next couple of years. Spence was heavily involved in the *Primer* and made many contributions. One point on which we could never agree was the role that physiology was to play in the theory. My mechanistic view led me to give such materials a central position. Spence argued, instead, that the formal mathematical theory was the only essential part of it and that physiology should be excluded. Marquis and Wendt were on my side, however, and the physiology stayed in. The book appeared in 1943 under the title of *Principles of Behavior*.

Reactions to the book were varied. Sigmund Koch wrote an embarrassingly positive review, but Lashley and Leeper took pot shots at it. The latter irritated Spence so much that he assigned the students in his graduate seminar the task of responding to it. None of these reactions was ever published. Probably they should not have been. Perhaps they should not even have been written. I have always thought that the time spent in bickering over theories could be better devoted to experimental work that would decide the worth of theories. However that may be, *Principles of Behavior* is my most important work to date. Counts of references have been made to show that my primer has stimulated more research on conditioning and simple learning than anything else that has ever been published.

CLOSING THOUGHTS: CLARK L. HULL

So, looking back on my life, I think that my major contributions have been these four:

Aptitude Testing	1928
Hypnosis and Suggestibility	1933
The Rote Learning Monograph	1939
Principles of Behavior	1943

As we all know, the work of science is never finished. Although *Principles of Behavior* was my best work, it had its flaws. Many of these were called to my attention by my strongest supporters, especially Kenneth Spence. Naturally I have also had my own further thoughts. They are recorded in my two later books, *Essentials of Behavior* (1951) and *A Behavior System* (1952). The resulting systematic account seems to me to be a great success. There are 178 formal theoretical propositions in the last book. There is empirical evidence on 123 of them. In this total, 106, or 86%, appear to be substantially validated; 16, or 13%, have some support, but it is not totally convincing. Only one (less than 1%), related to the Weber–Fechner function, is possibly wrong. But I saw the new man in the department yesterday – Kimble his name is, one of Spence's students. He is directing a dissertation by a student named Kessen on CS intensity. I asked him if there was anything in Kessen's results that went against my theory. He said no. So perhaps all 123 of the propositions are valid.

What to do next? Perhaps I should make a list of the $178 - 123 = 55$ propositions on which evidence is lacking, so that people in my laboratory can begin work on them. But what I would rather do is get back to work on what I always thought would be my magnum opus, my planned-for book on thinking. At least I can put down some possible titles. I could call it:

Psychology of the Thinking Process
Mechanisms of Thought
Mechanisms of Mind
Mental Mechanisms
Mechanisms of Mental Health
Psychology from the Standpoint of a Mechanist

CLOSING THOUGHTS: GREGORY A. KIMBLE

My first awareness of the work of Clark L. Hull came when I was an undergraduate student at Carleton College. I had a National Youth Administration (the 1930s equivalent of work study) job as a research assistant for Herbert F. Wright. Wright was a field theorist of Lewinian persuasion. He had read Hull's goal gradient papers and was convinced that the facts of the research were better interpreted in terms of Lewinian theory. Lewin had noted before Hull that proximity must increase the attractiveness of a goal and had used this idea to explain the paradoxical fact that attempted escapes from prison were at a peak just before the time when a prisoner was due to be released. In addition,

Lewinian theory made an assumption that was not salient in Hullian theory: that proximity to a goal narrows the organism's perceptual field. We set out to investigate these ideas with rats that ran a long, straight maze for food and were allowed access to a succession of blind alleys placed evenly along the true path. We recorded running times on a wax-paper kymograph and noted the animals' errors. Our predictions were that the animals would run faster near the goal and that they would enter the blind alleys near the goal less often and penetrate them less deeply.

Actually our expected results would have posed no great problem for Hull, as he would demonstrate in a 1938 paper that must have been in press even as we were conducting our research. But nothing ever came of it. Our laboratory at Carleton was in the attic of the college chapel. We had to leave the windows open, both to control the odors and to keep the room cool enough to work in. One night a fierce wind-rain storm tore through the attic, ruining many of our records and mixing up most of the rest. We gave up. I graduated in 1940 and went off to Northwestern for graduate study.

At Northwestern I took courses with Claude Buxton and G. L Freeman in which we read some of Hull's papers. The precision and style of Hull's theorizing made a deep and lasting impression on me. For reasons that were entirely a function of my own immaturity, however, things did not go well for me at Northwestern. After completing an MA degree, I decided to move on. I applied to Yale. Hull offered me a research assistantship and sent me a collection of the reprints that confirmed my earlier positive reaction. But, by then, World War II was under way. I backed out of the appointment and went home, expecting to be drafted. That never happened and, in 1943, I enrolled for graduate study at the University of Iowa.

At Iowa, Kenneth Spence was chair of the department and what came to be called "Hull–Spence" theorizing dominated the intellectual scene. In a spirit that is uncommon in psychology, however, Spence insisted that, in addition to mastering Hull's writings (particularly *Principles of Behavior*) students were expected to understand the important opposing points of view. We came away from that education knowing Hull's theory in detail and also where that theory stood in the larger scheme of things.

From Iowa, I went to my first job at Brown. There I directed a few theses on the Hull–Spence treatment of motivation and launched a program of research in which I extended Hullian theory to the acquisition of motor skill. This work and my dissertation caught Hull's attention and we carried on a brief correspondence concerning my research. Hull was working on the revisions of his theory that would be published as *Essentials of Behavior* and *A Behavior System*. He asked for details of data which may have had some indirect influence on the revisions.

It was not until I moved to Yale in 1950 that I met Hull face to face. By that time Hull's health was failing and he was not around the department very much. The only personal contact that I can remember having with him was the brief interchange related to William Kessen's dissertation. It was not such interactions, but Hull's elegant theorizing, particularly in *Principles of Behavior* that had the greatest influence on my intellectual life.

ACKNOWLEDGMENT

Earlier versions of this chapter were presented at conventions of the Rocky Mountain Psychological Association and APA. To develop these addresses, I began by assembling a large collection of verbatim quotes from Hull. Then, because the presentation would be oral, I paraphrased the quotes (as little as possible) to put them into language that was comfortable for me. I sent a first draft of the talk to several persons who had been students or on the faculty at Yale, requesting judgments of the accuracy of my statements and ideas for additional content. I owe thanks to many of them—Eleanor Gibson and Eliot Rodnick in particular—for their suggestions.

REFERENCES

Ammons, R. B. (1962). Psychology of the scientist: II. Clark L. Hull and his "Idea Books." *Perceptual and Motor Skills 15,* 807–882, Monograph Supplement 9-V15.

Ammons, B. (1987). *Psychology from the standpoint of a mechanist: The early life and work of Clark L. Hull.* Unpublished doctoral dissertation, Duke University, Durham, N.C.

Boring, E. G. (Ed.) (1952). *A history of psychology in autobiography* (Vol. IV). New York: Appleton-Century-Crofts.

Dollard, J. C., Miller, N. E., Mowrer, O. H., Sears, R. R., Ford, C. S., Hovland, C. I., & Sollenberger, R. T. (1939). *Frustration and aggression.* New Haven, CT: Yale University Press.

Hull, C. L. (1920). Quantitative aspects of the evolution of concepts: An experimental study. *Psychological Monographs, 28,* 123.

Hull, C. L. (1928). *Aptitude testing.* Yonkers, NY: World Book.

Hull, C. L. (1929). A functional interpretation of the conditioned reflex. *Psychological Review, 36,* 498–511.

Hull, C. L. (1933). *Hypnosis and suggestibility.* New York: Appleton-Century-Crofts.

Hull, C. L. (1938). The goal-gradient hypothesis applied to some "field- force" problems in the behavior of young children. *Psychological Review, 45,* 271–299.

Hull, C. L. (1943). *Principles of behavior.* New York: Appleton-Century-Crofts.

Hull, C. L. (1951). *Essentials of behavior.* New Haven, CT: Yale University Press.

Hull, C. L. (1952). *A behavior system.* New Haven, CT: Yale University Press.

Hull, C. L., Hovland, C. I., Ross, R. T., Hall, M., Perkins, D. T., & Fitch, F. B. (1940). *Mathematico–deductive theory of rote learning: A study in scientific methodology.* New Haven, CT: Yale University Press.

Miller, N. E., & Dollard, J. (1941). *Social learning and imitation.* New Haven, CT: Yale University Press.

Pratt, C. C. (1939). *The logic of modern psychology.* New York: Macmillan .

Tolman, E. C. (1938). The determiners of behavior at a choice point. *Psychological Review, 45,* 1–41.

Chapter 15

Edward Chace Tolman: A Life of Scientific and Social Purpose

Henry Gleitman

This chapter about Edward Chace Tolman is a presentation in two parts. The second part is essentially the speech I gave on the occasion of Tolman's centennial, held in Tolman Hall, on the Berkeley campus of the University of California in June, 1986. Since, on that occasion, I spoke primarily from the perspective of a student, I said very little about Tolman's life. To rectify this omission I am including, as the first part of this chapter, a brief biography. Most of it comes from Tolman's (1952) chapter in *A History of Psychology in Autobiography*. All of the quotations are from pages 323–339 of that publication.

TOLMAN'S BIOGRAPHY

Tolman was born in Newton, Massachusetts, in 1886 and received his early education in the Newton Public Schools. His family was of the class that the sociologists would call "upper middle" or possibly "lower upper." Tolman's father was president of a manufacturing company and his maternal uncle was president of a similar company. Because of his background, Tolman and his brother, who was 5 years older than he was, were both expected to go into their father's business, but neither of them did. Both went to the Massachusetts Institute of Technology and had successful careers in science and academics. Tolman notes that the fact that the brothers decided to pursue academic careers, instead of

---

*Photograph of Edward C. Tolman courtesy of Henry Gleitman

going into the factory, and the further fact that this led to no family quarrels—they were even financially supported during their college years—probably tells a good deal about the nature of his family situation and of the general cultural milieu in which he lived.

Family Life

Tolman's immediate family consisted of "a warm, loving, but in some areas puritanical mother and of a kindly and affectionate, but very much occupied father—who was depressingly energetic and excited about his business, so much so that when he tried to get us boys interested in it he merely wore us out." Tolman speculated that this may be "the sort of setup which the recent studies of ethnocentrism suggest may be conducive to the developing of ambitious, but non-authoritarian personalities."

Commenting on other aspects of the family situation that may have had an important impact on his life, Tolman says that,

> Although we lived in a well-to-do conventional suburb with stress on appearances, there still persisted in our family and in those of some of the neighbors the legacy of reformism, equal rights for Negroes, women's rights, Unitarianism and humanitarianism from the earlier days of the "Flowering of New England." These social tendencies were combined with the special Bostonian emphasis on "culture" together with, in our family, a special dose of moral uplift and pacifism.

Tolman thought that one significance of this family outlook was that

> the rebellion of my brother and myself against parental domination [by refusing to go into the family business] was in a direction which the parents themselves could not too greatly, or too consciously, disapprove. We were choosing the professions. We were set to increase the sum of human knowledge and presumably were to apply such an increase to the betterment of mankind. Furthermore, we would be living up to the puritan tradition of hard work and to the Quaker tradition, on our mother's side, of plain living and high thinking.

Education

However that may be, Tolman went to MIT and obtained a bachelor's degree in electrochemistry, noting that he went to MIT, "not because I wanted to be an engineer, but because I had been good in mathematics and science in high school and because of family pressure." Tolman's brother followed a similar route and became a world-famous theoretical chemist and physicist.

During his senior year at MIT, Tolman became more certain of his own interests and he made a career decision. At that time he read some of William James's work and decided that he wanted to become a philosopher. Upon graduating from MIT in 1911, he went to the Harvard summer session and "took an introductory course in philosophy with Perry and one in psychology with Yerkes—both then young assistant professors in the combined department of philosophy and psychology. I decided then and there that I did not have brains enough to become a philosopher, but that psychology was nearer my capacities and interests. It offered, at that date, what seemed a nice compromise between philosophy and science." The following fall, therefore, Tolman enrolled at Harvard as a full graduate student in philosophy and psychology. He reported in his autobiography that the courses he remembered most vividly were: Perry's course in ethics, which (reinforced by a reading of McDougall's *Social Psychology*) laid the foundation for his later interest in motivation, and gave him the main concepts that he used throughout his lifetime; Holt's course in experimental, "which proved to be a terrible letdown from the really humanly important problems which I had supposed psychology to be concerned with;" Langfeld's course in advanced general psychology, using Titchener as a textbook, "which almost sold me temporarily on structuralistic introspectionism;" Holt's seminar in epistemology, and Yerkes's course in comparative, using Watson's *Behavior—An Introduction to Comparative Psychology*.

After his first graduate year at Harvard, Tolman went to Germany for the summer to help prepare for the PhD examination in German. [Up until about 1950, most universities had French and German (with Russian an option) as requirements for the PhD degree]. Tolman spent a month at Giessen with Koffka, "and so got my first introduction to Gestalt psychology—although at that time I sensed only vaguely what it was all about. Nevertheless it prepared me to be receptive to Gestalt concepts when, after the first world war, we began hearing about them more fully in this country through the writings of Wertheimer, Köhler and Koffka." In the fall of 1923, Tolman returned to Giessen for a couple of months to learn more.

Academic Career

After receiving the doctoral degree in 1915, Tolman was an instructor [the entry-level rank of assistant professor became common only after World War II] at Northwestern University for 3 years. He describes himself in those days as being relatively self-conscious and inarticulate and afraid of his classes. Furthermore, Tolman's family background came back to haunt him:

[T]his was just before we got into the first World War and my pacifist training, plus my own problems about aggression, kept me in a terrific emotional turmoil. . . . I was called before the Dean sometime during the summer of 1917–18 because I had given my name to a student publication, circulated in the Middle West, that was concerned with "war aims," and which had, no doubt, something of a pacifist tinge. . . . I was dismissed at the end of the academic year on the grounds of war retrenchment and my not too successful teaching. . . . But I have always thought that my near pacifism had something to do with it.

At the beginning of the following academic year, in 1918, Tolman became an instructor at the University of California in Berkeley, where he remained for the rest of his life. From the very first, as Tolman recalls it,

California symbolized for me some sort of final freeing from my over-whelmingly too puritanical and too Bostonian upbringing. The "Freedom of the West," whether real or fancied, at once captured my imagination and loyalty and has since claimed them ever since—although with the years I have, of course, become aware that all is not gold that glitters, even in California. . . .Whatever my increasing psychological maturity—and there has been some—I like to credit most of it to the social, intellectual, and physical virtues of Berkeley plus an extraordinarily happy marriage.

Contributions to Psychology

During his years at Berkeley Tolman created a cognitive theory of learning, for which he is remembered, even at the present time. Tolman conceived of learning as involving the development of cognitions, or bits of knowledge, about the environment and the organism's relationships to it. In direct contrast to Thorndike and Hull, Tolman did not think of learning in terms of the strengthening of stimulus–response connections. He proposed, instead, that learning consists of the formation of what he called "sign–gestalt expectations," "sign–significate relations," or "hypotheses." All of these conceptions represent knowledge about "what leads to what" in any situation. They are very close to the currently popular concept of "representation."

Evaluation.   Tolman is best remembered as a pioneer in the history of cognitive psychology and for making that contribution in a day when the behaviorists were dominant in the field. Tolman, himself, in his characteristically self-effacing way, both minimized the importance of his contributions and gave others credit for whatever significance they may have:

In conclusion, it would seem [appropriate] to indicate the main sources from which I think my ideas have come. First of all most of the credit, if it be credit, should go to all the students whose ideas I have shamefully and consistently adopted and exploited throughout the years, and ended up by believing to be my own . . . . [I]t should go to my teachers at Harvard who taught me to think, to be critical, to be complicated but to remain naturalistic . . . . [I]t should go to the Gestalt psychologists but especially to Kurt Lewin whose ideas I have borrowed time and again and absorbed into my very blood . . . [I]t should go to my year's stay in Vienna and especially to Egon Brunswik who opened my eyes to the meaning and the viability of the European tradition [and] gave me new insights into the essentially "achievement" character of behavior. . . . Finally my thanks must go the Department of Social Relations at Harvard University, which during the year 1949–50 taught me something of sociology and of anthropology and of personality and of social psychology, and set me wondering about ways in which my rat concepts might eventually be amalgamated with those of scientists in these other fields. For, if we are to advance, we must first understand, and then attempt to incorporate into our own, the perspectives of our sister sciences—not merely of those sciences which pertain to physiology but also and even more of those which pertain to social living.

A TRIBUTE TO E. C. TOLMAN

My own speech at the 1986 Tolman centennial touched on some of the same topics as were covered in the preceding biography. The difference is that I used them in an effort to pay proper tribute to Tolman, as a psychologist, as a teacher and as a man. With some slight editing, my speech was as follows:

Today, or rather this year, when he would have been 100 years old, I want to pay tribute to my teacher, Edward Chace Tolman. Let me begin by saying that it feels rather odd for me to speak here at Tolman's centennial. It is odd for me, who was 21–or was it 22?–when I came to Berkeley to work with him in 1946. In that year Tolman had just turned 60. I now am older than he was then, and it feels exceedingly odd because that simply cannot be. You can't be older than your own father!

But then it always feels a bit odd to return symbolically to meet one's past: at reunions, memorial rituals, or at centennials. On all such occasions there is such a powerful tendency to reshape our memories of the past to fit our conceptions of the present. We do it personally, as we refashion the memories of our fathers and mothers and former lovers. And we do it intellectually, when we reshape our interpretations of our scientific forefathers (perhaps I should say, forepersons) and create them anew. In this regard, we are bit like Gilbert and Sullivan's Major General Stanley, that very model of a modern major general, who bought his commission and, having bought it, needed an ancestral home to go along with it. So he did what was required: He bought an ancestral home, complete with a set of ancestral pictures on its walls. We psychologists do this all the time as we remake our history, refashioning our past to make sense of our present. Is this what we are doing now? Certainly others have been doing it for (to?) Tolman, in ways that leave me quite uncomfortable. In the spirit that Tolman would appreciate, however, I want to look at these new assessments before I decide what to make of them.

A Footnote in the History of Psychology?

Revisionism seems inevitable in history. If it happened to George Washington and the major figures of the French Revolution, why not to Tolman? Such a revisionist approach to Tolman has been taken by Donald Campbell, one of Tolman's former students, and by David Krantz and his coworkers, who imply that, all in all, Tolman ended up as a rather minor character on the stage of psychology's history (Campbell, 1979; Krantz, 1972; Krantz & Wiggins, 1973). To be sure, they point out that Tolman's theory turned out to be much more correct than those of his erstwhile rivals; and they all grant that he was enormously beloved, by his students, by his colleagues, by his friends and, for that matter, by most of his professional rivals. One might conclude that one could do much worse than to be essentially right, as well as esteemed and much beloved.

But, according to Campbell and Krantz, Tolman could (and should) have done much better. For, as they see it, he failed to have much of an impact because he didn't fulfill what they call the role of a "tribal leader." To quote Campbell,

> The puzzle with which I start this study is that Tolman's students almost completely stopped doing recognizably Tolmanian studies or using Tolmanian concepts once they left the University of Berkeley. Instead, the books they dedicated to him (e.g., Krech & Crutchfield, 1948) [and this is certainly true of me as well] were devoid of specifically Tolmanian influence. In contrast, Spence's students continued loyally to use the Hullian paradigm long after they left the University of Iowa . . . . Still more puzzling puzzle: Why were Tolman's students the least loyal when of all the learning theories of the 1930s, Tolman's can now be seen to have been clearly the best?

Campbell then cites interviews from a study by Krantz and Wiggins (1973) with students of all the major learning theorists of the time. These interviews leave no doubt that Tolman and, for example, Kenneth Spence (one of Tolman's major rivals) presented themselves very differently indeed. Campbell sees this difference in the self-presentation of these men as the key to what later happened to their students. In contrast to Tolman, who defaulted on his tribal leadership role, Spence had no problems in assuming the leader's part. That may partly explain the remarkable loyalty of Spence's students to his theory long after they left his campus.

Up to a point, the evidence marshaled by these revisionists is quite convincing. There is no doubt that Hull, Spence, and Skinner tried to instill loyalty to a theoretical position and were quite successful in doing so. To quote one of Kenneth Spence's students: "[He] tried to save his students from the 'errors' of others as he had diagnosed them through considerable experience of his own. Thus, the intellectual climate was always one of 'us against them,' and we never really got to study 'them' . . . ." (This quote and those to follow are all from Krantz & Wiggins, 1973). Another said, "He demanded total acceptance of his position by students. Those who disagreed or questioned were viewed with disdain." Or take statements about B. F. Skinner from some of his former students. One points out that, "One of the unique features of Skinnerianism is that there are tasks for the apostles. There is so much work to be done, many experiments to be performed, numerous variables to explore, and procedures to try. . . ." A similar apostolic theme is sounded by another former student: "I've come to hold a rather different set of views from Skinner's under the influence of other men, other worlds, other thoughts. . . . [But, as much as I owe to him], I still have to recover from him. . . . Skinner's self-image combines certain features of Thomas Alva Edison, Bertrand Russell, and Jesus Christ. He has a legitimate claim to all three elements. . . ."

Are these descriptions accurate? There are undoubtedly distortions prompted by the sheer passage of time and by heaven knows what personal factors. (Was Plato fully accurate in his depiction of Socrates? Or Aristotle in what he said about Plato?) I have talked to some of Spence's students, including one of the editors of this volume. They feel that some of the statements made about their former teacher are in error. As they remember their days at Iowa, Spence always insisted that his students have a thorough understanding of alternative theories, especially Tolman's.

Whatever one makes of those arguments, the real issue may not be whether the descriptions of Spence are factually accurate; perhaps what really matters is their overall tenor. And in this regard, there is no doubt that Tolman presented himself quite differently from Spence (and for that matter from Hull and Skinner). For I would swear that none of the statements about Spence or Skinner could possibly have been made about Tolman by any of *his* students.

As evidence I cite the way Tolman's former students described *him*. One of them put it this way:

> There are 119 publications in my bibliography. One of these was a collaborative study with Tolman and another graduate student. That is the only one directly related to Tolman's position, but I would say that all my writing and research has been influenced by Tolman's systematic position and even more by his personality.

Another said,

> He wanted us to stand on our own feet and be our own men, not his. Any slavish adherence to his views would have been repugnant to him. So all of us who were fortunate enough to be associated with him have struck out for ourselves and hopefully we are better psychologists, and yet more hopefully, better people for having been associated with him. (Again, all quotes from Krantz & Wiggins, 1973)

In sum, Campbell, Krantz and Wiggins certainly have a point in arguing that in contrast to his theoretical rivals, Tolman failed to act as a tribal leader. Campbell rather regrets this fact; he feels that he and other Tolman students—and all psychology—would have been much better off had Tolman encouraged followership. He implies that, because of his rejection of the role of leader, Tolman became a rather minor figure and had little influence. There is no doubt that in this sense Tolman defaulted. The question is whether that default was a fault. In trying to answer this question, I want to consider Tolman under several rubrics: as a psychologist, as an educator, and as a man.

Tolman as a Psychologist

First, a few words about Tolman as a psychologist. To understand Tolman's legacy to psychology, you must begin by recognizing that he was a behaviorist and saw himself as a behaviorist. He had little patience with introspection, at least not of the sort practiced by Wundt and Titchener. But he was equally opposed to the kind of behaviorism espoused by Watson. In a broad sense, Tolman's own behaviorism, which he sometimes called "purposive behaviorism," was a blend, in which American pragmatism, an insistence on the all-importance of motivation, and a somewhat more relaxed way of being objective were merged.

Cognitive Behaviorism. Today Tolman is generally classified as a "cognitive behaviorist" and the originator of a "cognitive theory" of learning. He is clearly a forerunner of modern "cognitive psychology." We still say this, although the expression cognitive psychology is now so widely used that it's not at all clear exactly what the term, *cognition*, means or whether there is any one left who is *not* a cognitive psychologist.

Tolman of course knew what he meant by the term. For him, it referred to a number of central states or processes that intervene between knowledge and preformance. Tolman himself called them *sign–Gestalt expectancies*, one of the many neologisms he coined—the more hyphenated a term, the more he liked it. Today some of us call such central states "representations," and some of us even use the term "ideas." Another example of such a central process that remains in current use is Tolman's notion of cognitive maps—a clear forerunner of modern analogue conceptions of spatial memory, spatial thinking, and the like.

These central processes, however terminologized, may or may not be manifested in behavior, for Tolman made an important distinction between expectations and performance. This distinction is strongly reminiscent of the now-familiar competence–performance distinction, formulated years later, by Noam Chomsky.

Molar Behaviorism. Another crucial theme in Tolman's theorizing was the distinction between the molecular and molar aspects of behavior—between the actual muscle movements made by an animal on the one hand, and the more broadly defined, goal-directed act on the other. Tolman advocated theorizing at the molar level, a decision whose value was empirically demonstrated by dozens of studies showing that rats learn the place where they have been rewarded rather than the particular movements required to get there. These demonstrations of *place learning* also supported Tolman's view that learning did not entail the strengthening of stimulus–response connections.

For Tolman the molecular–molar distinction was clearly parallel to the distinction between proximal stimulus and percept made by the Gestalt psychologists, such as his colleague Egon Brunswik, and other students of perception. The Gestalt psychologists had shown that what one sees is not solely determined by the proximal stimulus, the stimulus defined in terms of receptor processes. First, they showed that two or more different proximal stimulus patterns can produce a kind of perceptual paraphrase, giving rise to the same percept (more or less)—as in the recognition of a melody when it is transposed to a different key—and the various perceptual constancies. Second, and conversely, the psychologists of perception had showed that the same proximal stimulus pattern can give rise to different percepts—as in various ambiguous figures. Well, Tolman asked, aren't those same things true of behavior? Isn't it true that the same act—that is the same behavior defined at a molar level—can be served by different molecular responses? The "muscle twitches" that occur when one of Skinner's rats presses the lever in the Skinner box, or when one of Tolman's rats runs a maze, may be very different on different trials. And, similarly, isn't it true that one and the same bit of behavior, described molecularly, can have different molar meanings—as when you slap a man's face in exactly the same way, but once because you hate him and once because he has a tarantula on his cheek? The examples are mine but the distinction is Tolman's.

Tolman as a Pioneer

The distinction just described appears to be identical to the distinction that the linguists and psycholinguists made much later, between surface and underlying structure in language. The mechanisms are surely different, but the distinction is established by the same basic tests: paraphrase and ambiguity. Two different surface structures can refer to the same underlying structure, as in *the dog chases the cat* and *the cat is chased by the dog*, or the same surface structure can refer to two or more underlying structures, as in *smoking volcanoes can be dangerous*.

To mention yet another area in which Tolman foreshadowed later developments, take the term "affordance," that is now so popular among Gibsonians. Just as J. J. Gibson knew, Tolman knew that objects have some kind of tendency to evoke certain actions in us and so he coined terms like manipulandum, discriminandum, sit-upon-able, eat-able—all these hyphenated neologisms with an *-able* or an *-andum* at the end that are vintage Tolman. Of course Gibson got there in his own way. But Tolman anticipated him as he anticipated so much else. To cite a single additional example, we have in Tolman a foreshadowing of the notion of modularity. In a 1949 paper, "There is More than One Kind of Learning," Tolman argued that, say, learning motor skills and solving problems are governed by different laws entirely.

One reason that Tolman was a forerunner in so many ways was that he was an essentially sane and sensible man. Unlike his many theoretical rivals, Tolman was not an imperialist; he never thought that one position, one point of view could be all-encompassing, and so he was able to accept concepts from such diverse sources as American functionalism, Gestalt psychology, Lewinian field theory, psychoanalysis, and Brunswikian probability learning. He was always ready to change his views, to revise his system, as new data, new interpretations and new interests dictated. Tolman was amazingly broad-minded, continually open to new ideas. He was the most *un*rigid psychological thinker I have ever met. Returning to our earlier theme: Was that a default, or was it a simple recognition that you can't be an imperialist if your would-be colonies refuse to be colonized?

It was Tolman's view (and now mine too) that the academic enterprise, all of it, but perhaps psychology in particular, must not be frozen. Hence there should never be too much of a commitment in the way of method, too much self-conscious metamethodologizing, too much commitment to even the most cherished theories of the moment. That antiprescriptive attitude of his came up again and again. He never engaged in the continual thou-shalt-be-scientific sermons of his theoretical rivals.

> I suppose I'm personally anti-pathetic to the notion that science progresses through intense self-conscious analyses of where one has got and where one is going. Such analyses are obviously a proper function for the philosopher of science and they may be valuable for many individual scientists, but I myself become frightened when I begin to worry too much as to what particular logical and methodological canons I should or should not obey. (Tolman, 1959, p. 93)

Tolman was also wary of too much reliance on methodology: "Psychology, given its many parts, is today such a vast continent of unknowns that it always seemed to me rather silly to be too precise, too quantitative, too deductive and axiomatic save in very experimentally overcontrolled and overlimited areas" (Tolman, 1959, p. 98). And he was wary of would-be scientific terms used vaguely. One of his peeves was the term "response":

> [I] still feel that "response" is one of the most slippery and unanalyzed of our current concepts. We all gaily use the term to mean anything from a secretion of ten drops of saliva, to entering a given alley, to running an entire maze, to the slope of a Skinner box curve, to achieving a Ph.D., or to a symbolic act of hostility against one's father by attacking some authority figure. Now I ask you! (Tolman, p. 1959, p. 95)

All of this has a very contemporary ring to it.

Tolman and the Psychology of his Times

Partly because Tolman was ahead of his time in many ways, his theorizing evoked criticism. In particular, his cognitive position was the target of attack from many rivals. Just what are these cognitive processes that are so central to the system, how does one tap into them, how are they related to action? Tolman recognized the challenge in Guthrie's famous quip about leaving the rat buried in thought at the choice point in the maze. It was a funny line. Tolman talked about it, and sometimes worried about it. Perhaps he should have answered that, all in all, it may be better to leave a rat buried in thought than to leave a man buried in his musculature. Or, more constructively, he could have pointed out that the learning–performance distinction and the insistence that the conditions that lead to learning are not the same as those that evoke performance represent a step toward an answer to this criticism. Although Tolman was a cognitive psychologist, he also sketched theories of action and motivation. A motive drives a creature's behavior until some kind of internal state is rectified. Until that happens, the creature continues doing things. And an animal behaving is not the kind of organism that Guthrie had described as having (according to Tolman's theory) nothing better to do than sit and contemplate its hypotheses.

If Tolman had a blind spot, it was one he shared with most other psychologists of his day: a neglect of the lessons of biology. He never entertained the possibility that different creatures might be different, rock-bottom different, in the ways they learn and behave. The closing comments of his presidential address to the American Psychological Association in 1937 set forth the credo of the major learning theorists of his time:

> Let me close, now, with a final confession of faith. I believe that everything important in psychology (except perhaps such matters as the building up of a superego, that is everything save such matters that involve society and words) can be investigated in essence through the continued experimental and theoretical analysis of rat behavior at a choice point in a maze... (Tolman, 1938)

In this pronouncement Tolman was in tune with virtually all of his behaviorist contemporaries. Of course he qualified, as he always did, and to be sure the exclusion of society and language is quite a qualification—one that neither Hull nor Skinner was prepared to make. But however qualified, Tolman shared the general belief in the cross-species generality of psychological laws. In the light of current knowledge, this perspective seems rather dated—one of the few aspects in which Tolman's thinking seems genuinely dated now.

Personal Style

So much for Tolman's substantive contributions. There are many I haven't touched upon, but I want to move on to say something about his style. Edward Chace Tolman was a remarkable human being—as a scientist, as an academic, and as a man. As a scientist he was constantly willing to question, to doubt, to regard himself and his ideas with a sense of humor. It is remarkable how rare that willingness has become—how rare for that matter it was in his own time. Tolman once gave a speech (it may have been his presidential address), and concluded with a short film of a rat in a maze with a half-minute bit from a *Mickey Mouse* cartoon spliced on at the end. That was so characteristic: take the field seriously, take the subject seriously, but as for yourself, be willing to kick yourself in the pants and smile. When Tolman described his system in a chapter in Koch's five-volume *Psychology: The Study of a Science* (which turned out to be his last publication) that same, wry, self-deprecating attitude appeared again:

> If in what follows I have not done a very clear or useful job, I would plead some half dozen reasons. First, I think the days of such grandiose or covering systems in psychology as mine attempted to be are at least for the time being pretty much passé. I feel, therefore, that it might have been more decent and more dignified to let such an instance of the relatively immediate past bury its own dead . . . (Tolman, 1959, p. 93)

But Tolman continually reminds you that, while he always hedges and wryly deprecates, this intellectual style is undertaken out of a kind of love. In talking about himself, he once said,

> I have liked to think about psychology in ways that have proved congenial to me. Since all the sciences, and especially psychology, are still immersed in such tremendous realms of the uncertain and the unknown, the best that any individual scientist, especially any psychologist, can do seems to be to follow his own gleam and his own bent, however inadequate they may be. In fact, that actually is what we all do. In the end, the only sure criterion is to have fun. And I have had fun. (Tolman, 1959, p. 152)

I am glad that Tolman could say this at the end of his life.

As an academic, Tolman felt passionate about the pursuit of truth. But he was never passionate about his own bets about this truth. He felt passionate about students, but never about their adherence to any one position. And finally, he felt passionate about the academic process, the process of searching for the truth; hence his refusal to sign the California loyalty oath. In 1949, toward the end of the McCarthy era, the university tried to impose loyalty oaths on the faculty, in conformity to state law. During the "Year of the Oath," 1949–1950, it was Tolman who became the leader of the faculty in the fight against the oath. He refused to sign it but, in his usual style, he made the point that he could afford the financial sacrifice if they were to fire him. He advised his younger colleagues to sign, and leave that battle up to others who were in a better position to conduct it. These courageous efforts brought Tolman widespread acclaim. He received honorary degrees at major universities and, when he died on November 19, 1959, the *Washington Post* wrote in an editorial: "His death last week is a loss to the nation as well as to the whole academic community."

Tolman as a Teacher

Let me end by talking about Tolman as a teacher. Students mattered much more to Tolman than his own beliefs or, rather, more than instilling his own beliefs in students. I recall one of my first years at Swarthmore College. Tolman was in the East and came to visit and looked at my laboratory with a mixture of pleasure and disapproval. It was in the cellar of the men's dormitory and the students complained of the smell—I told them about olfactory adaptation but that didn't make them any happier. From someone, Tolman had heard that I had become a Hullian. He was right; I did become a Hullian for a year or two. When you're in a department with giants like Wolfgang Köhler, Solomon Asch, and Hans Wallach, one way of getting out their shadow is to become as different from them as you possibly can. And becoming a Hullian was as good a way as any. Tolman's reaction to my defection was straightforward: "Gleitman, you son of a bitch, I hear you are becoming a Hullian! So okay. Just be a good Hullian!"

It was all so simple as I see it now. Tolman's view was that our students are a way of extending ourselves in time. We live in a world in which we are necessarily finite, in which we must come to an end both biologically and intellectually. Students are our intellectual progeny, and are one way of extending ourselves in time, perhaps as much or even more than our ideas. For our students beget students, their students beget students, and on and on. It's not given to many of us to be René Descartes. Or Hermann Helmholtz. Or Sigmund Freud. Or, for that matter, Edward Chace Tolman. The best we can do is to have a student who'll have a studcent, who'll have a student, and perhaps somewhere, down the line, one of them will be a Descartes, a Helmholtz, a Freud or a Tolman. Perhaps I'm projecting my own attitudes on him. I can't be sure. After all, I knew him when he was 60 and I was 20. But I do think that Tolman did believe something of that sort.

Revising the Revisionists

Because I believe that this view of the academic process is right, and that Tolman held it, I conclude that Tolman was an eminent success, not the charming, lovable failure of the revisionists mentioned earlier. This is not just because his substantive ideas about psychology turned out to be more correct than Hull's or Spence's. It is rather because of his personal qualities that allowed him to be more willing to hedge, to wonder, to be puzzled, and to be more open to the world and to other people. And it may be that it was because of this that he also turned out to be more correct in the long run. So, although I think that Tolman was a massively successful psychologist, he was not a master whose works we must still read to find the truth—in the way one can still read Helmholtz. Instead, I think of him as someone whose knowledge has been much surpassed but whose wisdom has not, someone perhaps like William James, or like Tolman's own teacher, Edwin Holt.

Let me conclude by asking you to rejoice and make a resolution: to rejoice because, for once, the revisionists are wrong; because both those who knew him personally and the many others who fell under his influence indirectly did not love a mere creation of their minds; because Tolman was Tolman and that, this time at least, Major General Stanley bought the right paintings. And, finally, on this year of Tolman's centennial, let us who are his students—for I believe that in some ways all modern psychologists are his students—make a resolution: to share his passion for the search for truth; to share his modesty and sense of humor about our own contributions to this search (for unlike Tolman, we have much to be modest about), to share his desire to teach rather than to indoctrinate, to refuse any tribal leadership, should any such be offered and, last of all to have some fun.

ACKNOWLEDGMENT

I want to express my thanks to Gregory A. Kimble for a massive and enormously helpful job of editing that went far beyond the call of normal editorial duty.

REFERENCES

Campbell, D. T. (1979). A tribal model of the social system vehicle carrying scientific knowledge. *Knowledge: Creation, diffusion, utilization, 1,* 181–201. Beverly Hills: Sage.

Krantz, D. L. (1972). Schools and systems: The mutual isolation of operant and non-operant psychology as a case study. *Journal of the History of the Behavioral Sciences, 8,* 86–102.

Krantz, D. L., & Wiggins, L. (1973). Personal and impersonal channels of recruitment in the growth of theory. *Human Development, 16,* 133–156.

Krech, D. & Crutchfield, R. (1948). *Theory and problems of social psychology.* New York: McGraw-Hill.

Tolman, E. C. (1938). Determiners of behavior at a choice point. *Psychological Review, 45,* 1–41.

Tolman, E. C. (1949). There is more than one kind of learning. *Psychological Review, 56,* 144–155.

Tolman, E. C. (1952). Edward Chace Tolman. *History of Psychology in Autobiography* (Vol. 4, pp. 323–339). Worcester: Clark University Press.

Tolman, E. C. (1959). Principles of purposive behavior. In S. Koch (Ed.), *Psychology: A study of a science, Vol. 2: General systematic formulations, learning, and special processes* (pp. 92–157). New York: McGraw-Hill.

Chapter 16

Leta Stetter Hollingworth: "Literature of Opinion" and the Study of Individual Differences

Stephanie A. Shields

When, in 1908, I set out to join my husband-to-be, Harry Levi Hollingworth, in New York City, my sense of what life would hold for me was quite different than the way the story actually unfolded. You see, I was leaving western Nebraska to become a writer. The plan was simple: I would teach school as I had in Nebraska while Harry established himself as a young professor of psychology at Barnard College. Meanwhile, I would set about establishing my writing career. From my young adolescence when my poetry helped me through the stormy and unloving years with an alcoholic and often absent father and a bitter and resentful stepmother, I knew that writing was my vocation in the fullest sense of the word. Perhaps the lovingly detailed baby biography that my mother wrote during my infancy was the model, perhaps it was my father's lively skill at storytelling, but I knew that I must be a writer. What I, like every young person, did not anticipate was that the world would not choose to cooperate with these ambitions.

Two important events changed the course of my professional life. First, I discovered upon arriving in New York, that the city would not employ married women as teachers. My plan to be an equal partner with my husband in providing for us evaporated simply because of my marital status! I had never taken kindly to the imposition of unreasonable limits and once again my sense of justice was deeply offended— why should artificial limits be imposed on an individual woman simply

---

*Photograph of Leta Stetter Hollingworth courtesy of Special Collections, Milbank Memorial Library, Teachers College, Columbia University.

because of a bureaucratic definition of the "natural" role of all women? As there was no way to contest the situation, I turned my energies to housekeeping and random literature courses. Neither was satisfying and the economic hardship of living on Harry's meager salary added injury to insult. The second event that was to set me on a new career path were my courses with Edward Lee Thorndike at Teachers College. Dr. Thorndike himself was not a stirring lecturer, but the questions he raised, the intellectual challenges that the material presented—even with my first courses in psychology—gave me a new purpose: Given no arbitrary social impediments, I would be a New Woman (curious that you do not use that term anymore) who would apply the study of psychology to the life of the New Woman (see also Benjamin, 1975; Benjamin & Shields, 1990; H. Hollingworth, 1943; Shields, 1975a; Shields, 1975b; Shields & Mallory, 1987.)

The Columbia Milieu

At that time, Columbia was immersed in an intense interest in testing and measurement. Testing promised scientific precision in description of purely mental traits. Many of the psychologists at Columbia had testing as a major or minor interest. I have no intention of reviewing the testing movement here, although its history is a fascinating story (e.g., Samelson, 1979). One finds real heroes and real villains in a field that grew within a span of 25 years from tentative ideas that intellect could be measured indirectly from sensory competencies to large-scale intelligence and personality testing of more than 1.8 million World War I army recruits. If anyone doubted testing's long-range potential, the war made secure the place of mental testing as a fundamental methodological tool for psychology.

Let me tell you what it was like as a new graduate student in 1911. As accustomed as I was to Harry's support and encouragement, I was not sanguine about the prospects of studying with a faculty that was convinced of female mental inferiority. Granted, Naomi Norsworthy (who had been Columbia's first woman graduate student in psychology) was on the staff of Teachers College, but her position held little status. When I began graduate study it was still uncommon to see women in graduate school. Columbia itself had not regularly allowed women to enroll for graduate study until just a dozen years before I began my work there. Nor were women eligible for any of the dozen full fellowships; they were allowed to apply for just four of the tuition-only scholarships (Rosenberg, 1982).

The atmosphere at Columbia is well described by Edna Heidbreder in

Seven Psychologies. She had been a student of Robert Woodworth and completed her PhD in 1924. She wrote:

> Psychology at Columbia is not easy to describe. A graduate student in psychology cannot spend many weeks at Columbia without becoming aware of the immense importance in that atmosphere of curves of distribution, of individual differences, of the measurement of intelligence and other human capacities, of experimental procedures and statistical devices, and of the undercurrent of physiological thought. [One] discovers immediately that psychology does not lead a sheltered life; that it rubs elbows with biology, statistics, education, commerce, industry, and the world of affairs. [One] encounters many different trends of thought, and frequently comes upon the same ones from different angles. But the separate strands of teaching are not knit together for [students] into a firm and patterned fabric. No one cares how [students arrange] the threads that are placed in [their] hands; certainly there is no model which [they are] urged to copy. Columbia students are as definitely marked as those of any other group, but the mark itself is straggling and irregular.(1933, pp. 191–192)

Edward Lee Thorndike and My Early Work on the Psychology of Women

When I came to work with him, I found Professor Thorndike's social views quite antithetical to my own. Even though my adviser's training had been very much influenced by Professor Cattell and even though he himself was a believer in sex prejudice, nevertheless Professor Thorndike proved to be sufficiently open-minded to data. But I'm getting ahead of my story.

You may associate Edward Lee Thorndike with the environmentalist stance that he took later in his career, but at the time I met him, he quite adamantly insisted that the individual's inheritance drove one's inevitable success or failure in life (Joncich, 1968). Still, his concern with clarity of logic, and his commitment to social benefit, made it impossible for me to discount him.

I think it is important to distinguish between "the literature of opinion" and "the literature of fact," opinion being "all written statements, made by scientific men and others, not based on experimental evidence," whereas the literature of fact is "based on experimental data, which have been obtained under carefully controlled conditions, and which may be verified by anyone competent to understand and criticize them" (L. Hollingworth, 1916a, p. 224). The scientific study of women in my day largely consisted of a literature of opinion parading as a literature of fact. Psychological science simply failed to see the fundamental significance of social roles, and instead blandly accepted explanations based on opinion rather than objective study.

My dissertation research grew out of a project in which I had assisted Harry in a contract study of effects of caffeine on various cognitive and motor performance tasks. It empirically confronted one of the most firmly entrenched literatures of opinion, that of "functional periodicity," the purported psychological impairment caused by menstruation. I completed two studies in which I tested women (in 1 I used 2 men as "controls") on a variety of perceptual and motor tasks over one to three months. I found no evidence of cyclical effects on performance, a finding that I am pleased to report has been corroborated by researchers after me. It was clear to me that the disparity between my results and mythologies of functional periodicity was a function of the taboos associated with menstruation, reliance on clinical observation for "data," and the unfortunate fact that "the tradition emanating from the mystic and romantic novelists, that woman is a mysterious being, half hysteric, half angel, has found its way into scientific writing" (L. Hollingworth, 1914a, p. 95).

I found it remarkable that Professor Thorndike was willing to sponsor my thesis work. I am sure he recognized me immediately as a competent student. But that someone so traditional would approve research on menstrual-cycle effects on learning and performance is, to my mind, quite impressive. In fact our values did not seriously clash until I took on one of his pet notions, a view of intelligence that seemed to me to be an elaborate attempt to explain biologically what could far more parsimoniously be explained with reference to social fact. It was the hypothesis he had picked up from Professor Cattell, who in turn had acquired it from the exceedingly sloppy scientist, but exceedingly popular writer, Havelock Ellis. Like other men of science, Thorndike assumed as factual the proposal that males of all species are inherently more variable[1] than females. In terms of evolutionary progress, then, it would be the females who preserve the integrity of the species, while males, through variation, would provide the progressive element, spurring on further evolution. As Professor Cattell once remarked, this would result in the distribution of women being "represented by a narrower bell-shaped curve." Psychologists assumed that greater male variability was true of mental as well as physical traits. The range of male mental ability seemed to be wider. The evidence for this assertion rested on the fact that more males than females inhabited institutions for the feeble-minded and more males than females achieved social eminence, a sign, Cattell and others felt certain, of natural mental superiority.

---

[1]For a more detailed discussion of the variability hypothesis see Shields (1982).

At first blush this might not seem a particularly noteworthy scientific proposal, but when applied, as it was, to generalizations about the actual intellectual capacities of men as a group and women as a group, it was time to take a closer look at this pseudotheory. I will not describe my empirical tests of the variability hypothesis, but suffice it to say I found no evidence to support it.

Now Professor Thorndike, being a man who was willing to face facts, accepted my findings, but then insisted that if I were to assume the equal intellectual capacity of the sexes, then I must be responsible for providing an explanation for sex differences in social accomplishment. Why are there so many fewer women than men of eminence? The alternate explanation was obvious to me:

> Why do we not consider first the established, obvious inescapable fact that women bear and rear the race, and that this has always meant, and still means that nearly 100% of their energy is consumed in the performance and supervision of domestic and allied tasks, a field where eminence is impossible. No one knows who is the best housekeeper in America. Eminent housekeepers do not and cannot exist. If we discuss at all the matter of sex differences in achievement, we should consider first the most obvious conditioning factors. Otherwise our discussion is futile scientifically. (L. Hollingworth, 1940, p. 16)

To anyone who might still have reservations regarding the validity of a social explanation, I suggest this simple exercise:

> Imagine if you please, a group of young men and a group of young women, all at the beginning of life, equally young, equally variable, equal in average capacity, allowed to compete over twenty years for a given social prize, say fame, or scientific achievement, or eminence in the arts, on the condition that every one should become the parent of two children. Have we any doubt as to which group will win? (L. Hollingworth, 1940, p. 16).

I believe that line of reasoning made an impression on Professor Thorndike. Unfortunately, the matter continued as an issue for debate despite much contrary evidence and occasionally you might still find it seriously considered today.

Clinical Psychology and Exceptional Children

After receiving my MA and a masters diploma in education in 1913, I continued my graduate studies and worked as a clinical psychologist. At that time clinical psychology was quite different than you think of it today because it was largely concerned with mental testing. I worked at the New York City Clearing House for Mental Defectives, where I was employed to administer Binet tests to "mentally inferior" individuals for commitment by the courts. I had taken the position as a temporary replacement for Emily T. Burr, one of the earliest workers in the field, and was kept on after her return. In 1914, the psychological examiners giving mental tests were put under civil service supervision, and after competitive exams I was at the top of the list and took the first opening, which was at Bellevue Hospital. I was later offered the position of chief of a psychological lab to be established at the hospital, but at about this time I completed the PhD and was offered the late Naomi Norsworthy's position in educational psychology. I held that position for the rest of my life, though I continued part-time work as a clinical psychologist until 1920. I was also involved in the effort to professionalize the status of clinical psychologists within the American Psychological Association (APA).

After World War I, applied psychology, particularly testing—"clinical psychology" in those days—was largely a "woman's profession," and it was everywhere. Nearly half of the APA's 300-plus members were active in some type of applied psychology. The APA had done little toward establishing standards for practitioners and, by repeatedly raising its requirements for membership, signaled its exclusive interest in experimental psychology. In 1917 a group of us at the annual meeting of the APA organized and attempted to form an independent professional organization, the American Association of Clinical Psychology. It was the first organized effort to do something about the status of psychology as a profession and was predictably met with argument and controversy. I am sorry to say that we had only limited success. Because feelings ran so high, action was postponed for a year, but at that time the APA did set up a committee to consider certification of "consulting psychologists" and to establish a clinical section within APA.

My work at the Clearing House did more than inspire me to organize applied psychologists; it introduced me to another area of psychology, the study of individual differences in intelligence which, like the psychology of women, was fraught with myth and misunderstanding (see also Pritchard, 1951). I tried to bring an objective, scientific point of view to address the unique needs and problems of these children in two books, *The Psychology of Subnormal Children* (L. Hollingworth, 1920) and *Special Talents and Defects* (L. Hollingworth, 1923). I also realized that many of the so-called "mentally defective" children that I tested were not intellectually limited, but were manifesting problems of social and personal adjustment, especially in adolescence. I developed courses on adjustment and on adolescence and published *The Psychology of the Adolescent* (L. Hollingworth, 1928), which, I am not unhappy to note, replaced Hall's textbook as a standard in the field.

In my capacity as a clinical psychologist, I became more and more frequently asked to help out with mentally gifted children who were experiencing educational or emotional problems. The prevailing notion at the time was that intelligent children need no special attention and should be able to take care of themselves, and that the exceptionally bright are fragile, clumsy, and eccentric. In fact, very bright children often do experience adjustment problems in school, not because of personality deficiencies, but because of inept treatment by adults and lack of intellectual challenge.

As often happens, a chance encounter with a single individual had an important impact on the direction of my work. A 7-year-old who was placed in the fifth grade, but was still insufficiently challenged, was brought in for a demonstration IQ test in my course on intelligence testing. Work with this boy was the first step in a research program that would occupy me for the rest of my career. At the time I began this work there were only a handful of psychologists and educators concerned with the high IQ child (or the child you would now call "gifted"). Lewis Terman, who is probably the best known to you, was largely concerned with the description of giftedness, while my interest lay in developing educational strategies for ensuring the gifted child's individual educational and developmental well-being. *Gifted Children* (L. Hollingworth, 1926) describes some of this work, and like my book on adolescence, it served as a standard reference work in schools of education for many years. I will save my discussion of my study of education for the intellectually gifted and the Speyer School experiment for another forum. I would like to mention, though, that I followed Child E (as I identify that highly gifted boy in our published work) and 11 other children to adulthood and my research on this exceptional group is summarized in *Children Above 180 I.Q.* (L. Hollingworth, 1942).

What Scientific Psychology Must Do

I credit my prairie upbringing for endowing me with a certain skepticism, with a need to test assertions empirically and independently rather than simply accept the "obvious" or the "traditional" for fact. The literature of fact is a literature based in science. Scientific progress can produce more than mere technological change; it can help us understand the social constraints that limit individuals—whether these limits are in the form of ignorance and tradition that place women in the impossible position of having to choose between intellect and nurturance, or are in the form of unfounded beliefs about intelligence that restrain gifted children from learning, doing, and achieving all that they can. Science can only contribute to the maintenance of ill-founded beliefs when it is used to "prove" a preconceived notion rather than to test that notion's legitimacy. For me the distinction between "applied" psychology and "scientific" psychology is absolutely artificial.

Throughout my career I have grappled with the problem of individual differences in the context of the group. How are we to understand the uniqueness of the individual as we go about the important job of identifying the special needs, abilities, and characteristics of the group? How are we to build a science that is nomothetically sound, and idiographically accurate? How can we best allow latitude for individual talents and predilections, while still serving the needs of the group to which that individual belongs?

The "problem" of individual differences requires us, as scientists, to maintain a steady effort to view the problem under study from the perspective of the individual whose life it touches. Here again my point is best made with an example of the often hidden loss of individual talent when the perspective of the individual participant is not remembered. One scene from my experience at Speyer School stands out vividly. I interviewed a bright young, 8-year-old and her mother regarding the girl's possible transfer to the school for gifted children. Jean had always been quick at finishing school assignments and the teacher would tell her to keep busy until the rest of the class should finish. How to keep busy? Each time that Jean finished early the teacher would tell her to take out her copy book and write numbers. "Jean had with her the copy books in which she had been writing for the past year, one digit after another by the hour. Jean's mother said, 'She can't stand the numbers any longer. Her hand gets stiff.' I wish you could see the thousands of rows of digits obediently inscribed by this intelligent child, till finally she burst out crying, 'I can't stand the numbers anymore'" (L. Hollingworth, 1940, p. 127). How many children like Jean are lost when we fail to look up from our standardized tests, measures of adjustment, and other global indexes of psychological attributes to be reminded of the individual who is being assessed?

The trend of studying the individual from a distance seems to increase directly in proportion to the size of a project and the money involved (L. Hollingworth, 1940, pp. 50, 51, 53). "To do first-class research requires the best brains and the best training. Unfortunately, today too many people are doing so-called research who lack one or the other, or both, of these requirements." Some tendencies that I've observed in child study must be brought to a halt if we are to maintain a general standard of excellence in research. I will mention only one here:

> [This unfortunate tendency] appears to be due to the demand *to get knowledge quickly*. . . . It has become a fashion in educational research to

rush forth hastily with a huge load of pencil-and-paper tests; to spend an hour or two on a hundred children; to rush hastily home to the adding machine, there to tabulate the performances of children, not *one* of whom has even been perceived as an individual child by the investigator. . ... But not only is there the tendency to get away from the individual child in favor of vague masses of children. There is the tendency for the investigator to get away from children entirely, so that all actual contacts with flesh-and-blood children are made through assistants only. . . . . If [investigators] of child psychology can be saved from ever having to manage and observe a child [they] can certainly thus avoid much fatigue. [They] will be saved from tedious contact with temper-tantrums, irrational negativisms, the expression of bodily needs, from contact with measles, whooping cough and chickenpox, from exhausting contact with parental prejudices, and so forth. The adding machine has tremendous advantages over the child as an object of intimate association. It has no parents; it does not lose its pocket-handkerchief; it has no measles; it does not kick or yell. All this we grant. Those who really study children—those who would study any individuals—*must* be prepared to "take pains."

Mrs. Pilgrim's Progress

These issues lead me back to the questions that framed my very earliest efforts as a psychologist and I want to close my remarks with a reprise. Although my research moved on to other concerns, my commitment to answering fundamental questions about the psychology and social role of women never wavered. In fact, I planned to write a book on the social psychology of women and even had chosen a title: *Mrs. Pilgrim's Progress*.

On the brink of the 21st century a fundamental re-examination of women's social role in industrial society is as clearly needed as it was 80 years ago. For example, it is essential to study pregnancy and child care. There are many crucial questions that were diligently ignored in my time but remain at the very center of human psychological well-being.

What are the best years for child-bearing—all things considered? Are the years 25–40 crucial for achievement of the distinctively human satisfactions— work, reputation, established security? If so, should children be borne before 25 or after 40? No evidence on any of these questions [is] available. Only tradition and superstition. (L. Hollingworth, 1940, pp. 59–60)

Women's social role is not an inevitable consequence of biological sex differences or natural preferences, but the action of outmoded laws and social norms whose sole foundation is custom.

The crux of the problem is obvious: Women bear children and, for centuries, have been trained to, expected to, and if need be, coerced to devote themselves to the care of their offspring. I want to emphasize that I am not criticizing motherhood or work within the domestic sphere—a facile reading would suggest this —I want to point out that the *real* problem is a "social order that has been built up on the assumption that there is and can be little or no variation in tastes, interests, and abilities within the female sex" (L. Hollingworth, 1914b, pp. 526, 528). Women's true potential can only be known if society recognizes a woman's right to choose career, maternity, or both. Through formal and informal education women have been taught by law and custom that motherhood is *the* appropriate adult female role (L. Hollingworth, 1916b).

I believe these questions are as pressing for you today as they were when I began my career as a psychologist, yet they are still considered "special interest" questions by mainstream psychology. A woman's right to choose career, maternity, or both, is immediately recognizable as a problem, but it has been neatly trivialized and transformed by social pundits into a selfish concern—the problem of "having it all." The problem of women's choice must be acknowledged as *central* to scientific psychology rather than outside the scientific canon. It cannot be set aside as one more "insoluble" problem.

> To affirm that it is insoluble is at the same time to affirm that there will always be a hard choice confronting women whose tastes vary from the mode; that there will be restlessness, unhappiness, and strife with the social order on the part of these individuals; and that society must tend to lose the work of its intellectual women or else lose their children. (L. Hollingworth, 1914b, p. 528)

"The essential fact about the New Women is that they differ among themselves, as men do, in work, in play, in virtues, in aspirations and in rewards achieved. They are women, not woman" (L. Hollingworth, 1927, p. 19). Each woman who deviates from the norms of the accepted role is faced with unique problems and is forced to produce unique solutions to them. It is the sum of these lived lives that will eventually produce, new, broader, and more suitable guidelines for the courses that a woman's life could take. Change itself can only accrue through the collected efforts of these "experimental lives," and that change happens with great struggle, but without open recognition.

> Only a few *see* that the New Woman is brave, however, because the deed she does is accomplished very, very slowly; [it] is therefore not spectacular; and especially because it is in conflict with fixed habits of thinking and acting. Such conflict irritates the near-sighted, instead of stimulating them to respect or applause. (L. Hollingworth, 1940, p. 60)

CONTRIBUTOR'S COMMENTARY

Leta Stetter Hollingworth has had a profound influence on my professional development, an influence at least as great as that of many fine teachers and colleagues I have known directly. I first encountered Leta Stetter Hollingworth's name and work in spring, 1972, while a first year graduate student at Pennsylvania State University. In the course of writing a term paper on the psychology of women (for a history of psychology course taught by Walter Weimer) I serendipitously found articles she had published early in her career—I had never encountered her name before. As a young feminist I was galvanized by the power in her description of the essential problem that women face in modern culture: how to make an intellectual and social contribution through work and, at the same time, fulfill one's capacity to nurture. As a young psychologist, I was puzzled by her belief that an objective science could help to provide the solution to this dilemma (by the early 1970's many were questioning the doctrine of the dispassionate stance of the scientist).

My interest in Leta Hollingworth led me to write a biography of her contributions to the psychology of women, which was published in 1975. Coincidentally, Ludy T. Benjamin, Jr., had also discovered Leta Hollingworth in the course of his work on Nebraska psychologists and also published a paper on her that year.

When Elizabeth Scarborough contacted me about participating in a lecture series celebrating the 50th anniversary of Edna Heidbreder's *Seven Psychologies* at the 1983 meeting of APA, I was deeply honored to play the role of Leta Hollingworth, the mentor I had never met. The experience was made doubly meaningful for me because it was to be held at the same APA meeting for which I had co-organized a symposium (with Margaret Signorella) honoring the memory of social psychologist Carolyn W. Sherif (1922–1982), who had also been a significant mentor to me in graduate school.

It was a very challenging lecture to prepare. The Heidbreder chapter I was to represent focused not on Leta Hollingworth, in whose voice the lecture was to be delivered, but on psychology at Columbia University, specifically Robert S. Woodworth's "dynamic psychology." Although I had done some research on psychology at Columbia in the course of gathering information on Leta Hollingworth, the testing movement, and the variability hypothesis, I knew little about Robert Woodworth's contributions, especially his extensive writings on dynamic psychology. I was most helped by Heidbreder's account in *Seven Psychologies* (she had been Woodworth's doctoral student at Columbia) and Woodworth's own self-effacing, clear, and cogent writing. The talk included in this volume has been substantially revised to focus on Hollingworth herself, primarily her early years as a graduate student, her contributions to the psychology of women, and her great concern that the individual not be lost at the expense of understanding the psychology of the group.

Leta Stetter Hollingworth is a well-known name among American feminist psychologists, but she also made major contributions to educational and school psychology, particularly the education of gifted children. Her contributions to that field have become increasingly recognized and in fall, 1989, there was a special conference at the University of Nebraska, celebrating her contributions to gifted education. The proceedings were published in a special issue of the *Roeper Review* (12(3), March, 1990). Recently I had the privilege of coauthoring with Ludy Benjamin a critical biography of her for Agnes N. O'Connell and Nancy Felipe Russo's *Women in Psychology* (Benjamin & Shields, 1990). A biography, written by her husband, Harry Levi Hollingworth was published in 1943 and has recently been reprinted by Anker Publishing Co. (Bolton, Mass.).

ACKNOWLEDGMENT

Parts of this chapter appeared in S. A. Shields and M. E. Mallory (1987) and are used with the publisher's permission.

REFERENCES

Benjamin, L. T., Jr. (1975). The pioneering work of Leta Hollingworth in the psychology of women. *Nebraska History, 56*, 493–505.
Benjamin, L. T., Jr., & Shields, S. A. (1990). Leta Stetter Hollingworth (1886–1939). In A. N. O'Connell & N. F. Russo (Eds.), *Women in psychology*. New York: Columbia University Press.
Heidbreder, E. (1933). *Seven psychologies*. New York: Appleton-Century-Crofts.
Hollingworth, H. L. (1943). *Leta Stetter Hollingworth*. Lincoln: University of Nebraska Press.
Hollingworth, L. S. (1914a). *Functional periodicity*. Contributions to Education, No. 69. New York: Columbia University Press.
Hollingworth, L. S. (1914b). Variability as related to sex differences in achievement. *American Journal of Sociology, 19*, 510–530.
Hollingworth, L. S. (1916a). The vocational aptitudes of women. In H. L. Hollingworth (Ed.), *Vocational psychology* (pp. 222–224). New York: Appleton.
Hollingworth, L. S. (1916b). Social devices for impelling women to bear and rear children. *American Journal of Sociology, 22*, 19–29.
Hollingworth, L. S. (1920). *The psychology of subnormal children*. New York: Macmillan.
Hollingworth, L. S. (1923). *Special talents and defects: Their significance for education*. New York: Macmillan.
Hollingworth, L. S. (1926). *Gifted children*. New York: Macmillan.

Hollingworth, L. S. (1927). The new woman in the making. *Current History, 27,* 15–20.

Hollingworth, L. S. (1928). *The psychology of the adolescent.* New York: Appleton.

Hollingworth, L. S. (1940). *Public addresses.* Lancaster, PA: Science Press.

Hollingworth, L. S. (1942). *Children above 180 I.Q.* Yonkers, NY: World Book.

Joncich, G. (1968). *The sane positivist: A biography of Edward L. Thorndike.* Middletown, CT: Wesleyan University Press.

Pritchard, M. C. (1951). The contributions of Leta S. Hollingworth to the study of gifted children. In P. Witty (Ed.), *The gifted child* (Chap. 4). Boston: D. C. Heath.

Rosenberg, R. (1982). *Beyond separate spheres: Intellectual origins of modern feminism.* New Haven, CT: Yale University Press.

Samelson, F. (1979). Putting psychology on the map: Ideology and intelligence testing. In A. R. Buss (Ed.), *Psychology in social context* (pp. 103–168). New York: Irvington.

Shields, S. A. (1975a). Ms. Pilgrim's progress: The contributions of Leta Stetter Hollingworth to the psychology of women. *American Psychologist, 30,* 852–857.

Shields, S. A. (1975b).Functionalism, Darwinism, and the psychology of women. *American Psychologist, 30,* 739–754.

Shields, S. A. (1982). The variability hypothesis. *Signs, 7,* 769–797.

Shields, S. A., & Mallory, M. E. (1987). Leta Stetter Hollingworth speaks on "Columbia's Legacy." *Psychology of Women Quarterly, 11,* 285–300.

Chapter 17

Natural Wholes: Wolfgang Köhler and Gestalt Theory

Robert Sherrill, Jr.

The following is an imaginary interview that I conducted with Dr. Köhler at his retirement home in New Hampshire in June 1967, shortly before his death. As I approached the house, Dr. Köhler was outside, chopping wood. His ax gleamed; it obviously was maintained carefully. Although he was doing manual labor, he was dressed impeccably in a suit and tie, very much the gentleman.

My initial impressions of Dr. Köhler were somewhat contradictory. His manner of relating was formal and polite. He spoke quietly, but with an intensity that commanded attention. He appeared very uncomfortable when discussing his personal life. He maintained some degree of aristocratic aloofness. I thought of the reports from several of Köhler's former assistants, that he could be extremely severe and demanding. At the same time, however, there was evidence of an artistic sensitivity, and a broad range of cultural interests. On one side of the living room there was a piano, and a stack of sheet music. Köhler admitted that playing the piano had always been one of his favorite pastimes. Near the door stood a well-worn pair of hiking shoes. Through the window, I could see a convertible parked in the yard, with its top down. Köhler appeared to be a man who had a zest for the outdoors. I thought of the romantic streak in German culture.

Dr. Köhler explained that he usually declined interviews, but had decided on his way back from a recent trip to Europe that he wanted to

---

*Photograph of Wölfgang Kohler courtesy of the Archives of the History of Psychology, Akron, Ohio

explain to psychologists in a less formal manner than in his scientific articles and lectures the full breadth of Gestalt theory, and to give some examples of how it forms the basis of a psychology that is both scientifically rigorous and humanly relevant. Now Dr. Köhler begins to speak.

FIRST YEARS

I was born in the city of Tallinn, Estonia, in 1887. My father was the headmaster of the local school set up by the community of German citizens living and working in the area for the education of their children. When I was about 6, our family returned to Germany, where I was raised. Education was important in our family. My older brother, Wilhelm, to whom I always felt very close, became a distinguished academician. My sisters were all trained as teachers or nurses. I always excelled in my academic studies. In addition, the German ideal of education at that time included a very broad cultural grounding. I was a lover of classical music from an early age. By the time I was an adult, I could converse knowledgeably about the arts and humanities, especially philosophy.

I attended the Universities of Tübingen, Bonn, and Berlin. At that time, the German university system was the envy of the world, with a long tradition of outstanding academic freedom, and a reputation for scientific excellence and academic rigor. There was an old saying about German university students that a third of them succumbed to the pressures of coursework and suffered nervous breakdowns; another third responded to the pressures with avoidance, got lost in alcohol, and generally went to the devil; and the last third went on to rule Europe. I received a thorough scientific background in physics, chemistry, and biology. I was deeply impressed by one of my physics professors at the University of Berlin, the great Max Planck. His lectures included such concepts as the entropy principle, and the dynamic self-regulation of physical systems, such as electrolytic media. Throughout my career, I found it useful to analyze psychological phenomena such as apparent movement or perceptual aftereffects in relation to such concepts. Several of my colleagues remarked over the years that I thought more like a physicist than a psychologist. I received my PhD in psychology from the University of Berlin in 1909. My earliest scientific papers were on the psychological analysis of audition, which for me was a happy marriage between my scientific training and my love of music.

RECONCEPTUALIZING SCIENTIFIC INQUIRY IN PSYCHOLOGY

In those days, there was much discussion in psychology about what was called the crisis of science. Although the natural sciences were all making impressive advances, many people doubted that the scientific method could be applied in psychology to solve significant human problems. Some psychologists wanted to abandon the scientific method entirely in favor of an intuitive "science of understanding."

It was difficult, in fact, to see much that was meaningful in the experimental psychology of that day. For example, the study of perception attempted to imitate the science of chemistry, by analyzing phenomena minutely into their simplest "elements." Lists of such so-called elements had been proposed, such as sensations and feelings, and attributes for each element, such as intensity or duration. Supposedly, the original phenomena of perceptual experience could be reconstructed by some process of simple addition or other combination of these elements. We called this the brick-and-mortar theory of perception. The trouble with the theory was that no one had been able to demonstrate how any combination of these rationally derived elements could produce a whole perception, with all its freshness and meaningfulness.

Koffka and Wertheimer

After receiving my doctorate, I had gone to the Frankfurt Academy to begin my academic career. My original intention was to continue with my psychological studies of audition, and I did publish several papers on this topic over the next few years. Kurt Koffka joined our staff the next year. Also, in the summer of 1910, Max Wertheimer appeared with some new ideas concerning the study of visual perception, and was offered laboratory space by an old professor of his from the University of Berlin to try them out. Koffka and I served as Wertheimer's first subjects.

Wertheimer's original experiment was very simple, but simple experiments can demonstrate important concepts. Imagine that you are seated in a darkened room, facing two strobe lights placed several inches apart, which are flashed in a regular, alternating sequence. If the time interval between the flashes is very slow, you will perceive each light flashing in an alternating sequence, as the brick-and-mortar theory of perception would predict. If the sequence of flashing is very fast, you will perceive both lights as remaining essentially on, with each lamp's intensity rapidly waxing and waning. However, at some intermediate frequency, you will perceive only a single light, which shuttles back and forth between the strobes. This perceived movement does not have the static qualities that had been previously ascribed to perceptual "elements." More importantly, it would not be predicted by any possible summation of these elements.

As Wertheimer, Koffka, and I discussed the implications of these experiments on the perception of movement, we agreed that studying the natural wholes of psychological phenomena permitted psychological science to regain human meaningfulness. We embarked on a project, which lasted our lifetimes, to demonstrate how this reconceptualization could apply to the entire breadth of scientific psychology, and beyond.

We began with the study of visual perception, because it was a stronghold of the brick-and-mortar theories we were attacking, and also because studies of visual perception allowed rigorous experimental control. Over the next several years, we published a series of papers that demonstrated that visual percepts are organized wholes whose subparts are not independent, but instead dynamically influence one another. Thus emerged our famous saying, "The whole is different from the sum of its parts." We showed in this way that it was scientifically necessary to perform analysis "from above," that is, from the whole, when first approaching a psychological problem. We analyzed a psychological phenomenon, such as a percept, into its naturally occurring subparts as a basis for further investigation. Such an approach preserved both scientific rigor and the human freshness of the original phenomenon. In our books and articles, we could demonstrate important points very simply, for example by using pictures with reversible figures and grounds in which the conclusions were self-evident from the reader's immediate experience of the phenomenon, rather than resorting to elaborate descriptions of perceptual elements, or statistics, and the like.

Gestalt Theory

The German word *Gestalt* means shape or overall configuration. The term can be applied more broadly outside of sensory experience to any organized entity, such as a memory trace, or the essence of a concept, such as justice. We adopted the term Gestalt for our theoretical approach out of our concern for respecting the natural wholes of percepts or other psychological entities. We believed that an analysis beginning with *Gestalten* would prevent scientific psychology from drifting into a myopic obsession with trivia, which had plagued the study of perception in the early 20th century, and which in my opinion, continues to hinder academic psychology today. Experimental psychology's naïve attempt to imitate chemistry in its search for "elements" had ignored two obvious facts known to any chemist. First, although in theory chemistry is ultimately reducible to physics, because the physical properties of compounds are entirely a function of the physical properties of the combining elements, the interactions among elements quickly become so complex that compounds have properties that could never be humanly predictable from a comprehensive knowledge of each element. Therefore, chemistry has remained a separate science, whose primary focus is on the behavior of compounds. Second, in many molecules, the atoms can combine in more than one structural configuration. Differences in this structural Gestalt cause very important differences in the properties of the molecule as a whole.

THE TENERIFE YEARS

My studies of the properties of Gestalten took an unexpected turn when I was appointed by the Prussian Academy of Science in 1913 to assume the directorship of an anthropoid research station on the island of Tenerife, off the coast of Africa. I remained there until 1920, in part due to World War I.

Perception and Insight

During those years, I performed naturalistic experiments which demonstrated that in apes both perceptions and cognitions are organized *Gestalten*. For perceptions, I showed that the apes learned *relationships* among stimuli, rather than a simple response to an isolated stimulus. For example, the apes learned to respond consistently to the smaller of two stimuli, even when the stimulus that had been rewarded in training trials became the stimulus to be avoided in the testing trials. This is the phenomenon of transposition, which is seen in many *Gestalten*, for example in melodies. For cognitions, I demonstrated that the solution of a problem required not just the gradual accumulation of new facts, but rather the reorganization of existing facts into a new, coherent structure.

I summarized these findings in my book, *The Mentality of Apes*, which was published originally in 1917, while I was still on Tenerife. I was proud to have demonstrated that cognitive restructuring is the essence of meaningful, more complex learning. For example, in one of my well-known experiments on problem solving, a chimpanzee was placed in a cage with a banana hung from a high beam. In the cage were two boxes. The chimpanzee could not reach the banana by standing on either box alone. His attempts at a solution began with considerable frustration, and numerous outbursts of temper. But suddenly, his behavior changed completely. His emotional distress disappeared. He quickly ran over to the smaller box; pulled it over to the larger box, which he had placed directly under the banana; stood the smaller box upright on the larger one; climbed immediately to the top of the smaller box; and plucked down the banana. Further trials with the same problem were solved quickly, even when the boxes were placed initially in very different locations in the cage. In other words, the animal's specific motoric behaviors were reorganized efficiently on each trial as subparts of a general solution. I emphasized in my book that a genuine achievement, as opposed to a chance solution, took place as a single continuous occurrence in space as well as in time. These experiences with the apes led me to define insight as the (often abrupt) appearance of a complete solution with reference to the whole layout of the perceptual or cognitive field.

A Whisper of Espionage[1]

It has been suggested (Ley, 1990) that after World War I broke out, I was recruited by the government of Germany to spy upon Allied naval traffic in the vicinity of Tenerife. It is true that Tenerife was an odd place to establish an anthropoid research station, since apes are not native to the Canary Islands. It would have been logistically simpler to study them in their home environment in the German Cameroons on the mainland of Africa, or simply to transport them to a large zoo in Germany. It is also true that Tenerife was strategically important during the first world war, because it was close to major shipping lanes in the Atlantic. Finally, it is true that there is considerable evidence from both the German and the British Naval Archives that the German government operated a very active espionage organization in the Canary Islands during World War I, and that the British suspected strongly that I was part of it, to the point of insisting repeatedly to the local Spanish authorities that my residence be searched. And it is very embarrassing that my former animal handler on Tenerife and two of my children from my first marriage have remembered that I operated a radio in a second story room of our house, where the children were never permitted to go, and that I would hide it carefully when I would be tipped off that the soldiers were coming again to search my home. Concerning all this, I will say only that I was a loyal citizen of my fatherland, Germany, until conditions there became intolerable; and that I have been equally loyal to my adopted country, the United States, from 1935 on.

THE BERLIN YEARS

In 1920, I returned to Germany to become the acting director of the Psychological Institute at the University of Berlin. Also in 1920, I published my book *Physical Gestalten*, which I continue to regard as one of my most important achievements. The book had a preface for physicists, and another for philosophers and biologists. In the book, I

---

[1]The title of this section is the title of Ley's (1990) book.

demonstrated that perceptual *Gestalten* exert a force toward an end-state characterized by completeness and equilibrium. For example, a visual stimulus of an incomplete circle will tend to be perceived as a complete circle. My colleague Wertheimer had proposed in 1912 that the Gestalt properties of visual perceptions must be reflections of similar structural relationships in underlying brain processes. I developed Wertheimer's insight in *Physical Gestalten* with detailed mathematical arguments that the dynamic character of psychological phenomena must be an expression of similar dynamic events among various regions of the brain that went beyond simple synaptic transmission of impulses, and obeyed physical laws of self-distribution and equilibrium. This identity of structure between psychological phenomena and underlying brain processes became the famous Gestalt theory of isomorphism. I consider it one of my most important contributions to science to have demonstrated that psychological processes can be analyzed with the methods and terminology of field physics.

In 1922, I received the additional academic appointment of professor of philosophy at the University of Berlin. Wertheimer was already there; and we stayed in close touch with Koffka, who was at the University of Giessen. During the 1920s and into the early 1930s, the Psychological Institute was lively and extraordinarily productive. We applied Gestalt principles to a wide variety of psychological issues and attracted students from all over the world. Our institute was located in one wing of what used to be the German emperor's palace. We worked in rooms with high, elaborately painted ceilings. Surely, psychological experiments have never been conducted in a more opulent setting! We attempted to instill in our students not only the highest standards of scientific excellence, but also an appreciation of the interrelatedness of the best that is human. On one occasion, when someone told me of a particularly elegant experiment in audition, I remarked, "Now that is an experiment worthy of Mozart!"

Nazi Disruption

But it was not to last. Outside of the universities, Germany's ferment was in part a reflection of serious economic and social disruption. Most of my academic colleagues viewed the National Socialists as thugs. Even when the Nazis took control of the government in January, 1933, it was difficult for most of us to imagine that they could force any important changes upon the university system or upon its cultural leadership of such a highly educated, sophisticated society. But almost immediately the Ministry of Culture began to dismiss professors who were Jewish. To my astonishment, almost none of my Christian colleagues was willing to protest this publicly. Many of them felt that it was improper to express an opinion outside of one's own subject of expertise, even in the role of an ordinary citizen.

In April 1933, I protested publicly in the form of an article for a Berlin newspaper. I pointed out that it was inconsistent of the Nazis to be both highly nationalistic and anti-Semitic, since many of the greatest contributors to German culture had been our country's Jewish citizens. My article caused quite a bit of public discussion as soon as it appeared, and the newspaper had to print extra copies of that day's edition. My friends predicted that the Nazis would respond to such a direct challenge by arresting me that very night. Knowing that the Gestapo typically made arrests in the wee hours of the morning, we decided to stay up all night and play chamber music. I was never arrested. However, the National Socialists continued to intimidate anyone who opposed them and to erode the academic freedom of the universities. It has been said that my newspaper article was the last openly anti-Nazi opinion to appear in print during the Third Reich.

In December 1933, troops interfered with persons leaving a colloquium at our institute. I protested strongly, and was promised that this would not occur again. In February 1934, however, it did occur again and in April 1934, the institute was searched for evidence of subversive activity. I protested even more sternly, to no avail. It was becoming increasingly unlikely that I would be able to protect the academic appointments of my assistants, and maintain the scholarly integrity of our institute. I offered to retire, but did not pursue this. Instead, with some sadness, I accepted an offer to deliver the William James lectures as a visiting professor at Harvard in the fall of 1934, and another to teach at the University of Chicago for the spring semester of 1935.

The ominous changes in German universities continued. While at Harvard, I received a written request to sign an oath of personal loyalty to Adolf Hitler. In January 1935, I was informed that a position at the institute had been filled without my permission. In May, I learned that all of the assistants whom I had trained had been dismissed. Convinced that the traditional academic freedom and cultural leadership of German universities had perished, I resigned from the University of Berlin in August 1935, and accepted a professorship at Swarthmore College in Pennsylvania.

THE SWARTHMORE YEARS

I taught at Swarthmore from 1935 until my retirement in 1958. I continued my study of dynamic vectors in areas of psychology in which experimental control was possible, such as perception and cognition. I saw this work as preparing Gestalt theory for the eventual study of human motivation. As I had at the University of Berlin, I attempted to relate psychological processes to underlying processes in brain tissue that obey the laws of field physics. I interpreted motivation as forces that operate between the person's perceptual and cognitive processes, on the one hand, and other processes that must be represented in other parts of the brain where physiological needs are represented.

Field Forces in Brain Processes

In an attempt to define scientifically the brain processes that must underlie all psychological processes, I began a long series of physiological experiments to demonstrate the field forces that underlie perception. Along with my students and colleagues at Swarthmore, I recorded electrical potentials from the visual cortex of cats, in which we showed that DC currents occurred, which corresponded with perceptual phenomena. For example, when a moving object was presented to the cat, electrical currents across the cortex shifted in the direction that would have been predicted from our knowledge of cortical representation of various parts of the visual field. These DC currents would not be predicted by atomistic theories of simple synaptic transmission of impulses. I was certain that they were caused instead by relatively steady electrical potentials maintained across cortical synapses.

Psychological Demands and Values

I also extended my work on the general importance of vectors in human life to the other side of psychology, that is, to issues of ethics and esthetics. I edited the lectures I had given at Harvard University in 1934 into a book I titled *The Place of Value in a World of Facts*, published in 1938. In it, I detailed how what we experience as the "requiredness" of a moral or ethical situation exerts a vector force upon us psychologically and neurologically, in exactly the same way that visual perception shows a psychophysical pressure toward completeness. Requiredness always occurs within a context of other facts, or human acts. It has a strongly demanding effect upon us, even when our personal needs are not involved. In fact, our responding to the requiredness can at times place us in physical danger. I saw such requiredness as being an objective basis of value, and therefore of human morality. In this way, Gestalt theory, with its emphasis upon dynamics and vectors, not only regrounded psychology in modern physiology, but also restored the possibility of scientific analysis of some of the most meaningful parts of human experience, such as ethics. It was always important to me that

Gestalt theory could be faithful both to the primary data of human experience and also to the unity of human life. In fact, my colleague von Hornbostel once wrote a delightful article that was titled, "The Unity of the Senses." Psychology is capable of being both rigorous and humanly meaningful, and those of us who were Gestalt theorists were proud to have been the first to demonstrate this.

MOTIVATION AND EMOTION

Now I depart from a chronicle of my personal history to discuss how we Gestalt theorists approach problems of human motivation and emotion. I want to do this in order to correct the impression held by many psychologists today that our primary concern has been the study of visual perception. Also, I want psychologists to understand that it was in our cautious approach to motivation and emotion that we parted company with similar theoretical systems which used our concepts and terms, but expanded upon them in ways in which I disapproved. I find great confusion among psychologists today with regard to who is and is not a Gestalt theorist.

Gestalt versus Figure–Ground Relationships

I will begin by emphasizing the distinction between a Gestalt and a figure–ground formation. Out of our concern for scientific rigor, we defined our terms very carefully. For Wertheimer, Koffka, and myself, a Gestalt was any naturally occurring organized entity or functional whole. A Gestalt could be a visual percept, a temporal pattern such as a melody or dance, a cognitive entity such as a memory trace, or a concept such as truth or democracy. Figure–ground formation is a special case of a Gestalt that occurs only in perception. In addition to the internal organization possessed by every Gestalt, a figure has a well-defined shape, a prominent contour, and greater "thing character" than the ground. Wertheimer and I used figure–ground formation only with regard to visual entities. My colleague Koffka was more liberal, and was willing to extend it to auditory percepts and to the other senses.

Affective Gestalten

We considered at least the cognitive components of motivational and emotional states to be *Gestalten*, and we were confident that a Gestalt analysis would be useful in understanding them. We discussed needs as forces that endow already-existing *Gestalten* with a personal vector that we called demand character. A Gestalt so endowed could be a percept, such as the sound of a waterfall heard by a person who is thirsty, or a cognition, such as the idea of water. Conversely, when a personal need is satisfied, the demand character attached to the Gestalt is destroyed. Koffka noted that after a copious meal, even the most delicious food has no attraction for us.

When the demand character associated with a problem is sufficiently strong, a person's problem solving suffers: elegant, correct solutions tend to be overlooked. In extreme cases, incorrect, maladaptive *Gestalten* can be organized. An example of this was described by one of our students, Schulte, in an article published in 1924 on the development of paranoid delusions. He outlined a sequence in which some situations demand a "we" relationship; the person is incapable of feeling and acting as a part of a "we," even though he is drawn poignantly toward group membership; and the cognition of a delusional relationship to others gradually forms, as a substitute fulfillment for the need. In one of my own papers, I described how an obsession could have the quality of a very lively being that seems to live inside oneself. Obsessions are often maladaptive, since they tend to crystallize a person's world around one theme. However, I added that sometimes obsessions can be harnessed in the service of a greater requiredness, such as that of the scientist or historian searching for truth. In that case, their power to force a uniformity upon one's world, and to maintain this focus for sustained periods, can cause new perceptions to emerge, or existing cognitions to reorganize into new, more creative structures.

Notes of Caution

We were confident that Gestalt analysis could clarify many other issues of motivation and emotion. I certainly considered cognitive structures such as having a sense of personal wholeness to be *Gestalten*. On one occasion, I went on a tour of a public mental hospital in New York. I was shaken badly by the sight of people who were struggling desperately to maintain any degree of organization of self. However, I insisted that problems of psychopathology be approached with proper caution and rigor. I had three reasons for such caution.

First, I wanted Gestalt theory to be established firmly in fields where experimental control was possible. This was especially important since in the earlier years of the Gestalt movement the academic behaviorists so often accused us of mysticism. Even so humane a scientist as Karl Lashley once asked me if I didn't have religion up my sleeve.

Second, we insisted that a perception or cognition is determined almost entirely by the objective structural organization of the stimulus or entity itself. As I have described, we attacked the brick-and-mortar theories of perception that explained away how we typically perceive whole, meaningful objects by assuming some process of synthesis within the perceiver such as "unconscious inference." We believed that organismic factors, such as fatigue or emotional needs, influence the actual formation of *Gestalten*, in the way in which Schulte described, only rarely. We saw organismic needs as special-case variables, which become important only when the objective stimuli are weak in their intensity or organization.

Finally, we were cautious about human motivation because it is so commonly believed to be only self-interest. I once remarked that my colleague Wertheimer was forever suspicious of mere selves, and I shared his rejection of the belief that human motivation is limited to the little voice that whispers, "Where do I get my share?" We preferred to concentrate upon aspects of Gestalt analysis, such as problem solving, which are less related to need-fulfillment, in order to avoid any misinterpretation that things make sense only with reference to a subjective I. Later, we thought, when the fundamentals were clear, self-interest would be recognized as the special-case variable in Gestalt formation that it is.

LEWIN AND GOLDSTEIN

With that prologue, I can describe Gestalt theory's relationship to the work of Lewin and Goldstein. I understand how easy it has been for many psychologists to confuse our work with theirs, in view of the similarity in use of terms and their close association with us in the 1920s.

Lewinian Field Theory

Lewin studied at the University of Berlin and became a faculty member at our institute after attaining his doctorate. He soon attracted his own crowd of enthusiastic students. He had enormous respect for Gestalt theory, but also felt free to criticize it when he believed that it was too narrow. I felt some personal kinship to him, since he thought about psychological problems in mathematical terms. For some years, our families were close. However, I disapproved of his willingness to use terms rather loosely in order to apply Gestalt analysis more quickly to problems of motivation. For example, he discussed a person's entire life-space as a Gestalt, including intrapsychic structures and processes that were far removed from direct observation or exact definition. For several years in the late 1920s, my students and his carried on a kind of running battle within the institute. The rivalry was enormously stimulating for us and for our students. I was proud to see that many of the American students who spent a year or two at our institute became eminent in psychology over the next several decades. By the time Lewin came to the United States in 1933, he believed that his theoretical system had diverged sufficiently from Gestalt theory to give it a separate name, field theory, or topological psychology. In a book with the latter title, he addressed a preface to me in which he expressed appreciation for my leadership of the happy and lively collective of friends at the University of Berlin. He then added impishly that he had tried his best to destroy the myth that Gestaltists do not attack one another in print. Because motivation was Lewin's main interest, and because he defined his terms more loosely, I agreed that his system was not Gestalt theory, and deserved a separate name.

Goldstein's Gestalt Neurology

Kurt Goldstein was a neurologist who worked at a rehabilitation institute for brain-injured soldiers in Frankfurt. Like Lewin, he was enthusiastic over the potential for applying Gestalt theory to complex human problems. He was one of the cofounders with Wertheimer, Koffka, and myself of the journal *Psychologische Forschung* in 1921, which published a considerable portion of the Gestalt theory literature during the years I lived in Berlin. However, like Lewin, he soon felt that a broader definition of Gestalt terms was necessary to accommodate the investigation of higher cognitive processes. As one example: he referred to a motor act in response to a stimulus as a figure formation, which occurred against the background of the organism's general physiological state. By the time Goldstein delivered a series of lectures at Harvard University in 1938–1939, he was referring to his theoretical system as organismic biology, or the holistic approach. He expressed appreciation to Gestalt theory, but made it clear that his theoretical emphases were different from ours. I agreed, and by the 1940s I was speaking of his work in a cool, distancing manner. I continue to view the work of both Lewin and Goldstein not as Gestalt theory, but as derivations of Gestalt theory.

GESTALT THEORY AND GESTALT PSYCHOTHERAPY

I now wish to talk about an important way in which the contributions of Gestalt theory have been distorted and abused. I am referring to a sloppy thinker by the name of Fritz Perls. Perls had been an assistant to Goldstein in 1926 at the neurological institute in Frankfurt. At that time, Goldstein and his colleague Gelb were already applying Gestalt concepts to the study of brain injury, with an expansion of the definition of Gestalt

terms that I have described. It was for this reason that they were beginning to speak of their adaptation of Gestalt principles as organismic
biology rather than Gestalt theory. Perls probably did not remember
correctly the distinction between these two systems, such as Goldstein's
broader use of the term "figure." It is certain that Perls did not read our
work before he wrote his own books, for he misrepresented us very
badly. For example, in one of his books he said that the choice of which
of all possible stimuli would stand out as figure for a person is the result
of many factors, which he lumped together under the general term
"interest." Such a statement implies that organismic needs exert a strong
influence upon perception. As I have mentioned, Gestalt theorists asserted repeatedly that perception is organized primarily by the dynamic
properties of the stimuli themselves. Much of what Perls describes as
perception would be described by us as selective *attention* to already-
formed *Gestalten*. It was astonishing for me to read that Perls attributed
to Gestalt theory the idea that organismic interest was a necessary condition for figure-ground formation. Also, I take strong exception to his
lumping together, as he put it, a number of factors under a term such as
"interest," without discussing what these factors are and under what
conditions they might act in the unifying way he suggests.

I give you one other example of how badly Perls misconstrued Gestalt
theory, out of his book entitled very appropriately *In and Out the Garbage
Pail* (1969, unpaginated). He says,

> [our answer] comes from a direction which never claimed the status of a
> philosophy [,] Gestalt psychology. . . . The formulation as expressed by
> the Gestaltists cannot possibly be correct. They say that the whole is more
> than the parts. In other words, something is added to the world simply by
> a configuration. This would ruin our picture of the energy balance of the
> universe. . . . [S]hall we then let the Gestaltists attribute to Gestalt
> formation more power than our pious ancestors gave to God?

For Perls to assert this of Gestalt theory is ridiculous. As I said earlier,
we recognized that Gestalt analysis could apply to a very wide range of
fields of study, spanning physics, biology, psychology and all of its
various subfields, ethics, and esthetics. We do, indeed, see ourselves as
promoting a general philosophical stance rather than a specialized
approach to visual perception. It is for this reason exactly that we
describe ourselves not as Gestalt psychologists but as Gestalt *theorists*.
As for Perls's assertions about energy balance, I demonstrated rigorously in my book *Physical Gestalten* that all Gestalten obey physical laws
of conservation of energy and of entropy. Finally, Perls's notion that a
Gestalt is something that is somehow added to a summation of parts

was precisely that part of the doctrine of earlier psychologists that my colleagues and I had rejected in our earliest papers on Gestalt theory, as I have described. What we did say was that the whole was fundamentally different from any possible summation of its parts.

In fairness to Perls, one could point out that his work might be a direct descendant of the theories of Lewin and Goldstein, since these researchers were willing to use terms such as "figure" far more loosely than myself and my colleagues in Gestalt theory. To my knowledge, such a careful exploration of these relationships has not yet been performed. I know that Paul Goodman made an attempt at a general theoretical formulation of Gestalt psychotherapy in the second part of the book *Gestalt Therapy*, which he co-authored with Perls and Ralph Hefferline (Perls, Hefferline, & Goodman, 1951). Unfortunately, he discussed the work of Lewin, Goldstein, and other psychologists as if it belonged to the mainstream of Gestalt theory. I hope I have made it clear that this is incorrect. Certainly, the books that Perls wrote by himself later in his life contain many gross distortions of our ideas, which would be comical except that they are taken seriously today by students of psychology. My colleague Mary Henle (1978) has written an article that discusses the ways in which the philosophy underlying Gestalt psychotherapy is different from that of Gestalt theory.

CONCLUDING PERSONAL NOTE

I believe that Gestalt theory's concern with the importance of human values has been vindicated in a backhand way by the modern academic behaviorists—I don't suppose that there is any other way that Gestalt theory could be vindicated by a behaviorist. The modern behaviorists now tell us that if we want to understand and change a person's behavior, we have to have some idea of what that person thinks and values. Isn't that marvelous! They call it "cognitive behaviorism." When I said similar things 40 years ago, they called it the pollution of scientific psychology with mysticism.

Also I am pleased to see that the modern psychology of perception continues to demonstrate that what we perceive is overwhelmingly determined by the objective properties of the stimulus. Motivation is influential in determining which of the available *Gestalten* we attend to and deal with, but most experimenters would agree that needs exert relatively little influence upon the actual formation of *Gestalten* or figures-on-ground. They would also agree that intense need states often interfere with the discovery of elegant and correct solutions to a problem.

On another point: Gestalt theory's emphasis upon the isomorphic relationships between perceptual phenomena and underlying brain processes continues to influence the experimental study of perception through research on figural after-effects. If a person is exposed to a figure, especially if the exposure is prolonged or intense, perception of subsequent figures will be affected. Such changes in perception reflect changes in the electrolytic medium of brain tissue caused by the first figure.

Finally, if there is any one idea that I would like to leave with young psychologists today, it would be that Gestalt theory began as a revolt against the naïve conception that science is limited to atomistic analysis. When my colleagues and I were students, we were shocked to find that the colorful, dynamic, meaningful aspects of everyday life, such as perception and memory, were described in terms of unrelated elements, which were somehow combined by mental associations. We were disturbed by the implication of this outlook that human life is intrinsically boring and senseless. American psychology has continued this tradition, with its suffocating emphasis on experimental methodology and theoretical analysis, at the price of great sacrifices in meaningfulness. This is a little bit like being preoccupied with aspects of your automobile, such as keeping your brakes maintained and your windshield clean. These services are necessary, of course, but they are not the main point of an automobile. In the same way, methodology and analysis are not the main point of psychological research. Allowing the vitality of humanness to become obscured in a quest for scientific understanding of human beings can easily shade into a subtle but pervasive philosophy of "nothing but." Karl Marx tried to tell us that human beings are nothing but the pawns of overpowering economic forces. Sigmund Freud tried to tell us that human love is nothing but a derivative of animal instinct. The experimental psychologists often act as though the essence of human learning is nothing but the associationistic laws that can be discovered in experiments with nonsense syllables.

This philosophy of "nothing but" has invaded every aspect of American culture. I call it "The Smog." It is contrary to the ideals upon which the United States was founded. The people who wrote the Declaration of Independence and the Constitution were highly optimistic about human nature. They believed that the capacities for rationality and simple humanness possessed by ordinary citizens are sufficient to guide a nation—that the most effective way to advance political and cultural life is to allow free citizens to follow their natural sense of what is just and necessary.

Science has made enormous strides in the past few centuries and it deserves the respect that it receives from lay individuals. However, the atomistic conception of science, which was so effective during the 19th century, still seems to some to be the only possible way to view life scientifically. Such an atomistic view of human beings and human society has badly undermined the optimistic view of human nature held by the Founding Fathers. I would hope that scientific psychology would broaden its conception of science, abandon atomism and help reverse the trend toward "nothing but." Just as the whole is qualitatively different from the sum of its parts, so also are human beings capable of being qualitatively different from, and far richer than, anything that can possibly be the result of economic forces impinging on their base instincts. If we can be alert to "The Smog" creeping on its atomistic cat feet into our work and thought, we will be able to keep ourselves focused on the richness of our experience of life and on the best that is human.

ACKNOWLEDGMENTS

This chapter is a revision of an invited address presented at the annual convention of the Rocky Mountain Psychological Association in April 1978. For purposes of the imaginary interview, the author has endowed Dr. Köhler with the capacity to comment on events that happened after his death, such as the later works of Fritz Perls and the account of his years on Tenerife by Ley (1990). The author is indebted to a variety of sources in addition to the works listed in the references: to Boring's (1950) presentation of the analogy of psychological *Gestalten* to chemical compounds, to Dr. Michael Wertheimer for his personal recollections of Dr. Köhler, and to Ms. Sue Van Riper for her transcription of the manuscript.

REFERENCES

Boring, E. G. (1950). *A history of experimental psychology*. New York: Appleton-Century-Crofts.

Ellis, W. D. (1938). *A source book of Gestalt psychology*. London: Routledge & Kegan Paul. (contains summaries of some of the important early Gestalt literature, including Köhler's *Physical Gestalten* and the articles by Schulte and von Hornbostel mentioned in this chapter).

Henle, M. (1978). Gestalt psychology and Gestalt therapy. *Journal of the History of the Behavioral Sciences, 14*, 23–32.

Köhler, W. (1917/1925). *The mentality of apes*. London: Routledge & Kegan Paul. [The original German publication was in 1917].

Köhler, W. (1938). *The place of value in a world of facts*. New York: Liveright.

Köhler, W., Held, R., & O'Connell, D. N. (1952). An investigation of cortical currents. *Proceedings of the American Philosophical Society, 96*, 290–330.

Ley, R. (1990). *A whisper of espionage: Wolfgang Köhler and the apes of Tenerife*. Garden City Park, NY: Avery.

Perls, F. (1969). *In and out the garbage pail*. Lafayette, CA: Real People Press.

Perls, F., Hefferline, R. F., & Goodman, P. (1951). *Gestalt therapy: Excitement and growth in the human personality*. New York: Julian Press.

Chapter 18

General Anthroponomy and Its Systematic Problems: A Tribute to Walter S. Hunter

Charles N. Cofer

When Professor Kimble invited me to prepare this tribute to Walter S. Hunter, he asked me for a title. I thought immediately of two: both were titles of Hunter publications. The first was "General Anthroponomy and its Systematic Problems," the second was "An Open Letter to the Anti-behaviorists." Kimble chose the second one but, in the process of the revision of the paper for publication, we agreed that, although I have things to say that pertain to both titles, the first is more appropriate.

In preparing this address, I have had access to Hunter's (1952) chapter in the *History of Psychology in Autobiography* and four obituaries that were written by Hunter's colleagues (Carmichael, 1954; Graham, 1958; Hunt, 1956; Schlosberg, 1954). Hunter directed my dissertation and I was a student in three of his courses, "Animal Behavior," "The Learning Process," and " Seminar in Systematic Psychology." I still have my class notes, to which I have been able to refer. A long letter from J. McV. Hunt, a faculty member at Brown, was very useful, as were conversations with Frank Finger, a fellow graduate student at Brown, 1937–1940, and Gregory A. Kimble and G. Robert Grice, junior faculty members at Brown immediately after World War II, and with their wives. In addition I have read or reread those of Hunter's papers that seem to me to have contained his major contributions to research, theory, and training in psychology.

In summarizing Hunter's contributions, I will, first, present a brief

---

*Photograph of Walter S. Hunter courtesy of the Archives of the History of Psychology, Akron, Ohio

biography. Second, I will describe his commitment to behaviorism and general anthroponomy. Third, I will review some of his work on the sensory control of the maze habit and his rejection of Crozier's tropistic analysis of behavior and Lashley's doctrine of equipotentiality. Fourth, I will consider the research by Hunter and his students on the delayed reaction and on double alternation in the temporal maze in several species, the results of which led him to postulate the existence of symbolic processes in some species of animals. Lastly, I will review his professional contributions, including his editorial work, his committee work, and his involvement as a psychologist in government in the two world wars.

BIOGRAPHICAL

The Hunter family was of Scottish origin and lived in Northern Ireland before coming to the United States in the 18th century, settling in the Middle West. Originally, most of them were farmers. Hunter was born on March 22, 1889, in Decatur, Illinois, where his father was in the real estate business. When he was 12 and in the sixth grade, his mother died and his father moved Walter and his older brother to Texas, to a farm near Saginaw, a town a few miles northwest of Fort Worth. Walter attended the two-room school during the 6-month term, and worked in the fields during the summers. He wrote (1952, p. 164), "I did a man's job in harvest, threshing and plowing in the summers" from 1901 to 1910. In addition to school and farming, probably with the encouragement of his father, Hunter found time to read Darwin's *Origin of Species* and *Descent of Man* and at least 15 paper-bound classics in American and English literature (some of which he memorized), to take a correspondence course on electrical engineering, to organize an Athenian society in Saginaw and to serve as the local correspondent for the North Fort Worth newspaper.

Education

Hunter had planned, on finishing the local school, to study electrical engineering at Texas A&M, but a teacher persuaded him to study the liberal arts first, so he attended the Fort Worth Polytechnical College for 3 years. At Polytechnical, a roommate lent him a text on psychology by the late Noah K. Davis of the University of Virginia. This aroused his interest in psychology, and he went on to read a text on psychology by William James (the abbreviated one in the "Briefer Course" series, the one that students called "The Jimmy," in contrast to "The James," their term for the larger two-volume *Principles of Psychology*). This reading led him to decide, at age 17, to become a psychologist. At the suggestion of a professor of philosophy and German, W. B. Rinker, he took courses in biology, chemistry, physics, mathematics, German and French as preparation for psychology. He continued to advocate such preparation throughout his entire career.

Hunter transferred to the University of Texas at Austin in 1908. There he attended all the courses that were offered in psychology, as well as courses in biology, German, and French. His mentor at Texas was C. S. Yoakum who had recently completed his doctorate at Chicago. In his second year at Austin, Hunter served as Yoakum's assistant for $15 per month, a sum that covered his room rent ($5) and his meals ($10). The course that interested him most at Texas was a course on animal behavior, using Margaret Washburn's *The Animal Mind* as the textbook. Hunter read extensively in the literature on animal behavior and, in his last quarter at Austin, he did independent research on the maze behavior of pigeons. Hunter conducted his experiments in the back yard of his rooming house every morning before breakfast, a program that recalls Thorndike's testing his animals in the basement of William James's house.

On graduation in 1910, Hunter went to Chicago, where James Rowland Angell had offered him a scholarship. He minored in philosophy although he would have preferred biology. As he commented later on, "it seemed necessary to take into account the fact that the only teaching positions for psychologists involved either a combination of psychology and philosophy or of psychology and education." In retrospect, however, he believed that the minor in philosophy gave him "a broad understanding of a fundamental branch of human thinking and an insight into various theoretical problems in psychology." In addition, "in the early years of my teaching I derived great satisfaction from the conduct of courses in ethics, Kant, and the history of English philosophy" (Hunter, 1952, p. 165).

Years later, Hunter told us graduate students at Brown that, after his arrival in Chicago, he did not leave the city until 2 years later, when he had finished his degree. He seemed to be suggesting that we do likewise but, among ourselves, we noted that Chicago must have been a much more interesting city than Providence, Rhode Island. An additional note on Hunter's opinions about proper graduate student conduct relates to E. G. Boring's famous comment that the standard workweek for graduate students at Harvard was 80 hours, a standard that Hunter probably would have evaluated with the remark, "That's Harvard for you." Hunter urged a 90-hour week on the graduate students, and most of us did come back to the lab almost every night (as did some of the faculty, especially Clarence Graham and E. H. Kemp).

Academic Career

After receiving his PhD at Chicago, Hunter returned to Austin and joined the faculty at a salary of $1,200. During his 4 years there, it never exceeded $2,000. Soon after arriving in Austin, Hunter was married and a daughter, Thayer, was born in September 1914. Unfortunately, Mrs. Hunter died in April 1915.

In Austin, Hunter's research program concerned the aftereffects of visual motion and the auditory sensitivity of the white rat. In the latter work he used a prototype of the later much-used T-maze. One of Hunter's graduate students at Texas was Alda Grace Barber, who did the research for her master's degree under his direction. They were married in 1917, and their daughter, Helen Barbara, was born in 1920. Mrs. Hunter told some of us at Brown that she had thought of doing her research with Yoakum, but that Hunter told her that, if she worked with him, she would have a more manageable problem. Mrs. Hunter gave the impression that Hunter minimized the actual difficulty of the research she did with him.

In 1916, at age 27, Hunter moved to the University of Kansas as a full professor and department head, succeeding R. M. Ogden. It was at Kansas that he developed his systematic position and began work on the reliability of the maze, the temporal maze, and the double alternation problem. He took a military leave of 16 months during World War I, during which he served as a captain in the Sanitary Corps, working as a psychological examiner. More of that later.

After 9 years at Kansas, Hunter accepted an offer to go to Clark University as the first G. Stanley Hall professor of genetic psychology. At Clark, Hunter worked with an excellent group of graduate students, including Norman Munn, Louis Gellerman, Wayne Dennis, Robert Leeper, E. H. Kemp, Frank Geldard, Lorrin Riggs, and Clarence Graham[1]. Hunter and his students did further work on the sensory

---

[1]Hunter was a visiting lecturer at Harvard from 1927 to 1929, commuting from Worcester. The course on animal behavior with its introduction to behaviorism was apparently a novel experience for the Harvard students, and one not without influence on their thinking and research (Hunter, 1952). The class roll included the names of D. W. Chapman, W. A. Hunt, F. S. Keller, B. F. Skinner, and R. W. White, all of whom became distinguished psychologists. In conversations with Professors Keller and Skinner, the writer was told of the high esteem that they had for Hunter and how much his course had influenced them.

control of the maze. They also made critical analyses of Lashley's concept of equipotentiality of brain areas and the work of Crozier and others on tropisms in the rat. After 11 years at Clark, Hunter moved to Brown University as professor and department chair. He retained these posts until his retirement in 1954. His death on August 3 of that year was sudden and unexpected.

When Hunter came to Brown, Harold Schlosberg, E. H. Kemp, and Herbert Jasper were already there. Clarence Graham and J. McV. Hunt came with Hunter from Worcester. When Jasper went to the Montreal Neurological Institute, Donald Lindsley replaced him. This was the faculty that I knew. When Kemp left, his replacement was Carl Pfaffman. Graham left for Columbia University in 1945, and Lorrin Riggs, who had worked in a wartime research capacity at Brown since 1941, became a regular member of the faculty. Of the nine psychologists just mentioned (including Hunter), six have been elected to the Society of Experimental Psychologists and five to the National Academy of Sciences.

Recognition and Honors

Hunter was a much-honored psychologist: the first G. Stanley Hall professor of genetic pychology at Clark (1925–1936), president of the American Psychological Association in 1931 and of the Eastern Psychological Association in 1941. He was vice-president of the American Association for the Advancement of Science and chairman of its section on psychology in 1933. He was elected as a charter member of the Society of Experimental Psychologists when it was formally organized in 1929, to the the American Academy of Arts and Sciences in 1933, to the National Academy of Sciences in 1935 and to the American Philosophical Society in 1941. Almost all of these honors came to him when he was in his 40s.

BEHAVIORISM AND GENERAL ANTHROPONOMY

In his "Open Letter to the Anti-behaviorists" Hunter asked, "Who are the behaviorists?" and answered that there were only two: John B. Watson and A. P. Weiss. He listed 23 antibehaviorists and concluded that the presence of so many "antis" meant that, "It is the power and incisiveness of [behaviorism] which you ["antis"] fear. . . . [T]his inclines one to believe that Watson has found the Achilles heel of your . . . psychology" (1922, p. 308). Hunter was convinced that the vulnerability of the antibehaviorists was methodological. His behavioristic position incorporated a severe attack on mentalism and introspection and the advocacy of the objective study of behavior (see the section on *Experience and Consciousness*).

General Anthroponomy

These strong views led Hunter to disassociate his position, which he called General Anthroponomy, from psychology. He defined anthroponomy as "the science of the laws which govern human action—the science of human nature." As distinguished from anthroponomy, Hunter claimed that psychology derives directly from Greek philosophy, and is concerned only with the study of mind, consciousness, or psyche, which is directly accessible only to the subject who possesses it, and is regarded as a separate and distinct aspect of the universe. The psychological viewpoint neglects everything about the human individual that cannot be interpreted as evidence for the existence of some type of psychic process. Anthroponomy, by contrast, examines observable human nature in order to describe and explain the phenomena observed. It is "essentially genetic and seeks to explain human nature from the simple to the more complex processes . . . . [The] relationship between anthroponomy and psychology is not unlike that between alchemy and chemistry and between astrology and astronomy." Hunter listed a number of categories into which the subject matter of anthroponomy could be divided. These classifications dealt with various types of S–R connections and with their integration, disintegration, retention, reinstatement, interference, and transfer from one situation to another (Hunter, 1925a, pp. 286–288).

Experience and Consciousness

Hunter quoted Madison Bentley, a student of Titchener, as saying that psychology "seeks to describe and understand experience and the activities of the total organism in which experience plays an essential part" (Hunter, 1926, p. 324). He took exception to that position. For, to understand experience in Bentley's terms required, for Hunter, an unacceptable definition of experience. If one listens to an orchestra and then describes the experience in terms of the instruments played, for Bentley this would be a description of the orchestra, not of the experience. To think otherwise is to commit the "stimulus error," the description of the stimulus or the object rather than of the elements in the experience itself, that is, the sensations, images, and feelings in the experience and, where appropriate, their attributes of intensity, extensity, quality, duration, and clearness. Another quotation from Bentley may help to clarify the issue. Bentley wrote, "It scarcely seems possible that such things as books and violins should be mistaken for the furnishings of the mind; but this is precisely the first error that the beginner drops into in his quest for component qualities" (quoted by Hunter, 1926, p. 325).

Of this approach, Hunter said that

> '[n]othing could be more barren than the Wundt–Titchener–Bentley psychology. It does not describe concrete things seen, heard or felt as these exist in the inner, i.e., the subcutaneous, environment. Nor does it give us a description of something mental which actually exists. [The mentalists attempt] to understand a phase of human nature by the indirect route of the environment. [For example] the Structuralists abstract qualities, intensities, durations and clearnesses (sometimes adding other attributes, sometimes dropping one or more) . . . from the environment and call the material selected experience. [Meanwhile] the Functionalists take concrete objects from the environment and call these experience. (Hunter, 1926, p. 327)

In the mid-1920s, Hunter was contrasting two methods of studying human nature: the indirect, subjectivist, or "psychological method," and the direct, objective, or "anthroponomical method." One of Hunter's examples may help to show the contrast as Hunter saw it. A beginner in the laboratory does not report the overtones that are present in a complex tone. If the experimenter presents the vibration frequency of the first overtone (SP, sensory process) by itself to such a novice, this stimulus elicits a language response, LR. After several presentations of this overtone, if the complex tone is presented again, the beginner gives the LR, indicating awareness of the overtone in the complex tone. Hunter writes with emphasis,

> *[J]ust as soon as the verbal response, LR, is made to the complex stimulus, just so soon does the subjectivist say that the "consciousness of the overtone" is present . . . . Why do we not say that LR is the subjectivists' 'consciousness' [or even] a criterion of its presence?* (Hunter, 1926, p. 331)

Hunter's answer to this question was that a simple verbal response (e.g., "yes") indicating the detection of a stimulus may not indicate "consciousness;" this would be especially the case when the response has become automatic as in a well-learned conditioned reflex. This kind of response Hunter called *A Behavior*, seen throughout the animal kingdom; it is a stimulus–response event in which there is an unambiguous stimulus, without involvement of symbols or substitute stimuli. The patellar reflex (knee jerk) provides a nonverbal example.

In contrast to *A Behavior*, *Type I Behavior* is limited to a small part of the animal series (e.g., raccoons, chimpanzees, human adults, and children) as demonstrated by their performances in the delayed-reaction situation and in double alternation in the temporal maze (more later). These situations involve two important language functions. Type I behavior occurs in situations in which LR in the sequence SP–LR leads to further receptor and effector activities; it is called an irreversible SP–LR and, for Hunter, this was "consciousness." Where LR–SP or R occurs, there is no "consciousness." Hunter emphasized that true language responses are symbolic and can be reinstated by the organism at any time (Hunter, 1924a, 1924b).

INSTINCT AND LEARNING

Hunter did not join Watson in the rejection of the concept of instinct but he (1920) did point out that "instinct could be modified by activity prior to, simultaneous with, and following the time of appearance of the instinct" (Graham, 1958, p. 135). In 1947, he was the discussant in a symposium on the heredity–environment issue at the annual meeting of the Society of Experimental Psychologists. In his comment, Hunter (1947) said that the other participants (Beach, Carmichael, Lashley, Morgan, and Stone) emphasized the role of heredity in behavior in contrast to the views expressed by Watson in his book *Behaviorism*, in 1925, and by Kuo (1924) in his paper, "A Psychology Without Heredity." Hunter argued that there is evidence for the inheritance of neural patterns, in the case of nest building in birds, and for inherited structures that make the voice of the mule more like that of the donkey than the horse.

VOLITION

Hunter did not deny the existence of voluntary behavior and pointed out that the criteria of voluntariness are threefold (Hunter & Hudgins, 1934, pp. 199–200): first, the response is acquired; second, the voluntary response is made to stimuli "generated by the organism itself. The kinaesthetic, tactual, and auditory stimuli involved in language are the most important self-induced stimuli in man" (p. 200). Third, there may well be differences in the latencies and form of voluntary and involuntary responses. Hudgins, working with Hunter, investigated whether responses not normally under voluntary control could be brought under such control through conditioning. He worked with the pupillary response and, among others, the self-administered commands to relax and contract. Hudgins found that conditioning did develop to such commands. Hunter and Hudgins (1934, p. 204) concluded "that the attempted classification of behavior into voluntary and non-voluntary forms of response is of less significance than a classification of corresponding behavior in terms of genesis, type of control, and temporal characteristics." They offered "the hypothesis that so-called voluntary behavior is essentially a conditioned response having a characteristic latency and temporal course and under the control of self-excited receptor processes." Hunter later reported that a voluntary response of not responding could be disinhibited by the occurrence of certain stimuli.

RELIABILITY AND SENSORY CONTROL OF THE MAZE

From the beginning of his career, much of Hunter's research had centered on the maze habit in rats. There were two main questions. One was the reliability of the maze: Are measures, such as time required to run the maze and number of errors, correlated across trials? After considerable research on this problem, Hunter (1952, p. 169) concluded that reliability could only be demonstrated by using the Spearman–Brown Prophesy Formula (which provides a measure of what reliability would be if the maze were very, very long) and that this formula is not appropriate for learning data.

The second question concerned the sensory control of the maze habit in rats: Which senses do rats use when they learn a maze? This was a problem that Watson had studied. Watson had shown (Hunter, 1919, p. 24) "that rats can learn this problem in terms of kinaesthetic. . .and organic sensory processes, sound, vision, and smell being unnecessary." Hunter used a variety of techniques in experiments on the problem and concluded in an address delivered as vice-president of the American Association for the Advancement of Science (AAAS) that no one sensory system was necessary for learning or performing the maze; that vision, olfaction, touch, and proprioception usually control the perfected habit; that there is no evidence that control is turned over to proprioception; and if these various senses are involved in the performance of the habit there is no reason to assume that they were not involved in learning (Hunter, 1934).

TROPISMS

Jacques Loeb (1918) made an interpretation of animal behavior in terms of tropisms in his book *Forced Movements, Tropisms and Animal Conduct*.

Loeb argued that an animal's movements are forced by patterns of tension in the body. For example, if the two sides are stimulated equally, the animal would proceed in a straight line but if the tensions are unequal the animal would turn to equalize the tension on its sides. In reviewing this book, Hunter commented that Loeb ignored many data in attempting to support his views.

In several papers, Crozier and Pincus (e.g., 1926) claimed to have found evidence for a negative geotropism in young rats when they were placed on an inclined plane. The claim was that these animals moved upward on the plane at an angle, theta, that was directly proportional to log sine alpha, the angle of inclination of the plane. Hunter (1927) attempted to replicate this work. He used rats before their eyes had opened and also both blinded and seeing older animals in his experiments. Hunter confirmed the general relationship for the mean data from his animals, but he argued that the function was meaningless because of the tremendous variability around the mean values. He concluded that his results did not support the negative tropism to gravity for which Crozier and Pincus claimed to have produced evidence.

EQUIPOTENTIALITY IN BRAIN FUNCTION

Hunter also criticized Lashley's claim (Lashley & Ball, 1929) of equipotentiality of parts of the brain to function in various behaviors. He said, "I hesitate to accept the authors' conclusions for several reasons: (1) The maze was a simple alternation [right–left–right–left] maze which would be easily learned and well retained. Therefore any lack of completeness in the severing of proprioceptive conduction paths might well fail to disturb the response by leaving a sufficient basis for executing this simple habit. (2) We cannot be sure that the proprioceptive impulses are confined to the tracts severed in any one rat. Lashley notes this possibility, but does not regard it as probable. (3) Maze habits are influenced by nonproprioceptive stimuli from the environment of the maze and from the maze itself. These stimuli may have played a sufficient role in the present simple habit to have supplied the deficiencies created in the proprioceptive processes" (1929, p. 507). Hunter argued, as noted earlier, that the maze habit is governed "by a multiplicity of stimuli rather than by a central neural engram as Lashley and Ball unjustifiably infer" (Hunter, 1930, p. 467).

THE DELAYED REACTION AND DOUBLE ALTERNATION

Turning now from systematic issues to empirical concerns, Hunter is best remembered for his research on the delayed reaction and the double alternation temporal maze. On both of these problems he used several species, from the rat to young children and, in that way, qualified as a true comparative psychologist.

Harvey Carr, Hunter's mentor at Chicago, suggested several possible dissertation topics to Hunter. The one that Hunter chose was called the delayed reaction. Specific procedures varied over experiments, but most commonly the subject first learned to go to that one of three boxes that was baited with food, the presence of food being indicated by a light on that box. On test trials, after this response had been acquired, the subject was restrained in a starting box from which it could see that one of the three boxes was lighted. Then the light was turned off. The critical question was whether and for how long the animal could wait and still go to the previously illuminated box.

Hunter's (1919) results showed that animals could master delays of from 5 seconds (rats) to 19 seconds (cats) to 3 minutes (dogs), if the animals kept "their heads or bodies oriented toward the proper box" (p. 33). Disruption of the bodily orientation led to failure to bridge the delay. However, raccoons, and children from 15 to 60 months of age, could lose their orientation during the delay and still react correctly. The length of delay for the raccoons was up to 20 seconds. For younger children it was 20 to 50 seconds and, for 5-year-olds, as much as 20 minutes. Hunter described his dissertation research at a meeting of midwestern psychologists at age 23 and reports that it was very well received (Hunter, 1952, p. 167). This report and the appearance of his monograph in 1913 no doubt gave a large boost to his reputation.

Hunter considered the possibility that the children's long delays might be the result of language. To test this idea, he repeated the experiment with his daughter, Thayer, when she was 13 to 16 months of age, at which time "she had no vocal language. She made many sounds. . .but in no case did she use them spontaneously, and in no case did she use them as symbols" (1917, p. 75). In this experiment Thayer watched her father put the lure into one of the three boxes, none of them illuminated. Hunter disturbed Thayer's bodily orientation during the delays, but she was able to perform correctly after delays as long as 24 seconds. He concluded that vocal language or bodily orientation was not essential to bridge the delays in raccoons and young children, and that they maintained some internal symbolic representation of the correct box over the interval.

Hunter continued to work on symbolic processes, in studies of double alternation in the temporal maze (Hunter, 1920a). In this maze, the animal goes first through a central alley to a choice point and is made to turn, say, to the right. After going through the same central alley on the next trial, a second right turn is required. On the next two trials the

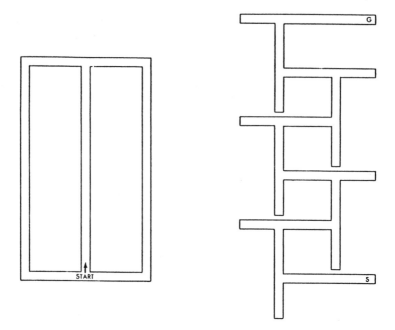

FIG. 18.1. *Temporal and Spatial Double-Alternation Mazes.* In the spatial maze (right) food is available at the point marked "g." If you trace the correct path in the spatial maze, you will discover that the sequence of correct turns is right, right, left, left, etc. In the temporal maze, the rat must go down the central path, turn right and right again, to return to "start" Then it must traverse the central path once more, taking two left turns to come back to "start" where food is now available. (Courtesy of Gregory A. Kimble)

requirement is to turn left. The path to be learned might be described as right–right, left–left, etc. This maze provides no differential stimuli in the central alley or at the choice point to cue the animal to turn one way or the other. Solution of this task depends on "the presence of symbolic processes" (Hunter, 1952, p. 171).

Even rats that are members of the 18th generation of Tryon's maze-bright animals cannot solve this problem although ordinary rats can perform a double-alternation sequence in a spatial maze and in a tridimensional maze where there are distinctive cues. However, raccoons can solve the double alternation problem, as can monkeys and children. No doubt, the results of these experiments on the delayed reaction and with the double alternation temporal maze account for Hunter's statement (1952–1960)[2] in his article on "Behaviourism" in

[2]Hunter's article appeared in the 14th edition of the *Britannica* in the printings made in 1952 and 1960.

Encyclopaedia Brittanica that, "Probably no one, other than the strict adherents of Loeb's theory of tropisms, has since maintained that behavior could be explained solely on stimulus-response grounds without taking into account the factors that arise within the organism." This statement together with his emphasis on representative symbolic processes might almost qualify Hunter as a cognitive psychologist!

PSYCHOLOGY IN THE PUBLIC INTEREST

Walter Hunter made contributions to psychology and to society in general in many ways: through his activities as an editor and his contributions to a nation at war, to the development of mental tests, to numerous scholarly organizations, and to education.

Contributions to Publishing

Early in his career Hunter had served as a consulting editor for such journals as *Journal of Animal Behavior, Comparative Psychology Monographs, Psychological Bulletin*, and *Behavior Monographs*. Hunter served on a number of committees of the National Research Council before becoming chairman of its Committee on Anthropology and Psychology. Among the achievements of the committee during his term, 1936–1938, was the establishment of the journal, *Psychosomatic Medicine*. He is particularly remembered, however, as the Editor, first of *Psychological Index*, from 1925 to 1936 (when it ceased publication) and then of *Psychological Abstracts*, from 1937 to 1947. He was one of the founders of the *Abstracts*.

Hunter was a member of an APA committee that, in cooperation with a committee of the National Research Council, obtained a 10-year subsidy of $75,000 from the Laura Spelman Rockefeller Memorial to develop plans for this new publication. Hunter was named the first editor and, in preparation for this responsibility, he and Mrs. Hunter made a trip to Europe to meet various foreign psychologists and to enlist their help in making the *Abstracts* truly international. During his editorship, Hunter received a great deal of help from Ray Willoughby (until his untimely death), Heinz Ansbacher, Alda Hunter and Esther (Mrs. J.) Hunt. To guarantee international coverage, younger faculty members at Brown were recruited to do abstracts of the foreign literature.

Mental Tests and other Applications

As mentioned earlier, during World War I, Hunter served as an officer in the Sanitary Corps, the division of the military that carried out its programs in psychology. One by-product of the program was the accumulation of a mass of data on national and racial differences in performance on the Army Alpha (verbal) and Beta (performance) tests of intelligence. Concerning the interpretation of the data from that program, Hunter (1952, p. 173) wrote, "These army findings [of the superior scores of people from Northern Europe over those from Southern Europe] were later used by C. C. Brigham in defense of Nordic superiority and other wild racial theories . . . ." Following the war, Hunter served as an adviser to certain foundations, including a Committee on Testing of the Carnegie Corporation and Carnegie Foundation, to which he recommended that various nonprofit testing groups be amalgamated into what became the Educational Testing Service.

Hunter's service in World War II, as a civilian was very extensive and involved, among other things, his serving as chair, in Washington, of the Applied Psychology Research Panel. Perhaps the best way to indicate something of Hunter's contribution is to quote from the citation accompanying the award of the President's Medal of Merit in 1948. Hunter was commended for recognizing "that research on the psychological and physiological capacities of man in relation to the new instruments of warfare could contribute materially to the more effective utilization of both military personnel and instruments" and for using psychological knowledge "in designing weapons to fit the man and to the selection and training of the man to utilize the particular weapon."

Education

Among the many committees on which Hunter served was the committee established by President Conant to study the role of psychology at Harvard. The result was the book, *The Place of Psychology in the Ideal University*. Some of Hunter's ideas about education in psychology are expressed in footnotes in the book. Others may be found in the address he gave as president of the Eastern Psychological Association (Hunter, 1941). As might be expected, he recommended a strong background in the other sciences as basic for work in the science of psychology, whether basic or applied.

Hunter was a strong advocate of the generalist tradition in psychology. Although an experimentalist himself, he believed that students who received the doctoral degree at Brown should be able to converse intelligently with psychologists of every specialty and background. To that end, he assigned papers in French and German in his courses and he encouraged young faculty members to offer seminars in areas of their expertise, even if the area were as remote from his own interests as projective tests of personality.

PERSONAL CHARACTERISTICS

I cannot finish this tribute to Walter S. Hunter without saying something about how people felt about him and about his personal life.
Hunter's life was not all work. At Clark, he and Mrs. Hunter developed
an interest in painting and he pursued the avocation to a considerable
level of skill, though not quite reaching Alda's level (Hunt, 1956). After
they came to Providence, the Hunters built a new house, which Hunter
once characterized as the most expensive piece of apparatus that he had
ever had. In that house, there was a table tennis room and Hunter, I
have been told, was the equal at that game of most of the younger
players who visited the house. At Brown, the Hunters belonged with
younger colleagues to a dancing club.

As mentioned earlier, Hunter had strong opinions about the behavior
that was appropriate for colleagues and for students. When a speaker
arrived intoxicated for a presentation at the weekly colloquium (that
Hunter organized and managed largely on his own), he told the
members of his department, including the graduate students that,
because of that behavior, that psychologist would never be invited to
visit Brown again. For graduate students, Hunter's expectations were
high, but he discouraged competition, often telling them that par
performance in the graduate program at Brown was the best that a
student could do, not better than the performance of the other students.
He expected students in his classes to be prepared and diligent but he
was never hostile and usually good-natured.

In his obituary, Graham characterizes the

> Walter Hunter many of us knew: the man of good humor and sound
> sense, a teacher, a colleague, a good companion, a man of great ability and
> one eminently fitted to play the role that he undertook so successfully, the
> representative of psychology in the councils of scientists . . . (1958, p. 127)

And, expressing a very similar judgment, J. Hunt (1956) wrote that "as
investigator, as theorist, as policy making committeeman" he made
many contributions. In addition, "Many a student and younger colleague owes both his scientific conscience and his professional confidence to Hunter, who could be critical of an argument or plan of attack,
sometimes devastatingly so, and yet encourage the person, be he
student or staff member."

ACKNOWLEDGMENT

Invited address presented August 12, 1989, at the convention of the
American Psychological Association in New Orleans on the program of

the Division of General Psychology (Division 1). I am indebted to Gregory A. Kimble for his work on the manuscript and to the 14 fellow graduate students and faculty at Brown University who wrote to me in response to a first draft of this chapter.

REFERENCES[3]

Carmichael, L. (1954). Walter Samuel Hunter, 1889–1954. *American Journal of Psychology*, 67, 732–734.

Crozier, W. J., & Pincus, G. (1926). The geotropic conduct of young rats. *Journal of General Physiology*, 10, 257–269.

Graham, C. H. (1958). Walter Samuel Hunter 1889–1954. *Biographical Memoirs of the National Academy of Sciences*, 31, 126–155.

Hunt, J. McV. (1956). Walter Samuel Hunter, 1889–1954. *Psychological Review*, 63, 213–217.

Hunter, W. S. (1913). Delayed reaction in animals and children. *Behavior Monographs*, 2(1), 86.

Hunter, W. S. (1917). The delayed reaction in a child. *Psychological Review*, 24, 74–87.

Hunter, W. S. (1919). *General psychology*. Chicago: University of Chicago Press.

Hunter, W. S. (1920a). The temporal maze and kinaesthetic sensory processes in the white rat. *Psychobiology*, 2, 1–17.

Hunter, W. S. (1920b). The modification of instinct from the standpoint of social psychology. *Psychological Review*, 27, 247–269.

Hunter, W.S. (1922). An open letter to the anti-behaviorists. *Journal of Philosophy*, 19, 307–308.

Hunter, W. S. (1924a). The problem of consciousness. *Psychological Review*, 31, 1–31.

Hunter, W. S. (1924b). The symbolic process. *Psychological Review*, 31, 478–497.

Hunter, W. S. (1925a). General Anthroponomy and its systematic problems. *American Journal of Psychology*, 36, 286–302.

Hunter, W. S. (1925b). The subject's report. *Psychological Review*, 32, 153–170.

Hunter, W. S. (1926). Psychology and anthroponomy. *Pedagogical Seminary*, 33, 322–346.

Hunter, W. S. (1927). The behavior of white rats on inclined planes. *Pedagogical Seminary*, 34, 299–332.

Hunter, W. S. (1928). The behavior of raccoons in a double alternation temporal maze. *Pedagogical Seminary*, 35, 374–389.

Hunter, W. S. (1929). Sensory control of the maze habit. *Journal of Genetic Psychology*, 36, 505–537.

Hunter, W. S. (1930). A consideration of Lashley's theory of the equipotentiality of cerebral action. *Journal of General Psychology*, 43, 455–468.

Hunter, W. S. (1934). The stimulus-neural control of behavior before and after learning. *Science*, 79, 145–151.

Hunter, W. S. (1941). On the professional training of psychologists. *Psychological Review*, 48, 498–523.

Hunter, W. S. (1947). Summary comments on the Heredity-Environment symposium. *Psychological Review*, 54, 348–352.

Hunter, W. S. (1952). Walter S. Hunter. In C. Murchison (Ed.), *A history of psychology in autobiography* (Vol. 4, pp. 163–187). Worcester, MA: Clark University Press.

---

[3] A complete bibliography of Hunter's writings may be found in Graham (1958, pp. 147–155).

Hunter, W. S. (1952–1960). Behaviourism. *Encyclopaedia Britannica, 3*, 327–329.

Hunter, W. S., & Hudgins, C. V. (1934). Voluntary activity from the standpoint of behaviorism. *Journal of General Psychology, 10*, 198–204.

Kuo, Z. Y. (1924). A psychology without heredity. *Psychological Review, 31*, 427–448.

Lashley, K. S., & Ball, J. S. (1929). Spinal conduction and kinesthetic sensitivity in the maze habit. *Journal of Comparative Psychology, 9*, 71–105.

Loeb, J. (1918). *Forced movements, tropisms, and animal conduct.* Philadelphia: Lippincott.

Schlosberg, H. (1954). Walter S. Hunter: Pioneer objectivist in psychology. *Science, 120*, 441–442.

Watson, J. B. (1925). *Behaviorism.* New York:Norton.

Chapter 19

Systems as Reconceptualizations: The Work of Edna Heidbreder

Mary Henle

Somebody once asked Edna Heidbreder how she and I had become friends. She replied with a smile, "John Stuart Mill brought us together." In a sense that was true. I had known and admired Edna's work since my undergraduate days at Smith College, and I had met her briefly on a couple of occasions. But the first opportunity for a serious talk came around 1963, when I was spending the year at the Institute for Cognitive Studies at Harvard. We were having dinner at the Wellesley Faculty Club; and the thing I, too, remember best about that conversation was our talking about J. S. Mill. I was immersed in the *Logic* at the time and had just read his autobiography, and Edna was, of course, totally familiar with both. We talked, too, about teaching and about the women's colleges and many other things. I was impressed and stimulated, and I was charmed by her friendliness, her graciousness, and her perceptiveness.

Other dinners followed the John Stuart Mill occasion. Then, after another year in the area, at Educational Services, Inc., I had to return to New York to erase my reputation as a "visiting professor" at my home institution, the Graduate Faculty of the New School for Social Research.

I don't remember when the "foliage trips" to Wellesley began. Elizabeth Fehrer, a longtime friend of both Edna's and mine, and I drove up to Wellesley to see Edna. After this first one, spring and fall visits became "traditional." Elizabeth called it one-trial learning. We came home stimulated and exhilarated, not exhausted, as the busy trip might

*Photograph of Edna Heidbreder courtesy of Mary Henle

have led us to expect. The visits continued, after Edna moved to Bedford, Massachusetts, up to the time of her death in 1985.

A REMARKABLE PERSON

I do not remember when I first conned Edna into going to meetings again, a practice she had let lapse. These were meetings, not conventions, of the Cheiron Society, then a rather new and small society for the history of the behavioral and social sciences. I remember a Wellesley meeting in 1977, notable for the presence of Edna Heidbreder and Sigmund Koch. Earlier there had been one at Akron, home of the Archives of the History of American Psychology, in 1970. The campus was occupied by student protesters, and we had to shuttle by bus to improvised meeting places. Improvised in style, I should say, because arrangements were made by John A. Popplestone and Marion White McPherson. Edna and I had been talking; her foot on the step of the bus, with her usual perceptiveness, Edna turned and said: Just what do you want of me, Mary? I said: An invited address at the next Cheiron meeting. It was to be held in New York, sponsored by the New School, New York University, and Fordham University. Edna let herself be persuaded. I remember the standing ovation for Edna Heidbreder before her talk at that meeting, I remember the talk, and the second standing ovation after it. On that occasion we presented to her three thick volumes of manuscript that were to become a Festschrift. She was nevertheless pleased with the not quite finished manuscript, and in due course the Festschrift, *Historical Conceptions of Psychology*, was published. The volume also contains reprints of several essays by Edna Heidbreder. (Henle, Jaynes, & Sullivan, 1973).

Unknown to her, the society, of course, picked up the hotel bill for its distinguished guest. Edna later wrote to me her experience in checking out. It went something like this:

Manager: This bill has been paid.
E.H.:   By whom?
Manager: I don't know.
E.H.:   Was it the Cheiron Society?
Manager: I don't know. Who is its president?
E.H.:   It has no president.
Manager: Where are its offices?
E.H.:   There are no offices.

"You can imagine," Edna wrote, "how the conversation continued."

I turn now to another dimension of our relationship. When I was a graduate student at Bryn Mawr, Harry Helson, my teacher, once said to me: "The last time you will get good criticism is in graduate school." He was almost right, but not quite. After those days, I have had excellent criticism from several people: Edna Heidbreder, Wolfgang Köhler, Solomon E. Asch—and more recently from a group of young psychologists who were once my students. Good criticism is hard to come by, and I have been most fortunate.

On our last visit (and at times in letters), Edna and I discussed naïve realism, an issue of concern to both of us. But our talks were not confined to psychology and its neighboring disciplines; we enjoyed talking about people, books, peace and politics, small adventures. Although her dislike of cats was intense, she could somehow understand my deep attraction to them; I remember a black cat on a Christmas card from her. It must have been hard for her, but she knew it would mean a lot to me.

There are many things to say about Edna Heidbreder. She was indeed remarkable: a remarkable psychologist, a remarkable thinker, a remarkable person, one of the finest human beings I have ever known. Here I will confine myself to her work, specifically her systematic work.

EDUCATIONAL AND PROFESSIONAL BACKGROUND

Heidbreder is best known for her book *Seven Psychologies*. If you are wondering what kind of education and experience would make it possible to write *Seven Psychologies*, you would find them in her life. Her education came at a time which practically assured the excellent student a broad and serious education. Her college major and master's thesis were in philosophy, in a period when psychology was experiencing the transition from mental philosophy to a scientific discipline. Then she taught history to high school students for a few years, an experience that gave her an appreciation of history and its problems; serious teaching of young students also forces one to clarify one's own thinking. After much self-education in philosophy and psychology, her intellectual travels next took her to New York City and Columbia University, where she encountered a diversity of points of view and a lively intellectual scene in psychology and beyond it. Her first psychological teaching was at another lively but very different university, the University of Minnesota, where behaviorism was popular and where the psychology department was heavily involved in the testing movement.

Of course, all these influences were influences on a particular person, Edna Heidbreder. I will not attempt to describe to you the characteristics of her remarkable mind, lucid, vigorous, cultivated and judicious, disciplined and generous, a mind that penetrated to the heart of the matter before it. These qualities are best appreciated by reading her work.

EMPIRICAL WORK

Before I come to her theoretical or systematic work, I will mention that she contributed to the testing movement, especially to personality testing. And both before and after *Seven Psychologies*, she was engaged in experimental work on thinking, mainly on the attainment of concepts. It would be a mistake to separate her experimental from her systematic work, because the empirical studies of thinking led her to consider the relations among perception, concept formation, and other cognitive functions, as well as their relations to the individual's motivation and motor behavior. Her empirical work necessarily led her to systematic thinking. Her interest was not in developing a system of psychology, but her experimental work led a systematic thinker to sketch a dynamic theory of cognition.

For purposes of today's talk, I will, nevertheless, neglect the experimental work and discuss *Seven Psychologies* and the theoretical papers that followed it.

SEVEN PSYCHOLOGIES

Seven Psychologies was published in 1933 and is still in wide use. It has been read by many thousands of psychologists and students of psychology. Thus I am in the fortunate position of discussing a work that practically every psychologist knows. I will not have to supply background; I can assume it.

In 1933 Heidbreder wrote: "Psychology today is addressing itself to a material very different from that which formed its subject matter a century or even a half-century ago." Surveying our contemporary field, we would see the same large differences between the subject matter addressed today and that of the time of *Seven Psychologies*. Why, then, is this book still so widely read? I have dealt with this question elsewhere (Henle & Sullivan, 1974), but I cannot omit it in an account of Edna Heidbreder's work, and I think the matter is clearer to me now.

Psychologists' Reactions

Of course nobody would read *Seven Psychologies* today if it were not faithful to its subject matter. Heidbreder remarks in her preface:

"Naturally I offer this book with many misgivings. The difficulties involved in the attempt to portray accurately and to estimate justly the thoughts of others require no comment." How well did she succeed in overcoming these difficulties? Perhaps those best qualified to answer this question are the psychologists whose thoughts she portrayed and estimated. Several of them wrote to her about her book. These letters are in the archives of Wellesley College, to which I am grateful for making them available to me.

Although he had not yet read all of *Seven Psychologies*, James Rowland Angell wrote:

> If you have succeeded half so well with the other movements as you have with the functionalists at Chicago, you will have rendered a highly important and permanent service to psychology. Yours is the only account I have ever seen which really grasps the intellectual background of the matter and the motives which inspired those who contributed. I feel a very real sense of personal gratitude for your rescue from the fogs of misunderstanding and misrepresentation a movement which had thoroughly sound scientific foundations, was conceived in a thoroughly scientific spirit and, so far as I am aware, was wholly free of any desire for recognition as the only orthodox church. . . .

Robert S. Woodworth commented: "I think you have 'got me straight.' I wouldn't ask for any more accurate and adequate presentation of my views." He adds:

> Next year for the first time I am to give a course on my own ideas of systematic psychology. I am calling the course 'Dynamic Psychology.' Your analysis of my work will be of great value not only to my students but even to me in critically re-examining my position . . . . Your extended discussion gives me the opportunity to see the system in some perspective . . . . Your book throughout is clear, logical, remarkably objective and beautifully written.

Another comment came from Kurt Koffka:

> Throughout I was struck by the clearness, impartiality, and fairness of your exposition. You have the progress of psychology at heart, and you try to present the different and conflicting systems in such a way that psychology may derive some benefit from your stock-taking. You are also clearly aware of the intellectual background of American psychology, you discern the trends in the American character which are favourable and which are hostile to a development of our science. Thus I find the summing up of the American attitude towards, or shall I say against, Gestalt psychology, on p. 374, truly excellent.

Koffka also expressed delight at the "fair and understanding presentation of Titchener."

Continued Usefulness

Such comments indicate why *Seven Psychologies* was so successful in its early years. Its purpose was "to enable a reader somewhat new in the field to become acquainted with some of the different points of view from which the facts of psychology may be regarded." Why does it continue to orient such a reader to a field whose contemporary points of view are greatly different?

Even the seven psychologies treated were not complete in 1933, so the same question arises for them. Woodworth had not nearly finished his work by that time. It is hard to think of Gestalt psychology without Wertheimer's *Productive Thinking*, without Köhler's *Place of Value in a World of Facts*, his *Dynamics in Psychology*, his work on figural after effects and on brain physiology, without Koffka's great systematization in the *Principles of Gestalt Psychology*. None of these had appeared by 1933, yet all can be fitted into the framework of the chapter on Gestalt psychology. Likewise the corpus of Freud's work was not quite complete in 1933. Even the *Project for a Scientific Psychology* of 1895, from which Freud's thinking never really freed itself, had not yet found its reluctant way into print. Restatements as late as the posthumous *Outline of Psycho-analysis* cast a different light on some issues. And yet the new developments would fit into the framework of *Seven Psychologies* because it viewed and treated a system as "an envisagement of the total field of psychology as a consistent and unified whole." Later parts could be fitted in if the whole was correctly perceived.

But a fuller answer is needed to the question of the continued usefulness of *Seven Psychologies*. A vague comment about the value of knowing history for an understanding of the contemporary scene will not do. To answer our question fully would require an extended analysis of contemporary points of view in comparison with those dominant in 1933, as one example, the relation of behaviorism to neobehaviorism to methodological behaviorism to radical behaviorism to cognitive behaviorism, to cognitive science, and so on. And even that would not give us a complete answer. I will content myself, therefore, with one or two characteristics of the book, and of Heidbreder's later systematic articles, that are responsible for its vigorous longevity.

First, an account of a system that does it justice is not only a narrative, but an analysis. A system is not just an aggregate of ideas; as E. B. Titchener once said, "a system must be systematic throughout." Heidbreder was fully aware of the nature of systems. I have already quoted her definition as "an envisagement of the total field of psychology as a consistent and unified whole." She adds (1933, p. 18):

It assumes that the apparently chaotic particulars which lie within its domain can, if properly understood, be brought into order and clarity: that the subject-matter can be defined, the central problem stated, the methods of investigation agreed upon, the relations to other bodies of knowledge determined, the elements or basic processes identified, the distinctive features brought into relief, the general outline or characteristic movement indicated.

What I have just quoted is the outline of the discussion of each of the seven psychologies selected. It is present unobtrusively, but it ensures that neither the author nor the reader will miss anything important. For a full understanding of *Seven Psychologies*, each chapter should be read with this outline in mind.

Heidbreder saw her task as not only portraying accurately, but also estimating justly the thoughts of the psychologists selected for inclusion in *Seven Psychologies* and the later systematic articles. About criticism, the protagonists of her book, in the passages already cited, seem well satisfied. I think the secret of this excellent criticism has been stated in a different connection by Robert B. MacLeod: In order to criticize a theory, he remarked, you must understand it so well that you are able to defend it. Edna Heidbreder was able to do both because she understood these psychologies so well. I have not yet mentioned Heidbreder's paper on William McDougall (Heidbreder,1939), but it seems relevant at this point to quote a letter from William Ernest Hocking, the Harvard philosopher, who knew McDougall at Harvard: "I don't know when I have read any estimate of a man's work, which seemed to me so just and discerning in stating his strengths and his weaknesses."

LATER SYSTEMATIC WORK

In *Seven Psychologies*, Heidbreder asks," What is the central problem for this thinker? What is this psychologist trying to accomplish?" A much-quoted example, "Whereas Titchener was intent chiefly on making the new psychology a science, James was more concerned that the new science be psychology." This theme reappeared in her later systematic work. For example, in a book review in 1964 (Heidbreder,1964), she wondered, "Just what are computer psychologists trying to do for psychology?" About Mary Whiton Calkins (Heidbreder, 1972),

"Why . . . did Calkins believe that the conceptual geography of her field needed recharting?" Her notable article on "William McDougall and Social Psychology" contains the remarks,

> The chances are that he will be remembered as a man sufficiently insistent on the special character of psychological facts as he saw them to demand that accepted principles of explanation be adjusted to receive them . . . . The point he refused to yield was the special character of the observed facts. That the theory be adjusted to accommodate the facts was his ever-recurring demand . . . . To solve the problems he raised was not McDougall's role in psychology. His achievement was to bring them to light in a manner so disturbing as to force them upon the attention of a generation of psychologists trained to ignore them.

Heidbreder on Freud

I would like to pay special attention to Heidbreder's treatment of Freud, not only in *Seven Psychologies*, but in a review of the New Introductory Lectures in 1934 (Heidbreder, 1934), and particularly in an article of 1940, "Freud and Psychology," originally published in the *Psychological Review* and reprinted, along with others of her papers, in the Festschrift presented to her by the Cheiron Society. In a culture then steeped in Freudian ideas, indeed staggering under the influence of Freud, Heidbreder was somehow able to step aside and ask: What was the nature of Freud's influence on psychology? What was his appeal? Why was he at once so strange and so familiar? Specifically, what had Freud done that nobody else had done? Her answers seem to me to deserve a special place in the vast body of Freudian commentary; they are fresh, penetrating, and to me totally convincing. To take a new look at Freud in such a climate is a major achievement.

Heidbreder sees Freud's influence on psychology—as his influence on so many other fields, including psychiatry—as an influence from outside. He was, of course, not a psychologist, although some of the problems on which psychologists were working were ones that interested him: for example, problems of emotion, of memory, of association. He preferred to go his own way even in these fields. In sharp contrast, psychologists could not, and did not, ignore him; that he exerted an enormous influence in this field hardly bears restating.

And yet Freud's influence was not produced by scientific evidence for his theories. As Heidbreder writes, "Freud's talent is for that part of the labor of science which consists in making observations and forming hypotheses; for the testing and verification of observations and hypotheses he shows no aptitude." Further:

Freudian theories found their way into psychology without the backing of accepted, or acceptable, scientific evidence. They entered with no support but that of common knowledge about human nature, knowledge neither more nor less accessible to psychologists than to anyone else. There is a sense in which Freud's teachings were unfamiliar to few, in which despite their boldness and originality, they were often heard even at first with something like recognition.

Freud's insights are not, of course, to be identified with those of common sense.

Rather, they were the outcome of explorations into the subsoil of common sense . . . . Freud's task required the difficult and delicate adjustment of focusing just off the usual fixation point; of maintaining a line of regard almost coinciding with, yet always distinct from, the one favored by habit and common practice.

Look at Freud from these standpoints and you will see a new Freud, a basic Freud, one that the contemporary controversies have missed.

An interesting point in connection with Freud is Heidbreder's remark that "he never worked out a very clear position with respect to the intellectual processes." I would like to amplify this cryptic statement in a direction of which I am not sure she would have approved. Freud may be regarded as the supreme irrationalist of his day at the same time that he ranks equally high as a rationalist. The first statement requires no support in view of Freud's slight interest in the intellectual processes and his continued emphasis on the primal urges. And yet the goal of psychoanalysis, for Freud, is a rationalistic one: Where id was, there shall ego be. Freud appears to have experienced no conflict between his rationalism and his irrationalism; the two seem not to have met in his thinking.

Heidbreder comments: "At any rate, a field of inquiry is indicated concerning lines of relationship between cognitive activities and the primal urges." Although not stated in these precise terms, this problem has concerned psychology almost ever since. Heidbreder herself reminded psychologists of the relationship in her paper, "Toward a Dynamic Psychology of Cognition" (1945). Soon afterwards, the so-called "new look" movement came to the fore, dealing flamboyantly with this relationship. The movement more or less fizzled out but, in an appropriately subdued form, the problem has remained with us.

On Kurt Lewin

Another notable paper appeared as a special review of Kurt Lewin's *Principles of Topological Psychology* (1937). Lewin has traditionally been treated as presenting just another theory of personality. Heidbreder who, I believe, was the first psychologist to understand the task Lewin set for himself, points out:

> And yet, in a sense, Lewin does not present a system at all, certainly not a system as that term is commonly understood. What he does present is primarily a conceptual tool, but one by means of which he hopes to give psychology the unity, coherence, and articulation that system-makers regularly try to achieve.

Lewin is still commonly treated as presenting a "dynamic theory of personality." It is time to think of him, as Heidbreder did some 50 years ago, as making "an attempt to reconceptualize the subject matter of psychology."

On Functionalism

We are fortunate in having from Heidbreder's pen two accounts of functionalism, one in *Seven Psychologies*, the other nearly 35 years later, presented on the occasion of the 75th anniversary of APA in 1967 (in Krantz, 1969). The first is well described by Angell in the letter from which I quoted earlier. It deals with the intellectual background and the scientific foundations of the movement, with the motives of the functionalists; and it attempts to clear up the then prevalent misunderstandings of this psychology. Of course it sets forth the central problems and distinctive features of functionalism. Since functionalism was not a system in the usual sense of system, there was no attempt to treat it as one. The second paper is obviously not addressed to persons relatively new to psychology. It raises the questions with which we are now familiar: How did the functionalists try to reconceptualize psychology? Why did they think that a reconceptualization was necessary?

Heidbreder brushes aside as superficial the common conception that functionalism was important as a transitional movement that made it possible for psychology to change from a science of consciousness to a science of behavior. It did that, of course (though it did not discard consciousness), but more important: "Their essential innovation consisted in taking a different conceptual approach to the problems of psychology, in placing its subject matter in a different conceptual perspective." Their conceptual framework, as we know, was Darwinian theory; and "in the concept of function they found a straightforward way of treating psychological processes as natural events in the natural world." Unlike their predecessors who, as Heidbreder points out, defined their subject matter on methodological grounds, on the question of what psychologists should observe, the functionalists also asked: "About what shall we as psychologists ask our questions?"

Where did the functionalists find their questions? I would like to quote again, because I think we tend today to overlook this important point. Such questions arise

> from the prescientifically organized knowledge which, for lack of a better name, may be called the commonsense knowledge of the culture in which psychology arose, developed, and changed, and is still developing and changing. There is an important sense in which psychologists, like natural scientists generally, do not initially select their own subject matter. They begin by accepting it as it has been prescientifically selected and conceptualized in the commonsense knowledge of the culture in which they operate; although, as they operate, they may depart widely from the knowledge with which they began: extending, refining, and altering it, sometimes in a manner that is radically revolutionary.

It must not be thought that the functionalists were presenting a commonsense psychology or that Heidbreder saw them as doing so. One more quotation will make this clear:

> Commonsense knowledge of this domain is, of course, subject to the limitations, inconsistencies, and obscurities, to the implicit assumptions, downright errors, and other faults that characterize common sense generally. In a sense it is the enemy—the obstructionist to be overcome. But for all its faults . . . such knowledge is an indispensable basis for the *questions* that give rise to genuinely scientific inquiry.

RECONCEPTUALIZING PSYCHOLOGY

I have hardly mentioned Heidbreder's paper on Mary Whiton Calkins (1972) or the one on William McDougall (1939), partly because of lack of time and partly because it is my impression that these psychologists are seldom read today. This is an unfortunate neglect, and I have the hunch that if you read these authors, you will profit from the articles and, conversely, that if you read the articles, you will go on to the authors they treat.

We can see explicit in all of Edna Heidbreder's later systematic articles a thread that runs through *Seven Psychologies*, though the earlier terminology is different. These psychologies are not set forward, as I have said, as narratives, but each psychology is treated as an attempt to reconceptualize the field. Thus, in each case, Heidbreder asks why each thinker believed that the field needed to be reconceptualized and what conceptual framework was developed.

How are we trying to reconceptualize psychology today? At least in that part of the field traditionally called experimental psychology, the computational approach is dominant—and I believe it is spilling over into other parts too. Although Heidbreder did not discuss this approach except in the brief review already mentioned, her *Seven Psychologies* can help us to evaluate it. Why do so many psychologists today think that their field needed to be reconceptualized? "Just what are computer psychologists trying to do for psychology? From one point of view, they are trying to conceptualize its subject matter—or a part of it." What basic processes are assumed? What distinctive features? What assumptions are being made about the subject matter of psychology? We might add another question: Have these contemporary theorists considered the reasons why their predecessors thought it necessary, in their day, to reconceptualize the subject matter of psychology?

It is not my task today to try to answer these questions. What I would like to suggest is that *Seven Psychologies* can help us to do so. It is unnecessary to point out that we need to get a perspective on the thinking of our own time as well as on that of earlier times. The analyses of *Seven Psychologies* provide models for us today.

Heidbreder herself suggests that this is the use she wants us to make of her book. In a discussion of the material she selected—why 7 systems rather than 70?—she comments: "To present seven different conceptions of psychology, seven conceptions in actual use, is not only to indicate the function and significance of those particular seven, but to suggest the function and significance of systems in general."

And in the 1967 paper on functionalism, she remarks: "One way of looking at schools of psychology is to regard each of them as proposing some conceptual scheme, some reconceptualization of the subject matter of psychology."

CONCLUSION

Now I can return to *Seven Psychologies*, and to the question from which I started, after this detour through Heidbreder's later systematic papers. If we consider a system in the way she does, we will ask the right questions about it. To repeat: What conceptual scheme does a particular psychology propose? Why did it consider it necessary to reconceptualize the subject matter of psychology? These questions will bring us to the centers of the systems of the turn of this century and no doubt to those of the next century. I think I have finally come to an understanding of *Seven Psychologies* and its long life. To ask the right questions seems to be the secret of a long and happy life.

REFERENCES

Heidbreder, E. (1933). *Seven psychologies.* New York: D. Appleton- Century.

Heidbreder, E. (1934). Review of S. Freud. New introductory lectures on psycho-analysis. *Journal of Abnormal and Social Psychology, 29,* 106–109.

Heidbreder, E. (1937). Special review [Lewin's *Principles of topological psychology*]. *Psychological Bulletin, 34,* 584–604.

Heidbreder, E. (1939). William McDougall and social psychology. *Journal of Abnormal and Social Psychology, 34,* 150–160.

Heidbreder, E. (1940). Freud and psychology. *Psychological Review, 47,* 185–195.

Heidbreder, E. (1945). Toward a dynamic psychology of cognition. *Psychological Review, 52,* 1–22.

Heidbreder, E. (1964). Logic, imagination, engineering and hope [Review of E. B. Hunt. *Concept learning: An information processing problem*]. *Contemporary Psychology, 9,* 40–41.

Heidbreder, E. (1969). Functionalism. In D. L. Krantz (Ed.), *Schools of psychology: A symposium.* New York: Appleton-Century-Crofts.

Heidbreder, E. (1972). Mary Whiton Calkins. *Journal of the History of the Behavioral Sciences, 8,* 56–68.

Henle, M., Jaynes, J., & Sullivan, J.J. (Eds.). (1973). *Historical conceptions of psychology.* New York: Springer.

Henle, M., & Sullivan, J. (1974). *Seven psychologies* revisited. *Journal of the History of the Behavioral Sciences, 10,* 40–46.

Chapter 20

Integrations of Lashley

Darryl Bruce

Karl Spencer Lashley (1890–1958) was the pre-eminent scientist of brain and behavior during the first half of the 20 century. Beach, Hebb, Morgan, and Nissen (1960) have assembled 31 of his slightly more than 100 publications in a book entitled, *The Neuropsychology of Lashley*. In doing so, they focused on his scientific work. In keeping with the spirit of this volume, I attempt a more personal account of the man and his science. To this end, I have divided Lashley's life into four stages: (1) his upbringing, 1890–1905; (2) his preparation for a career in psychology, 1905–1917; (3) his appointments at universities, 1917–1942; and (4) his directorship of the Yerkes Laboratories of Primate Biology and subsequent retirement, 1942–1958. The first of these periods is treated lightly; the remaining three are given more attention.

LASHLEY'S UPBRINGING, 1890–1905

Lashley was born on June 7, 1890, in Davis, West Virginia, the only child of Charles Gilpen Lashley and Margaret Blanche Spencer. His father was a merchant, banker, and municipal politician. His mother, a descendant of the American philosopher and educator Jonathan Edwards, had been a schoolteacher prior to her marriage. She was an avid reader and under her tutelage, Lashley developed an early aptitude for reading and learning and an abiding love of nature. He also proved

---

*Photograph of Karl S. Lashley courtesy of B. R. Hergenhahn

mechanically inclined and as a youngster, learned sewing (using his mother's sewing machine) and woodworking.

The Lashleys made a series of moves from 1894 to 1898 that took them ultimately to Seattle. During this time, Karl's formal education, which began at the age of 4, was in a mixture of public and private schools. From Seattle, the family traveled to Alaska and the Klondike in 1898 during the gold rush. It was a memorable experience for the young Lashley and he made two return visits to the area in the later years of his life. By 1899 the Lashleys had returned to Davis, where Karl entered the public school system, graduating from high school at the age of 14.

PREPARATION FOR A CAREER IN PSYCHOLOGY, 1905-1917

> My training has been atypical for psychologists. As an undergraduate I specialized in comparative histology; my master's thesis was in bacteriology and my doctor's in genetics . . . . I did not choose psychology as a career until two years after the Ph.D. I never attended a course in physiology or neurology, which have become my major interests.

So wrote Lashley in reply to an inquiry into his professional training. In this section, I shall describe Lashley's atypical preparation more fully and introduce the reader to the individuals who influenced him.

Undergraduate Study at West Virginia, 1905-1910

Lashley entered the University of West Virginia in 1905 and after a preparatory year (required because the high school in Davis was not accredited), began study toward the AB degree. As a freshman elective, he took beginning zoology, taught by the comparative neurologist, John Black Johnston. This course set Lashley on his way to a career in the life sciences. He later commented that the lectures in comparative anatomy were his only training in neurology. So, in a sense, he was Johnston's student.

Johnston left West Virginia after Lashley's freshman year and was replaced by Albert M. Reese. Reese hired Lashley, who by then had decided to major in zoology, as his laboratory assistant. Lashley worked 3 years in this position, performing tasks that ranged from boiling out human skeletons to teaching a laboratory course in neurology. He received minimal direction from Reese in carrying out these responsibilities and in conducting research for an undergraduate thesis on the histology of the digestive tract of chimeroid fish. Lashley's association with Reese, his ability to work independently, and his intensive preparation in zoology were undoubtedly instrumental in his being awarded a graduate teaching fellowship in biology at the University of Pittsburgh.

Graduate Study at the University of Pittsburgh, 1910–1911

The training in biology at Pittsburgh was not to Lashley's liking because of the heavy emphasis on bacteriology. Nevertheless, he obtained a master's degree with a thesis on the bacteriology of rotten eggs. At Pittsburgh, he came into contact with Karl Dallenbach, who was a teaching fellow in psychology. Lashley took Dallenbach's undergraduate laboratory course in experimental psychology. Although this appears to have been his first formal contact with psychology, it probably did not play much of a role in his later shift to the field, because the course was in the nonbiological tradition of Wundt and Titchener.

Graduate Study with Herbert S. Jennings, 1911–1914

Lashley left Pittsburgh to spend the summer of 1911 conducting genetics research at the Cold Spring Harbor Biological Laboratory on Long Island. In the fall, he began doctoral study in zoology with the geneticist Herbert S. Jennings at Johns Hopkins University in Baltimore. Initially, Lashley assisted Jennings in his research on reproduction in paramecia. Subsequently, he carried out his dissertation research and then a separate follow-up study on the question of the degree to which variation in the number of tentacles in clones of hydra was inherited. Both investigations indicated a limited role for inheritance. Lashley received the PhD degree in 1914.

The influence of Jennings on Lashley was substantial, not only because of what he learned about genetics research from Jennings, but also because under Jennings he developed an aversion to vitalism—the notion that living things contain an intangible life force in addition to physicochemical elements—and to the ideas of Jacques Loeb. Loeb interpreted the behavior of lower organisms solely by appeal to tropisms (forced reactions toward or away from a stimulus). He believed that the understanding (and control) of behavior required nothing more than identifying the causative external stimuli. By contrast, Jennings sought internal, sensorimotor, physiological explanations of behavior, and he recognized the importance of questions about the function and evolution of behavior. Lashley was more in sympathy with Jennings's position than Loeb's.

Graduate and Postdoctoral Study with John B. Watson, 1911-1915

A major influence on Lashley at Hopkins was John B. Watson, who at the time was approaching the height of his reputation in psychology. Moreover, his science had not yet been ruined by his ambition to establish a behavioristic system of psychology. Thus the timing of the collaboration could not have been better. And what a partnership it must have been! Watson—ambitious, enthusiastic, brash, outgoing, and a comparative psychologist of the first rank; Lashley—energetic, independent, resourceful, vastly intelligent, with a superb background in zoology. Certainly the 4-year association was productive, at least from Lashley's standpoint. He published 14 articles in psychology during this period and 9 of them reflect the influence of Watson. Moreover, there can be little doubt that it was research with Watson that converted Lashley to a career in psychology and that laid the foundations for many of his later scientific interests in development, primatology, sensory capacities of animals, comparative psychology, and the psychology of learning. I shall concentrate here on the last two topics.

The important comparative research on which Watson and Lashley collaborated was fieldwork carried out in the spring of 1913 on Bird Key in the Dry Tortugas, a cluster of small islands in the Gulf of Mexico some 70 miles west of Key West, Florida. Two species of birds were studied, noddy and sooty terns. One of the projects continued Watson's earlier work in 1907 and 1910 on the homing abilities of these birds. Watson sought evidence that they could home over long, unfamiliar stretches of water. Lashley's task was to transport and release the birds during two trips westward in the Gulf, the first to Mobile, Alabama, and the second to Galveston, Texas. These were challenging assignments. A major problem was keeping the birds alive until they could be released for the flight back to the Tortugas. Lashley's skill at doing so was instrumental to the demonstration that the terns could in fact home over long distances.

In a separate but complementary project, Lashley investigated the nest-finding ability of terns on Bird Key when they were removed from their nests and released within the immediate vicinity on the island. His description and analysis of how the birds returned to their nests was very much in the nature of ethology—the study of species-typical behavior in natural settings—and foreshadowed his acceptance of the European ethological tradition long before it was recognized by most North American comparative psychologists.

The notable learning research conducted by Watson and Lashley was on conditioning. Lashley attempted to condition the salivary reflex in human beings, a preliminary to his later interest in the neurophysiology of the conditioned reflex. In Lashley's recollection, the research got started this way:

> In [the fall of] 1914, I think, Watson called attention of his seminar to the French edition of Bechterew [published in 1913] and that winter the seminar was devoted to translation and discussion of the book. In the spring I served as a sort of unpaid assistant and we constructed apparatus and planned experiments together. We simply planned to repeat Bechterew's experiments. We worked on withdrawal reflexes, knee jerk, pupil. Watson took the initiative in all this . . . . I did much of the actual experimental work. I devised drainage tubes for the parotid- and submaxillary ducts and planned the salivary work which I published.

Watson's presidential address to the American Psychological Association in 1915 was a progress report on this research. He said little about conditioning the salivary reflex, other than to describe the apparatus that Lashley had constructed for measuring salivation in human beings. He concentrated instead on the conditioning of motor reflexes, in particular the conditioning of withdrawal responses to auditory stimuli.

In early 1916, the collaboration between Watson and Lashley came to an end, chiefly because they developed different interests in conditioning research. Watson saw the conditioned response as the basic unit of habit and considered conditioning as a framework for understanding the development of all behavior. Lashley's interest was in finding out how conditioned reflexes are represented in the nervous system. In Lashley's words:

> Watson saw [the conditioned reflex] as a basis for a systematic psychology and was not greatly concerned with the nature of the reaction itself. I got interested in the physiology of the reaction and the attempt to trace conditioned reflex paths through the nervous system started my program of cerebral work.

Even though the two men traveled different paths from 1916 on, they maintained a friendly and mutually respectful relationship that persisted long after Watson was fired from Johns Hopkins. It is not difficult to understand why Lashley would want to keep in touch with Watson. Watson's influence on him had been substantial. Their joint research, especially on conditioning, led Lashley to shift to a career in psychology and was the basis for most of his later scientific interests. At the same time, however, the difference between the two was fundamental, and perhaps even predictable. Watson's emphasis on conditioning as a method, on the conditioned reflex as the basic unit of habit, and ultimately on behavioral control as a theoretical objective was in keeping with the ideas of Jacques Loeb, one of his teachers at the University of Chicago. Lashley's wish to understand the physiological basis of conditioned reflexes reflected the explanatory approach of his mentor, Jennings. Thus the contrasting views of Watson and Lashley on the conditioned reflex were a quiet replay of the earlier clash between Loeb and Jennings.

Postdoctoral Study with Shepherd I. Franz, 1915–1917

Lashley's initial efforts to determine the neural changes taking place during conditioning and learning were unsuccessful. He was unable to establish stable conditioned salivary reflexes in human beings and work on the effects of drugs on maze learning in rats was inconclusive. A more fruitful approach to the problem, brain ablation studies with animals, was provided by Shepherd I. Franz, who worked at the Government Hospital for the Insane in nearby Washington, DC.

When Lashley proposed collaborative research, Franz agreed. They conducted a number of projects, but two in particular are significant because they mark the beginning of Lashley's programmatic studies of the cerebral bases of learning. In both investigations, rats were trained by Lashley at Johns Hopkins and ferried to and from Franz's laboratory in Washington for the operations and the later histology to assess the damage caused by the operations. The first study examined the effect of frontal lobe injuries on the retention of a one-choice maze habit after varying amounts of overlearning—learning beyond the point of the first correct run through the maze. The evidence suggested that frontal lobe destruction had little effect on the retention of the habit. In a second investigation, other areas of the brain were lesioned as well as the frontal lobes. The tasks were, again, the simple one-choice maze and, in addition, a more complex, inclined-plane problem. Acquisition and retention of the maze habit were not significantly affected by any of the lesions. The inclined-plane problem was another matter. Here, Lashley and Franz found that (1) Retention was impaired or absent when the frontal lobes were completely, but not partly, destroyed—there was localization of function; and (2) When destruction of the frontal lobes was partially, the particular part preserved was immaterial—the parts were, in Lashley's terms, *equipotential* in the functioning of the habit. Franz's combination of brain ablations and laboratory procedures for the study of learning and retention in animals provided Lashley with the methods that he needed to begin his research on the cerebral mechanisms of learning, research that spanned the stage of his career that we consider next.

UNIVERSITY APPOINTMENTS, 1917-1942

In 1917, Lashley was hired as an instructor at the University of Minnesota. He spent 1 year there and then took a leave of absence to work in Baltimore with Watson on a study of motion pictures in sex education. He and Watson traveled around the towns of Maryland showing a film designed to educate the public against the dangers of venereal disease and collected data on its effectiveness. The investigation had its humorous moments, but probably it also was responsible for Lashley's longstanding interest in research on sexual behavior. In 1920, he was persuaded to return to Minnesota by the newly hired chair of the department, Richard M. Elliot. Elliot saw to it that Lashley was well supported in his research, protected as much as possible from routine duties, given a light teaching load, and promoted as rapidly as possible. By 1924 he was a full professor.

In 1926 Lashley took a position as research psychologist with the Behavior Research Fund at the Institute for Juvenile Research in Chicago. The move may have been motivated by the hope that a change in environment would improve the health of his wife, who suffered severely from asthma, but Minnesota's inability to meet Lashley's need for more research support may also have been a factor. After 3 years with the Behavior Research Fund, Lashley accepted an appointment in the Department of Psychology at the University of Chicago, where he remained until 1935.

Studies of Cerebral Function in Learning

Lashley's studies of the cerebral bases of learning led to 13 major research articles, the majority of them completed during the Minnesota and Chicago years. Significant parts of the research formed the basis of three of Lashley's synthetic publications: (1) his only book, *Brain Mechanisms and Intelligence*, published in 1929; (2) his address as president of the American Psychological Association given to the ninth International Congress of Psychology at Yale University in 1929, the published version of which appeared in 1930; and (3) a review article, "Integrative Functions of the Cerebral Cortex," published in 1933. I present the important themes of these writings because they represent much of what Lashley is remembered for.

Brain Mechanisms and Intelligence.   This monograph (Lashley, 1929) summarized the results of investigations carried out at Minnesota and at the Behavior Research Fund in Chicago. Their objective was to analyze the neural mechanisms that play a role in learning. The word "intelligence" in the title of the book reflected Lashley's belief that learning could not be divorced from the broader problem of intelligence.

The research examined the effects of cerebral lesions in rats on the acquisition and retention of different kinds of habits, mainly those for mazes of varying difficulty but also the learning of brightness discrimination and inclined-plane problems. Animals were operated upon and allowed time to recover. They were then tested on their abilities to learn and retain the different kinds of habits, using time and accuracy as measures. Each animal was ultimately sacrificed and the extent of the brain injury determined by sectioning and staining brain tissue. Location of the lesion was carefully ascertained. Its extent was expressed as a percentage of total surface area.

A major finding was that maze learning was affected by brain damage. What was especially noteworthy, however, was that the effect depended on how much cortical area had been destroyed and not where the destruction had occurred: "The magnitude of the injury is important; the locus is not" (Lashley, 1929, p. 60). "For learning of the mazes no part of the cortex is more important than any other" (p. 68). The correlation between learning and the amount of cortical damage was strongest for the most difficult of the maze problems. Lashley also examined the retention of maze habits when brain lesions were made following learning. Again, performance was found to depend on the amount of remaining cortex rather than its locus. "It is certain that the maze habit, when formed, is not localized in any single area of the cerebrum and that its performance is somehow conditioned by the quantity of tissue which is intact" (p. 107).

To summarize these findings, Lashley used two related shorthand expressions: (1) *equipotentiality* (all parts of a functional area of the brain are equally capable of carrying out the functions of the whole area) and (2) *mass action* (performance of a function is reduced in proportion to the amount of damaged functional tissue). In reaching these conclusions, Lashley considered and rejected the possibility that the negative effects of brain lesions on maze habits were due to interference by a purely sensory or motor deficit. Evidence that we need not consider here persuaded him that some more general deterioration in learning as a whole had occurred.

Lashley emphasized that his antilocalization results and conclusions were of restricted generality. They did not apply to all problems. For example, acquisition of the brightness discrimination habit was largely unaffected by lesions of any extent or of any locus. Evidence from other studies indicated that habits for this task, when formed by normal animals, are localized. Lashley suggested that such habits are less complex than the maze habit and that performance is therefore not dependent on large amounts of cortical tissue.

"Basic Neural Mechanisms in Behavior."   The International Congress of Psychology in 1929 was notable for two addresses, one by Ivan P. Pavlov, who described his recent work on the role of subcortical centers in unconditioned reflexes. The other was the talk that Lashley published as "Basic Neural Mechanisms in Behavior" (1930). Pavlov spoke first; Lashley, 2 days later. Pavlov was present at Lashley's talk, but Lashley apparently did not hear Pavlov. To the best of my knowledge, the two did not meet at the congress.

Lashley began his address by lamenting the inadequacies of current notions concerning the mechanisms of the brain. There are basically two theories, he said. One states that functions are localized in certain parts of brain. But even if that were true, such a theory gives no insight into how the parts function or influence one another.

The other hypothesis Lashley termed reflex theory.

> It states that the mechanism of cerebral function is essentially the same as that of the spinal reflexes, involving the conduction of nerve impulses from the sense organs over definite, restricted paths to the effectors. The performance of a habit, whether of speech or of manipulative movement, is determined by the existence of definite connections between a limited number of nerve cells, which are always functional in that habit. The model for this theory is a telephone system. Just as two instruments can be connected only by certain wires, so the sense organs and muscles concerned in any act are connected by nerve fibers specialized for that act . . . . [T]he essential feature of the reflex theory is the assumption that individual neurons are specialized for particular functions. The explanatory value of the theory rests upon this point alone, and no amount of hypothetical elaboration of connections alters the basic assumption. (Beach et al., 1960, pp. 192–193)

Lashley then presented evidence to refute both theories. He argued that equivalence of stimuli—different stimuli can call out the same response—would not be possible if areas of the brain or single cells respond to specific stimuli. Similarly, equivalence of responses—the same stimulus can be responded to in a variety of ways—would not be possible if areas or single cells have very specific functions. Finally, plasticity (recovery of function) of the nervous system after injury constituted additional negative evidence (in this context, Lashley described his own findings reported in *Brain Mechanisms and Intelligence*). Then, coming down hard on reflex theory, he asserted that it was becoming an obstacle to understanding how cerebral integration really works.

Lashley sketched an alternative hypothesis, but it was vague and was not the important part of the address. Rather, the significance of the talk was the vigorous attack on Pavlovian reflex theory, an attack in which, curiously, Pavlov's name was never mentioned. Afterwards, Pavlov denounced Lashley's lecture so vehemently that his interpreter, trying to keep up with the 20-minute tirade, finally gave up and said simply at the end of it, "Professor Pavlov said: No!" (Windholz, 1983, p. 399). Pavlov was undoubtedly wounded by Lashley's criticisms, because he had expected a better North American reception of his conditioning work. Pavlov thought it perfectly suited to the new behavioristic spirit in psychology. To have had one of the foremost behaviorists of the time reject his ideas so thoroughly must have been a bitter disappointment.

"Integrative Functions of the Cerebral Cortex."   This article (Lashley, 1933) contains practically all of Lashley's data (as well as those of others) and arguments in support of the concepts of mass action and equipotentiality. He concluded that the evidence pointed to the mutual interdependence of parts of the brain and that specialization of structures was perhaps less important than the amount of brain tissue—mass action. Furthermore, the evidence indicated that for the entire cortex (for certain functions) and for specialized areas (for other functions), the constituent parts were all equally capable of carrying out the actions of the whole—equipotentiality. Lashley now believed that equipotentiality applied even within highly specialized areas such as those for vision and motor activity.

Harvard University, 1935–1942

In 1935, Lashley became professor of psychology at Harvard University. The public story is that James B. Conant, president of Harvard at the time, charged the search committee with finding "the best psychologist in the world." The committee recommended Lashley and he was appointed, even before the offer was made to him. The implication is that the call to Harvard came out of the blue. The facts are, however, that the university had approached Lashley as early as 1927 about a position and again in late 1928. So it could not have been a surprise when Harvard made a third overture in 1935. This time Lashley accepted. Always irreverent, he was fond of saying later that the main reason he went to Harvard was for the sailing, which was one of his loves.

Things began to unravel for Lashley soon after arriving at Harvard. He was burdened with more administrative work than he wanted. He did not have the dominant voice in the department that he expected he would. Promised financial support to establish a research institute of neurology and psychology did not materialize. Some political decisions within the department went against him. And the sailing wasn't that great either. After a year or so of this, Lashley withdrew intellectually from the department. He wrote a severely critical letter to President

Conant, demanding that he be given a "roving" professorship, and offering his resignation as an alternative. Harvard acquiesced and he was appointed Research Professor of Neuropsychology in 1937.

In 1942, the separation from Harvard became more pronounced when Lashley became director of the Yerkes Laboratories of Primate Biology in Orange Park, Florida. Still a member of the Harvard faculty, his association with the university from that time on was limited to supervising PhD students who chose to work with him at Yerkes and to brief teaching assignments at Harvard—initially during the summers but eventually for annual 2-week stints in the graduate proseminar.

DIRECTOR OF YERKES LABORATORIES AND THEREAFTER, 1942–1958

The move to Yerkes seems to have agreed with Lashley. He had no heavy teaching demands. He was free of university bureaucracy and politics. The weight of administrative responsibilities at Yerkes was not onerous because much of it was shouldered by the assistant director, Henry Nissen. The lab attracted stimulating graduate students and postdoctoral associates, notably, Frank Beach, Donald Hebb, Karl Pribram, Austin Riesen, and Roger Sperry. He was in a setting where most of his scientific interests could easily be pursued; indeed, it was almost as though he were back as a graduate student at Johns Hopkins, a situation in which he had thrived. The isolation of north Florida, which many people who came to work at Yerkes found difficult to adjust to, may even have appealed to him. It was probably similar to the isolation that he had enjoyed when he and Watson were on the Dry Tortugas conducting their studies of bird behavior. Finally, the warmer climate of Florida was probably beneficial to his wife's health; it certainly suited Lashley. And yes, the sailing was probably better, too.

By the time Lashley took up his appointment at Yerkes, a great deal of his empirical research on brain and behavior had been completed and most of his publications had appeared. Yet significant work was still to come. In this segment of the chapter, I emphasize Lashley's comparative psychology, notably, his commanding theoretical articles on the topic and his connections to European ethology. I conclude with excerpts from Lashley's correspondence to convey an idea of his personal interests and professional values.

Important Publications in Comparative Psychology

Lashley made two very significant contributions to comparative psychology before arriving at Yerkes. One was the field research described earlier that he carried out with Watson on the nesting and homing behavior of noddy and sooty terns. The other was his presidential address, "The Experimental Analysis of Instinctive Behavior," delivered at the 1938 meeting of the Eastern Psychological Association. North American psychology of the 1920s, 1930s and 1940s stressed learning rather than instinct and environmental rather than genetic determinants of behavior. Lashley argued that the anti-instinct bias was misguided:

> I am well aware that instincts were banished from psychology some years ago, but that purge seems to have failed of its chief objective. The anti-instinct movement was aimed primarily at the postulation of imaginary forces as explanations of behavior. It was only incidental that these had also been assumed to be constitutional. The psychology of instincts was a dynamics of imaginary forces and the anti-instinct movement was primarily a crusade against such a conceptual dynamism. Somehow the argument got twisted. Heredity was made a scapegoat and the hypostatization of psychic energies goes merrily on. Desires and aversions, field forces and dynamic tensions, needs and vectors, libidoes and means-end-readinesses have the same conceptual status as had the rejected instincts and, besides, lack the one tie to physiological reality which the problem of genetic transmission gave to the latter . . .

> Although the distinction of genetic and environmental influences has little importance in many fields of psychology, it is of real significance for problems of the physiological basis of behavior. This is true because information concerning the mechanics of development and the histological organization produced by growth is far more exact than any available data concerning the changes produced by learning. Fundamental principles of neural integration may be inferred from innate structure and the behavior dependent upon it. The plasticity and variability of learned behavior precludes any similar correlations with structural patterns. (Beach et al., 1960, pp. 373–374)

From that splendid opening, Lashley went on to consider a variety of instinctive behaviors (e.g., the honey-dance of the bee, kin recognition, reproductive activity, discrimination of visual patterns, jumping behavior of rats, and egg retrieval of gulls), their underlying sensory organization, and their probable control by a complex of stimuli. At a neurological level, Lashley suspected that all instincts would turn out to be a matter of the activation of very specific sensory–motor mechanisms. As a first step in understanding these mechanisms, he called for specification of the adequate stimuli for instinctive behaviors.

Lashley returned to the heredity–environment problem in a symposium held at Princeton University in 1947. The address was later published as "Structural Variation in the Nervous System in Relation to

Behavior" (1947). This article applies to a variety of areas within psychology and is as pertinent today as it was when Lashley wrote it. The argument is simple and compelling: Individual variations in the brain within species are similar to differences between species. Since we have no hesitancy in attributing interspecies differences to genetic determinants, it may be assumed that individual variations within species, and the individual differences in behaviors dependent on them, are similarly determined. Lashley then described the evidence for considerable variation in every aspect of the brain that had been measured. Conceding that the hereditary basis of such variation had not been studied, he claimed its genetic determination by analogy with the known hereditary basis for other structures and went on to argue that individual variation in the brain must have functional significance and, at the very least, cannot be ignored as possible causes of individual differences in mental abilities and behavior.

Lashley's presidential address to the American Society of Naturalists, published in 1949 as, "Persistent Problems in the Evolution of Mind," was the third and last of his important theoretical statements on comparative psychology. In this article, Lashley's materialism, behaviorism, emphasis on genetic determinants of behavior, and ethology are forcefully stated. On materialism: "The evolution of mind is the evolution of nervous mechanisms . . ." (Beach et al., 1960, p. 461). On behaviorism: "A comparative study of the behavior of animals is a comparative study of mind, by any meaningful definition of the term" (p. 457). On the genetic determinants of behavior, Lashley argued that the distinction between instinctive behavior as the product of genes and intelligent behavior as the product of experience was overdrawn and that both are genetically determined. The differences are a matter of degree, not kind. On ethology: "A study of complex instincts requires a detailed analysis of the exact stimulus or combination of stimuli which call forth the behavior, combined with descriptions of the behavior elicited" (p. 473). Finally, Lashley asked, what is it that differentiates animals in an evolutionary sense? And answered: More highly evolved animals have a greater capacity to perceive relations, a greater variety of types of perceptual organization to draw on. Such organization is an inherent property of the nervous system, even though at this time we have only the vaguest notion of the underlying neural mechanisms.

Lashley as a Bridge to Ethology

Until the middle 1960s, there was much antagonism and misunderstanding between North American comparative psychology and European ethology. In a sense, Lashley was a bridge between the two camps.

Although a comparative psychologist, he valued the ethologists, especially Lorenz and Tinbergen, for their careful analyses of effective stimuli and for their acute observations of response patterns. At one time he even recommended that the Department of Psychology at Harvard consider Tinbergen for an appointment, but the recommendation fell flat.

The reciprocal respect for Lashley from the ethologists was undoubtedly helped by his status as director of Yerkes, a leading center for primatology in the world. During his tenure as director, Yerkes hosted a wide range of visitors, among them most of the prominent ethologists of the time: Karl von Frisch, Konrad Lorenz, Niko Tinbergen, W. H. Thorpe, and Paul Schiller. Schiller came to work at Yerkes in 1947 and died in a tragic skiing accident 2 years later. He had begun to translate some of the important ethological articles so that they would be accessible to American comparative psychologists. The work was later brought to fruition by his wife, Claire Schiller, in an edited volume entitled *Instinctive Behavior*. Lashley wrote the introduction to this book.

SELECTIONS FROM THE CORRESPONDENCE OF LASHLEY

Lashley's correspondence makes stimulating and demanding reading and is an inestimable source of information about his personal characteristics and professional values. The following selections, all from letters that he wrote during the last 16 years of his life, are intended to give a more complete measure of the man.

In an exchange of letters with William A. Kepner, a retired professor of biology from the University of Virginia, Lashley debated the value of purpose as an ultimate cause (Kepner) versus mechanism (Lashley):

> Basically I suppose our difference is one of values. You would like to save beauty, truth, and mother-love from profanation. I was nursed on Melon's Food and Nietsche [*sic*]. I can determine mother-love with pituitary hormone and find truth only a matter of statistics. Yet I am sure that I get as much out of living as the most religious and risible. It is not the mechanist who fears the atom bomb, but those who dread the eternal life of bliss in which they believe. There is no record in the psychiatric literature of a neurotic mechanist. (letter to Kepner, April 29, 1952)

> Why seek purpose in nature? So far as I can analyze the motive, it is to add to the importance of things we think admirable; to find that they were planned for, as we plan for the things we want. God created the universe in order to start evolution in order to produce man in order to produce the

hydrogen bomb in order to destroy all that he had produced. I can readily understand the psychology of such a schizophrenic deity . . . .

I once liked to play poker and I still prefer a universe ruled by chance. [I also] once computed the probability of producing the Andante in Beethoven's Op. 131 by throwing dice. That particular permutation might occur if all people in the world threw dice for a million years, 8 hours per day. That computation does not prevent me from feeling that I would rather be able to play the movement well than anything else in the world. Ideal? No, a simple reaction to frustration. Values are queer habits, easily established and hard to change. (letter to Kepner, May 14, 1952)

On the alleged evidence for telepathy Lashley had this to say:

The basic principle of scientific method is that the conditions of observation shall be so stated that any adequately trained observer can reproduce them and obtain the same results [but] studies of telepathy have never met this criterion. The reasons given for failure to meet the accepted standards of scientific demonstration approach the realm of religious mysticism; the possession of the power by only a few inspired individuals, etc. . . . . [T]he absence of testable theories of telepathy is a further weakness of the investigations. It has been said and with justice that the greatest disappointment for an advocate of telepathy would be to have it explained. (letter to R. E. McConnell, October 3, 1954)

On comparative psychology and dualism:

I question the psychology which denies to animals the functions of imagination and reasoning. The differences even between the rat and man are of degree, not of kind. (letter to Bhajan S. Schmi, January 5, 1953)

On the limits of science:

We should not deceive ourselves with the belief that the solution of society's problems can come from science. Science can affirm means but not ends and my pessimism makes me believe that our values will always be dictated by those who can play on emotions, the poets, preachers, spellbinders, the Huey Longs and Cardinal Newmans. (letter to Roger J. Williams, June 19, 1946)

On his enjoyment of the role of critic:

The Laurentian Symposium was great fun, since I found myself playing the post of devil's advocate in opposition to almost all the other members of the Symposium. Some of my more pungent remarks seem to have suffered the editorial axe. Toward the close of the meeting Penfield remarked rather wistfully, "I am glad to see that Lashley is as critical of himself as of everyone else". (letter to F. M. R. Walshe, January, 28, 1955)

CONCLUDING COMMENTS

Lashley retired as director of Yerkes in 1955 but was a member of its board of directors until his sudden death on August 7, 1958, while vacationing in France. Although his research and theory on the neurophysiological mechanisms of learning and in comparative psychology would have been enough to establish anyone's claim to scientific fame, remarkably, there are other contributions, and I would be remiss if I did not make at least brief mention of three of them.

One was his research on the neural bases of vision, which resulted in 18 published articles, the first in 1930 and the last in 1948. These papers cover considerable ground, including a method for studying vision in rats, the role of cortical structures in the rat's performance of brightness and pattern discriminations, and numerous studies of the anatomy of the visual system in rats.

A second important contribution in 1946 (with George Clark) was an influential critique of the reliability with which the cortex could be anatomically subdivided into purported functional areas.

Third was one of Lashley's most admired theoretical statements, "The Problem of Serial Order in Behavior." In this 1951 article, he rejected the notion that an action sequence is an associative chain in which each element (whatever it might be) arouses the next by direct association. Drawing on a wide range of behavior, he hypothesized instead that serial actions are organized in advance of their performance and at a higher level, that is, by a generalized plan or schema of integration. He hastened to add, however, that this was merely a statement of the problem, not its solution.

As a final note, it sometimes seeems that Lashley's contributions to science were largely negative, that he only attacked theories without offering alternatives. While it is true that he enjoyed the role of critic, and no doubt believed, with the philosopher Karl Popper, that knowledge progresses only through criticism, he was more than just a critic. Whatever the subject matter, Lashley identified the fundamental problems to be addressed. For example, his contributions to comparative psychology, while critical of extant theory, had a positive effect. They redressed the bias against instincts, emphasizing heredity as a determinant of behavior. They promoted the detailed description of behavior and the careful analysis of the stimuli that elicit it. Perhaps the best expression of Lashley's position on such matters is his own: "The scientist's one prayer should be: Lord preserve me from all reverence of authority, both thine and mine" (letter to Sigmund Koch, April 6, 1953).

REFERENCES[1]

Beach, F. A. (1961). Karl Spencer Lashley: June 7, 1890–August 7, 1958. *Biographical Memoirs of the National Academy of Sciences, 35*, 162–204.
Beach, F. A., Hebb, D. O., Morgan, C. T., & Nissen, H. W. (Eds.). (1960). *The Neuropsychology of Lashley.* New York: McGraw-Hill.
Bruce, D. (1986). Lashley's shift from bacteriology to neuropsychology, 1910–1917, and the influence of Jennings, Watson, and Franz. *Journal of the History of the Behavioral Sciences, 22*, 27–44.
Kelly, B. N. (1990, June). *"The Best Psychologist in the World": Karl Lashley and Harvard, 1927–1935.* Paper presented at the meeting of the Cheiron Society, Medfield, MA.
Lashley, K. S. (1929). *Brain mechanisms and intelligence.* Chicago: University of Chicago Press.
Lashley, K. S. (1930). Basic neural mechanisms in behavior. *Psychological Review, 37*, 1–24.
Lashley, K. S. (1933). Integrative functions of the cerebral cortex. *Physiology Review, 13*, 1–24.
Lashley, K. S. (1947). Structural variation in the nervous system in relation to behavior. *Psychological Review, 54*, 325–334.
Lashley, K. S. (1949). Persistent problems in the evolution of mind. *Quarterly Review of Biology, 24*, 28–42.
Lashley, K. S. (1951). The problem of serial order in behavior. In L. A. Jeffress (Ed.), *Cerebral mechanisms in behavior* (pp. 112–136). New York: Wiley.
Orbach, J. (Ed.). (1982). *Neuropsychology after Lashley: Fifty years since the publication of Brain Mechanisms and Intelligence.* Hillsdale, NJ: Lawrence Erlbaum Associates.
Windholz, G. (1983). Pavlov's position toward American behaviorism. *Journal of the History of the Behavioral Sciences, 19*, 394–407.

---

[1]Biographies of Lashley are available in a number of sources. Those that I have used most are the one by Beach (1961) and the first five chapters of the book by Orbach (1982). The section on Lashley's preparation for a career in psychology is based on an earlier article (Bruce, 1986). Materials on the cerebral basis of learning and comparative psychology come from Lashley's publications, many of which appear in the book of Beach et al. (1960). Page numbers in this chapter, for quotations from articles included there, refer to that volume. Publications by Lashley that are not in Beach et al. and that are mentioned in the text are listed separately in the references. Excellent treatments of the controversy between Lashley and Pavlov are to be found in Orbach, Chap. 1, and Windholz (1983). The paper by Kelly (1990) furnishes a behind-the-scenes account of Lashley's appointment to Harvard. The letters of Lashley from which extracts have been made are in the archives of the Yerkes Regional Primate Research Center in Atlanta. I am grateful to Fred King and Nellie Johns for allowing me access to this resource. The picture of Lashley was provided by Professor B. R. Hergenhahn of Hamline University. My review of Lashley's contributions to comparative psychology has benefited from the observations of Don Dewsbury. Finally, I should say that my interest in Lashley dates from an evening in 1980, when I had a most pleasant conversation with Mrs. Claire Lashley (Lashley's second wife), in the Lashley home on Fiddler's Cove in Jacksonville, Florida. I thank the History of Psychology Foundation, the Southern Regional Education Board, the Florida State University Foundation, and the Marjorie Young Bell Fund of Mount Allison University for supporting the research that underlies this chapter.

Chapter 21

Harry Stack Sullivan:
The Clinician and the Man

Kenneth L. Chatelaine

"I probably shall not return, but remember this and do not forget it. I shall be controversial. There was no way to avoid it." (Sullivan's last words to his foster son, James Inscoe Sullivan, on January 2, 1949)

Harry Stack Sullivan made major contributions to the history of personality theory. He outlined an interpersonal approach to personality, the idea that an individual's concept of selfhood is a reflection of others' attitudes toward that person. Influenced by the social psychology of George Herbert Mead and Charles Cooley, Sullivan understood a person's ego-concept to be the result of what is mirrored back to that person by mother, family, and social surroundings.

Contemporary American theories of personality find their origins in the work of Sullivan. For example, Sullivan's personality theory served as a precursor to the work of Carl Rogers. The idea of the "phenomenal self" in Rogers's thinking was anticipated in the work of Sullivan, and Rogers built his theory on the Sullivanian idea that the self-concept is a sociological product. Sullivan's theory also was a forerunner to the developmental personality theory of Erik Erikson. According to Sullivan, every individual traverses seven stages of development during life: (1) infancy, (2) childhood, (3) the juvenile period, (4) preadolescence, (5) adolescence, (6) late adolescence, and (7) adulthood. Although Erikson used a somewhat different classification of psychological stages, he was

---

*Photograph of Harry Stack Sullivan courtesy of the Washington School of Psychiatry

preceded by Sullivan's idea that personality must be viewed in evolutionary perspective.

In addition to his seminal ideas regarding the interpersonal origins of personality and his promotion of a developmental approach to personality, Sullivan also pioneered in the investigation of anxiety. Life, according to Sullivan, is a dialectic between homeostasis and anxiety. Homeostasis has both an organic and psychological aspect. On the organ level, the individual tends toward a homeostatic condition, toward a state of "euphoria" in which all psychical needs are gratified. On the psychological level, the individual strives for a frictionless adjustment to the environment. The psychological mechanism which allows an individual to feel at peace with the environment and the self is high self-esteem.

The force that negates "euphoria," that introduces unrest and disquietude in a person's life is anxiety deriving from low self-esteem. Anxiety is the great human plague; it is the force of contradiction that disrupts and distorts one's ability to relate to the environment. It is the root source of mental illness and one of Sullivan's goals in psychiatric therapy was the alleviation of anxiety.

Sullivan's theory of personality derived from his ideas regarding the evolution of the self-concept, a perception of the self that is gradually developed and elaborated from appraisals showered upon us by others. Although the personal self-concept develops slowly, the need for personal security is present from the very beginning of existence. Sullivan hypothesized that threats to an individual's self-respect are experienced as anxiety, which in turn produces defensive measures to relieve that anxiety and protect the self. These assaults on self-esteem emanate from sources outside the person, most importantly from the mother who is a person's principal nurturing other. The origins of this way of thinking are very probably in Sullivan's life experience.

BIOGRAPHY

Born in Norwich, New York, on February 21, 1892, Harry Stack Sullivan was the only surviving child of Timothy J. and Ella M. (Stack) Sullivan. From analysis of Sullivan's relationship with his parents one can understand the development of his revolutionary psychological insights.

Called upon from an early age to support and direct the family, following his father's death in a railroad accident, Timothy J. Sullivan grew to be a serious and introspective man who was withdrawn and shy. Unhappily forced by circumstance to live on and work the Stack land, the elder Sullivan appeared unreachable to the son, who preferred solitary reading to the daily chores required of a farmer. It was only after the death of his mother and his becoming a doctor and attaining some professional standing, that Harry was able to develop satisfying communication with his father.

A few years older than her husband, Harry's mother came from a family of educators, lawyers, doctors, and priests and was said to have "suffered" because she felt she had married beneath herself. According to A. H. Chapman (1976, p. 20), throughout Sulllivan's childhood his mother "unloaded on her son her helpless anger, her tales of her family's former prominence, and impractical dreams of a better future." Convinced of the superiority of her own family over her husband's, Ella told her son tales of the glorious past. Especially fascinating to young Harry was one of his mother's stories of an ancestor supposedly known as West Wind, a horse that ran toward the sunrise to meet the future. Sullivan, with his sentimental, humorous Irish mind, is said to have partly believed the story. Whether he did or did not, his strong feeling for horses is evidenced by his personal symbol of two horses' heads enclosed within a circle, one looking upward and the other down.

Although entertained by her tales, Sullivan seemed to feel that he was never really loved by his mother. The woman's unhappiness with her lot in life must have been communicated to the child. In a striking statement Sullivan later (1974, p. 49) wrote:

> I escaped most of the evils of being an only child by chief virtue of the fact that mother never troubled to notice the characteristics of the child she had brought forth. And her son was so different from me that I felt she had no use for me except as a clothes horse on which to hang an elaborate pattern of illusions.

One stark phrase in that paragraph testifies to the tragedy of Sullivan's childhood and to the source of most of his later suffering: "She had no use for me." What could provide a more graphic indication of the man's loneliness, alienation, and anger, and of the perverse source for his inspirational genius?

At home in Smyrna on the Stack family farm, to which he moved at the age of 3, young Harry was surrounded by fields and livestock. He was the single child in the only Catholic family in an old Yankee Protestant community where intense prejudice then existed against the Irish. Patrick Mullahy (1973) writes that the boy's closest friends were the farm animals, with whom he felt comfortable and less lonely. Likewise Clara Thompson, Sullivan's colleague and close friend, in her memorial address in 1949, described Sullivan as "a lonely person from his earliest childhood." Thus was the boy isolated, with a disgruntled, complaining mother and an uncommunicative father, who may have been resentful of his wife's rejection; with no companionship from children his own age, lost within the spatial expanse of the farm. One can only conjecture as to his unfulfilled, half-conscious yearnings for a paradise lost, his need to search for that which he must pursue until the end of his life; or until the horse (West Wind) and the sunrise meet.

When Sullivan, the man, became Sulivan the clinical master of interpersonal relations, he produced his best-known work, *Schizophrenia as a Human Process* (1974). In this work he described what he himself referred to as the loneliest of the lonely, the schizophrenic. If genius is derived from understanding, and if the understanding of self is the basis of all other understanding, the genius of Harry Stack Sullivan lay in his awareness of the impact of personal experience upon the development of mental illness.

EDUCATION

Sullivan received his grade and high school education at the Smyrna Union School, entering in 1897 or 1898. Although early records were destroyed by fire, later files show him to have been a superior student. Yet, because he did not know how to be part of a group and had no friends, young Harry felt out of place and turned to books for companionship. The only source of positive self-esteem for him during these years was his continued scholastic excellence, which did little to decrease his shy loneliness.

There is no question that Sullivan while growing up felt crippled by this isolation from boys of his own age. His writings about this stage of

FIG. 21.1.   *Sullivan's Personal Seal*
(Courtesy of Kenneth L. Chatelaine)

life are not just those of a theorist, they are the insights of someone calling upon personal experience and writing from within the self. For example, in *Conceptions of Modern Psychiatry* (1953, pp. 42-44), Sullivan wrote this about preadolescence:

There are the most excellent reasons why true social orientation takes a long time coming. But it comes in preadolescence. The capacity to love in its initial form makes its appearance as the mark that one has ceased to be juvenile and has become preadolescent. What this means in the outline of situations which it brings about is this: at this point the satisfactions and the security which are being experienced by someone else, some particular other person, begin to be as significant to one as is one's own satisfaction or security, then the state of love exists. . . .

The appearance of the capacity to love ordinarily first involves a member of one's own sex. . . .When this has happened, there follows in its wake a great increase in the consensual validation of symbols, of symbol operations, and of information, data about life and the world. . . .

One's security is not imperiled by one's love object. One's satisfactions are facilitated by the love object. Therefore, naturally, for the first time, one can begin to express onself freely. If another person matters as much to you as you do to yourself, it is quite possible to talk to this person as you have never talked to anyone before.

The freedom which comes from this expanding of one's world of satisfaction and security to include two people, linked together by love, permits exchanges of nuances of meaning, permits investigations without fear or rebuff or humiliation, which greatly augments the consensual validation of all sorts of things, all in the end symbols that stand for—refer to, represent—states of being in the world.

It was this stage of personal development that Sullivan himself sorely missed and wished to re-create for his patients by his famous milieu therapy treatment.

After graduating as valedictorian from high school at the age of 16, Sullivan was awarded a state scholarship and left his community for the first time to attend Cornell University in Ithaca, New York. At the end of his first semester, Sullivan's grades were average but during his second semester they fell dramatically, and in June of 1909 he was suspended for failure in all his subjects.

Nothing definite seems to be known about the 2 years following Sullivan's suspension from Cornell. There is speculation that during this time Sullivan suffered some kind of mental illness, possibly a brief schizophrenic episode and that he may have been hospitalized at Binghamton State Hospital, where Dr. Ross McClure Chapman (who later hired Sullivan to work at Sheppard Pratt Hospital) was first assistant physician. Sullivan himself is reported to have told people that in his early years he had been a patient in an unspecified psychiatric hospital. Unfortunately, however, all of the Binghamton State Hospital records for the years 1909–1910 have been destroyed by fire, and intensive research reveals no hard evidence for this suggestion.

In 1911 Sullivan turned up in Chicago to attend the Chicago College of Medicine and Surgery, and went on to become a practicing psychiatrist. Of Sullivan the clinician at Sheppard Pratt, Dr. Dexter Bullard, Sr., a colleague, has said:

> I've never gotten a clear picture of how he worked with patients—I think particularly schizophrenic patients. I've heard many vignettes about patients, but I've never had a very clear idea as to whether he saw them regularly for individual sessions or whether his emphasis was somewhat more on the total work. He had this knack of picking his staff quite carefully and then if an alienated patient was sitting over in the corner and happened to look up and follow with his eyes the passage of one of the attendants, Harry would go to that attendant and coach him in the ways of making tentative advances to the patient . . . . [H]is use of his staff was phenomenal, sensitive—and he had a recovery rate of about 86%, I think . . . higher than any place I've ever heard of. He did not do much individual work in the years here at Sheppard. (personal interview, April 9, 1977)

Utilizing his specially selected staff, Sullivan established a milieu therapy treatment ward at Sheppard Pratt Hospital in the year 1929. In 1930 he ceased his work with schizophrenics at the hospital and moved to New York to work with obsessional neurotics in a private practice setting. For Sullivan this change represented merely a logical progression in clinical approach. According to his own theories, he was now addressing a disease with a dynamism more akin to that of schizophrenia than any other impaired response to anxiety.

SULLIVAN'S THEORY OF SCHIZOPHRENIA

In his 1931 article, "Environmental Factors in Etiology and Course Under Treatment of Schizophrenia," Sullivan states that the occurrence of this illness must be explained primarily on the basis of experiential rather than hereditary or organic factors. Because of personal experience, some people, caught up in the course of difficult events, undergo a change in total activity, behavior, and thought. This he identified as schizophrenic psychosis. Sullivan felt that, although heredity and genetic factors may contribute to a person's illness, once measured these factors will be found to be of little importance in the etiology of the disease.

The basis of schizophrenia's etiology, according to Sullivan, must be discovered within actual events involving the person and other significant individuals. The realization that dealings with other people are decidedly the most difficult actions for anyone to handle does not occur until a person's early teen-age years. While the individual may have learned to manage parents and other authority figures during childhood, it is only after a need for real, interpersonal intimacy appears that delicate adjustments of personality are developed, which foster relationships with others. Such a subtle level of personality growth is never achieved by the schizophrenic.

Sullivan stressed that the most primitive and perhaps most important aspect of the personality is contributed by the infant's mother or her surrogate. If these infantile parts of the self are too distorted, ensuing growth will be damaged as well and a pathological personality may result. If distortions transmitted to the child are not too pronounced they may take, in boys, the form of an ongoing juvenile appraisal of the self as reflected by the mother. In such cases neurotic dependency on the mother is great, and weaning from it difficult even during adult years when mother substitutes may take the form of a marriage partner or "close" friend.

In an extreme case the boy may experience a wholesale incorporation of his mother's values and attitudes, and may find it impossible to progress to a normal interests in girls. Either the mother alone or only older women will then be attractive to him for what Sullivan refers to as "interpersonal intimacies." The boy will not be able to progress smoothly to biologically ordained heterosexuality, and may in fact by psychologically crippled in all of his future interpersonal relations. In Sullivan's experience such lack of success in heterosexual adjustment often also led to failure in preadolescent socialization with other boys, and was of prime importance in causing the schizophrenic break.

Sullivan found that it was in mid- or true adolescence, with the advent of "frank sexuality," that such youths begin having serious problems. Once they have established a good status within a peer group, it becomes necessary for them to proceed to an interest in girls. Such growth, however, is precluded by the stunted development and organization of the personality. As a result the individual's status within his social group, and thus his self-respect, is seriously endangered. To preserve both status and esteem the youth must either resort to lies about his sexual life, or isolate himself from the group and continue a nonheterosexual sociality with other such handicapped (nondeveloped) individuals. Due to increasing pressure of the sexual drive, the outcome of such a choice could well be a homosexual life-style. In other youngsters, coping may take the form of regression to an earlier type of interpersonal living, which stresses renewed dependence on the parental and associated adult environment.

In Sullivan's theory such an overidentification with the mother (or mother surrogate), coupled with a severe rebuff in interpersonal relations during adolescence, could result in what he calls the outcropping of schizophrenic processes. For the schizophrenic male who has suffered a disastrous loss of self-esteem, the universe is without integrity. It is to him unpredictable. To escape the anxiety brought about by this realization he retreats into a dreamlike state, thus building a barrier between himself and other people who threaten him. And since the development of such a barrier deprives the individual of consensual validation, the schizophrenic becomes interpersonally incompetent. As his behavior becomes increasingly inappropriate, he may begin to feel persecuted and his behavior gradually deteriorates. Sullivan prescribed a sympathetic environment as the cure for such progression of the disease.

THE CLINICIAN ON THE WARD

Acccording to Sullivan the persons with whom the schizophrenic patient has personal contact are of great importance in determining the course and outcome of the illness. Likewise, persons significant in causing the illness—usually found in the home situation in which the onset of the disease occurred—are unlikely to be helpful to the patient during the acute stages of the psychosis. All of Sullivan's clinical experience (of which he had considerable) in the institutional care of acutely schizophrenic males between the ages of 14 and 25 confirmed both deductions, as he reported in 1974 (p. 246): "I have come to feel that the personality qualifications of all those with whom the acute schizophrenic patients come in contact should be primary considerations in any attempt to achieve good results from treatment."

As demonstrated time and again in his clinical experience, Sullivan felt that even a great deal of good work done with a schizophrenic patient could be ruined by only a brief contact with unsuitable personnel. This mode of thinking often precipitated the elimination of visits by relatives and others associated with the onset of the illness, and a restriction of visitors during its acute stages. This type of "segregation," with strict monitoring of personal contacts, placed the patient in the company of only highly qualified personnel immediately upon admission to the mental hospital and was essential in arresting or stabilizing the schizophrenic state in process.

Team treatment by specially chosen personnel was essential to the successful care of the schizophrenic patients on Sullivan's ward. Since personality, to his way of thinking, was not a product of good intentions acquired later in life, trained mental health professionals—including his colleagues—were deemed totally inadequate for and incapable of handling the job to be done. More explicitly on this topic, Sullivan stated that physicians came to him seeking insights into problems of the mind. They came to him as well-trained physicians and therefore, according to him, with an acquired inability to understand anything that he might say to them. He didn't believe that if they stayed with him from now 'til Gabriel blows his horn that they would acquire much notion of what he was talking about—or privately give a damn. They were already educated, they had an MD, and they had a whole system of ideas about psychiatry that had its origins in misunderstandings about physical chemistry.

Sullivan thus insisted on training his own personnel and, for the most part, excluded highly trained professionals from his ward. He instead turned to subprofessionals for work and interaction with his patients, claiming that the capacity of these staff members to do more than wish the patient well was a product of personality that had been established years before they became interested in caring for the mentally ill. He coordinated a team selected on the bases of personalities that were suited, in his mind, to dealing with schizophrenics. The utilization of such a treatment team, he felt, could achieve results at complete variance (at least in cases of acute onset) with the schizophrenic patient's poor prognosis.

IMPLEMENTING THE TREATMENT MILIEU

In order to implement the technique of therapy that he labeled "treatment milieu," Sullivan established and operated a special ward for schizophrenic men during his final 12 months at Sheppard Pratt Hospital. Housed in what was then known as the Reception Building, this ward functioned as a patient receiving service designed according to his own specifications as a clinical social structure. Management of the area was totally Sullivan's responsibility, in a unit remarkably divorced from the various hierarchical structures usually governing hospital administration. Always controversial, in 1929 Sullivan was almost fired from his professional position by the hospital's board of trustees for what their perceptions were of his work on the ward.

Entirely removed from the supervision of the Nursing Service, no woman except for a female housekeeper was ever allowed access to the area. All attendants were specifically chosen and intensively trained by Sullivan himself, and although classified as subprofessional came to operate in a truly professional manner. The team developed a high esprit de corps, even holding its own informal staff conferences either at a local bar or in the house established by their mentor near the hospital grounds. Sullivan's theory was that these attendants who were so successful with schizophrenic patients were potentially schizophrenic themselves, a concept aligned with the clinician's belief that some of his own skill likewise derived from early personal encounters with schizophrenic processes.

Sullivan's reasons for eliminating the registered nurse from his ward stemmed from certain important theoretical considerations. He was convinced that the schizophrenic patient had in his formative years suffered humiliation within his family structure, as a result of which he was now enduring an acute sense of low self-esteem. To expect such an individual to find a cure within an institution riddled with outworn codes of hierarchical values was to Sullivan nonsensical and self-defeating. The presence of the registered nurse on his all-male ward would also have represented a prototype of the high-status female in an inferior male society. Thinking of the power struggle conducted in the home, where the mother pays deference to the authority of the father, but in fact governs the household, Sullivan perceived the hospital as a place where the nurse often pays deference to the physician yet in fact rules the ward. These was no place for interaction such as this on Sullivan's unit. His initial and foremost concern was for the already damaged self-esteem of his patients.

Sullivan's theory was that a patient's treatment should begin with removal from the situation causing his difficulty. His intent was to encourage the schizophrenic to renew efforts at adjusting to others, and felt that this could be accomplished only with a ward that was homogeneous in sex, age, and diagnosis. Since he felt strongly that the first 24 hours of hospitalization are the most critical for the patient, he could not in good conscience subject them to an institution devoid of "protection" and privacy, where the individual's feelings of utter humiliation and degradation would only be reinforced. He instead encouraged his special attendants to spend a great deal of time with the new patients, and to give them as much reassurance as possible. A protective wall was constructed at Sullivan's request, which served to shield his patients from the view of any outsiders entering the building. Unless admitted to the other side, no one could see any interactions taking place on the ward. To Sullivan, the routine daily life of the individual was more crucial to his clinical progress than any single hour spent with a therapist.

Sullivan was aware, however, that the role of the physician is of critical importance in treatment. Feeling that the small amount of time shared between doctor and patient is crucial, he utilized the crude recording devices available at that time to assure that all interactions taking place could be analyzed and investigated. Microphones hidden on his desk, in the ceilings, and in the bathroom were controlled with switches concealed within his desk drawers, while a secretary stationed one floor below recorded all that transpired.

Fundamental to Sullivan's theory was the notion that the psychiatrist or therapist is inescapably involved with all that is happening during the course of the session. He also felt, as expressed in his book *Clinical Studies in Psychiatry*, that no one has grave difficulties in living if he has a very good grasp on what is happening to him. Because of this, Sullivan's emphasis in therapy was not upon uncovering and bringing to the surface unconscious content, nor was it upon the encouragement of a dependent clinical relationship. It was clear communication that he sought. To Sullivan the mission of the therapist lies in assisting the patient to grasp and articulate his experience. Returning to his concept that it is the interaction of people with other people which causes anxiety, he emphasized the impact of a significant other (the therapist) upon the development of the individual (the patient) by utilizing a therapeutic tool he called "participant observation." By studying his own role as psychiatrist, he developed the theory of the analyst as one who not only observes, but also participates.

Since for Sullivan all personality handicaps are manifestations of anxiety produced by an individual's significant others, it followed that anxiety could only be revealed and understood in the presence of a significant other as portrayed by the therapist. The kind of person that the therapist is, what he does, what he says, and how and when he says it, are all things that relate directly to a patient's success in treatment. While both patient and therapist are strongly motivated to meet, they are both equally driven by anxiety to withdraw from each other. An interplay of movements—multiple variations of advance and retreat—characterize the clinical interview. Recognition of these movements and an exploration of their origins is the goal of the time spent together in the interview, a process which, Sullivan hoped, would lead to an understanding of their significance within the existing situation.

Sullivan observed in working with schizophrenic patients that language is often used more as a defense than as a means of communication. The individual who experiences a great deal of anxiety in contacts with others can keep them at a distance, either by withdrawing physically or by speaking in a way that makes the listener withdraw. This is not a conscious or planned action on the part of the patient, but is a complicated response to anxiety, resulting in a successful avoidance of people. Sullivan termed this type of defensive pattern (along with others such as selective inattention, dissociation, paranoia, and obsessions) a "dynamism of difficulty." To him such reactions were an indication that mental patients are no different from other people, but are in fact striking examples of common human experience.

Sullivan felt that few people, and certainly no patients, come into the presence of others without considerable caution and some expectation of rebuff. For him the understanding of the resulting communication blocks established between individuals is necessary to the comprehension of humanity's common underlying anxiety and anticipation of hurt, and is a major goal of the treatment interview. The clinical interview was to him a miniature of human communicative processes, containing the essential qualities of all interpersonal relationships. During it the person being observed could be comprehended only in terms of his relationship to others influencing him, and in terms of the behavior of the observer (the therapist) who is a part of that field of influence. According to Sullivan there could be no situation in which the interviewer (therapist) exists as a "neutral" figure. He is inevitably a participant, and the entire field of social action is thus altered by his presence. Sullivan's approach is known as "field theory" in clinical therapy today.

THE CLINICIAN AT WORK

Throughout his practice, Sullivan treated even the most severely schizophrenic patients as the "normal" human beings he perceived them to be. Although aware always of the individual's state of mind (alert, confused, angry, distorted, whatever), he still hammered away at each subject during the interview process in an effort to bring about an awareness of reality. Knowing how painful awareness could be for some, he nonetheless attempted to heighten each patient's ability to test and deal with the actual world. By causing the individual to face the facts about his life, he led both subject and interviewer to a perception of reality that would reduce the threatening level of anxiety within the patient.

The following interview between Sullivan and a patient at the Sheppard Enoch-Pratt Hospital was recorded in or about the year 1927. The 23-year-old male schizophrenic was interviewed during his fifth day of hospitalization. Confused and somewhat depressed, he seemed to require urging before he would do anything. He had quite strongly expressed the idea that anyone who came into contact with him would be poisoned. Eating only under supervision, he had to be tube-fed three times on the day the interview was conducted.

Sullivan: What is the situation? Why don't you talk? Do you mind telling me what it is all about? (moves about in natural fashion and continues to gaze at recorder) What is the idea?

Patient: Sir?

S.: What is the idea?

P.: The idea?

S.: Why are you sitting there so silently? If you don't mind, I should like to know why you act so odd. Do you think you know the gentleman there? You are looking at him a great deal.

P.: I know who you are, all right.

S.: This is very fortunate. Tell me about it. Tell about it. I don't think you know. I don't think you have the faintest idea who I am.

P.: I know you are a policeman all right. (grins)

S.: And what makes you think I am a policeman?

P.: Isn't that what you have been doing all the time—trying to get me in prison?

S.: Who? Who has been trying that?

P.: Everybody.

S.: Any why? Why has everybody been trying to get you in prison? Are you supposed to have done something that was wrong? Why has everybody been trying to get you in prison? Have you any idea? Would you mind telling me why you think everybody is trying to get you in prison?

P.: Just because I said it, that's all.

S.: Do you believe everything you say? Do you never make mistakes in what you say? Are you one of those people who is always right? Are you always right? (shakes head negatively) I am glad you are not conceited. Now quite honestly, do you think I am a policeman?

P.: Sure. I remember one of those from the times I have been to the city.

S.: What makes you think I am a policeman? What makes you think I am a policeman? Because I have large feet? (grins) Or merely because you like to think I am a policeman? Well, whenever you feel like it, answer me. It doesn't cost any more than keeping quiet, you know. Did the police bring you to the hospital?

P.: My mother brought me. Mother and brother.

S.: Why should you connect me with the police? I should love to know. Isn't that a little bit cuckoo? (grins faintly) Isn't it a little bit weird to connect me with the police? Doesn't that require considerable imagination on your part? Or, maybe you have seen the blue cross on my car. Is that it?

P.: I know your car—sure.

S.: You know those blue crosses are physician's permits from the police.

All the doctors who want them can get blue crosses from the police in Baltimore. The same as ambulances. Did you know that or didn't you? They are what are known as right-of-way signs. I put mine on the tail end because I want right-of-way over the speed cops. But the fact that I have a blue cross that says "Police Permit" doesn't make me a policeman. Mr. (patient's name) do you feel that everyone is against you—that you have no friends—that everybody has it in for you—is that the notion? (shakes head negatively) Are you a stubborn person? Are you naturally stubborn?

P.:   No sir.

The transcript clearly shows that in 1927 Sullivan was already employing what is today called "reality testing." The many questions that Sullivan puts to the patient in rapid order are an attempt to force the patient to test reality. The goal of Sullivan's questioning is to force the patient to juxtapose his idea of reality against reality itself in order to disclose the patient's own idea of reality as distorted. By constantly drawing patients to examine what is real, Sullivan wishes to display to them how their own idea of reality is deformed. The assumption is that when patients understand this disparity they will start to correct their own distorted conceptions. Sullivan's creativity was demonstrated in the use he made of reality testing as early as 1927. Several decades before reality testing became standard practice in clinical treatment, Sullivan was already making innovative advances in this form of psychiatric treatment.

Sullivan felt, and ensuing results showed that good clinical work completed within a hospital unit should be extended into the postinstitutional life of the convalescent patient. Unfortunately, however, such patients were all too often taken back into the unhealthy environment (usually the home situation) that had precipitated the illness to begin with, long before enough insight had been consolidated to enable the patient to avoid immediate damage. The end result of such detrimental circumstance was often a recurrence of the illness.

Sullivan believed that in order for the relapse situation to change for the better, much rethinking is needed in regard to the etiology and institutional care of schizophrenia. His clinical vision concerned the creation of convalescent communities in which the young schizophrenic patients could pause long enough after leaving the immediate care institution to become secure in meeting and solving future interpersonal problems.

CONCLUSION

Sullivan was one of the major American personality theorists of the 20th century and contributed to the modification of Freudian psychoanalysis.

Sullivan was a neo-Freudian (though he rejected the term as applied to him), but it is important to stress the significant revision that he introduced into Freudian theory. Whereas Freud believed in an intrapsychic model of personality, the idea that inner-psychological forces determined personality, Sullivan held to an interpersonal model of the self, the idea that personality is a product of the mutual interaction between the human organism and the familial-social. While Freud emphasized libidinal forces as determinate of personality, with particular focus on the Oedipal complex, Sullivan shifted attention to the area of self-esteem and adjustment. Both Freud and Sullivan understood the adult personality as an arena upon which the unresolved conflicts of earlier life were played out and this idea of a past haunting a present was their common grounding in psychoanalysis. Freud, however, emphasized the Oedipal, the libidinal, and the idea that personality was predominantly shaped by the age of 3. Sullivan saw life, not as a mere repetition of an Oedipal conflict, but as a process of continuous and progressive development until death. In a lasting reconstruction of psychoanalysis, he demonstrated how the self is not only the product of inner forces but a result of the image of ourselves that society reflects back to us.

Within American psychoanalysis, Sullivan was a primary force, along with William Alanson White and Adolf Meyer, of refocusing the center of psychoanalytic theory. Sullivan helped shift the center of gravity from neuropsychology to social psychology. Freud maintained that human personality was both intrapsychic and determined primarily by neurological drives. The libido was the primary physiological drive. Sullivan, by contrast, stresses the sociological and interpersonal shaping of personality rather than the neurological determinants. Twentieth-century philosophical developments emphasized the crucial role of society in the molding of human attitudes and character. Sullivan adjusted psychoanalytic theory to these 20th-century philosophical currents. Sullivan brought about a greater correspondence between psychoanalysis and the larger background of 20th-century sociological theory.

AUTHOR'S NOTE

My first experience with Harry Stack Sullivan occurred in 1970, during the course of my research for the first major paper required of my doctoral program at the University of Maryland. Entitling my paper "The Contributions of the NeoFreudians to the Social Definitions of the 1930's," I intended to address the works of Karen Horney, Erich Fromm, and Harry Stack Sullivan. The first two individuals I read and reported on with great ease; then I began to read what is considered to be Sullivan's greatest work, *The Interpersonal Theory of Psychiatry* (1953). I read the first chapter and understood nothing. I read it again and understood nothing. After a third try I gave up and left him out of my paper, hoping that my adviser would not notice. He did, and marked me down accordingly.

I did not read Sullivan again until I was asked to consider doing my doctoral dissertation on him. Needless to say, I had my doubts after my first experience, but my adviser suggested that I visit Edith Weigert at her home in Bethesda, Maryland. Dr. Weigert had known and worked with Sullivan for years. Between patients, this 85-year-old woman psychoanalyst spoke of him for an hour in a soft voice. As I rose to leave, she related one final incident. Out riding together one day, Sullivan put his hand on her shoulder and said, "Edith, you do not know how lonely I am." This was the great theorist on loneliness speaking, the one who had once defined the schizophrenic as "the loneliest of the lonely." And so my odyssey began.

REFERENCES

Chapman, A. H. (1976). *Harry Stack Sullivan: The man and his work.* New York: Putnam's.
Mullahy, P. (1973). *The beginnings of modern American psychiatry: The ideas of Harry Stack Sullivan.* Boston: Houghton Mifflin.
Sullivan, H. S. (1931). Environmental factors in etiology and course under treatment of schizophrenia. *Medical Journal and Records,* 19–22.
Sullivan, H. S. (1953a). *Conceptions of modern psychiatry.* New York: Norton.
Sullivan, H. S. (1953b). *The interpersonal theory of psychiatry.* New York: Norton.
Sullivan, H. S. (1956). *Clinical studies in psychiatry.* New York: Norton.
Sullivan, H. S. (1974). *Schizophrenia as a human process.* New York: Norton.

Chapter 22

Robert Choate Tryon:
Pioneer in Differential Psychology

Kurt Schlesinger

My name is Robert C. Tryon. I died many years ago and I must say that your invitation to come and talk to you took me very much by surprise. Incidentally, you did not send me a plane ticket, and travel to New Mexico from my new place of residence is very expensive. It is also very difficult to obtain an exit visa; they don't even quite know what sort of passport to issue. Anyway, it is for these reasons that I hesitated before accepting your kind invitation, although it is still not clear to me why you asked me to come. I finally did decide to come, motivated largely by curiosity over your invitation. I assume that you wanted me to come because you felt like hearing something about my time, my life, and my work. I will try to oblige.

BIOGRAPHY

I was born on September 4, 1901, in Butte, Montana. I came from what may be described as "poor working stock." My father earned his living as a plumber. Neither my father nor my mother was well educated, both having finished only elementary school. None of my siblings, of which I had seven, went beyond high school. We were always poor, and to the day I died I always thought of myself as a "working stiff." I died on September 25, 1967, in Berkeley, California, at 66.

---

*Photograph of Robert C. Tryon courtesy of the Archives of the History of Psychology

Education

When I was still very young my family moved to Los Angeles. I don't remember the move at all; it must have occurred sometime during 1904 or 1905. I grew up in Los Angeles, then a very lovely small town with the mountains in the background and the ocean not too far away. I was a good student, finishing high school with top grades. As a reward, and as the first member of my family ever to do so, I entered college—the University of California, Southern Branch, today known as UCLA. My major was in English. At that time one could only do one's freshman and sophomore years there, and if one wished to continue one had to transfer north to Berkeley.

This is what I did and I continued to major in English. My ambition then, and always, was to become a writer. During my career as an English major I met some very interesting people. They were mostly San Francisco journalists who formed a stimulating "Bohemian" crowd. We would discuss politics, philosophy, and literature endlessly, consuming enormous amounts of beer. Beer, I must tell you, became and remained one of my great passions. Parenthetically, I might just add that during the last 30 or so years obtaining a cold glass of beer has been very difficult. I also met my first wife, Carolyn, who introduced me to psychology, which was her major. She convinced me to take a class from one of her professors. I did. I was fascinated. I gave up my ambitions to become a writer—when one is young one's ambitions change rapidly—and I began to read and major in psychology. The professor's name was Edward Tolman.

Upon graduation I was invited to become a graduate student at Berkeley. I accepted and obtained my PhD jointly in psychology and genetics in 1928. My fellow graduate students were people some of whom you might remember; let me mention the names of some of those who were my friends: Yoshioka, Macfarlane, and Tinklepaugh. Our teachers were Tolman, Franzen, and Stratton. From Tolman I learned psychology, from Franzen I learned statistics, and from Stratton—well from Stratton I did not learn very much.

While a graduate student, I published two papers, both on the effects of unreliability of measurement on the differences between groups (Tryon, 1926, 1928). Both papers were published in the *Journal of Comparative Psychology*, and both papers made something of an impression on the psychological community in general, and on Professor Tolman in particular. My dissertation, titled "Individual Differences at Successive Stages of Learning," was accepted by the psychology department in 1928.

In those days, most psychologists studied learning. Multifarious experiments on the learning process per se were being published. In addition, Lashley used learning in his attempts to study cortical localization of function, in his search for the engram. Using learning experiments, other psychologists were studying drives and incentives, and so it went, on and on; everyone was studying learning.

At that time people thought it necessary to study learning as a means of measuring mental capacity. Therefore, or so one would have thought, an accurate and quantitative description of learning would have been available. But that was not the case. Learning was always described in terms of a "learning curve," which represented the average performance of subjects plotted against successive stages in the learning process. This seemed to me inadequate and I resolved to do something about it. I tested hundreds of rats in two very difficult mazes, investigating individual differences in learning very carefully, and correlating performances at various stages of the learning process.

My dissertation was a modest success. It convinced me that reliable and valid measures of learning could be obtained, and that one could learn a good deal about the process of learning by a careful examination of animals at various stages of acquisition. My dissertation also convinced Professor Tolman that I knew statistics and that I should be hired to teach this subject to my fellow graduate students. We discussed an offer for me to become instructor of psychology at Berkeley.

Early Career

Stratton, then the department's chairman, had very different ideas. It seemed that he was dead set against me. I don't know why, but I suspected that he considered me less than a gentleman, unworthy of holding an academic appointment, especially one in his department. Stratton pointed out that I always wore a shirt to work, and the same shirt at that. Worse, he thought that my fingernails were dirty. This was proof that I was not a gentleman. In any event, he strenuously opposed my appointment.

Events conspired to frustrate Professor Stratton's wishes. Tolman had been offered the chair at Harvard in 1928. He took the offer very seriously, and went to see President Sproul, of the University of California. Tolman agreed to stay if three conditions were met. First, that Charlie Honzik be appointed his full-time research assistant. Honzik had worked as the departmental "shop man," and in an accident had lost some of the fingers on his right hand. Worker's compensation did not exist, and Tolman felt obligated to help him find other employment. Second, he asked for a small salary increment for himself. And, third, he insisted that I be appointed instructor of psychology. All three requests were granted, and I—son of a plumber, dirty shirt, dirty nails and all—was appointed to the distinguished position of instructor of psychology, University of California, Berkeley. I never left, except during the war, and to give lectures here and there.

I began to teach. I never liked it—- formal classroom teaching, that is— although some have said that I was pretty good at it. In those early days my graduate students were Ghiselli, who went on to make quite a career for himself as an industrial psychologist; Crutchfield and Ballachey, who became social psychologists; Charlie Honzik, who became a clinician; John Gardner, who went on to become secretary of health, education, and welfare in the Kennedy and Johnson administrations, and some others. In later years my graduate students included Jerry Hirsch, a behavioral geneticist now at Illinois, and Dan Bailey, a quantitative psychologist now at Arizona State.

RESEARCH

I also began to do research, and a lot of it. I was interested in two inter-related issues in psychology. I wanted to study the heritable causes of behavior, and I wanted to describe the learning process quantitatively. Quantitative descriptions, I always thought and still think, would provide an adequate theory of learning. I published such a description, in fact I published 12 such descriptions, all in the *Journal of Comparative Psychology* (Tryon, 1930, 1931a, 1931b, 1931c, 1931d, 1939, 1940a, 1940b; Tryon, Tryon, & Kuznets, 1941a, 1941b). I will describe some of my findings in a minute, but here I would like to interject that it always was one of the keenest disappointments of my life that no one took these descriptions for what I thought they were, namely a comprehensive theory of learning. And not a bad one at that because one could make important predictions about the behavior of rats in mazes based on my theory.

I think that I have made contributions to several domains of psychology. I have contributed to behavioral genetics, I have contributed to our understanding of the learning process, I have made some modest contributions to statistical procedures useful in the behavioral sciences, and I have used these statistical procedures to contribute to what others have called behavioral ecology. Let me describe my work in each of these areas very briefly.

Behavioral Genetics

When I first arrived at Berkeley, Tolman had just published the results of a selective breeding experiment, in which he had tried to obtain two populations of animals one of which learned easily and another which made many errors. The experiment was a qualified success: Animals in the first selected generation responded to the selective pressure; however, animals in the second selected generation regressed to the mean.

I thought that Tolman had made two mistakes: Most seriously, the selective breeding was based on performance in a maze of questionable reliability. Second, he stopped the experiment too soon. Those of us with training in genetics knew that interpretations based on only two generations of selective breeding are pretty shaky. In fact, Tolman made a third mistake. He inbred while trying to breed selectively. This is a serious error because inbreeding exhausts genetic variance on which selective breeding depends. I made the same mistake myself, not knowing that it was an error. This mistake was pointed out to me years later, by Jerry McClearn, who joined the faculty here at Berkeley in the later 1950s.

My Selective Breeding Study.   In any event, Jeffress, another student, and I convinced Tolman to try again, this time with a maze of known reliability. We built a 17-unit T-maze that was indeed reliable. When running 22 hours hungry and for food reinforcement, the odd–even reliability of our measurements, in terms of the number of errors the animals made, was 0.93. We published our results, to my knowledge the first time that reliabilities of the measuring instrument used in animal learning studies had ever been reported (Tryon, Tolman, & Jeffress, 1929).

Tolman and Jeffress became impatient. Selective breeding experiments take a long time. I proceeded with the remainder of the experiment by myself, not realizing that the experiment would last for more than a decade.

As things turned out, my first job was to run all over the Berkeley campus to find rats: to the Anatomy Department to pick up a few, to the Zoology Department to pick up a few more, and so on until I had collected a base population, a *heterogeneous* base population, of about 100. As I have already indicated, selective breeding depends on genetic variability in the population, so the fact that my base population was heterogeneous is important. In the genetic sense, the word heterogeneous has Greek origins, *hetero* meaning different and *geneous* referring to the genetic material, genes. I tested these heterogeneous animals in my maze and obtained a distribution of error scores, some rats making many errors as they learned the maze, others relatively few. I then selected for breeding the *brightest* rats and mated them *inter se*, and I did likewise with the *dullest* rats. In due course, these matings produced offspring, which I again tested in the maze when they were of the appropriate age. I then mated the brightest rats from within the bright line, and the dullest rats from the dull line, and tested the progeny, and so on, for 21 generations of selective breeding.

The experiment was a success. The lines I had selected differed from each other greatly in terms of the number of errors they made in learning the maze. In fact, by the seventh selected generation the distribution of error scores was so different that they no longer overlapped. The dullest rat from within the bright line made fewer errors than the brightest rat from within the dull line (Tryon, 1940c).

Significance and Generalizability.   The experiment, as I have said, was a success. It was also an immediate success and it remains a success today, judging by the number of references to the experiment that continue to appear. The experiment is discussed in almost every introductory psychology textbook published these days, much to my delight.

The results of the experiment were significant, and for three reasons: First, because they demonstrated that learning ability, which clearly is a phenotype that depends heavily on environmental factors, has a genetic substrate. Second (and please remember the times, the heyday of behaviorism and American learning theory), these results were important because they clearly indicated that Watson's, and Kuo's, and Dunlap's idea of writing a psychology in which heredity had no place plainly would not work. Third, and most important, these results were significant because we had created biological material on which we, and others, could perform many other experiments.

We did just that; we performed many experiments on the rats we had selected. One question we felt compelled to answer was whether the differences in our selected lines could be accounted for by drive variables. We showed that they could not. Rather, the animals differed in terms of habit strength, to use the language of the 1940s.

Searle, another graduate student at Berkeley, showed that rats selected as bright and dull, respectively, were *not* generally bright and dull. Rather, we had selected for a very special trait, namely, for performance in mazes the mastery of which depended on the correct utilization of spatial cues. This reaffirmed my belief that mental capacity, intelligence, needs to be conceptualized in terms of clusters of independent, though correlated, abilities (Tryon, 1932a, 1932b, 1935). In this regard I differed from Spearman, who thought in terms of generalized intelligence, some sort of "g" factor. We engaged in a public debate about our different views. This was the only "scientific" fight I ever had with Spearman. The other fight was more personal: He was the editor of a journal to which I had submitted an article, which, when it appeared, contained a spelling error. Given my undergraduate training in English, this caused me considerable grief—this and Spearman's glee in pointing out the error. I went back to my original manuscript to discover that I had spelled the word correctly, and that the mistake was the printer's. Spearman never believed me and continued to make fun of my spelling.

Lastly, these experiments also had an impact on learning theory. Tolman, when he presented his new theory of learning during his presidential address to the American Psychological Association in 1937, felt obliged to introduce four individual difference variables in his account of learning. These individual difference variables were (1) *Heredity*, (2) *Age*, (3) previous *Training*, and (4) special *Endocrine*, drug, and vitamin conditions (or HATE).

Learning Experiments

During these years, the 1930s, I also worked on the learning process. In all I published 10 papers in this area, and 2 more manuscripts remained on my desk. The first paper in this series was published in 1930; it was titled "Studies in Individual Differences in Maze Learning Ability: I. Measurement of the Reliability of Individual Differences." The last paper was published in 1941; it was titled "Studies in Individual Differences in Maze Ability: X. Ratings and other Measures of Initial Emotional Responses to Novel Inanimate Objects" (Tryon, Tryon, & Kuznets, 1941b).

Structure of Learning.   The best paper in this series was the seventh one (Tryon, 1940a), in which I tried to formulate what I called a general theory of learning. My theory was an attempt to account for individual differences in maze learning on the basis of the general psychological components of learning that were deducible from observing the behavior of animals at various stages of learning. The particular psychological components underlying learning, I thought, could be inferred on the basis of the behavior of rats, provided that the performance satisfied criteria of internal consistency, goodness of fit, prediction of other behaviors *in situ*, and in other relevant situations. In total, I inferred the existence of 10 such components, some examples of which are directional set, exit gradients, conflicts, and food pointing.

As the animals learn the maze, these psychological components form higher order coalitions, which are dynamic, changing with practice. In order to explain these changes in components with practice, I was required to make six assumptions: (1) retention, or memory, of the components, (2) memory of the consequences of the components, (3) memory of the effort entailed in utilizing the components, (4) existence of multiple goals, (5) weighing some of the components because of emotional support, and (6) selection of those components that involve the least effort.

In sum, my theory of learning involved a shift in the way these components were put together into higher order coalitions with practice.

TIME OUT FOR WAR AND ADMINISTRATION

My research in learning and behavioral genetics was interrupted by the entry of the United States into World War II. Gardner Murphy, the eminent personality theorist, had read some of my statistical works, and called me to Washington to work for the Office of Strategic Services, the equivalent of the CIA. I was appointed deputy chief of the planning staff of the OSS, charged with developing measuring instruments that would be useful in selecting individuals who would make good spies, saboteurs, liaison officers with the various resistance movements in occupied Europe. Now I can tell you that selecting bright and dull rats is quite different from selecting good spies, but we were successful. Very few of the men we dropped behind enemy lines were ever caught.

World War II ended, and I returned to Berkeley. Because of my administrative experience, or so I was told, I was elected chairman of my department. The previous individuals, Stratton and Tolman, had been heads rather than chairs and I insisted on becoming a chair. I began to introduce democratic procedures into the administration of the department. I thought of this as progressive, and so it was, but it did not work. Given our faculty, everyone wanted his or her own way, and when they got their way, as a result of my enlightened democratic regime, chaos was the result. The department suffered, suffered greatly, and it took a very long time to recover.

CLUSTER ANALYSIS

After the war I never really went back to my research in behavioral genetics or learning. Rather, I became very interested in computers, in statistical procedures, especially in their application to "relevant" problems in the social sciences. I introduced the computer into my classes, into both my undergraduate and graduate courses in differential psychology. Computers removed dreary hours of desk calculator work, which previously had had a deadening effect on students. They could now spend more time on ideas. Let me give you one example: One of my graduate students, Stevenson, broke new ground when he studied the structure of creativity in a sample of 33 engineers, then cross-referenced these finding across *all* of them by a master cluster analysis. We calculated that this study would have taken 15 years of analysis by desk calculator. It was done in 8 hours by the computer. Here we have an illustration of how the computer permits one to tackle an experimental problem that would never have been attempted without it.

I worked very hard on cluster analysis (Tryon, 1967, 1968a, 1968b). This method, in its final form, was my last public accomplishment. In fact, it was published posthumously (Tryon & Bailey, 1970). Cluster analysis serves four goals: (1) The condensation of many variables into a few basic dimensions that capture the general covariation among variables, (2) Selection of homogeneous subsets of variables that are observable representations of the basic dimensions, (3) Description of the statistical properties of the dimensions and clusters, and (4) Geometrical, or graphic, descriptions of the cluster structure of the data.

In the mid 1950s, I began to work full time on the development of cluster analysis, although some of you may recall that I had written my first monograph on the subject way back in 1939. Now, however, I really went to work on cluster analysis *and* on developing the computer program to run it. This required me to spend literally thousands of hours in front of my desk calculator. The final result of this painfully difficult work, painful because I was never very good at programming, was my book on cluster analysis, written with Dan Bailey, *The BC TRY System of Analysis.*

BEHAVIORAL ECOLOGY

I now had the tools in hand with which to study how human beings group together in large metropolitan areas. Living and working in Berkeley, I naturally chose the Bay Area as my laboratory. I used the 1940 and 1950 census data for my investigations.

In this work I made only one assumption: that in large urban areas people aggregate, or form social groups, on the basis of certain defining behavioral characteristics. I gave these social groupings names such as "The Segregated," "The Workers," and "The Exclusives." This research yielded three interesting findings. First, these social groupings remained relatively constant. There was a remarkable similarity in the data based on the 1940 and the 1950 census, and this despite the socially disruptive intervening world war. Second, these social groupings were to a certain extent differentiated in a biological sense; the groups were reproductively isolated. One can imagine the consequences of such assortative matings in human populations, especially if these conditions persist over long enough periods of time. And, third, I found this work in behavioral ecology interesting because it allowed me to investigate the incidence and the characteristics of psychiatric disorders in these social areas.

CONCLUSION

During those years, the 1950s and 1960s, I also started work on a general introductory psychology text. I had always felt that there was a real need for a short book of this type, say 200 pages or so, which would present the main concepts of general psychology and illustrate these with the solid methods of our field. My feelings were that students get terribly confused by the crazy quilt of "this experiment shows . . . ," and "that theory states . . . " style of writing, a style that is more or less characteristic of many present-day encyclopedic general textbooks. I thought that I could write my style of book, and in fact I did. The page proofs were on my desk the day I died. The manuscript was never published.

To summarize, my substantive contributions have all been in the area of individual differences. I tried to understand the learning process by investigating individual differences. And I tried to develop quantitative methods to describe and understand individual differences. I am a differential psychologist, and I hope that I have made this clear. I hope that I have also given you something of the flavor and content of my academic life. Thank you very much and good luck.

AUTHOR'S PERSONAL COMMENT

I now feel obliged to speak to you as Kurt Schlesinger, more or less in order to establish my "credentials" as a biographer and expert on Robert Choate Tryon. Please allow me these few personal remarks.

I did know Professor Tryon, albeit not very well. I was not one of Professor Tryon's graduate students, although he had many, and you would have done much better inviting one of them to give this lecture. I was, however, a graduate student at the University of California at Berkeley, and I did audit several classes that he taught. We often had discussions about the state of psychology in general, and about one of his great interests, behavioral genetics, in particular. He served as a member of my comprehensive examination committee.

Although Robert Tryon was not one of my official teachers, he served as an academic advisor. I think of him as a friend, but I do not know whether this feeling was reciprocated. Nevertheless, I have lasting memories of Robert Tryon, memories that are now more than 25 years old, and memories that are very warm. I have always held him in the highest regard. He was a dedicated scholar, a first-rate psychologist, and a truly gentle man.

I would like to share one personal experience with you, an experience that I now remember, many years later, with considerable amusement. The incident I am about to relate occurred in 1962. It was a day on which the Bay Area was in the middle of a heat wave, one of the worst on record. It was also the day scheduled for the oral part of my doctoral comprehensive examination, to take place at 1 P.M. in Tolman Hall. The custom, in those days, perhaps it was even a requirement, was for candidates to appear in their best suit, which in my case made little difference since I possessed only one. I am wearing the jacket of the suit I wore on that occasion, but the pants and vest that went with it have long since disappeared. I don't know whether you agree with me that it is/was a very handsome suit, but as you can see it was clearly meant for a winter wardrobe. The heat of the day, the winter suit, and the emotions one feels when one is about to take an oral examination, all made me perspire a good deal.

As I said, my examination was scheduled for 1 o'clock, and I was punctual, but my committee, out to lunch, was not. After I had been pacing the halls for about an hour, they appeared around the corner of the hall and entered the room set aside for my orals. I was told to wait outside while the committee planned their tactics. A few minutes later I was asked to enter and I witnessed the following scene. There were the five members of my committee, seated around a table, my chairman in the middle. His head was on the table and I swear that he was sound asleep. The committee chairman's function was to run the examination and, as much as possible, to keep the student out of trouble. My chairman's "position" added to my distress. The proceedings continued, another member of the committee took charge, and decided that the proper way to continue would be to let people ask me questions, beginning with Professor Tryon. He asked me a fine question, fine not the least because I happened to know the answer. Having asked the question, Professor Tryon got up and left the room. At this point I did not know how to proceed, but I was instructed to answer Professor Tryon's question. I gave what I think was a very good answer, the conclusion of which coincided exactly with Professor Tryon's entry into the room, coffee cup in hand. The remainder of the examination proceeded without any other untoward incident; my chairman never woke up, I passed, and everyone congratulated me.

Others have written,

> Tryon was a tolerant man. His acceptance of the human condition was almost that of a naturalist. He was rarely censorious of human frailty. His friends knew him as gentle, affectionate and playful. His humor was tender and self-mocking. To a remarkable degree, he lived and worked and judged himself by his own standards. He was his own man. (Krech, Crutchfield, & Ghiselli, 1969)

Let me now apologize for these lengthy personal reflections. In his introduction to *The Comic Mark Twain Reader* (1977), Charles Neider discusses Twain's essay *How to Tell a Story*, reminding us that there are essentially three ways to tell a story. The comic story is English, the witty story is French. Both these ways of telling a tale are short and both end in a point, and both are told with "pathetically eager delight." The third way of telling a story is humorous, and Twain called it "the American yarn." It is told at great length, in a deadpan style, and it "wanders as it pleases and it need not arrive anywhere in particular. A yarn is most successful if it goes on and on, the audience is most attentive, but the teller, now tired, goes to sleep, to awaken to an audience still spellbound, waiting to hear the end of the tale." Well, my remarks certainly did not arrive anywhere in particular, but of this I am certain: Robert Tryon definitely liked to tell and listen to yarns.

REFERENCES

Krech, D., Crutchfield, R. S., & Ghiselli, E. E. (1969). *In memoriam*. Berkeley: University of California Press.

Neider, C. (1977). *The comic Mark Twain reader*. New York: Doubleday.

Tryon, R. C. (1926). Effect of the unreliability of measurement on the differences between groups. *Journal of Comparative Psychology, 6*, 449–453.

Tryon, R. C. (1928). Demonstration of the effect of unreliability of measurement on a difference between groups. *Journal of Comparative Psychology, 8*, 1–22.

Tryon, R. C. (1930). Studies in individual differences in maze learning ability: I. Measurement of the reliability of individual differences. *Journal of Comparative Psychology, 11*, 145–170.

Tryon, R. C. (1931a). Studies in individual differences in maze ability: II. Determination of the individual differences by age, weight, sex, and pigmentation. *Journal of Comparative Psychology, 12*, 1–22.

Tryon, R. C. (1931b). Studies in individual differences in maze ability: III. Community of function between two maze abilities. *Journal of Comparative Psychology, 12,* 95–116.

Tryon, R. C. (1931c). Studies in individual differences in maze ability: IV. Constancy of individual differences: Correlation between learning and re-learning. *Journal of Comparative Psychology, 12,* 303–345.

Tryon, R. C. (1931d). Studies in individual differences in maze ability: V. Luminosity and visual acuity as causes of individual differences: A theory of maze ability. *Journal of Comparative Psychology, 12,* 401–420.

Tryon, R. C. (1932a). Multiple factors vs. two factors as determinants of abilities. *Psychological Review, 39,* 324–351.

Tryon, R. C. (1932b). So-called group factors as determinants of abilities. *Psychological Review, 39,* 403–439.

Tryon, R. C. (1935). Interpretation of Professor Spearman's comments. *Psychological Review, 42,* 122–125.

Tryon, R. C. (1939). Studies in individual differences in maze ability: VI. Disproof of sensory components: Experimental effects of stimulus variation. *Journal of Comparative Psychology, 28,* 361–415.

Tryon, R. C. (1940a). Studies in individual differences in maze ability: VII. The specific components of maze ability, and a general theory of psychological components. *Journal of Comparative Psychology, 30,* 283–338.

Tryon, R. C. (1940b). Studies in individual differences in maze ability: VIII. Prediction validity of the psychological components of maze ability. *Journal of Comparative Psychology, 30,* 535–582.

Tryon, R. C. (1940c). Genetic differences in maze-learning ability in rats. 39th *Yearbook of the National Society for the Study of Education,* 111–119, (Pt. I).

Tryon, R. C. (1967). Predicting group differences in cluster analysis: The social area problem. *Multivariate Behavioral Research, 2,* 453–457.

Tryon, R. C. (1968a). Comparative cluster analysis of variables and individuals: Holzinger abilities and the MMPI. *Multivariate Behavioral Research, 3,* 115–144.

Tryon, R. C. (1968b). Comparative cluster analysis of social areas. *Multivariate Behavioral Research, 3,* 213–232.

Tryon, R. C., & Bailey, D. E. (1970). *Cluster analysis.* New York: McGraw-Hill.

Tryon, R. C., Tolman, E. C., & Jeffress, L. A. (1929). A self-recording maze with an auto-delivery table. *University of California Publications in Psychology, 4,* 99–112.

Tryon, R. C., Tryon, C., & Kuznets, G. (1941a). Studies in individual differences in maze ability: IX. Ratings of hiding, avoidance, escape, and vocalization responses. *Journal of Comparative Psychology, 32,* 407–435.

Tryon, R. C., Tryon, C. & Kuznets, G. (1941b). Studies in individual differences in maze ability: X. Ratings and other measures of initial emotional responses to novel inanimate objects. *Journal of Comparative Psychology, 32,* 447–473.

Index

A

Adams, C., 81
Adaptation, 33, 34, 35, 128, 129, 134, 135, 218
Adjustment, 126, 128, 132, 135, 219, 248–250, 326, 331, 339
Adler, A., 163
Adler, G., *168, 169*
Advertising, Watson's career in, 179–180
Agassiz, L., 15
Alexander, I. E., 153–169, *168*
Allen, G. W., 14, 16, *25*
Alma College, 211, 212, 213
American Academy of Arts and Sciences, 279
American Association for the Advancement of Science, 279, 283
American Association of Clinical Psychology, 248
American Association of University Professors, 81
American Association of University Women, 110
American Philosophical Association, 13, 66, 279
American Psychological Association (APA), 13, 23, 28, 55, 66, 85, 171, 177, 178, 180, 184, 206, 217, 224, 238, 248, 279, 287, 289, 302, 311, 313, 349

American Society of Naturalists, 319
Ammons, B., 214*n, 224*
Ammons, R. B., 211, 214, 224
Analysis, 33, 34, 93–95, 127, 133, 192, 197–199, 265, 267, 268, 270, 272, 298, 350–351
Anderson, J. R., 194, *206*
Angell, J. R., 23, 24, *25,* 121–126, *136,* 175, 277, 297, 302
Ansbacher, H., 287
Anthropometric Laboratory, 7
Anthroponomy, 276, 279–281
Anxiety, 326, 335, 336
Apes, 34, 35, 38, 261, 262
Apparent motion, 190, 258–259
Applied psychology, 91–99, 102, 103, 126, 136, 215, 248, 250, 287–288
Applied Psychology Research Panel, 288
Army Alpha and Beta, 288
Archetype, 165
Archives of the History of American Psychology, 294
Aristotle, 101, 233
Arithmetic, 141–142
Arizona State University, 346
Art, psychology of, 107, 109, 110
Asch, S. E., 240, 295
Ash, I., 83
Association, 5, 7, 31, 65, 66, 130–135, 140, 146, 156, 158, 190–196, 272, 322
Association of Collegiate Alumnae, 110

357

Astor, J. J., 14
Atomism, see Elementism
Attitude, 63, 93, 94
Atwood, M. E., 201, 206
Austen Riggs Foundation, 77, 85
Ayer, A. J., 17, 25

B

Bacon, F., 94
Bailey, D. E., 346, 351, 355
Baldwin, J. M., 61, 177, 178
Ball, J. S., 284, 291
Ballachey, E. L., 346
Barber, A.G., 278
Barnard College, 243
Bartlett, F. C., 192, 206
Barzun, J., 14, 22, 25
Basel, University of, 155
Batesburg Institute, 174, 175
Batson, J., 186
BC TRY System of Analysis, 351
Beach, F. A., 282, 307, 318, 323n, 323
Bechterew, V., 311
Beers Society, 21
Behavioral genetics, 9, 346, 350, 353
Behaviorism, 34, 58–62, 84, 129, 171–184,
    192, 216–219, 230–238, 267, 271,
    276–286, 295–302, 310–319, 348
Beier, E. G., 43–55
Bellevue Hospital, 248
Benjamin, L. T., 244, 253, 254, 254
Bentley, M., 280, 281
Bergman, E. O., 144, 151
Bergmann, G., 171, 186
Berlin, University of, 34, 109, 190, 191,
    258–269
Bettelheim, B., 44
Binet, A., 7, 19, 248
Binghamton State Hospital, 329, 330
Biopsychology, 307–323
Birds, 310–311, 318
Birmingham General Hospital, 2
Blackwell, G., 186
Bledstein, B. J., 69, 71
Bleuler, E., 156, 157
Blondlot, N., 29
Blumenthal, A. L., 75–87, 86
Bonn, University of, 258
Bonner, F., 186
Boring, E. G., 66, 72, 209, 224, 273, 273,
    277

Borstelmann, L. J., 185
Bottom-up processing, 198–199
Brain Institute, Moscow, 39
Breuer, J., 20
Brewer, C. L., 171–186
Brick-and-mortar theory, 259, 260, 268
Brigham, C. C., 288
Brill, A. A., 44
British Psychological Association, 67
Broadus, J. A., 171
Brown University, 223, 275–279, 287–290
Bruce, D., 307–323, 323n, 323
Brunson, M., 173
Brunswik, E., 231, 235, 236
Buckley, K. W., 175, 186, 186
Bryn Mawr College, 295
Buist, G., 172
Bullard, D., 330
Burgess, M. W., 186
Burghölzli, 155, 156
Burr, E. T., 248
Buss, A. R., 255
Buxton, C., 223

C

Calculators, 141, 142; see also Computers
California at Berkeley, University of,
    227–239, 344–352
California at Los Angeles, University of,
    344
Calkins, C., 64
Calkins, M. W., 57–72, 110–112, 299–300,
    303
    biography, 64–67
Calkins, W., 64
Cambridge, England, 2
Campbell, D. P., 84, 86
Campbell, D. T., 232, 233, 241
Carleton College, 222, 223
Carmichael, L., 275, 282, 290
Carnegie Corporation, 288
Carnegie Foundation, 288
Caro, A., 191
Carr, H., 121–136, 285
Castellan, N. J., 206
Castration anxiety, 44, 51
Cattell, J. M., 23, 79, 81, 245, 246
CEEB Scholastic Aptitude Test, 145
Cely, M., 174
Cerebral function, 313–314, 315, 316
Chamberlain, T., 81

Chapman, A. H., 327, *340*
Chapman, D. W., 278*n*
Chapman, R. M., 329
Charcot, J. M., 18
Charles University, 190
Chatelaine, K. L., 325–340
Cheiron Society, 294, 300
Chicago College of Medicine and Surgery, 330
Chicago, University of, 121–136, 175–176, 264, 277–285, 297, 312, 313
Chicago World's Fair, 82
Chomsky, N., 192, *206*, 235
Clark, G., 322
Clark University, 20, 44, 45, 65, 69, 90, 102, 159, 278, 279, 289
Clayton, G., 186
Clinical psychology, 166, 247, 248, 249; *see also* Psychiatry
Cluster analysis, 350–351
Cobb, M. V., 144, *151*
Cocaine, 53–54
Cofer, C. N., 275–291
Cognition, 132, 134, 192, 230, 235, 236, 246, 261–269, 296, 301
Cognitive psychology, 39, 45, 189–205, 235–238, 271, 287, 298, 301
Cold Spring Harbor Biological Laboratory, 309
Colorado, University of, 122
Columbia University, 66, 81, 90, 139–145, 244, 245, 253, 279, 295
Commire, A., 176, *186*
Comparative psychology, 81, 144, 217, 229, 310, 317, 319, 320–322
Compensation, 163, 164
Complex (Jung), 157
Compounds, 124, 127
Computers, 192–205, 299, 304, 350–351; *see also* Calculators
Conant, J. B., 316, 317
Concepts, 213–215, 296
Conditioned reflexes, 30–37, 218–221, 281–283, 310–312, 316
Conditioning, *see* Conditioned reflexes
Connectionism, 140, 146–147
Consciousness, 58, 61, 62, 126, 129, 167, 280–282, 302
Cooley, C., 325
Cornell University, 81, 82, 90, 329
Correlation, 8, 94, 144, 150
Corsini, R. J., *207*

Crabtree, J., 186
Croton oil, 2
Crozier, W. J., 276, 279, 284, *290*
Crutchfield, R. S., 232, *241*, 346, 354, 355

D

Dallenbach, K., 309
Darwin, C., 2–3, 9, 21, 29, 94, 276, 302
Darwin, E., 2
Davis, N. K., 172, 276
Day-care centers, 115, 117
Delayed reaction, 276, 284, 285
Dellarosa, D., 202*n*
Demarest, J., 185–186
Dementia praecox, 156–162, 328–336, 338, 340
Democracy, 51–53
Dennis, W., 278
DePauw University, 122
Descartes, R., 240
Dessoir, M., 109
Determinism, 16, 25, 49
Development, 48–50, 128–131, 145, 178, 181, 248–251, 325, 326, 339
Dewey, J., 18, 122, 123, 175
Dewsbury, D., 186, 323*n*
Dictionaries, 143
Differential psychology, 343–355; *see also* Individual differences; Psychological tests
Digestion, 29–30, 36
Dollard, J., 221, 224, *225*
Donaldson, H. H., 175
Double alternation, 276–286
Dreams, 159–163, 166, 168
Driesch, H., 216–217
DuBois-Reymond, E., 17
Duke University, 76, 77, 79, 83
Duncker, K., 192, 200, *206*
Dunlap, K., 348
Durant, H., 67–68
Durant, P., 67–68
Dynamics, 92, 128, 161, 190–198, 253, 258, 260, 265, 296–302

E

Eastern Psychological Association, 279, 288, 318
Ebbinghaus, H., 213
Eder, N. D., *168*
Edinburgh University, 146

Educational psychology, 103, 143–150, 250–254, 288
Educational Services, Inc., 293
Educational Testing Service, 288
Edwards, J., 307
Effect, law of, 128, 146–148, 216
Einstein, G., 186
Elementism, 34, 126–130, 147, 190–197, 259, 260, 272, 273, 280, 322
Eliot, C. W., 15, 17
Elliott, R. M., 209, 313
Ellis, H., 246
Ellis, W. D., 273
Eminence, 4–5, 247
Entropy, 258, 270
Epstein, W., 76
Equipotentiality, 33, 276, 279, 284, 312, 314, 316
Ericsson, K. A., 191, 192, 194, 206
Erikson, C. W., 147n
Erikson, E. H., 325
Ernst, G. W., 201, 206
Estes, W. K., 207
Esthetics, 107, 109, 110
Ethology, 317, 319, 320
Evans, R. B., 89–103, 103
Experimentalists, The, see Society of Experimental Psychologists
Experimental psychology, 22–23, 65–66, 78–84, 90–102, 122, 124, 144–148, 175, 192, 215, 229, 245, 248, 259–272, 304, 309
Extraversion, 161, 165, 166
Eugenics, 10, 96

F

Fact, vs. opinion (Hollingworth), 245, 246, 249
Family, 106, 115
Father, 52, 160, 165, 328
Federal Emergency Relief Administration, 108
Federal Public Housing Administration, 108
Fehrer, E., 293
Feminism, 253, 254
Ferenczi, S., 54
Field, B., 174
Figure and ground, 266, 270, 271
Finger, F., 275
First Baptist Church in Greenville, 175

Fitch, F. B., 225
Fixation, 199, 200
Flournoy, T., 20
Ford, C. S., 244
Fordham, M., 168, 169
Fordham University, 294
Forrest, D. W., 11
Fort Worth Polytechnical College, 276
Framingham Academy, 107
Frank, L. K., 115, 117
Frankfurt Academy, 259
Frankfurt, University of, 191, 269
Franz, S. I., 312
Franzen, R. H., 344
Freedom, 48, 49, 53
Freeman, G. L., 223
Free will, 17
Freiburg, University of, 109, 110
Friedan, B., 105, 119
Freud, A., 45
Freud, S., 6, 20, 43–55, 84, 102, 154–163, 240, 272, 298, 300, 301, 305, 338, 339
  break with Jung, 154, 159–163
From above down, 197–198, 199, 260
From below up, 197–198, 199
Fromm, E., 339
Functionalism, 34, 59, 121–136, 218, 236, 281, 293, 302, 303
Furman University, 172–174, 179, 183, 185
Furumoto, L., 57–72, 72, 106, 108, 111, 119, 119

G

Galton, F., 1–11
  biography, 2–4
Galton, S., 2
Galton, V. D., 2
Gantt, W. H., 186
Gardner, J., 346
Garner, J., 176
Gazda, G. M., 207
Geer, B., 173
Gelb, A., 269
Geldard, F., 85, 278
Gellerman, L., 278
Gender, 43, 113
General Problem Solver, 192, 193, 202–203
Genetics, 9–10, 309, 318, 319, 344–348; see also Heredity; Inheritance
Genius, 4

Gestalt psychology, 34, 35, 59, 127, 189–207, 217, 218, 229–236, 257–273, 297, 298
"g" factor, 145, 348
Ghiselli, E. E., 346, 354, *354*
Gibson, E. J., 224
Gibson, J. J., 236
Giessen, University of, 217, 229, 263
Gifford, G. E., *25*
Gleitman, H., 227–241
Goldstein, K., 268, 269, 271
Goodman, P., 271, *273*
Goodnow, F. J., 178
Government Hospital for the Insane, 312
Graham, C. H., 275, 278, 289, *290*
Greeno, J. G., 194, 202, 203, *206*
Greenville Woman's College, 173
Grice, G. R., 275
Grosse, E., 110
Gruber, H. E., *206*
Guthrie, E. R., 238

H

Habit, 19, 24, 131–132, 200, 216, 217, 284, 311–315, 348
Hadassah Society, 78
Hagen, E., 150, *151*
Halasz, F., 203, *206*
Hall, G. S., 18, 22, 78, 83, 248
Hall, M., *225*
Hamline University, 323n
Hannah, B., 153, *168*
Harris, B., 186
Hartley, M., 176, *186*
Harvard University, 13, 15, 17, 65–70, 79–85, 90, 107–112, 140, 144, 229, 231, 264, 269, 277–288, 293, 316–320, 323n, 345
Hawkins, H., 69, *72*
Hawkins, Hampton, 174, 175
Hawkins, R., 174
Hayden, D., 105, 114, 116, *119*
Hays, R., 209, 220
Hebb, D. O., 307, 317, *323*
Hefferline, R., 271, *273*
Heidbreder, E., 58–70, *72*, 244, 253, *254*, 293–305
Heidenhain, R., 29
Held, R., *273*
Helmer, B. B., *119*
Helmholtz, H., 240

Helson, H., 295
Henle, M., 271, *273*, 293–305, *305*
Heredity, 9, 282, 318, 319, 322, 330, 348
Hergenhahn, B. R., 323n
Herrnstein, R. J., 66, 70, *72*
Higher mental processes, 210, 215, 220, 269
Hilgard, E. R., 121–136
Hinkle, B. M., *168*
Hippocrates, 37
Hirsch, J., 346
History of science, 91, 93, 100
Hitler, A., 38, 86, 264
Hocking, W. E., 299
Höffding, H., 197, 204, 205
Hollingworth, H. L., 243, 244, 246, 254, *254*
Hollingworth, L. S., 243–255
Holt, E. B., 229, 241
Homosexuality, 54, 331, 332
Honzik, C., 345, 346
Hormic psychology, 59, 127, 128, 234
Horney, K., 339
Horses (Sullivan), 327, 328
Hovland, C. I., *224*, *225*
Howell, W., 177
Howes, B., 108, 112, 115, 117
Howes, E. P., *see* Puffer, E.
Hudgins, C. V., 282, 283, *291*
Hull, C. L., 39, 75–84, *86*, 209–225, 230–241
  biography, 210–214
Hull, R. F. C., *168*, *169*
Hunt, E., 287
Hunt, E. B., *305*
Hunt, J. McV., 275, 279, 289, *290*
Hunt, W. A., 278n
Hunter, A., 287, 289
Hunter, H. B., 278
Hunter, T., 278
Hunter, W. S., 275–291
  biography, 276–279
Huxley, T., 21
Hypnosis, 20, 47, 79, 80, 219, 220
Hypochondriasis, 14, 16, 20
Hypothetico-deductive method, 212
Hysteria, 20

I

Ickes, H., 176
Ickes, M. A., 175, 176, 178

362 INDEX

Id, 51
Idea books (Hull), 210, 211, 212
IER Intelligence Examination, 145
Illinois, University of, 346
Imagery, 6, 7, 167
Imagination, 133–134, 204
Incest, 44–45, 52, 160
Individual differences, 6, 36–38, 144, 145,
    243–252, 319, 344–352
Individuation (Jung), 166, 167
Information processing, 24, 45, 192–205
Inheritance, 7
Inhibition, 24, 32–33, 36, 218, 219
Insight, 193–205, 262, 338
Instinct, 19, 24, 48, 164, 282, 318, 320, 322
Institute for Cognitive Studies, 293
Institute for Juvenile Research, 313
Institute for the Coordination of Women's
    Interests, 114, 119
Institute of Educational Research, 144
Institute of Human Relations, 209, 220
Intelligence, 34, 143–149, 215, 244–249,
    288, 313–314, 348
International Psychoanalytic Association,
    159, 161
Interpersonal approach to personality,
    325–340
Introspection, 7, 62, 229, 234, 280
Introversion, 153, 165, 166
Iowa, University of, 223, 232, 233
Irradiation, 32, 33, 36, 218
Isomorphism, 263, 271
Iutzi, B., 213

J

James, H., Jr., 14, 15, 79
James, H., Sr., 14, 15
James, Harry, 19
James,W., 13–25, 61, 65, 79, 84, 107–111,
    140, 212, 218, 229, 241, 276, 299
    biography, 13–18
Janet, P., 18, 19, 20
Jasper, H., 279
Jastrow, J., 75–87, 213
    biography, 76–86
Jastrow, M., 76, 77
Jastrow, R., 84
Jaynes, J., 294, 305
Jeffress, L. A., 347, 354
Jeffries, R., 201, 206

Jennings, H. S., 309, 312
Johns Hopkins University, 69, 78,
    177–179, 184, 309, 311, 312, 317
Johns, J., 186
Johns, N., 323n
Johnston, J. B., 308
Jones, M. C., 186
Joncich, G., 139, 151, 245, 255
Jung, C., 102, 153–169
    biography, 154–166
    break with Freud, 154, 159–163
Junghans, E., 77
Jung Institute, 153n, 166
J. Walter Thompson advertising agency,
    179

K

Kansas, University of, 278
Katona, G., 192
Keller, F. S., 185, 278n
Keller, H., 82
Kelly, B. N., 323n, 323
Kemp, E. H., 278, 279
Kepner, W. A., 320
Kessen, W., 222, 224
Kihlstrom, J., 80, 86
Kimble, G. A., 1, 27–40, 209–225, 241,
    275, 290
King, F., 323n
Kingsbury, F. A., 136
Kings College, London, 2
Klein, R., 186
Kline, P. J., 194, 206
Koch, S., 221, 239, 241, 294, 323
Koelsch, W. A., 102, 103
Koffka, K., 35, 190, 192, 217, 229, 259,
    263–269, 297, 298
Köhler, Wilhelm, 258
Köhler, Wolfgang, 34, 35, 190–200, 206,
    229, 240, 257–273, 295, 298
Kornhauser, A. W., 136
Krafft-Ebing, R., 155, 156
Krantz,D., 232, 233, 234, 241, 302, 305
Krech, D., 232, 241, 354
Kretschmer, E., 38
Kuhn, T., 59
Külpe, O., 190
Kuo, Z. Y., 282, 291, 348
Kuznets, G., 346, 355

L

Lane, W., 83
Lange, C., 24
Langfeld, H. S., 229
Larson, C., 186
Lashley, C. G., 307, 323n
Lashley, K. S., 33, 34, 221, 267, 276–284, 291, 307–323, 345
  biography, 307–319
Laura Spelman Rockefeller Memorial Fund, 114, 287
Laurentian Symposium, 321
Learning, 31–38, 134, 140–150, 195–199, 209, 217–221, 230–238, 246, 261, 282, 283, 310–322, 344–352
Le Clair, R. C., 20, 25
Leeper, R., 221, 278
Leipzig, University of, 77
Levin, J., 76
Lewin, K., 222, 223, 231, 236, 268–271, 301–302, 305
Ley, R., 262, 273, 273
Leys, R., 91, 103
Libido, 44, 48, 50, 54, 160
Lieb, R., 186
Liébeault, A. A., 19
Lindsley, D., 279
Loeb, J., 283, 284, 287, 291, 309, 312
Logic, 95–102, 192, 212, 213, 293
Lorenz, K., 320
Lorge, I., 143, 149, 150, 151
Ludwig, K., 29

M

Macfarlane, J. W., 344
MacLeod, R. B., 299
Mallory, M. E., 244, 254, 255
Manheim, R., 169
Manly, I., 174
Marbe, K., 190
Marks, L., 79, 87
Marquis, D., 221
Marriage, 106, 112–114, 116, 118
Marx, K., 272
Maryland, University of, 339
Maslow, A. H., 24
Massachusetts General Hospital, 16
Massachusetts Institute of Technology, 108, 227, 228, 229

Mass action, 314, 316
Masson, M. E. J., 201, 206
Materialism, 23, 28, 53, 319
Mayers, L., 119
Maze, 217, 223, 236–239, 276–284, 312, 345–349
McCarthy, J., 239
McClearn, G. E., 1–11, 347
McConnell, J. V., 185
McConnell, R. E., 321
McDougall, W., 63, 180, 229, 299, 300, 303
McGeoch, J. A., 121
McGuire, W., 162n, 163, 169
McPherson, M. W., 294
Mead, G. H., 325
Meaning, 132, 143, 196–205, 260–272
Mechanism, 209–225
Melton, A. W., 121
Memory, 66, 70, 133–134, 213, 215, 272
Mendel, G., 9
Menninger Clinic, 46
Menstruation, 246
Mental activity, 126–136, 195, 213
Mental disorder, 38, 44–48, 80, 248, 267, 328–330, 333
Mental health, 20, 79, 116, 126, 166
Meteorology, 3
Mexico, University of, 177
Meyer, A., 91, 339
Michigan, University of, 213, 214
Milieu therapy, 329, 330
Mill, J. S., 293
Miller, N. E., 221, 224, 225
Mind-cure movement, 21–22
Minnesota, University of, 295, 313
Mohraz, J. J., 119
Montreal Neurological Institute, 279
Mood, 135–136
Moore, A. W., 175
Moore, G. B., 172, 173
Morgan, C.T., 282, 307, 323
Moss,R. A., 217
Mother, 64, 106, 111, 116, 252, 326–337
Motivation, 128–131, 150, 217–229, 234, 238, 265–271, 296
Mowrer, O. H., 220, 224
Mullahy, P., 327, 340
Müller, G. E., 70
Munn, N., 278
Münsterberg, H., 61–66, 107–112, 116
Murchison, C., 122, 151, 186, 290

Murphy, G., 350
Myers, C. S., 20
Mysticism, 14–15, 160, 161, 216, 267, 271
Myths, 159, 160, 161

N

Nanney, L., 186
National Academy of Sciences, 279
National College Equal Suffrage League, 108
National Committee for Mental Hygiene, 21
National Research Council, 287
National Youth Administration, 222
Nature vs. nurture, 9–10, 282
Nazis, 263, 264
Nebraska, University of, 254
Neider, C., 354, 354
Neilson, W. A., 115, 117
Neuropsychology, 307–323
Neves, D. M., 194, 206
Newell, A., 192,193, 201–204, 206
Newton, I., 94, 221
New York City Clearing House for Mental Defectives, 247, 248
New School for Social Research, 179, 191, 293, 294
New York World's Fair, 86
Nietzsche, F., 320
Nissen, H. W., 307, 317, 323
Nobel prize, 29, 30, 185
Normal curve, 5
Norsworthy, N., 244, 248
Northwestern University, 223, 229
Number two (Jung), 154, 157, 160

O

O'Connell, A. N., 254, 254
O'Connell, D. N., 273
Oedipus complex, 45, 165, 339
Office of Strategic Services, 350
Ogden, R. M., 278
Orbach, J., 323n, 323
Origin of Species, 3–4, 276

P

Paired associates, 57, 66, 70
Palace of culture (Jastrow), 81, 83

Palmieri, P., 67–69, 72
Park, Miss, (medium), 216
Part-whole relations, 198–199
Pavlov, I. P., 27–40, 315, 316, 323n
    biography, 28–29, 38–39
Pearson, K., 4, 11, 95, 103
Peirce, C. S., 78
Pennsylvania State University, 253
Pennsylvania, University of, 77
Perception, 122–134, 190–198, 213, 235–236, 258–272, 296, 319
Perkins, D. T., 225
Perls, F., 269–273, 273
Perry, R. B., 24, 25, 25, 229
Personality, 47, 60, 62, 166, 167, 244, 249, 296, 302, 325–339
Personnel, selection of, 144; see also Vocational guidance
Pfaffman, C., 279
Phi phenomenon,190, 258, 259
Pilzecker, A., 70
Pincus, G., 284, 290
Pisoni, D. B., 206
Pittsburgh, University of, 309
Planck, M., 258
Plato, 233
Pleasure in the symptom (Freud), 49–51, 54
Point of view, 92–99
Polson, P. G., 191–201, 206
Polya, G., 192, 207
Popper, K., 322
Popplestone, J. A., 294
Popularization of psychology, 80–86, 112, 179, 184
Potts, G. R., 206
Pratt, C. C., 219, 225
Pribram, K., 317
Prince, M., 18
Princeton University, 175, 177, 318
Principles of Psychology, 13, 22–23, 61, 79, 212, 276, 277
Preston, J. H., 77–78, 87
Pritchard, M. C., 248, 255
Probability, 146, 147
Problem solving, 38, 191–203, 261, 268
Productive thinking, 148, 191–205
Prussian Academy of Science, 261
Prytula, R., 186
Psychiatry, 19–22, 325–340; see also Clinical psychology
Psychical research, 23, 156, 216–217, 321

Psychoanalysis, 18, 20, 43–55, 59, 102, 160–166, 220, 236, 298, 301, 335–339
Psychological tests, 136, 144, 149, 215, 219, 220, 244–253, 287, 295, 296; *see also* Individual differences
Psychopathology, *see* Mental disorder
Psychophysics, 79, 80, 222
Psychotherapy, 22, 46–53, 166, 167, 269, 271, 329–338
Puffer, E., 105–119
Punishment, 146–149
Purpose, 59, 127, 128, 234, 320
Putnam, J. J., 18

Q

Quantification, 140–141, 150, 244, 245, 346, 352
Quantz, J. R., 83, *87*
Questionnaire method, 6, 7
Quetelet, J., 4

R

Radcliffe College, 70, 108–119
Rats, 217, 223, 236–239, 276–284, 312, 318, 345–349
Ray, I., 21
Rayner, R., 178, 180
Razran, L., 201, *206*
Read, H., *168, 169*
Reality testing, 338
Reason,J., 80, *87*
Reddy River Baptist Church, 174
Reductionism, *see* Elementism
Reese, A. M., 308
Regression, 8
Reinforcement, 33, 146, 148, 217
Reliability, 283, 322, 344–349
Religion, 14–23, 83, 173, 210–213, 267
Renouvier, C., 17, 18
Reputation, 4, 7
Reward, 146–148
Richmond Normal Schol, 213
Richter, C., 186
Rickert, H., 110
Riesen, A., 317
Riggs, L., 278
Riklin, F., 157
Riley, R. W., 185
Rinker, W. B., 277
Roback, A., 77, *87*

Robinson, E. S., 121
Robinson, F. R., 121
Rockefeller Foundation, 115, 116
Rocky Mountain Psychological Association, 55, 224, 273
Rodnick, E., 224
Roe, T., 186
Rogers, C. R., 325
Roosevelt, F. D., 176, 179
Rosenberg, R., 244, *255*
Rosenberg, S., 163, *169*
Ross, B., 13–25, *25*
Ross, R. T., *225*
Royal Geographical Society, 3
Royce, J., 61, 64, 112
Ruckmick, C. A., 126, 127, *136*
Russell, A., 115, 119, *119*
Russell Sage Foundation, 115
Russo, N. F., 254, *254*

S

St. Petersburg, University of, 29
Samelson, F., 57–58, 72, 186, 244, *255*
Sanford, E. C., 65
Santayana, G., 18, 111
Scarborough, E., 65, 72, 105–119, *119*, 253
Schema, 193, 194, 322
Schiller, C., 320
Schiller, P., 320
Schizophrenia, *see* Dementia praecox
Schlager, M., 199*n*
Schlesinger, K., 343–355
Schlosberg, H., 275, 279, *291*
Schmi, B. S., 321
Scholastic Aptitude Test, 145
Seaberg, E., 83
Searle, L. Z., 348
Sears, R. R., *224*
Selective breeding, 346–348
Self, 19–24, 43, 48, 57–72, 155, 166, 267, 325–339
Seven Psychologies, 295–305
Schulte, H., 267, 268, *273*
Sechenov, I. M., 29
Second signal system, 31, 34, 36
Self-actualization, 24
Sellars, R. W., 213
Sex, 43–48, 53, 54, 160, 313, 331, 332
Shakow, D., 18, *25*
Shapiro, K., 153, *169*
Shaw, J.C.,192, 202, *206*

Shepard, G.F., 214
Sheppard Pratt Hospital, 330, 333, 336
Sherif, C., 253
Sherrill, R., 257–273
Shields, S. A., 243–255, *254*
Sidis, B., 18
Siegfried dream, 162, 163
Sign-gestalt expectation (Tolman), 230, 235
Signorella, M., 253
Similarity, 197, 205
Simmons College, 108
Simon, H. A., 192, 193, 202, *206, 207*
Skinner, B. F., 147, 149, 185, 233–238, 278*n*
Smith, C., 186
Smith College, 64–67, 106–119, 293
Smith-Rosenberg, C., 64, 67, *72*
Smoking, 215
Smyrna Union School, 328
Social Security Administration, 150
Society of Experimental Psychologists, 90, 279, 282
Socrates, 46, 233
Sollenberger, R.T., *224*
Solomon, B. M., 65, *72*
Southern Society for Philosophy and Psychology, 185
Space perception, 122–124, 132, 133
Spearman-Brown Prophesy Formula, 283
Spearman, C., 348, 349
Spence, K., 217, 221–223, 232–234, 241
Spencer, H., 21
Spencer, M. B., 307
Sperry, R., 317
Speyer School, 249, 250
Spread of effect, 147
Sproul, R. G., 345
Stanford University, 145
Statistics, 5, 7–8, 346, 350
Stein, G., 18
Stenquist, J. L., 149
Stevenson, G., 351
Stimulus and response, 130, 141, 146, 192,216, 230, 235, 280, 281, 287
Stimulus generalization, 32, 218
Stocks, E. H., 117, 118
Stone, C. P., 282
Stout, G. F., 125
Stratton, G. M., 127, 132, 133, *136*, 344, 345, 350
Stream of consciousness, 23, 61

Strong Vocational Interest Test, 84
Structuralism, 58, 102, 125–129, 132, 229, 281
Stumpf, C., 109, 190
Sullivan, E. M. S., 326, 327
Sullivan, H. S., 325–340
  biography, 326–330
Sullivan, J. I., 325
Sullivan, J. J., 294, 296, *305*
Sullivan, T. J., 326
Swarthmore College, 240, 264, 265
Swedenborg, E., 14
Symbolic processes, 276, 282, 285–287
Symbols, 158, 159, 162, 329
Systematic psychology, 296–304, 311
Szold, B., 78
Szold, H., 78
Szold, R., 78

T

Talent, 6–7
Technology, 89–103
Teleology, 59, 127, 128, 234, 320
Temperament, 37–38
Temporal maze, 276, 278, 282, 285, 286
Tender-mindedness and tough-mindedness, 17
Tenerife, 261, 262, 273
Terman, L. M., 149, 249
Terrell, G., *206*
Tests, *see* Psychological tests
Texas, University of, 277, 278
Thinking, 45, 133–135, 148, 159, 190–205, 222, 296
Thompson, C., 327
Thompson, G., 145
Thorndike, E. R., 18, 34, 35, 139–151, 216, 230, 244–247, 277
Thorndike, R. L., 139–151, *151*
Thorpe, W. H., 320
Thurstone, L. L., 209
Time machine, 1
Tinbergen, N., 320
Tinklepaugh, O. L., 344
Titchener, E. B., 59, 89–103, 125, 126, 229, 234, 280, 281, 298, 299, 309
Tolman, E. C., 39, 209, 217, 219, *225*, 227–241, 344, 346–350, *354*
  biography, 227–230
Top-down processing, 198–199

Tough-mindedness and tender- minded-
  ness, 17
Townes, C. H., 185
Transfer, 150,197, 200, 280
Trial and error, 34, 35, 134, 219
Tropism, 276, 279, 283, 287, 309
Tryon, C., 344, *355*
Tryon, R. C., 286, 343-355
  biography, 343-346, 350, 352
Tsyon, E., 29
Tübingen, University of, 258
Twins, 144
Twitmeyer, E. B., 30
Types (Jung), 165

U

Unconscious mental processes, 6, 21,
  45-54, 79, 157-164, 268, 335
Understanding, 192-197, 201-205
Union College, 14
United States Housing Authority, 108
Ustimovich, K. N., 29

V

Value, 21, 100,101, 265, 271, 321
van der Post, L., 153*n*
van Kleeck, M., 114, 116, 117, 118
Van Riper, S., 273
Variability hypothesis (Hollingworth),
  246, 247, 253
Varigny, H., 81, *87*
Vassar College, 178
Vienna, University of, 44, 231
Virginia, University of, 276, 320
Vitalism, 101, 309
Vocational guidance, 149, 150, 215, 219,
  220
Volition, 282-283
von Ehrenfels, C., 190
von Frisch, K., 320
von Hornbostel, E. M., 266, *273*

W

Wallach, H., 240
Walshe, F. M. R., 322
Ward, J., 61
Warren, H. C., 177, 178
Washburn, M. F., 277

Watson, E., 173, 174, 175
Watson, E. K. R., 171, 174
Watson, J., 176
Watson, J. B., 58, 84, 123, 124, 171-186,
  216-219, 234, 279-283, *291*, 310-318,
  348
career in advertising, 179-180
Watson, Jim, 180-183, 185, 186, *186*
Watson, J. N., 186
Watson, M., 176
Watson, P. B., 171, 174
Watson, S., 185
Watson, W. R., 180
Weaver, A., 83
Weber, A., 172
Weigert,E., 340
Weimer, W., 253
Weisberg, R.W., 199-201, *207*
Weiss, A. P., 279
Wellesley College, 65-71, 108, 293, 294,
  297
Wells, H. G., 1
Wendt, G. R., 221
Wertheimer, L., 191
Wertheimer, Max, 189-207, 229, 259,
  263-269, 298
  biography, 190-191
Wertheimer, Michael, 1, 189-207, *206*, 273
Wertheimer, V., 191
Wertheimer, W., 190
West Virginia, University of, 308
West Wind (Sullivan), 327, 328
Whewell, W., 94
White, C. L., 1
White, R. W., 278*n*
White, W.A., 339
Wiggins, L., 232, 233, 234, *241*
William Esty Company, 179, 182
Williams, R. J., 321
Willoughby, R., 287
Windholtz, G., 186, 316, 323*n*, *323*
Wisconsin, University of, 75, 76, 79-84,
  213, 215-219
Witmer, L., 13, *25*
Witty, P., *255*
Women, 43, 44, 57-72, 90, 105-119,
  244-254, 293-305
Women's studies, 105
Woodworth, R. S., 128, 245, 253, 297, 298
Woodyard, E., 144, *151*
Word counts, 142-143
Work, 155, 160, 161, 252

World War I, 108, 144, 178, 230, 244, 248, 261, 262, 278, 287
World War II, 10, 166, 223, 229, 275, 288, 350
Wright, H. F., 222
Wright, S., 150
Wundt, W., 59, 79, 89, 107, 125, 126, 172, 190, 192, 234, 281, 309
Würzburg, University of, 190
Wyers,E., 186

Y

Yale University, 75–82, 121, 209–224, 313
Yerkes, R. M., 229
Yerkes Laboratories of Primate Biology, 307, 317, 320, 322
Yerkes Regional Primate Research Center, 323n
Yoakum, C. S., 277, 278
Yoshioka, J. G., 344

DATE DUE

MAR 0 8 1998	
MAR 0 1 2001	
MAY 1 0 2001	

GAYLORD   PRINTED IN U.S.A.